CONSTRUCTING A NEW FRAMEWORK FOR RURAL DEVELOPMENT

RESEARCH IN RURAL SOCIOLOGY AND DEVELOPMENT

Series Editor: Terry Marsden

Recent Volumes:

Volume 7: Focus on Migration

Volume 8: Dairy Industry Restructuring

Volume 9: Walking Towards Justice: Democratization in Rural Life

Volume 10: Nature, Raw Materials and Political Economy

Volume 11: New Directions in the Sociology of Global Development

Volume 12: Between the Local and the Global

Volume 13: Gender Regimes, Citizen Participation and Rural Restructuring

Volume 14: Beyond the Rural-Urban Divide: Cross-Continental Perspectives on the Differentiated Countryside and Its Regulation

Volume 15: Welfare Reform in Rural Places: Comparative Perspectives

Volume 16: From Community to Consumption: New and Classical Themes in Rural Sociological Research

Volume 17: Globalization and the Time-Space Reorganisation: Capital Mobility in Agriculture and Food in the Americas

Volume 18: Rethinking Agricultural Policy Regimes: Food Security, Climate Change and the Future Resilience of Global Agriculture

Volume 19: Agriculture in Mediterranean Europe: Between Old and New Paradigms

Volume 20: Labor Relations in Globalized Food

Volume 21: Alternative Agrifood Movements: Patterns of Convergence and Divergence

RESEARCH IN RURAL SOCIOLOGY AND DEVELOPMENT
VOLUME 22

CONSTRUCTING A NEW FRAMEWORK FOR RURAL DEVELOPMENT

EDITED BY

PIERLUIGI MILONE
DICA, Perugia University, Perugia, Italy

FLAMINIA VENTURA
DICA, Perugia University, Perugia, Italy

JINGZHONG YE
COHD, China Agricultural University, Beijing, China

Emerald

United Kingdom – North America – Japan
India – Malaysia – China

Emerald Group Publishing Limited
Howard House, Wagon Lane, Bingley BD16 1WA, UK

First edition 2015

British Library Cataloguing in Publication Data
A catalogue record for this book is available from the British Library

ISBN: 978-1-78441-622-5
ISSN: 1057-1922 (Series)

Printed and bound by CPI Group (UK) Ltd, Croydon, CR0 4YY

ISOQAR
REGISTERED
Certificate Number 1985
ISO 14001

ISOQAR certified Management System, awarded to Emerald for adherence to Environmental standard ISO 14001:2004.

INVESTOR IN PEOPLE

CONTENTS

LIST OF CONTRIBUTORS *vii*

CHAPTER 1 INTRODUCTION
Pierluigi Milone, Flaminia Ventura and Jingzhong Ye *1*

CHAPTER 2 RURAL DEVELOPMENT: ACTORS AND PRACTICES
Jan Douwe van der Ploeg, Jingzhong Ye and Sergio Schneider *17*

CHAPTER 3 ACTIVITIES, ACTANTS AND ACTORS: THEORETICAL PERSPECTIVES ON DEVELOPMENT PRACTICE AND PRACTITIONERS
Norman Long *31*

CHAPTER 4 IS MULTIFUNCTIONALITY THE ROAD TO EMPOWERING FARMERS?
Pierluigi Milone and Flaminia Ventura *59*

CHAPTER 5 PEASANT INNOVATION AND GRASSROOTS ACTION IN CHINA
Jingzhong Ye and Huiyang Fu *89*

CHAPTER 6 SEEDS AND SPROUTS OF RURAL DEVELOPMENT: INNOVATIONS AND NESTED MARKETS IN SMALL SCALE ON-FARM PROCESSING BY FAMILY FARMERS IN SOUTH BRAZIL
Sergio Schneider and Marcio Gazolla *127*

CHAPTER 7 HIDDEN TREASURES: RECONNECTING CULTURE AND NATURE IN RURAL DEVELOPMENT DYNAMICS
Paulo F. Petersen 157

CHAPTER 8 RURAL DEVELOPMENT FROM THE GRASSROOTS: TWENTY YEARS OF THE EU "LEADER APPROACH"
Laurent Van de Poele 195

CHAPTER 9 THE DISTINCTIVENESS OF RURAL DEVELOPMENT PRACTICES IN NORTH WEST EUROPE
Rudolf van Broekhuizen, Bart Soldaat, Henk Oostindie and Jan Douwe van der Ploeg 209

CHAPTER 10 TOWARDS THE CHARACTERIZATION OF ACTORS ENGAGED IN RURAL DEVELOPMENT PROCESSES IN THE NORTH WEST OF EUROPE
Henk Oostindie, Rudolf van Broekhuizen, Bart Soldaat and Jan Douwe van der Ploeg 239

CHAPTER 11 WEAVING THE INSTITUTIONAL MARKET: THE POLITICS OF FOOD PRODUCTION IN LAND REFORM SETTLEMENTS IN BRAZIL
Claudia Job Schmitt 255

CHAPTER 12 REVISITING EVOLVING WEBS OF AGRI-FOOD AND RURAL DEVELOPMENT IN THE UK: THE CASE OF DEVON AND SHETLAND
Jessica Paddock and Terry Marsden 301

CHAPTER 13 CONCLUSION: REPRODUCING FUTURE IN RURAL AREA
Pierluigi Milone, Flaminia Ventura and Jingzhong Ye 325

ABOUT THE AUTHORS 335

LIST OF CONTRIBUTORS

Huiyang Fu	College of Humanities and Development Studies (COHD), China Agricultural University, Beijing, China
Marcio Gazolla	Colegio Agricola de Frederico Westphalen, Universidade Federal de Santa Maria, Santa Maria, Brazil
Norman Long	Wageningen University, Wageningen, The Netherlands
Terry Marsden	Cardiff School of Planning and Geography, Cardiff University, Cardiff, UK
Pierluigi Milone	Dipartimento di Ingegneria Civile ed Ambientale, Perugia University, Perugia, Italy
Henk Oostindie	Rural Sociology Group, Wageningen University, Wageningen, The Netherlands
Jessica Paddock	Sustainable Places Research Institute (PLACE), Cardiff University, Cardiff, UK
Paulo F. Petersen	AS-PTA – Agricultura Familiar e Agrocologia, Rio de Janeiro, Brazil
Claudia Job Schmitt	Departamento de Desenvolvimento Agricultura e Sociedade, Universidade Federal Rural do Rio de Janeiro, Rio de Janeiro, Brazil
Sergio Schneider	Grupo de Estudos e Pesquisas em Agricultura Familiar e Desenvolvimento Rural (GEPAD), Universidade Federal do Rio Grande do Sul, Porto Alegre, Brazil

Bart Soldaat	Independent consultant for agriculture and rural development, Wageningen, The Netherlands
Rudolf van Broekhuizen	Rural Sociology Group, Wageningen University, Wageningen, The Netherlands
Laurent Van de Poele	Centre for European Studies, KU Leuven University, Leuven, Belgium
Jan Douwe van der Ploeg	Rural Sociology Group, Wageningen University, Wageningen, The Netherlands
Flaminia Ventura	Department of Economics and Food Sciences, Perugia University, Perugia, Italy
Jingzhong Ye	College of Humanities and Development Studies (COHD), China Agricultural University, Beijing, China

CHAPTER 1

INTRODUCTION

Pierluigi Milone, Flaminia Ventura and Jingzhong Ye

ABSTRACT

This book is the result of a selection of papers presented in the seminar held in Beijing in 2012. It is the third in chronological order of a seminar series on the comparative analysis of rural development in China, Brazil, and the EU. In previous seminars (2010 in Rome, 2011 in Porto Alegre) the focus was, first, on the nature and dynamics of rural development processes and, second, on the performance of rural development policies. In the third seminar (held in Beijing in November 2012), the focus was on actors and practices. What motivates the actors who are actively involved in rural development? And how do they structure their new practices? In this chapter, different stories on rural development practices between China, Brazil, and the EU are illustrated, highlighting the differences and also commonalities and similarities. In this story, the figure of the peasant appears crucial and in different dimensions: from the manager of natural resources who takes the greatest care of their condition in order to achieve the largest profits; to the innovator who builds on age old methods to find novel solutions with the available conditions, resources, and technologies, and who creates the right synergies for harmonious and positive impact solutions; to the rural villager who does with what he/she has and knows, but who at the same time is curious

Constructing a New Framework for Rural Development
Research in Rural Sociology and Development, Volume 22, 1–16

ISSN: 1057-1922/doi:10.1108/S1057-192220150000022021

about innovations; to the father who is aware that he is responsible for building a future for his children. Peasant agriculture seems to go beyond its own limits through a transition process that has led to a paradigm shift moving away from the modernization and creating new opportunities and alternatives in terms of practices, products, and markets. These alternatives are now representing the base for a new autonomy and competitiveness of rural areas in an increasingly globalized world.

Keywords: Peasants; rural development; multi-functionality; culture of progress; local knowledge; globalization

During the last decade, international debates about food sovereignty, new markets that link producers and consumers of food in novel ways, agroecology (an innovative way to produce food), and new rural development processes have revived a set of questions that had seemingly disappeared forever: Who are the peasants? How do they produce? How do they link to wider society and especially to consumers? What is their relevance when it comes to food security and food sovereignty?

These questions (and especially the first) constitute the primary focus of this introduction which emphasizes the relevance of peasants in modern times, the importance of their production models, and their capacity to create a future for generations to come. Peasants and their production models have always been strongly criticized for being stuck in their history and for dealing with crucial issues with obsolete and old-fashioned tools not able to fully meet the needs of modern times, especially in terms of world hunger, quality and wellbeing of populations, and the scarcity and condition of resources. Using the classical rhetoric of modernization theories, the peasant lifestyle is viewed as no response to such issues since it guarantees neither adequate productivity, profits, and levels of wealth, nor proper solutions for overcoming the limits caused by the shortage of resources. Instead, it has been argued that such questions must be tackled within advanced or, economically speaking, "modern" models that can impact on three issues:

1. overcoming the limits of the factors of production;
2. the growth of activities and related margins within increasingly "risky" economies of scale; and
3. the replacement of resources and their limiting factors (i.e., land).

However, this "modern" model fails to address two fundamental aspects. In the first place, it provides linear solutions that barely touch upon the complexities that arise whenever an action is undertaken; and second, regardless of what skeptics believe, peasants have been reformulating their model of growth for over 2000 years, resisting, modifying, and readjusting to changes over time and to a large extent contributing to the identification of innovations that favored the birth of the so-called modern era (Ye, 2002). Indeed, the long history of peasant resistance is sufficient to prove not only that the peasant model is unlikely to disappear but also that such a model might well be a real alternative to addressing the key contemporary issues highlighted above.

But before illustrating some elements prevailing in the peasant model, we feel obliged to clarify more specifically what we mean by "peasants." To this end, we mention the story of Yacouba Sawadogo from the village of Gourga in northern Burkina Faso who "*in the mid-1970s started to plant trees in the desert of Sahel and in no time he gave birth to a forest.*" This is what emerged in an interview with Tamara Ferrari, a journalist of Vanity Fair. In the interview Yacouba reveals what led him to change his life: "*one day I dropped everything and told my fellows that I wanted to be a peasant. Everybody thought I was mad. The mid-1970s were not a good time as the entire area of Sahel was affected by a severe drought. The desert swallowed hectares of cultivated lands. Thousands of people were starving, while others were running away. I thought that if had abandoned my land too nothing would have remained here. So an ancient farming technique I learnt in Mali came to my mind*" (Vanity Fair 12/2013).

The technique used was known as *Zai*, which consists of preparing the land during the dry season and digging holes able to catch water. To this Yacouba added an innovation by increasing their size and filling them with manure and leaves. The manure attracted termites but instead of fighting them he favored their presence as he thought their tunnels would help to catch water, thus reducing the need for irrigation. Later, he also discovered that the termites digested the manure in such a way that they contributed to soil remineralization. In this way, over 38 years, Yacouba turned 23 hectares of wasteland into a forest and his model was adopted by the States of Mali and Niger, where several forests were created thanks to the *Zai* technique. Today, Yacouba is now contributing to the spread of this practice by participating in many initiatives across Africa and worldwide and has achieved an international reputation. At present, he is focused on activities aimed at saving endangered plants: "*One year ago a man came to my farm with a medicinal tree, the last one left in Niger. Here it remultiplied and I gave it back to him with interest. I started to wander around Burkina Faso to gather the seeds of the plants used to heal every disease. This news spread and I started to receive plants from all over Africa. In this way, I save the species and preserve traditions.*"

In this story the figure of the peasant appears in different dimensions: from the manager of natural resources who takes the greatest care of their condition in order to achieve the largest profits; to the innovator who builds on age old methods to find novel solutions with the available conditions, resources, and technologies, and who creates the right synergies for harmonious and positive impact solutions; to the rural villager who makes do with what he/she has and knows, but who at the same time is curious about innovations; to the father who is aware that he is responsible for building a future for his children.

These are all dimensions developed over time, but today they represent the real revolution of modern agriculture. Throughout the world the peasant model is strongly re-emerging in response to crises derived from the phenomena of both globalization and population growth. This capacity of tackling newly emerging issues with innovative responses is constant over time. It is the real core of the peasant model which, unlike the models of "modern" agriculture, does not admit to failure or delocalization of production which is the cause of territorial deserts, but favors the constant improvement of resources and of the condition of its territories. However, the peasant model meets both the skepticism of institutions that are bound to seek great solutions to globally generated problems, and the power of large industries that in order to survive and sustain a high return on investment, need to increase profit margins and hold down the costs of production resources, with the consequent delocalization and exploitation phenomena.

In this book, the above assumption is supported by empirical evidence from the EU, Brazil, and China, three countries with very different rural development policies, but which identify in peasant solutions similarities in the processes, methods, and products obtained from very different starting points. How this happened remains a mystery, but on the other hand, it is the confirmation of an increasingly flourishing peasant model.

THE CIRCULARITY OF THE MODEL AND REPRODUCIBILITY OF RESOURCES

The peasant model can be represented as a circular model in which the inputs used become outputs and then inputs again. Such a model relies on the ancient concept of "throwing nothing away." Reusing products or elements considered as waste generated during production processes has always been the key feature of such a model. It is worth underlining that the pattern of "modern" agriculture, linked to unilinear solutions to various farm objectives (i.e., increase of production and reduction of costs and environmental impact) has led to excessive specialization due to which the achievement of one of its objective causes a negative impact on the others. For instance, the increase of the productivity of the factors of production often intensifies the negative impact on the environment – which sometimes cannot be identified in the short term, as in the case of genetically modified seed use, or in the reduction of the demand for labor. In many areas tending towards specialized agriculture, as in the "*Pianura Padana*" in Italy, the effects of these forms of agriculture are clearly visible. Indeed, some farms considered as best masters for their capacity to follow the "modern" pattern are being forced to shut down in the face of the current crisis, or move to territories where economies of cost can take advantage of backward conditions, as in the case of eastern Europe where many agricultural entrepreneurs of the Padan Plain and of other countries such as the Netherlands and Germany, are investing.

Returning to the peasant model, it can be represented by Fig. 1 (van der Ploeg, 2003), which shows how peasants take advantage of the circularity element to tackle urgent issues or to respond to their and their family needs. In economic terms, this capacity has often been referred to as the capacity of implementing economies of scope (Milone & Ventura, 2000; Teece, 1980) or of proximity (Ventura, 2000). The rediscovery of this capacity has allowed the formalization of a new paradigm of rural development (Milone, 2009; van der Ploeg et al., 2000; Ventura, 2000) within which farmers redefine the boundaries of their farms (Milone & Ventura, 2004).

The new element emerging from such a model is that today the possibility of reusing the resources within production processes applies also to the market or better to the income dimension, while in the past it was applied exclusively to environmental or social dimensions. This assumption is supported by many examples given in detail in the following chapters. The peasant model has indeed made it clear that what is considered as waste can be reused as product within new or nested markets that over the years can turn into competitive or contestable markets (Milone & Ventura, 2014).

The new dimension of nested markets gives substance to the peasant model and strengthens both its stability and credibility against those who

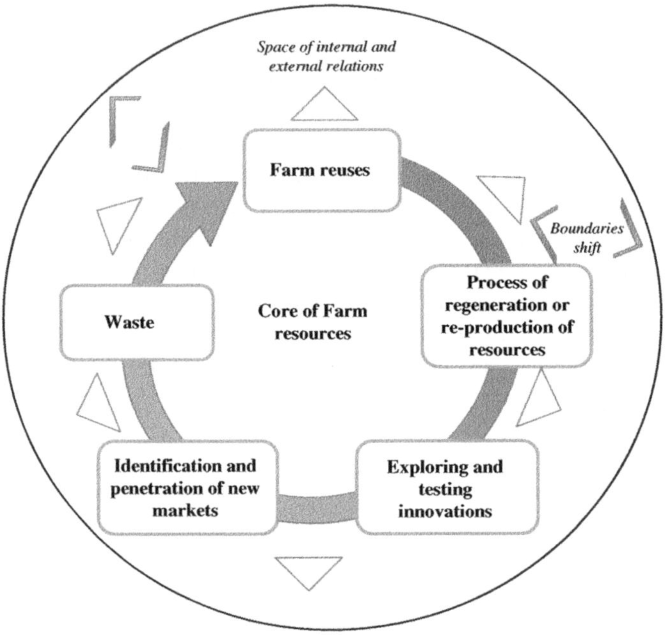

Fig. 1. The Peasant Model.

have always supported the disappearance of the peasantry. Peasants reflect the context in which they live and from which they derive silent and ongoing forms of development, that enable dynamic improvements, over time, in the quality of life, family wellbeing, natural resources and the environment, and of society in general.

Moreover, the circularity of the model makes it strongly flexible and adjusted to what van der Ploeg (1994) defines as "farming style," as well as strongly resistant to the superstructures that Benvenuti identified as TATE – Technological-Administrative Task Environment (Benvenuti, 1975, 1982). This resistance stems from the fact that peasant farms have to define an autonomous space enabling them to be less affected by pressures from the market, input providers, and financial capital. Such pressures are causing the shutdown of many European farms that follow the "modern" or "entrepreneurial" model of agriculture.

THE MULTIFUNCTIONAL UNIT AND VALORIZATION OF LABOR

Analysis of the peasant model starts from the assertion that the basic productive unit is a multifunctional one, namely, where the internal resources are destined for multiple and synergistic uses. Among the resources used, the labor force is the most flexible, as it can be placed in different activities according to needs, times, and market demands. Therefore, peasant labor gives a great flexibility that relies on the capabilities and knowledge developed through the ages and transferred from generation to generation. Today, such knowledge may seem superfluous, but it could be useful in the years to come. Unlike the patterns of "modern" agriculture, where knowledge stems from predetermined recipes, training actions, or technical assistance, in the peasant model knowledge is an integral part of labor, it develops with labor and the farm, becoming an essential component of farm heritage.

Capabilities and knowledge are at the root of the inclination of peasants to constantly test new solutions or innovations in practices, products, and farm functions. This is the way novelties, namely "new configurations that promise to work" are born (Milone, 2009; Rip & Kemp, 1998; van der Ploeg et al., 2004). And this is also the way "field laboratories" are born (Stuiver, van der Ploeg, Leeuwis, 2003), where peasant wisdom and ability engage with the laws of nature, give birth to processes of coproduction that Chayanov included in the concept of Social Agronomy (1924) and which van der Ploeg identifies as the existence of different farming styles:

> The individuality of the direct producer, his creative energy, the particularities of his farm and the quality of his fields, mean that the individual farm will always deviate from the average type. Curiosity and the search for novel solutions characterize all farmers. Consequently, all farms are in a kinetic condition; they are permanently changing due to the widely spread experiments, searches and creative trials. (Chayanov, 1924, p. 2)

> The actively created heterogeneity (condensed here as different farming styles) constantly interacts with the many changes in the context in which farming is embedded. The impact of these changes will have a different effect on farms practicing different farming styles. Hence selection will occur; some styles will show themselves to be better adjusted to facing and dealing with the changed environment, others will become marginalized. (van der Ploeg, 2013, p. 65)

Thanks to the above mentioned tendency, heterogeneity of agricultural practices has been maintained, practices that by means of novel solutions try to control the laws of nature in favor of a productive and livable space. In short, the multi-functionality of the peasant farm can be summarized as having:

1. Different functions that respond to needs of farmers and civil society;
2. Multiple use of resources aimed at their preservation and reproducibility;
3. A portfolio strategy and diversification;
4. A capacity for coordination of multiple functions that need original and flexible solutions.

The above characteristics are today the central elements of a new paradigm of rural development that tries to combine the sustainability of environmental, social, and economic dimensions of rural life.

A key role in the multifunctional peasant farm is that played by the labor of the peasant and his family. The farm's main objectives are built upon this resource, which means that, over time, farm boundaries may be extended (or contracted) as required. The evolution of farm functions is thus determined and defined on the basis of the human resources available and used. Therefore, the concept of labor as a resource ranges from that of being a mere productive factor, characterized by specialization and replaceability, to that of immovable capital on which the dimension and mission of the enterprise is outlined. In economic terms, moving the objective from production profitability to valorization of labor allows the peasant farm to strengthen its autonomy, though this is strictly linked to keeping full control of the labor resource to better respond to external shocks in terms of both market and increased competition in resources use. Thanks to this autonomy that European agriculture is overcoming one of the most serious financial and economic crisis in the last 100 years, or that peasant farms of South America and China are contributing to solving the ancestral issue of the free access to food, or that peasant farm production in Africa represents 80% of the total agricultural production and more than 70% of total workers. This model must be respected and safeguarded as the European Commissioner for Development and Cooperation, Mr. Piebalgs, stressed in an interview with the journalist Eleanor Whitehead published in the magazine "This is Africa" in its December–January 2012 issue.

> We should not be arrogant against the smallholder – 80 percent of Africa's agricultural production today is actually created by these smallholder farmers, so it gives employment and these are the traditional structure. – We should not say that the EU

> agricultural pattern will be replicated in Africa or the Caribbean and Pacific. We should not think that it will be just a couple of farmers, hundreds of hectares of land and huge productivity. It should be looked on with respect that they will use a model which suits their needs, and that they will not necessarily repeat our pattern. – We must strengthen countries' resilience towards food price shocks and changing climate patterns. (Piebalgs, This is Africa, Dec/Jan 2012)

Therefore, with the purpose of maximizing the remuneration of the factors on which the entrepreneur exercises property rights, the peasant model implements multi-functionality in agriculture through a real revolution also in the production processes in which what was considered as byproduct or even waste is instead, with full rights, a resource for the production of new goods and services characterized by substantial positive externalities for society and the environment. A clear example of this is represented by the "good manure" of Dutch environmental cooperatives, where the problem of slurry disposal linked to nitrate pollution was solved by some peasants of Northern Friesland who started to produce an "improved slurry" (Reijs, Verhoeven, van Bruchem, van der Ploeg, & Lantinga, 2004). This gave them exemption from having to comply with national regulations for disposal and led to an overall improvement of the environment and of animals welfare. In peasant farms, the launching of strategies of multi-functionality has implied a considerable change not only in terms of practices but also in terms of organization and relationships. The need to go beyond traditional models has entailed alliances with new actors able to oppose the lobbies of food empires. And thanks to such new alliances, today the peasant model has managed to come out of its niche and overcome the skepticism expressed, especially by international development institutions, on their capacity to represent a credible alternative to increasingly industrialized agricultural models. The peasant model has therefore evolved from a multifunctional unit to comprise a rural web that now reaches beyond the boundaries of national states. This web acquires a "normative" dimension since it allows one to identify the interrelations that lead to more sustainable development, namely to promote a mode of development in which environmental conservation and economic development become interdependent and strengthen each other on a mutual basis. In other words, in a sustainable development the needs of the economy, society, and nature, which are usually in competition between each other, are redefined with special attention to economic growth, social justice, ecological protection, and intergenerational equity (Kitchen & Marsden, 2009).

GOING BEYOND THE MYTH OF MARGINALITY: PEASANTS AND THE CULTURE OF PROGRESS

Peasants have always been placed within the concept of marginality. Being a peasant has often meant being seen as out of touch with modern time and thus unable to change, discover, or accept progress and its opportunities, especially vis-à-vis what industry, technology, and chemistry had to offer them in terms of overcoming environmental obstacles or what in agronomic terms are considered as limiting factors (such as soil fertility, employment availability, and work productivity). In short, peasants have always been viewed as conservative actors destined to disappear.[1] In various studies carried out over the years in different parts of the world, the invalidity of such assertions has clearly emerged. What has been discovered is very simple:

1. The process of modernization is based on the linear overcoming of factors limits through new incremental solutions mainly tending to safeguard investments in capital made by the large agro-food empires. The organization of the process has been placed within hierarchical structures offering standardized solutions easy-to-implement and replicate and aimed at cost minimization. This has led to a denial of the history of different territories and of their complex realities and to the proposal of a uniform model able to create the competition much beloved by the economy of global markets on which the strategy of wellbeing of the last 50 years is based. Here, we will not dwell on the failures of such models that have been clear for long a time in Europe and many other areas of the globe. What we wish to underline is that the concept of "modernization" conjures up the image of a repetitive process of codified and often linear actions that, thanks to technological advances, are able to overcome the limits placed by a scarcity of resources and their differential nature, thus increasing our overall knowledge and productivity. However, overcoming the limits of the known is conceived exclusively within the framework of linear laboratory experimentations that hardly ever tackle the complexity of problems in their entirety such as those relating to limited or scarce natural resources. In this manner the notion of modernization is confined within the broader concept of a self-celebratory culture obsessed with demonstrating its capacity to overcome limits regardless of their side effects. Evidence of this is given by the phenomena of food empires that move as grasshoppers across pristine lands exploiting their resources until they reach the limits imposed by both technological progress and the surrounding environment. Only then do they move on to more promising territories, generating

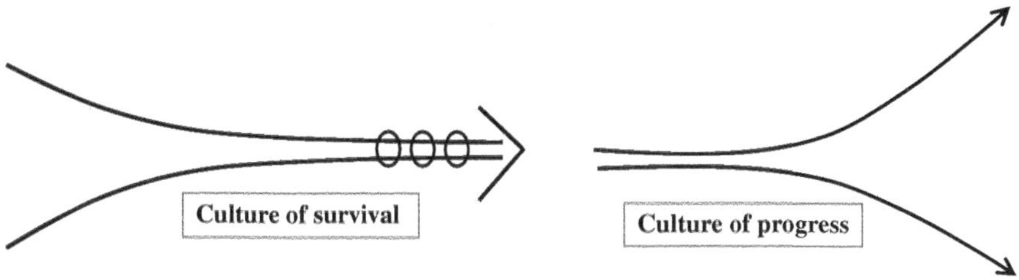

Fig. 2. The Peasants Culture. *Source*: Berger (1979): Pig Earth.

phenomena such as "land grabbing," child exploitation or miserly wages, social degradation, and the loss of agro-ecological knowledge and entrepreneurial capacities.

2. Peasant resistance and conservatism is nothing but the capacity to look to the future, especially to their children, and to acknowledge the scarcity of resources over long-term temporal dynamics. Indeed, what peasants do is revolutionary if compared to predictive unilinear models that tend to exploit resources within a "cage of knowledge" whose shortsightedness is due to the limits of the known. Therefore, as shown by Berger (1979), peasants have constantly adopted dynamic behaviors that allow them to move from a culture of survival, where scientific knowledge often defines them as guardians of traditions, to a "culture of progress" in which they are able to develop plans for the future (see Fig. 2).

In this book, the authors highlight the different ways in which peasants deal with complex situations and identify the potential solutions that can contribute to them and their family's wellbeing. Over the years, such solutions have strongly influenced the birth of modern civilization which has a tendency to deny its historical origins, but, at the same time, continues to have very strong connections to it. Evidence of this can be found across Europe, Latin America, and Asia. It reveals as many similarities as differences that look to the future as open and heterogeneous, leaving room for multiple realities that are neither subordinate nor hierarchized.

POLITICAL ACTION BETWEEN PEASANT AND SCIENTIFIC KNOWLEDGE

Politics was born as a method for expressing citizens' needs aimed at creating collective points of view and places for discussion or congregation, where one could share one's own needs and identify solutions able to equally satisfy everyone. Going back to the birth of nation states, founded upon democratic bodies of government, such a method was aimed at generating the necessary actions to give equitable responses to common needs. However, over the years, common needs have been increasingly shaped by economic lobbies[2] that have crossed the boundaries of rights and equity and above all of States assuming influential roles at international level through which they impose decisions at the local level. Such lobbying action has often been supported by scientific knowledge that justifies technological solutions and productive processes that promote uniform solutions primarily aimed at increasing productivity and competition. However, due to their very nature, these solutions tend to simplify the complexity and diversity of both territories and agricultural practices. A striking example of this is the case of Parmalat milk production, cited by van der Ploeg (2008), which from a company committed to quality and the needs of its milk producers has turned into a multinational corporation able to obtain funds for its expansion and the required legislative solutions for modifying basic production concepts, such as those characterizing "fresh milk" in Italy. In order to justify these processes and technological solutions the company argued it would be able to implement important economies of scale resulting in the offer of a cheaper "fresh milk" product in the form of micro-filtrated milk (van der Ploeg, 2008). The story is well known and eventually the dairy giant Parmalat took on the dramatic role of a "virtual Empire" that in the end collapsed, to the detriment of millions of savers, investors and of course producers, leaving a gap of billions of Euros that to date has not been fully bridged. Yet, paradoxically, the Parmalat system was acclaimed by the scientific knowledge lobby as a successful model of internationalization of companies and competitiveness in global markets.[3]

This leads to two fundamental topics:

1. The concept of knowledge; and
2. Political action as a result of local knowledge.

Over time the concept of knowledge has increasingly been confined to the level of science, and has thereby become locked into a cage of knowledge which is gradually less and less permeable to external demands and more and more self-referential. Furthermore, such knowledge plays a key role in the formulation of programs and policies for economic, social, and environmental growth in many rural areas of the world. But here we wish to underline the importance of another kind of knowledge, namely what we designate as "peasant knowledge." Such knowledge pertains to daily experiences and relations and evolves over time and space according to the circumstances, events, and decisions taken more or less consciously, though always considered the most appropriate at the time. It may also to some extent be codified, though in expressive modes that are hardly ever characterized by elegance and formal correctness as is the case with "scientific knowledge," but unlike the latter it responds in a reliable, original and topical way to current matters occurring in different territories. In short, it is hardly ever "virtual" knowledge. It is superfluous to underline that peasant and scientific knowledge are two sides of the same coin brought together by a mutual recognition and synergic and coherent relation in which the success of the first means the success of the second. This is what is happening in the new paradigm of rural development, where recognition of a peasant model implies the success of advanced and sustainable scientific solutions in territories characterized by scarcity of natural and energy resources, food, and climate change. In the paradigm of modernization, scientific knowledge has forgotten the existence of a peasant knowledge confining it to history and replacing it with what is considered technical progress through which a broadening of the space of the known is achieved. Two consequences however have been overlooked:

1. The broader the space of the known, the wider the boundaries of the unknown;
2. In its implementation phase, scientific and technological progress curbs the originality of solutions that might stem from human ingenuity and from the capacities of both man and "peasant knowledge" that reflect an "irrational" capacity to adjust to external shocks or to unpredictable events. In other words it has the capacity to step outside of positivistic thinking. It is in life circumstances that peasant knowledge takes shape and has a capacity to formulate or experiment with novel solutions that often go beyond the boundaries of the known thanks to the intuitive ability to act on beliefs and on the will to enhance their own, their family's, and wellbeing of the community in general. In short, we should acknowledge that peasants, besides representing a central part of the history of agricultural development, remain a solid foundation for a more prosperous agro-economic future for everyone.

After clarifying this aspect, we can now move to the second issue, namely: can political action derive from or be the result of local modes of knowledge? Recent studies in Brazil, China, and Europe, and documented in this book, provide strong evidence that peasant knowledge offers solutions to problems of livelihood and wellbeing and responds to the newly emerging needs of civil society in this third millennium. It does this primarily in terms of offering alternative solutions to agricultural industrialization. Examples of this are family farming in rural areas of China to combat poverty and improve access to food; the proved capacity of European peasantry to conserve territory and protect the landscape and make rural areas become more habitable and produce quality food; and by peasant and collective solutions in relation to the management of water resources and the construction of nested markets in Brazil.

However, what needs to be highlighted is that in many cases political action and the scientific world still have difficulty in recognizing the said solutions as promising, placing emphasis instead on programed actions within programmatic frameworks that are still strongly oriented toward solutions of modernization rather than of multi-functionality, or, even worse, having multi-functionality as the main objective, but demanding solutions typical of technological modernization (i.e., issues regarding food safety, commercial quality and access to markets, and waste management).

In conclusion, peasants alone are unable to start a revolutionary process against current practice. Clearly multilevel changes are needed that include support from both private and public institutions aimed at creating new synergic and coherent policy frameworks and objectives. And in some situations, it will be necessary to establish new institutions aimed at strengthening peasant action and promoting its development and involvement in new rural networks where rules, roles, responsibilities, and shared objectives are defined. Today, it is imperative that political action and relevant planning procedures fully embrace these issues and play a decisive role in the mediation and defense of local interests in this era of globalization.

NOTES

1. In the early 1970s, the Mansholt Plan declared that the small farmers of Europe would disappear by the end of the century.
2. With respect to the agro-marketing system, van der Ploeg identifies such international lobbies with Food Empires (2008).
3. The continued discussion of such issues is now somewhat irrelevant since the concept of market competitiveness is nowadays completely empty, outdated, and not appropriate for describing economic matters occurring in a global era in which also the notion of nation states is outmoded (Bauman, 2011).

ACKNOWLEDGEMENT

We wish to thank Professor Tony Fuller for the helpful comments and English revision and Nick Parrott for the English revision of Chapters 1, 2, 4, and 13.

REFERENCES

Bauman, Z. (2011). *Collateral damage, social inequalities in a global age*. Cambridge, UK: Polity Press.

Benvenuti, B. (1975). General systems theory and entrepreneurial autonomy in farming: Towards a new feudalism or towards democratic planning? *Sociologia Ruralis*, 15, 46–64. doi:10.1111/j.1467-9523.1975.tb00162.x

Benvenuti, B. (1982). Dalla mano invisibile a quella visibile: l'azienda agraria olandese in una gabbia istituzionale. In *QA La Questione agraria* (Vol. 5, p. 27). Milano: Franco angeli.

Berger, J. (1979). *The pig earth, first vintage international edition*. New york, NY: Pantheon books.

Chayanov, A. (1924). *Die Sozial Agronomie, ihre Grundgedanken und ihre Arbeitsmetoden*. Berlin: Verlagsbuchhandlung Paul Parey.

Kitchen, L., & Marsden, T. (2009). Creating sustainable rural development through stimulating the eco-economy: Beyond the eco-economic paradox? *Sociologia Ruralis*, *49*(3), 273–293.

Milone, P. (2009). *Agriculture in transition: A neo-institutional analysis*. (1[a] ed., p. 256). Van Gorcum: Assen, The Netherlands.

Milone, P., & Ventura, F. (2000). Theory and practice of Multi-product farms: Farm Butcheries in Umbria. In Sociologia Ruralis (Vol. n° 40/4, pp. 452–465). Oxford, UK: Blackwell Publishers.

Milone, P., & Ventura, F. (2004). Novelty as redefinition of farm boundaries. In J. S. C. Wiskerke & J. D. van der Ploeg (Eds.), *Seeds of Transition*. Assen: Van Gorcum.

Milone, P., & Ventura, F. (2014). The visible hand in building new markets for rural economies. In P. Hebinck, S. Schneider, & J. D. van der Ploeg (Eds.), *Rural development and the construction of new markets*. London: Routledge.

Reijs, J. W., Verhoeven, F. P. M., van Bruchem, J., van der Ploeg, J. D., & Lantinga, E. A. (2004). The nutrient management project of the VEL and VANLA environmental Co-operatives. In S. C. Wiskerke & J. D. van der Ploeg (Eds.), *Seeds of transition*. Assen: Van Gorcum.

Rip, A., & Kemp, R. (1998). Technological change. In S. Rayner & E. L. Malone (Eds.), *Human choice and climate change* (Vol. 2), Columbus, OH: Battel Press.

Stuiver, M., van der Ploeg, J. D., & Leeuwis, C. (2003). The Vel and VANLA environmental co-operatives as field laboratories. *NJAS – Wageningen Journal of Life Sciences*, *51*, 27–40.

Teece, D. J. (1980). Economies of scope and the scope of the enterprise. *Journal of Economic Behavior and organization*, *1*, 223–247.

van der Ploeg, J. D. (1994). Styles of farming: An introductory note on concepts and methodology. In J. D. van der Ploeg & A. Long (Eds.), *Born from within-practice and perspective of endogenous rural development*. Assen: Van Gorcum.

van der Ploeg, J. D. (2003). *The virtual farmer*. Assen: Van Gorcum.

van der Ploeg, J. D. (2008). The new peasantries. In *Struggles for autonomy and sustainability in an era of empire and globalisation* (p. 356). London: Earthscan Publication Ltd.

van der Ploeg, J. D. (2013). *Peasants and the art of farming, a chayanovian manifesto*. Agrarian Change and Peasant Studies Series, Halifax and Winnipeg: Fernwood Publishing.

van der Ploeg, J. D., Bouma, J., Rip, A., Rijkenberg, F. H. J., Ventura, F., & Wiskerke, J. S. C. (2004). On regimes, novelties and co-production. In J. S. C. Wiskerke & J. D. Ploeg van der (Eds.), *Seeds of transition* (pp. 1–30). Assen, The Netherlands: Van Gorcum.

van der Ploeg, J. D., Renting, H., Brunori, G., Knickel, K., Mannion, J., Marsden, T., ... Ventura, F. (2000). Rural development: From practices and policies towards theory. *Sociologia Ruralis*, *40*(4), 391–408.

Ventura, F. (2001). *Organizzarsi per sopravvivere*, PhD thesis, Wageningen University.

Ye, J. (2002). *Processes of enlightenment, farmer initiatives in rural development in China*, PhD thesis, Wageningen University, Wageningen.

CHAPTER 2

RURAL DEVELOPMENT: ACTORS AND PRACTICES

Jan Douwe van der Ploeg, Jingzhong Ye and Sergio Schneider

ABSTRACT

From a more general point of view the initiatives and novel practices of farmers represent 'seeds of transition'. They are the 'sprouts' out of which new socio-technical modes for organizing production and marketing emerge – 'sprouts' that, taken together can be described under the term 'rural development'. The examples are, on the whole, well-known; they include agro-ecological production, on-farm processing, agro-tourism, new credit associations and cooperative forms of commercialization. But it remains important to develop a more sociological interpretation of these new forms: since they are produced by social actors and are constantly redefined and modified through the relations and interactions implied by these new forms. This chapter defines the outline on actors and practices that will be discussed in later chapters of the book.

Keywords: Rural development; peasants; innovation; Brazil; China; Europe; rural sociology

Constructing a New Framework for Rural Development
Research in Rural Sociology and Development, Volume 22, 17–30

ISSN: 1057-1922/doi:10.1108/S1057-192220150000022001

INTRODUCTION

Rural development is not the self-evident outcome of the interplay between rural markets and agricultural technologies. Rather, rural development is *actively* shaped by the many actors, social movements and/or state apparatuses that are involved in it. Rural development is *constructed* through the many encounters that take place at the decisive interfaces where these agents meet and engage in complex and often contradictory practices (see Long, 2015). This applies a fortiori to the current materializations of rural development processes, which are evolving as, more or less, coherent sets of responses to the squeeze on agriculture (and, more specifically, to the economic and financial crisis that is now threatening agriculture), socio-economic and spatial inequalities and the poverty, deprivation and backwardness that these engender. In short: rural development is a (highly variable) *set of responses to market failures* (van der Ploeg et al., 2000; van der Ploeg, Ye, & Schneider, 2010). These responses assume, and create, new relations between the rural and the urban. They often occur through (and materialize as) the production of *new goods and services* that satisfy emerging new societal values. At the farm level this translates into multi-functionality.

At a wider level it translates into the construction of *new markets* (van der Ploeg, Schneider, & Ye, 2012). These new products and services are channelled through new markets which provide better remuneration to the farming population. Rural development also materializes as a social struggle aimed at defending the resources and regulatory space needed for these new products, services and markets. In this sense rural development represents a 'counter development': it differs from the development of agriculture and the countryside (and, consequently, the development of food processing, distribution and consumption) that is induced and shaped by the main agricultural and food markets. In hegemonic discourse rural development is understood as merely correcting or complementing market-led development. But it may well go beyond this and can replace market-led development – not in and through a sudden change – but through a complex and contradictory process of transition. Careful empirical research is needed to assess how rural development really *operates* (and particularly whether it should be understood as being complementary to market-led development or as a counterforce that might transform market-led development).

In other publications we have focussed on the nature and dynamics of rural development *processes* (van der Ploeg et al., 2010) and on the performance of rural development *policies* (Hebinck, Schneider, & van der

Ploeg, 2014). Here, the focus is on *actors* and *practices.*[1] This book explores who the actors are that operate as driving force in these processes, what motivates them, how they relate to each other and how they structure their practices. And, echoing the contribution of Long to this volume, we ask how the newly emerging practices, and more generally rural development processes as a whole, shape the actors that are involved in them. For, we argue, it is not only the actors that shape new practices, but the practices equally shape actors involved.

Naturally, there are major differences in rural development practices between China, Brazil and the EU (which we documented in the special issue of *Rivista di Economia Agraria*, 2010). Equally there are major differences between 'pioneers', those who instigate novel activities, and 'followers', those who apply elements and ingredients that have already proven their validity. But, alongside the many dissimilarities, this book also identifies some commonalities and the authors attempt to distinguish the commonalities from coincidental similarities.

THE MAIN ACTORS IN RURAL DEVELOPMENT

It is important to note that in this book we do not talk about actors or practices in general. We restrict our investigation to those actors who are actively involved in rural development processes, constructing new practices and, therefore, new relations, networks, resource constellations and identities that are central to, and strategic for, the further unfolding of rural development.

As mentioned before, there are major differences, both temporal and spatial, in how rural development processes are socially constructed. In Europe rural development is generally driven by farmers' ongoing search for new possibilities that enhance the likelihood of maintaining the continuity of their farms.[2] Thus, new rural development activities are first born as individual initiatives and only then tied together into new networks. By contrast, in Brazil, social movements play a central role in triggering rural development processes, whilst in China the state clearly plays the leading role (Ye, Rao, & Wu, 2010). This does not imply that the state does not play a role in Brazilian and European rural development processes, or that there is an absence of individual initiatives (of the type that dominates in Europe) in Brazil or China. Far from it. The point is that the gravitational centre of rural development processes clearly differs between China, Brazil and Europe.

This has major consequences for any attempt to characterize the main actors involved in rural development processes. These actors are socially shaped by the relationships that they engage in. These relationships are often developed through necessity, although actors can also sometimes choose (or even construct) these relationships in a voluntary, goal-oriented and knowledgeable, way (Long, 1985, 2001). Actors can even be involved in different 'multiple structures' which may wholly or partly contrast with each other. They may spend part of their time engaged in 'conventional' farming (and being subordinated to unequal power relations) and another part being involved in creating new patterns (new contrasting structures) that allow them to go beyond their historically inherited situation.

In Europe, *pride* is an important keyword that describes the motivation of the actors involved in rural development processes. Their pride stems from their capacity to show that they are not just a victim of circumstance, but are able to make a difference, to *construct* (rather than to find) new responses, even if they are only partial ones. Fig. 1 shows a mother and her

Fig. 1. An Expression of Pride.

son who have changed their farm into a very attractive multi-functional enterprise whose portfolio includes providing berths for passing yachts and their passengers. *Rebelliousness* could be another keyword. Many rural development practices are, especially initially, deviations from the rule.

They involve actors explicitly contesting the existing rules of the game and the seemingly immutable regularities associated with them.[3] In so doing they construct new practices and new networks. Once the value of these is proven, this can create a sense of pride. Finally, we should also mention *passion*. These actors are usually people who love farming and who have a strong desire to continue with it, to renew it, to make it match new societal demands and be viable for the next generation. Needless to say the balance between passion, rebelliousness and pride has to be continuously adjusted over time, especially in the face of the setbacks that often have to be dealt with.

In Brazil *resistance* is one of the forces that motivates rural development actors (Schneider & Niederle, 2010). This, of course, is related to the leading role played by social movements. Actors' relationships with each other (and others) are primarily defined through their involvement in the social movements through which they construct rural development. Yet, there is no absence of resistance in Europe – but it is more underground in Europe than in Brazil, where it is more overt. This is partly because rebelliousness is more a feature of individuals and resistance is more carried by organizations and movements (Scott, 1985, 1998). Equally there is no absence of pride and passion in Brazil.

There is pride when common endeavours bring practical results or when distinction is created, for example when productive employment, a certain level of self-regulation and acceptable incomes are created where they were previously lacking. These elements flow together in one carefully coordinated balance, summarized in Fig. 2, taken in one of the settlements created through an extended struggle by one of the social movements. *Ocupar* translates as occupation (of the land) to open up (create) space for manoeuvre. This is followed by *resistir* (resistance), which is required to remain on the occupied lands and to obtain titles, credit, access to markets, etc. Then comes *produzir* (production), the next stage in the struggle. Underlying all these key words, there is *cooperar* (cooperation), not only between the actors involved but also with state agencies that might be led to view the movements and settlements in a positive light.

In China many of the actors actively involved in rural development are driven by a carefully regulated balance of *tradition* and *renewal*. To understand this, one has to take into account that multi-functionality has always

Fig. 2. An Image from a Brazilian Settlement.

been an important feature of Chinese farms.[4] The current generation is building on this tradition and is strengthening and renewing it. Another important balance is that between *local initiatives* and *central intervention.* Some rural development practices in China have started from local initiatives. These are often daring and highly novel. Others stem from government initiatives and are often backed up by considerable state support. On the whole, most initiatives involve strong cooperation between the state and peasants. Fig. 3 shows the construction of new terraces in the hills surrounding a peasant village. Once constructed these new fields will be used for walnut production, an attractive form of diversification. Elder farmers are investing considerable amounts of money here to create new opportunities for their children. In this they are supported by government subsidies and co-ordination from the local village committee.

These descriptions, and the associated pictures, initially seem to suggest major differences between Brazil, China and Europe. The actors differ, as do their main motives. Nonetheless, there is also an important commonality. Time and again we see *agency*: the capacity to make a difference, to get actively involved and to (jointly) shape the course of events. This agency translates into new *material realities* that are co-constructed by the actors involved. These may take the form of new settlements, new fields or new agritourism facilities, etc. In turn, these new material realities

Fig. 3. Rural Development in China.

provide new employment opportunities, increased and diversified production (and improved incomes) and new flows of people coming into the countryside. These new material realities (new objects and new networks that generate new and viable constellations) are the basis of pride and help partially transform the identities of those involved. It should be emphasized that without active agency these new realities would not emerge. They are not the outcome of the 'self-regulatory capacity of markets'; nor the outcome of a blueprint elaborated by state agencies. They are the result of agency: the capacity to actively intervene in (or create new) markets and to negotiate and/or to mediate state intervention.[5]

In the case of rural development such agency often requires *doggedness*. The chosen trajectory seldom represents the easiest way forward and often goes against the grain. Hence, insistence is needed. The trajectory might involve a long time span, which again requires doggedness as well as a certain amount of *stubbornness*. *Endurance* is also needed to see things through over a long time span. Such features appear, we believe, in China and Brazil as much as they do in Europe.

We do not want to romanticize the actors involved in rural development practices, nor do we want to represent them as some kind of folk heroes. What we want to do is to develop understanding of what motivates and drives them. We know very well that there is, on the whole, far more opportunism than doggedness and endurance in the countryside, whilst modernization and education have wiped out much traditional stubbornness. Nonetheless, deviations are created through doggedness, stubbornness and endurance and the convergence of many such deviations forms the basis of emerging new rural development processes.

We neither want to analyse persistence, endurance, doggedness, etc., as mere psychological attributes and/or as behavioural characteristics of individual farmers. The point is that individual behaviour can be conditioned by social phenomena, and thus becomes a social fact in the Durkheimian sense of the word. The external pressures on farmers in Brazil, China and the EU might differ considerably, as might the actions and reactions developed to modify or change these external pressures. However, to understand the multiple and diverse strategies that farmers use to build their responses, it is necessary to use an analytical approach that recognizes the active role of social actors. Norman Long rightly described this active role of actors in terms of 'agency', which he defined as '*the ability of an actor to process social experience and to devise ways of coping with social life, even under the most extreme forms of coercion*' (Long, 1985). It is quite possible that specific 'coping' strategies that (co-)shape social identities and features, such as doggedness, etc., emerge from this. Thus, tradition, pride, resistance, stubbornness, etc., might be viewed as important *social attributes*. Whilst the 'peasant model' may be most commonly outlined in terms of economics and/or resource-flows (see Milone, Ventura, & Ye, 2015), it can also be described in sociological terms, that is in the terms used above. In this respect it is important to signal that such features are *relational* terms that are at the core of specific 'activity systems' (see Long, 2015). Doggedness, for instance, describes the relation between something that shows itself to be resistant to change and a person wanting to change it despite that resistance. Pride also emerges, as a relational element, after the desired change has finally been realized, after expending much energy, insistence and creativity, and so forth.

Rural development does not happen 'automatically'. The less so since it occurs through, and as, an evolving set of, more or less, coherent responses to market failures and the poverty, marginality and lack of prospects that these engender. The design and subsequent implementation of such responses critically requires doggedness, passion, resistance and the like. Thus, it can be argued that rural development practices very much (co-)shape the actors involved into the people they are. If rural development is counter-development – as we argued above – then it shapes people into rebellious people. This is inevitable, especially when actors attempt to launch initiatives and practices that run against the grain.

In summarizing a series of detailed biographies, Ye (2002, p. 1)[6] concluded that rural development occurs through farmers' initiatives. Such initiatives are an expression of their agency: 'a farmer's initiative is the impetus that sufficiently and necessarily drives a farmer to formulate a realistic strategic plan and to implement it as an attempt to create space for manoeuvre and to pursue change'. Ye argues that there is something special in such initiatives: 'In the Chinese case we can identify farmer initiatives when actions go beyond the potentialities and opportunities of the existing farm household economy to embrace new livelihood pursuits' (*ibid.*). Ye also argues that such initiatives are widespread: 'There is the ubiquity of farmer initiatives in all agrarian sectors and all rural communities. It is farmer initiatives that intrinsically drive local development and social change' (*ibid.*). We have studied similar processes of novelty production in Europe and in Brazil (Milone & Ventura, 2009; Schneider, Gomes da Silva, & Bezerre, 2014; Schneider & Niederle, 2010; Wiskerke & van der Ploeg, 2004). It is remarkable to discover that novelties are being produced everywhere – one can almost say that they are ubiquitous.

The sets of motives (the different balances) described separately for Europe, Brazil and China, are tentative, as is our attempt to identify common elements. We present them here as mere hypotheses, hoping that they will stimulate and provoke more detailed inquiries and comparisons for discussion.

RURAL DEVELOPMENT PRACTICES

The rural development *practices* in which these actors are involved also merit discussion. It is important to note that these practices are shaped by the actors, just as the latter are shaped, to a degree, by the former. We assume that (a) these practices have certain traits in common, and (b) that there are important and intrinsic relations between the actors and practices, that is between the specific features of the actors and the specific characteristics of the practices they construct. Both (a) and (b) are still to be unravelled. In so doing we will need to keep in mind that each one informs and influences the other.

The new practices that are constructed in, and as part of, rural development processes contain several distinctive features. A first one is *autonomy*. There are two aspects to this. Rural development practices are usually (but not always) autonomously generated. More importantly, they are a strategy for *regaining* and/or *enlarging autonomy*. Even when there is considerable state support, the unfolding of these practices represents a search for enlarging autonomy. This search for autonomy subsequently translates into a search for *endogeneity*, building as much as possible (but not exclusively) on locally available resources in order to avoid getting entrapped in new dependency relations. It also translates into novelty production, the search for local and original solutions which helps to avoid dependency on externally developed innovations.

The search for (if not the active construction of) *synergy* is a second important characteristic of rural development practices. This search is intimately related to multi-functionality, which is essentially about using one and the same set of factors of production to make a wider (and expanding) range of products and services. Marsden (2009, p. 124) defines this as 'the relative capability for the local rural economy to do more than one thing at the same time from the same (and necessarily restricted) resource base'. Synergy involves doing this in such a way that the economic effects grow more than proportionally.[7] If and when sufficient synergy is created, rural development practices can become self-propelling.

A third important characteristic is that the different practices increasingly interlink through *horizontal networking* (as opposed to vertical hierarchies). Within these networks *reciprocity* plays a major role. Newly created economic relations are embedded in reciprocal frameworks (Sabourin, 2011).

In the fourth place, we argue that most rural development practices explicitly carry the stamp of the *rural*. They make use of available resources (often mobilized through non-commodity circuits and often part of local ecosystems) and this makes it easier to start new enterprises. It seems to be far easier to start new entrepreneurial activities in rural areas than in urban ones, not only because there nearly always are at least some resources available but possibly also because people in rural areas are more able to draw on collective memories, available local knowledge and social networks. Trust, credibility, reputation and personalized interactions (as opposed to the 'liquidity' and anonymity of social relations in the urban sphere) are probably also important ingredients here. They are also often enhanced through rural development practices.

Typically, many rural development practices also adopt a remarkably long-term perspective (reflecting the stubbornness and endurance of the actors involved). They are often seen as contributing to the prospects of the next generation, offering them employment opportunities, attractive working conditions and considerable autonomy. Finally, it is important to note that many rural development practices seem to contribute significantly to the quality of life – not only of those who are directly involved in them, but more broadly.

We believe that these characteristics, or at least most of them, are common to rural development practices (as they unfold at the micro-level) in Brazil, China and Europe, and that they are probably particularly characteristic of the new and novel practices being constructed 'at the frontier' of rural development processes.

ON ACTORS AND PRACTICES

So far we have talked about local people constructing local responses to global processes and the problems they bring. These responses (or 'initiatives' as they are called in Chinese studies) result in (and occur through) new productive practices and new networks that link producers and consumers in novel ways (van der Ploeg et al., 2012). In this respect they are highly distinctive. They are not merely an expression of protest and contestation; nor are they forms of sabotage or foot dragging. Instead, they represent a struggle of the 'third kind' (van der Ploeg, 2008) that goes beyond contestation and/or sabotage. They are *productive* responses, creating not only new goods and services but also generating new forms of production, distribution and consumption.

We believe that the 'fingerprint' of those creating these new practices can, in one way or another, be discerned in these practices and vice versa; the identities of those involved will be affected by the distinctive practices in which they are engaged.

Although some of the interrelations seem to be self-evident (we have already pointed to the possible convergence of stubbornness and long-term perspectives that are built into the new practices), we are still far from understanding the complex intertwinements and mutual transformations of actors and practices. We hope that the collection of chapters contained in this volume will help to formulate research questions to help people navigate through this difficult area.

In synthesis, this book discusses the ways in which farmers look for, and create, new ways of getting things done, in order to resolve everyday problems that emerge in the productive processes, the management of their properties, their access to markets, etc. Farmers invent new ways to face up to, and go beyond, the difficulties related to their material survival and to the continuity of their social group. These ways build on the repertoires, practices and initiatives that farmers have developed to face the many contingencies, mostly unexpected, that undermine their autonomy and increase their vulnerability. The agrarian sector is increasingly enmeshed in market circuits, through which farmers have to mobilize the required productive resources and to sell their produce. The capacity to innovate and create space for manoeuvre within these circuits provides farmers with flexibility, learning capabilities and knowledge, all strategic requirements for their interactions with the general economy and society at large.

From a more general point of view the initiatives and novel practices of farmers represent 'seeds of transition' (Wiskerke & van der Ploeg, 2004). They are the 'sprouts' out of which new socio-technical modes for organizing production and marketing emerge – 'sprouts' that, taken together, form the basis of rural development (Schneider et al., 2014). The examples are generally quite widely reported on; they include agroecological production, on-farm processing, agritourism, new credit associations and cooperative forms of commercialization. But it remains important to develop a more sociological interpretation of these new forms: since they are produced by social actors and are constantly redefined and modified through the relations and interactions implied by these new forms.

What we seek to develop, then, is an overall view of these new practices: one that views them not just as *reactions* but also as *new and creative constructions* that promise far wider changes. In this respect the metaphor of 'seeds' is central. The seeds need to be put in fertile soil in order to germinate and produce new harvests. Some of them are already beyond 'sprouting' and have already clearly shown themselves to have a far-reaching impact.

NOTES

1. The contributions to the volume were first presented and discussed in the 'Third Seminar on the Comparative Analysis of Rural Development in China, Brazil and the EU' held at the College of Humanities and Development Studies (COHD) at China Agricultural University (CAU) in Beijing between 30 October and 3 November, 2012.

2. Apart from the search for farm continuity, rural development practices may be spurred by a wide range of other motives. Some of these are discussed in Oostindie et al.'s contribution to this volume.

3. An example of such 'seemingly immutable regularities' is the commonly held idea that only large farms can be continued, whilst smaller farms must necessarily disappear. Many relatively small farms have disproved this notion by employing rural development practices and converting themselves into solid enterprises with strong prospects for continuity.

4. Whilst in Europe and Brazil it had to be reconstructed.

5. Ye (2002, p. 2) refers to the farmers actively engaged in rural development as being 'enlightened'. This word would strike a strange chord in Europe and Brazil, but it nicely expresses a general feature: 'it not only refers to being inspired by ideas from others, but more importantly, from engaging in and learning from social interactions with others, with events, and everyday experiences'.

6. A summary can be found in Ye, Wang, and Long (2009).

7. To put it simply: if activity A renders 10 euros, and activity B also renders 10 euros when organized separately, then the judicious combination of A and B within one multi-functional enterprise might render 25 euros. The additional benefit of 5 euro is the synergetic effect of well-organized multi-functionality.

REFERENCES

Hebinck, P., Schneider, S., & van der Ploeg, J. D. (2014). *Rural development and the construction of new markets*. London: Routledge.

Long, N. (1985). Creating space for change: A perspective on the sociology of development. *Sociologia Ruralis*, *XXIV*(3–4), 168–184.

Long, N. (2001). *Development sociology: Actor perspectives*. London: Routledge.

Long, N. (2015). Activities, actants and actors: Theoretical perspectives on development practice and practitioners. In P. Milone, F. Ventura, & J. Ye (Eds.), *Constructing a new framework for rural development* (Vol. 22). Research in Rural Sociology and Development. Bingley, UK: Emerald Group Publishing Limited.

Marsden, T. (2009). Mobilities, vulnerabilities and sustainabilities: Exploring pathways from denial to sustainable rural development. *Sociologia Ruralis*, *49*(2), 113–131.

Milone, P., & Ventura, F. (2009). *I contadini del Terzo Millennio*. Perugia: AMP Edizione.

Milone, P., Ventura, F., & Ye, J. (2015). Introduction. In P. Milone, F. Ventura, & J. Ye (Eds.), *Constructing a new framework for rural development* (Vol. 22). Research in Rural Sociology and Development. Bingley, UK: Emerald Group Publishing Limited.

Rivista di Economia Agraria. (2010). Special Issue "A comparative analysis of rural development processes in China, Brazil and the European Union" (in English language), *LXV*(2).

Sabourin, E. (2011). *Sociedades e organizações camponesas – uma leitura através da reciprocidade*. Porto Alegre: UFRGS Publisher.

Schneider, S., Gomes da Silva, M. A., & Bezerre, I. (2014). *Sementes e brotas da transiçao: Innovaçao e desenvolvimento em areas rurais do Brrasil*. Porto Alegre: PGDR.

Schneider, S., & Niederle, P. (2010). Resistance strategies and diversification of rural livelihoods: The construction of autonomy among Brazilian family farmers. *Journal of Peasant Studies*, *37*(2), 379–405.

Scott, J. C. (1985). *Weapons of the weak: Everyday forms of peasant resistance*. New Haven, CT: Yale University Press.

Scott, J. C. (1998). *Seeing like a state: How certain schemes to improve the human condition have failed*. New Haven, CT: Yale University Press.

van der Ploeg, J. D. (2008). *The new peasantries, struggles for autonomy and sustainability in an era of empire and globalization*. London: Earthscan.

van der Ploeg, J. D., Renting, H., Brunori, G., Knickel, K., Marsden, T., de Roest, C., ... Ventura, F. (2000). Rural development: From practices and policies towards theory. *Sociologia Ruralis, 40*(4), 391–408. UK: Blackwell Publishers.

van der Ploeg, J. D., Schneider, S., & Ye, J. (2012). Rural development through the construction of new, nested markets. *Journal of Peasant Studies, 39*(1), 133–173. UK: Routledge Publishers.

van der Ploeg, J. D., Ye, J., & Schneider, S. (2010). Rural development reconsidered: Building on comparative perspectives from China, Brazil and the European Union. *Rivista di Economia Agraria, LXV*(2), 163–189.

Wiskerke, J. S. C., & van der Ploeg, J. D. (2004). *Seeds of transition: Essays on novelty production, niches and regimes in agriculture*. Assen: Royal Van Gorcum.

Ye, J. (2002). *Processes of enlightenment, farmer initiatives in rural development in China*. PhD thesis, Wageningen University, Wageningen.

Ye, J., Rao, J., & Wu, H. (2010). Crossing the river by feeling the stones: Rural development in China. *Rivista di Economia Agraria, LXV*(2), 261–294.

Ye, J., Wang, Y., & Long, N. (2009). Farmer initiatives and livelihood diversification: From the collective to a market economy in rural China. *Journal of Agrarian Change, 9*(2), 175–203.

CHAPTER 3

ACTIVITIES, ACTANTS AND ACTORS: THEORETICAL PERSPECTIVES ON DEVELOPMENT PRACTICE AND PRACTITIONERS

Norman Long

ABSTRACT

This chapter falls into two parts. The first offers a theoretical overview of three actor perspectives on issues of development intervention: (a) activity theory, (b) actor-network theory and (c) actor-oriented interface analysis. The second provides an illustrated discussion of the usefulness of actor perspectives for understanding the encounters that take place between 'development experts' (local and foreign) and so-called 'beneficiaries'. The argument draws upon ethnographic data relating to issues of development interface, actor identities, networks and discourse.

Keywords: Rural development; rural sociology; actor network theory; actor oriented approach; interface analysis

Constructing a New Framework for Rural Development
Research in Rural Sociology and Development, Volume 22, 31–58

ISSN: 1057-1922/doi:10.1108/S1057-192220150000022002

SIMILARITIES AND DIFFERENCES BETWEEN THE PERSPECTIVES

In highly condensed form, the basic tenets of the three approaches can be summarised as follows.

Activity theory[1] builds upon cultural-historical activity theory developed originally as a multidisciplinary paradigm for comprehending the relationship between action and cognition. It has been used for understanding transformations in work, organisation and technology. It models activity systems and their developmental contradictions, and includes a theory of cycles of expansive learning in organisations and communities. It adopts an applied interventionist methodology based upon detailed case-study research (see *Learning by Expanding* by Engeström, 1987). The latter has been used extensively in developing, on a participatory basis, improvements in the management of industrial organisations as well as public services in Finland and elsewhere.

It starts from the assumption that an activity is composed of a 'subject' and 'object' mediated by some 'instrument'. The subject (person or group) is motivated by an object or 'objective' to engage in some activity. This process involves mediation through certain tools, such as technologies, texts, cognitive schema, cultural symbols and modes of organising. The theory then proceeds to map out what is called the 'hierarchical structure of activity' in terms of the distinctions between activity (defined as the engagement of a subject towards the solution of a problem or need), action (more clearly goal-oriented and entailing implicitly or explicitly relations with other subjects and framed by social and cultural commitments) and operations (habitual, taken-for-granted or automatic responses driven by the conditions and tools at hand). Attention is also given to explaining the relation between 'context' and 'behaviour' in terms of a unity rather than an opposition of elements. 'Context is not an outer container or shell inside of which people behave in certain ways' (Nardi, 1996). Instead the activities become the context in which possible future individual or collective actions take shape cognitively and organisationally, thus allowing for both 'internal' and 'external' mediating processes. This, in turn, enables one to take account of the ways in which rules regulate actions and interactions within the activity system, leading to an analysis of how, for example, divisions of labour and systems of power and status may underpin activity and shape social consciousness (Engeström, 2001).

In the model proposed by activity theory the 'subject' refers to the individual or subgroup relevant to the specific activity or activities; and the 'obj' to the 'raw material' or 'problem space' at which the activity is directed and which is moulded and transformed into outcomes with the help of physical and symbolic, external and internal mediating instruments, including both tools and signs. The community comprises multiple individuals or subgroups who share the same general object and who construct themselves as distinct from other communities. The division of labour refers to both the horizontal division of tasks between the members of the community and the vertical division of power and status. Finally the rules refer to the explicit and implicit regulations, norms and conventions that constrain actions and interactions within the activity system. A concrete illustration of these components would be that of a health care clinic composed of a variety of medical and non-medical professional staff organised in different practice units and marked off from each other by specialist technologies and administrative styles, and of course by a wide range of different kinds of patients.

An activity system is always heterogeneous and multi-voiced. Due to differences in life histories and positions in the division of labour, the various subjects construct 'objects' and the other components of activity relevant to them in different, partially overlapping and partially conflicting, ways. There is constant construction and renegotiation within the activity system. Coordination between different versions of the object must be achieved to ensure continuous operation. Tasks are reassigned and redivided, rules are bent and reinterpreted. There is also incessant movement between the various nodes of the activity, such that what initially appears as the object may soon be transformed into an outcome, then turned into an instrument, and perhaps later into a rule (Engeström, 1996). Thus, for instance, an unusual medical case first appears as a problem, is transformed into a successful diagnosis and treatment, the account of which is used instrumentally as a prototype or model for similar cases, and is gradually sedimented and petrified into a rule requiring certain procedures in all cases that fit the category. On the other hand, rules may be questioned, reinterpreted and turned into new tools and objects.

Thus activity is fundamentally a collective, systemic formation that has a complex mediational structure. An activity system produces actions and is realised by means of further actions. However, activity is not reducible to action. Actions are relatively short lived and have a clear-cut beginning and end, whereas activity systems evolve over lengthy periods of historical time, often taking the form of institutions and organisations. And Leont'ev (1978, p. 52) further points out that the concept of object is already contained in the very concept of activity itself; hence there is no such thing as 'objectless' activity. An object is both something given and something projected or anticipated. A thing or phenomenon becomes an object of activity as it meets a human need. The subject constructs the object, that is, 'singles out those properties that prove to be essential for developing social practice' (Lektorsky, 1984, p. 137). In this constructed, need-related capacity, the object gains motivating force that gives shape and direction to activity. It is the object that determines the horizon of possible goals and actions.

An activity system does not exist in a vacuum; it interacts within a network of other activity systems, and is articulated with external systems which – borrowing from the language of historical materialism – often generates dialectical contradictions. These processes point to the importance of studying how expansive joint learning processes come about within heterogeneous actor networks and thus lead to concrete modes of collaboration and their associated tools, concepts and rules. This also requires the study of where ideas for projects (e.g. technology or development aid projects) originate and how their contents and modes are negotiated. Central to all this is the question of identifying a 'shared object' of activity and the underlying dialogicality of multiple voices and points of view. In this way activity theory comes close to recognising the significance of the dynamics of interface relations, although, as Kontinen (2004) rightly stresses, it underestimates the complexities entailed in diverse groups negotiating shared objects of activity. This arises primarily because it lacks a solid conceptualisation of power relations and questions of agency in respect to both human and non-human components, although this deficiency is now acknowledged and partly resolved (see Engeström, 2009). Nevertheless, it continues to be largely wedded to a structure-oriented, systemic view of social order and change, which uncovers its strong roots in historical materialist thinking.

Furthermore, it depends heavily on a deductive method of analysis that takes as given the existence of activity systems with clearly demarcated parameters. A central difficulty concerns the identification of so-called 'shared objects' that mediate between actors and activity systems. This arises because of the existence of a multiplicity of actors with diverse world-views, meanings and interests. Hence 'shared' or 'common' views about which activities are required to solve the problem(s) encountered will likewise vary greatly. In fact a great deal of negotiation and renegotiation is necessary for formulating and achieving anything like a common view and means of action. Moreover, what looks like a 'shared' position frequently turns out to be nothing more than a temporary and fragile coalition that shifts as events move on.

All this is reminiscent of Checkland's model of 'soft systems' thinking which is likewise based on participatory modes of identifying some common problem or problems for resolution. Having arrived at some common understanding of the problem then a plan of action (or set of activities) is defined in order to bring about a solution (see Checkland, 1988; Röling, 1988). 'The idea is that participatory processes almost automatically become consensus and cooperation-oriented (providing that sufficient attention is given to social learning), and that consensus is a precondition for development and innovation' (Leeuwis, 2004, p. 163). Note also the issue of what Röling calls 'platforms' whereby 'different stakeholders are brought together to overlook the situation and learn and negotiate towards more productive outcomes (i.e. co-ordinated action)' (Leeuwis, 2004, p. 34; Leeuwis & Aarts, 2011).

While, in some respects, *actor-network theory* is similar to activity theory in that actor-network theory (ANT) also accords central importance to material objects, technological artefacts, texts and discourses in the making of 'the social', it rejects outright systems thinking, structuralism of various kinds and social constructivism, in favour of an undifferentiated, hybrid socio-technical, cultural-cum-natural mode of understanding and in this way it challenges the very foundations of *social* science.

Actor-network theory can be traced to the early work of Michel Callon and Bruno Latour at the Ecóle des Mines in Paris in the early 1990s. Their analysis focuses upon the progressive constitution of networks in which both human actors and non-human actants assume identities in accordance with prevailing strategies of interaction. Actors' identities and qualities are defined during negotiations between the 'representatives' of different kinds of actors. In this perspective, representation is to be understood in its political dimension, that is, as a process of delegation. The most important of these negotiations is what they call 'translation'. This consists of multifaceted interactions in which actors (1) construct common definitions and meanings, (2) define representativities and (3) co-opt each other in the pursuit of individual and collective objectives or 'projects'. In ANT, both actors and actants share the scene in the reconstruction of these network interactions leading to the stabilisation of the system. But the critical difference between them is that only actors are able to put actants into circulation.[2]

The core components of heterogeneous networks consist of an assemblage of human, social, material, technological and textual elements (Callon & Law, 1995; Latour, 1993). This view attempts to dissolve the common-sense distinction between 'things' and 'people' by arguing that 'purposeful action and intentionality are not properties of objects but neither are they properties of human actors. Rather, they are properties of institutions, of *collectifs*' (Verschoor, 1997, p. 27). That is, they are emergent effects generated by the interaction of numerous human and non-human components, not by a group of individuals who decide to join together to undertake some common endeavour (Long, 2001, p. 57).

This approach concentrates on constructing accounts of 'how the [human and non-human] actants they identify function as signifiers in a discursive field' (Golinski, 1998, p. 40). Hence the emphasis in ANT rests on semiotic dimensions rather than on the close-up study of situated social practice, or what Golinski describes as 'incidents of practical engagement with the material world'.

As Mosse (2005, pp. 34–35) points out, the central processes of 'translation' and 'enrolment' of ANT may usefully be applied to the 'subtle relationship between the framing of problems and the social process of enrolment in the design [and, one might add, the implementation] of a development project'. Framing enables key (i.e. 'authoritative') actors to engage the interest of larger constituencies that provide various ideas and storylines that serve to legitimise the 'collective' effort. Project design is a bid for political support and involves translating a range of different perspectives and interests into one (apparently) coherent whole or container of many notions and texts. In order to achieve this, a degree of ambiguity and imprecision is necessary, otherwise 'the project' would be unsustainable. And Latour (1996) goes on to stress that it is critical to turn 'the project as a world of signs into a world of objects'. Hence, as Mosse underlines (2005, p. 35), 'a project design becomes complex and contains irreconcilable perspectives; but in order to persuade it requires unity, coherence and simplicity' (or what Latour has labelled 'blackboxing').

This is achieved in a variety of ways: through repositioning one's standpoint so that one's values and interests are more compatible with those of the other actors, succumbing to strategic pressure or manipulation, and/or allowing oneself to be seduced by rewards of various kinds (the carrot effect). In addition, therefore, to the various symbolic mediations (highlighted in both activity theory and ANT) associated with specific material, technical and cultural signifiers, it is also necessary, of course, to acknowledge the critical role played by various types of 'brokers' and 'gatekeepers' who occupy critical nodes within a specific network or activity field. The latter operate within the spaces (often 'informal') between the different organisations and interest groups within particular arenas of development intervention.

Let me conclude this brief overview of ANT by discussing the issue of what Latour has designated as the 'symmetry' of human and non-human components. This point of view arises methodologically from the need to show how technologies, discourses (verbal and non-verbal) and other texts, material resources, symbolic elements, government policies and human and non-human life forms enter the development scene. But how do these various non-human elements relate to people? Can we ascribe an equal degree of agency to non-humans as to humans? Does the approach advance our understanding of heterogeneous networks and collective forms of social action? And if we are committed to the idea of *collectifs* being somehow actors in their own right, why do we need to differentiate between 'individual' and 'collective' actors? How does one, indeed, distinguish between *collectif* and collective action? Surely we should give some more detailed attention to 'coalitions' of actors and how they are formed and consolidated?

A further niggling matter is why should we be so seduced by the language of Latour et al.? In fact the use of the word 'language' in this respect is highly pertinent since the research method developed by AN theorists seems to stress semiotic dimensions to the neglect of a close-up study of situated social practices. Indeed rather than grounding one's findings on in-depth ethnography and thus stressing the pragmatics of everyday life and intervention processes, we encounter a fascination for story-telling based on key narratives designed to unlock processes of translation, enrolment and the formation of *collectifs*. Moreover, this is often done from the point of view of heroic translators (or authoritative or dominant actors – including the researchers themselves), rather than in terms of the dynamics of conflict and accommodation between the multiplicity of actors and the differential frameworks of meanings and values entailed. Actually the blackboxing of *collectifs* does not help. What does help is the opening of these so as to reveal the many intricate and entangled social relationships, networks and multiple discourses involved.

Let me now turn to the *Actor-oriented Approach to Development Intervention*.

This approach is based on the simple idea that different social forms develop under the same or similar structural circumstances. Such differences reflect variations in the ways in which actors attempt to come to grips, cognitively and organisationally, with the situations they face. Therefore an understanding of differential patterns of social behaviour must be grounded in terms of 'knowing, active subject[s]' (Knorr-Cetina, 1981, p. 4), and not merely viewed as due to the differential impact of broad social forces (such as ecological change, demographic pressure or incorporation into world capitalism). A main task for analysis, then, is to identify and characterise differing actor strategies and rationales, the conditions under which they arise, how they interlock, their viability or effectiveness for solving specific problems and their wider social ramifications.

Agency refers to the knowledgeability, capability and social embeddedness associated with acts of doing (and reflecting) that impact upon or shape one's own and others' actions and interpretations. Agency is usually recognised ex post facto through its acknowledged or presumed effects. Persons or networks of persons have agency. In addition, they may attribute agency to various objects and ideas, which, in turn, can shape actors' perceptions of what is possible. Agency is composed, therefore, of a complex mix of social, cultural and material elements. And 'strategic agency' signifies the enrolment of many actors in the 'project' of some other person or persons.

Social actors are all those social entities that can be said to have agency in that they possess the knowledgeability and capacity to assess problematic situations and organise 'appropriate' responses. Social actors appear in a variety of forms: individual persons, informal groups or interpersonal networks, organisations, collective groupings and what are sometimes called 'macro' actors (e.g. a particular national government, church or international organisation). But care must always be taken to avoid reification; that is, one should not assume that organisations or collectivities such as social movements act in unison or with one voice. In fact 'collective' and 'organisational' endeavours are better depicted in terms of 'coalitions of actors', 'interlocking actor projects' and 'the interplay of discourses'.

In order to advance such an analysis it has been necessary to generate a number of interconnected concepts – some borrowed from other writers and recast in accordance with 'new' evolving research questions (e.g. social 'fields', 'domains', 'arenas' and 'networks'), others in response to specific research findings' (e.g. 'confederations of households', 'multiple enterprises', 'interlocking actor-projects' and 'knowledge repertoires') and yet others arising out of a process of rethinking or 'demythologising' existing sociological notions and metaphors (e.g. 'planned intervention' as a socially constructed and negotiated process, 'commoditisation' as reformulated in terms of contests over social value and 'interfaces' as seen in terms of 'discontinuity' rather than linkage[3]). The value of an actor-oriented vocabulary, I argue, is that it opens up perspectives that are productive for future research and theoretical thinking. It also aims to challenge practitioners as well as other stakeholders and actors involved in development arenas, so that they might better grasp the ongoing complexities, 'battlefields of knowledge' and opportunities for negotiating socio-political space. Acquiring a new way of talking about conflicting interests and common dilemmas is, I believe, one important step towards promoting more equitable modes of development and resource distribution.[4] It also offers an open agenda for exploring new ways of conceptualising 'structures' as 'boundary markers that become targets for negotiation, reconsideration, sabotage and/or change' (Long, 2001, p. 63).[5] Hence, it rejects outright frameworks based on a priori assumptions and 'driving forces' or explanans, and instead focuses on the 'social life of development' which is highly diverse and replete with 'multiple realities'. This requires us to reach beyond the semantics of structure-oriented or policy-defined understandings of development in order to encompass a wide range of modes of human action centred on conflicts and negotiations over meanings and resources (Arce, 2003a, 2003b; Arce & Fisher, 2003).

This directs attention to the importance of identifying actors' self-organising strategies (cf. Sally Moore's (1973) notion of 'semi-autonomous fields') that are largely independent of externally conceived plans or programmes of development; though they may of course derive benefits directly or indirectly from the presence of project personnel or government officials and the resources they bring. At the same time, the latter have the capacity to develop their own spaces for manoeuvre and to build their own support and exchange networks. Nevertheless, there remains an important distinction between social actions resulting from relatively autonomous self-organising processes and those that are 'mandated' by government or some other authoritative body. Put simply, the former focuses on the capacity of actors/groups to define their own goals and tactics vis-à-vis other actors and interests, with the aim of imposing, wherever possible, their own demands or powers. In contrast, the latter focuses on how to convince or enrol others into accepting or supporting more actively the efforts of project personnel or agencies to implement externally formulated policy objectives. Obviously, development processes necessarily entail a complex mixture of both. Indeed, there are strong arguments for including in project evaluation studies not only policy implementation processes initiated by government or other external bodies, but also those less formal 'policy' goals and 'projects' formulated and carried out by local groups and organisations. Furthermore, it is crucially important that one explores not only the effects of planned intervention on 'target groups' and other so-called 'stakeholders' but also the strategies and actions of what one might call 'hinterland' actors. That is, those who appear to be 'bystanders' or who remain on the periphery of the formal intervention process. A related matter concerns the need to acknowledge that much of what happens in the context of development programmes, and especially in respect to specific localised development projects, requires understanding the significance and impact of a range of individual and collective memories of previous development scenarios. These memories often recall examples of previous state–civil society relations, local initiatives and inter-institutional struggles, and in so doing they shape actors' understandings and responses. These dimensions stress the 'added value' of detailed ethnography as against project evaluation studies (cf. Crewe & Harrison, 1998; Mosse, 2005).

A major advantage of actor-oriented analysis is that it aims to explore a wide range of actor capacities that may shape the social and material world, giving special attention to the kinds of conflicts and negotiations linked to forms of social interface and to the emergence of practices that change existing livelihoods and identities and which cannot easily be assimilated into existing everyday routines. Such social relationships and interfaces enrich the life experiences of actors through the ways in which they affect individual attachments and feelings.[6] These latter cannot simply, as Olivier de Sardan (2005) has argued, be reduced to the 'entanglement of social logics'.[7]

Instead, I suggest we view these complex entanglements of social relationships and practices from an interface perspective since these form an intrinsic part of social life and reveal the malleability of boundary markers that are assumed to fix and integrate actors and their sense of belonging and security. The notion of 'interface' entails comprehending social relations and value commitments as forever 'on the move'. That is, it highlights the alliances, diversions, conflicts and negotiations that arise as actors develop strategies and reposition their interests vis-à-vis specific events and social struggles (Gluckman & Devons, 1964).[8] Here it is important to emphasise that social life and social structures are never totally fixed or integrated. Therefore, methodological devices, such as the interface concept, are not simply there to depict the capacity of 'structures' to functionally reproduce themselves or accommodate to increasing incompatibilities but rather to identify the potentiality of the different actors to innovate, and thus to create the conditions for people and resources to realign themselves in different combinations.

The conceptual repertoire of actor-oriented analysis contributes to the understanding of development policy processes and state-civil society relations. Actor-oriented research has a long pedigree of analysing the effects of state intervention and tracing out how various actors act vis-à-vis these expert-designed initiatives. This work dovetails with similar research carried out by Olivier de Sardan and his APAD colleagues on the nature of administrative practice, political brokerage and the dynamics of decentralised forms of government (see, e.g. Bierschenk & Olivier de Sardan, 1998 and the follow-up review by Batterbury, 2002).

As I suggested earlier, using as an entry point the notion of 'interface', we can look at the role of policies in the reshaping of meanings and relationships as they emerge within the social encounters and dialogues that take place between the various actors involved. This approach gives attention to the indirect mechanisms and discourses that link the conduct of various individuals and organisations to the political projects of others located within and beyond the state domain. The key elements of an interface perspective can be depicted as follows:

1. *Interface as an organised entity of interlocking relationships and intentionalities*

   Interface analysis focuses on the linkages and networks that develop between individuals or parties rather than on individual or group strategies. Continued interaction encourages the development of boundaries and shared expectations that shape the interaction of the participants so that over time the interface itself becomes an organised entity of interlocking relationships and intentionalities.
2. *Interface as a site for conflict, incompatibility and negotiation*

   Although interface interactions presuppose some degree of common interest, they also have a propensity to generate conflict due to contradictory interests and objectives or to unequal power relations. Negotiations at the interface are sometimes carried out by individuals who represent particular constituencies, groups or organisations. Their position is inevitably ambivalent since they must respond to the demands of their own groups as well as to the expectations of those with whom they must negotiate.

   In analysing the sources and dynamics of contradiction and ambivalence in interface situations, it is important not to prejudge the case by assuming that certain divisions or loyalties (such as those based on class, ethnicity or gender) are more fundamental than others. One should also not assume that because a particular person 'represents' a specific group or institution, that he or she necessarily acts in the interests or on behalf of his/her fellows. The link between representatives and constituencies (with their differentiated memberships) must be empirically established, not taken for granted.

3. *Interface and the clash of cultural paradigms*

   The concept of interface helps us to focus on the production and transformation of differences in worldviews or cultural paradigms. Interface situations often provide the means by which individuals or groups come to define their own cultural or ideological positions vis-à-vis those espousing or typifying opposing views. For example, opinions on agricultural development expressed by technical experts, extension workers and farmers seldom completely coincide; and the same is true for those working for a single government department with a defined policy mandate. Hence agronomists, community development workers, credit officers, irrigation engineers and the like, often disagree on the problems and priorities of agricultural development. These differences cannot be reduced to personal idiosyncrasies but reflect differences laid down by differential patterns of socialisation and professionalisation, which often lead to miscommunication or a clash of rationalities. The process is further compounded by the coexistence of several different cultural models or organising principles within a single population or administrative organisation which create room for manoeuvre in the interpretation and utilisation of these cultural values or standpoints.

   It becomes necessary, therefore, to identify the conditions under which particular definitions of reality and visions of the future are upheld, to analyse the interplay of cultural and ideological oppositions, and to map out the ways in which bridging or distancing actions and ideologies make it possible for certain types of interface to reproduce or transform themselves.

4. *The centrality of knowledge processes*

   Linked to the last point is the importance of knowledge processes. Knowledge is a cognitive and social construction that results from and is constantly shaped by the experiences, encounters and discontinuities that emerge at the points of intersection between different actors' life-worlds. Various types of knowledge, including ideas about oneself, other people and the context and social institutions, are important in understanding social interfaces. Knowledge is present in all social situations and is often entangled with power relations and the distribution of resources. But in intervention situations it assumes special significance since it entails the interplay or confrontation of 'expert' versus 'lay' forms of knowledge, belief and value, and struggles over their legitimation, segregation and communication.

An interface approach then depicts knowledge as arising from 'an encounter of horizons'. The incorporation of new information and new discursive or cultural frames can only take place on the basis of already existing knowledge frames and evaluative modes, which are themselves reshaped through the communicative process. Hence knowledge emerges as a product of interaction, dialogue, reflexivity, and contests of meaning, and involves aspects of control, authority and power (pottier et al., 2003).

5. *Power as the outcome of struggles over meanings and strategic relationships*

   Like knowledge, power is not simply possessed, accumulated and unproblematically exercised. Power implies much more than how hierarchies and hegemonic control demarcate social positions and opportunities, and restrict access to resources. It is the outcome of complex struggles and negotiations over authority, status, reputation and resources, and necessitates the enrolment of networks of actors and constituencies. Such struggles are founded upon the extent to which specific actors perceive themselves capable of manoeuvring within particular situations and developing effective strategies for doing so. Creating room for manoeuvre implies a degree of consent, a degree of negotiation and thus a degree of power, as manifested in the possibility of exerting some control, prerogative, authority and capacity for action, be it front- or backstage, for brief moments or for more sustained periods. Thus power inevitably generates resistance, accommodation and strategic compliance as regular components of the politics of everyday life.

6. *Interface as composed of multiple discourses*

   Interface analysis enables us to comprehend how 'dominant' discourses are endorsed, transformed or challenged. Dominant discourses are characteristically replete with reifications (often of a 'naturalistic' kind) that assume the existence and significance of certain social traits and groupings, pertaining, for example, to 'communities', hierarchical or egalitarian structures and cultural constructions of ethnicity, gender and class. Such discourses serve to promote particular political, cultural or moral standpoints, and they are often mobilised in struggles over social meanings and strategic resources. Yet, while some actors 'vernacularise' dominant discourses in order to legitimate their claims upon the state and other authoritative bodies, others choose to reject them by deploying and defending countervailing or 'demotic' (lit. 'of the people') discourses that offer alternative, more locally rooted points of view.[9]

THREE ETHNOGRAPHIC CASES

Philippine NGO Study: Actors, Discourses and Interfaces

The first example draws upon Hilhorst's (2003) highly readable study of the everyday politics of a Philippine NGO, which exposes both the cut and thrust of office life as well as its dealings with clients and donors. A central theoretical thread running throughout the study is the use of discourse and actor-oriented concepts and analysis.

Discourse analysis concerns itself with how people construct narratives about and attribute social meanings to their experiences and predicaments. Although most existing studies of discourse draw upon formal institutional narratives and statements (taken from documentary sources or public debate) and often adopt socio-linguistic or textual modes of interpretation, here the approach is applied imaginatively to the study of a series of critical events as well as everyday practices (e.g. past and present political struggles, the minutiae of social status and management problems in the NGO office, and the implementation of village-level projects). From this it is concluded that NGOs (and other similar organisations) are composed of an amalgam of different discourses, ideological repertoires and social relations and interests, which 'push and pull' actors in different directions, thus creating a diversity of incompatible commitments and social discontinuities. Any attempts, therefore, to establish order out of this apparent chaos, through the imposition of so-called 'rational' modes of control and accountability or the promotion of unified political and ethical positions are, almost certainly, doomed to failure. Linked to this is the point that languages of discourse in effect create their own 'realities', upon which decisions and justifications are enacted, and particular interpersonal social networks and divisions reinforced. (Mosse, 2005 makes a similar point.)

This emphasis on the multiplicity and malleability of discourse runs counter to the 'received wisdom' that there are hegemonic (or authoritative) discourses that structure society and fundamentally limit the potentialities for change. Contrary to this latter position, the study convincingly shows that, while so-called hegemonic representations (e.g. of 'modernity', 'progress', 'development', 'village life' and 'ethnicity') may be promoted by powerful external institutions – even international bodies such as the World Bank or Greenpeace – it is local groups and intermediate organisations that reassemble these ideas in line with their own interests and understandings, and in so doing formulate counter-discourses. Hence the necessity of according local actors (including NGO workers and experts) with the capacity to organise their own experiences and respond creatively to external interventions.

The research uses a variety of methods: ethnographic studies undertaken in the office of the NGO and in different field sites where local projects and events were located, interviews with staff and workers, situational analysis of conflicts and everyday routines, social network studies and the analysis of various official and unofficial texts and documents concerning the work of the NGO and regional political history. The central task is to document in detail how specific discourses (hegemonic ones too) become 'realities' (or 'shared objects') through an array of actors' practices. As Hilhorst (2003, pp. 82–83) explains, '[T]hese are subtle processes, occurring over long stretches of time and difficult to isolate in the complexities of everyday social life'. She goes on to argue that in the context of development intervention these are often ambiguous and combine a number of different and sometimes contradictory interpretations of 'development', 'modernity' and 'participation', which are best revealed and interpreted through strategic interface studies.

The Dynamics of Rural Development in Benin

My second example derives from the work of Roch Mongbo (1995) who offers a detailed analysis of a government-initiated rural development programme in Benin, which was implemented during the last years of the Marxist-Leninist regime (1989–1993). The programme was officially presented as inspired by the desire to turn 'dying villages into dynamic places'. The Ministry of Agriculture was made responsible for organising a series of new development initiatives based upon people's participation in local enterprise. Yet, despite these laudatory aims and a well worked out plan of action, the programme – as Mongbo graphically documents – quickly acquired its own dynamic, both within the offices and corridors of the bureaucracy as well as within the public and private domains of village life. Precisely how and why this came about are the pivotal questions of this anthropological study.

In exploring these dimensions, the study lays bare the historical antecedents and trajectories of the programme. It also probes the everyday rationales, politics and transformations of specific development projects and encounters; and it identifies the cultural dispositions and livelihood interests of the different social actors involved. The ethnographer's lens is focused throughout on the ongoing cultural and social constructions of what Mongbo calls the 'field of rural development'. This field is composed of an assortment of variously connected and counterposed types of discourse and social practice, whose *raison d'etre* is provided by planned intervention, though never completely framed by the strategies and language games of the state. At the centre of this field is a multiplicity of actors who are thrown together in a melody of relations based on cooperation, conflict and alliance. The actors include bureaucrats, field officers, peasant producers, women's group leaders, traders, local political figures and foreign development experts and donors.

In unravelling some of the details of this process, Mongbo skilfully guides the reader through a series of social situations that range from routine meetings, everyday encounters, to points of mounting political struggle. In so doing, he is able to identify a number of key issues and concepts that advance our understanding of development interfaces and of arenas of struggle and symbolic contestation. The study embraces a thorough documentation of the livelihoods, personal predicaments and status concerns of both government officers and different strata of the village population. The overall effect of the narrative is to convey the urgency of the problems, passions and interests of the individual people and families involved.

In addition, the account brings to light the significance of emic ways of talking about differences in 'well-being' and 'social esteem', thus showing not only how villagers depict internal social differences but also how they juxtapose the priorities of people's livelihoods with the goals of 'development' as defined by outsiders. A further interesting observation made by the researcher is that, despite these evident differences between 'local' and 'external' socio-cultural orientations and representations, issues of status and livelihoods – and likewise witchcraft and family commitments – clearly preoccupy bureaucrats as much as they do villagers. Hence, while it might seem logical to expect a marked separation between their lifeworlds and knowledge repertoires, there are in fact as many points of cultural convergence and accommodation as there are of divergence and opposition. This is repeatedly manifested in several of the case studies elaborated in the study where, for example, local development workers align with women's groups or other village actors in a collective effort to hoodwink foreign development practitioners and donors or senior government officials; while, on the other hand, agreements are struck between certain expatriate personnel and local officials and politicians.[10]

The author – both researcher and ex-agricultural extension practitioner – also reflects on his own capacity to move between the worlds of the office and the village, gliding between being both 'outsider' and 'insider'. Yet such a 'split personality' life heightens the sense of underlying conflicts of loyalty and a betrayal of confidences. Although such concerns must have been troublesome for the researcher, both during fieldwork and in deciding what to make public in the text, one is left with a strong feeling for the authenticity of the account.

The central theme running throughout the study is that of the 'appropriation' and 'dismemberment' of the government policy programme – its discourses, resources and organisational practices. The language of development is produced and transformed at critical development interfaces, thus revealing aspects of intervention processes that usually remain outside of analysis. These congealed or ignored areas (such as the minutiae of everyday livelihoods and family political struggles) – not often understood or encompassed or even envisaged within the framework of intervention programmes – are usually pigeon-holed by policy analysis as 'side-effects', that is, if they are mentioned at all. But, for Mongbo, they are critically important for understanding policy outcomes and constitute the everyday unseen politics of development negotiations. Checking policy outcomes only against formally designated goals and objectives necessarily leads to the obfuscation or deliberate marginalisation of the many ways in which the local actors, as well as other actors such as government or NGO staff, handle the problematic situations they face and attempt to improve their own living circumstances. It also ignores the significance of existing cultural and socio-political commitments and values that remain undetected or poorly understood by implementers. Indeed local people often devise methods for concealing their own lifeworlds and will do so strategically if their activities or priorities run at odds with the conditions and goals set by donor or implementing agencies.

Mongbo's study, then, is especially interesting for the way he documents how various local actors ('the intervened') become 'intervenors' themselves by taking the initiatives of intervention into their own hands and deciding the orientation of affairs for themselves, even to the extent of utilising and bending the images and language of the intervenors. This is illustrated by the arrival of an extension worker who sees his mission as that of dynamising village life. He quickly becomes embroiled in local relationships and interests, and eventually manages to negotiate the insertion of the programme into the village. In doing so, he becomes enroled by local groups, though still promoting his own identity as a government officer, specialist on cooperative matters, orthodox Christian and a 'forceful' man. He even pushes through some personal projects such as the implementation of a cooperative plan that he had designed as part of his master's degree. In this way the government blueprint for village plans was rewritten according to the priorities of particular villages and the negotiating capacities of the rural development officer.

Such appropriation processes also take place in the bureaucracy when ministerial orders or policy changes are filtered down and reworked by officials within the institution. Such changes become the source for conflict bargaining among administrators and between them and other staff. Coalitions congeal around ethic, religious, family and patron–client relationships, and sometimes evoke witchcraft and counter-witchcraft accusations and practices. In one case it emerges that the director's best allies are not his senior administrative staff, nor the technical officers, but drivers, night watchmen and village agents who become important resource persons in decisions on technical/professional matters. It is as the result of the combination of these relationships that government staff are able to give policies their own historical imprint and make them more compatible with and manageable in everyday social and administrative reality. At the same time they develop a 'new', 'fashionable' participatory written and spoken discourse that gives legitimacy to the actions they take. Mongbo shows how all the actors involved, local or otherwise, appropriate those parts of the rural development programme that are most meaningful to their own life trajectories.

Because of this it is difficult to speak of 'project failure'. Also projects and programmes themselves lose their substance in the minds of people dealing with or using components of them in their everyday lives. As life goes on, pieces of programmes become part of ongoing social interactions and routines. Actors, including planners, do not of course constantly retain uppermost in their consciousness the overall project plan. Instead, they keep it alive piecemeal through the material and symbolic updating that takes place in the seminars and similar public rituals and missions they attend, as well as through the circulation of official documents and the payment of project per diems, rewards and incentives. In the village it is the rural development officer who keeps the programme alive. Bits and pieces of the programme are grafted onto the arenas of everyday life in the village; for example, women's groups attach new meanings and uses to items originally associated with the rural development programme by grafting them onto other resources that derive from earlier interventions and experiences.

Looking at intervention from an actor-oriented perspective, then, brings out its dynamic face. It also highlights the way in which 'deviant' or 'counter-development' processes are a central part of the transformative nature of development intervention itself. This leads to the treatment of development intervention as a constructed social field made up of a multiplicity of interests, values, discourses, strategic practices and emergent outcomes – that is, something quite different from that represented in policy-speak.

Participatory Development, Local Leaders and Development Implementors in Rural China

My final ethnographic snapshot relates to issues of participatory development in present-day rural China. Compared to the conventional top-down approach to planned development intervention, the participatory approach is widely regarded as much more democratic in nature and therefore much more acceptable to local people. However, the case of a participatory project in rural China highlights how leadership and authority relations may still play a critical role in shaping the contours and contents of the participatory process. Although critical of certain features of socio-political life, local villagers placed higher priority on maintaining good relations with their local and township leaders (especially party secretaries) than opting for less familiar forms of governance (such as new externally derived notions of democratic practice). Moreover, the study concludes that what goes for 'participation', in the end reinforces existing socio-political power fields. Since the late 1980s, international development aid discourse in China has focused on participation and local governance (Li, 1999; Plummer & Taylor, 2004; Wang, 2003) and, over the last two years, the approach has been gradually incorporated into national development programmes such as participatory village planning. Thus development workers and researchers who promote the idea of participation believe that, compared to existing types of top-down State planning, participatory approaches will be more democratic in nature and therefore more easily accepted by local people (Li, 1999; Liu, 2003). It is argued that by adopting such an approach farmers' interests are likely to be reflected maximally in village projects. Hence it is taken for granted that farmers will fully accept and definitely benefit from participatory projects. Yet, experience has shown that this idea of what 'participation' can do is often not realised as expected.

Applied field research carried out by researchers at CIAD/CORD (Centre for Rural Development), China Agricultural University, Beijing, during the late 1990s/early 2000s has provided critical insights into these participatory issues. The case I want to briefly explore here concerns a two-year German-funded poverty alleviation project entitled ‘Participatory Community Development in Pocang Township, Hebei Province’, which CORD itself was contracted to carry out. Being a ‘participatory’ project, two principles central to the implementation process were to be adopted by the CORD team. The first required the implementors to publicise the project locally so that local inhabitants would become informed as to its objectives, contents, financial arrangements and organisation. The second stressed that intervenors and implementing agencies should not impose their own interests and ideas but empower local people to make their own decisions about project activities. However, from personal experience the implementors were already well aware that such notions of participation, transparency and local decision-making could not be introduced without unforeseen consequences. As one member of the team put it, ‘even when carried out in a very prudent way, outsiders must pay the price for what they do to local people’.

Four villages were to be covered, each having its peculiarities. Pocang Township leaders categorised two of the villages as ‘good villages’ and the other two as ‘problematic’, the implications being that the first two had ‘solid’ (that is well organised) village committees with few conflicts among their residents. Thus they would be ‘easy to manage’ because they would ‘follow their leaders’ instructions – in one of them this meant that authority and loyalty were vested in the village party secretary and in the other that ‘all village committee members had a voice’. In contrast, the other two villages were riven with internal disputes: one involving long-term struggles between two political factions and the other centring on hostility towards the village party secretary, who it appeared had a long history of manipulating local households to accept whatever he felt was the thing to do. In this sense, he was of course a strong leader.

These circumstances did not bode well for the future outcomes of the project. Indeed, each village scenario threw up its own specific challenges for the implementation team. I do not of course have space here to lay out the differences but only to give a flavour of the difficulties encountered.

Eventually the practitioners had to come to terms with their own failure to effectively sell the ‘participatory package’. Yet, despite this disappointment they gradually reached a level of self-reflexivity that was both helpful analytically as well as practically for designing more effective intervention strategies. Let me now address a central issue, namely the struggles that took place over the funding of water resource projects as against rotating credit groups.

After several discussions concerning how to use the German funds, Ye, the lead practitioner/researcher, spoke out strongly, saying:

> Dear participants, oh, you are so used to having others make the decisions! Try to make them yourselves. For example, Nandugang and Baoshi [two of the villages] may have fewer funds for a water resource system but you will have more revolving funds. The total amount for each component will therefore be the same. What is the difference? Mr. Xu (village party secretary of Sanggang), please invite your friend Liu Zhenqun to drink some liquor after the meeting, then he may give his share to you, you are both friends ...

Here he was suggesting that they negotiate a series of trade-offs between those villages that prioritise improvements in water resources and those that stress rotating credit. The German donor had stressed funds for establishing household credit rotating groups, but several local groups wanted to use the money for improving their water resources.

At this point, Liu Zhenqun, the village party secretary of Nandugan, immediately stood up and in a very excited voice declared:

> Our village also needs a water resource system. My villagers have to collect water from far away every day for drinking and cooking. We want to have more funds to construct a water system ...

In succession other village leaders also expressed their strong interest in water systems.

The reasons for this vis-à-vis revolving funds became clear. First, a water resource system would benefit more villagers. Second, it would be more visible in the short term to both villagers and visiting government officials. Third, it would be an obvious and generally noteworthy improvement for a village, but more importantly it would underline the achievements of the village leader and his committee charged with launching such a project. Indeed in each administrative village of the project area one encounters a large information board which records village demographic and educational data and lists successful local development projects, naming those responsible. Most of the items in such a list relate to improving basic infrastructure. Local people often judge party secretaries and their associates in terms of their abilities to implement such schemes. These assessments play a major role in determining the outcome of local elections.

In contrast, revolving funds are seen to benefit only a small segment of the village population, namely the poorer households; and the funds themselves become invisible once they are distributed. Furthermore, poor farmers do not really bring benefits to the village, nor can they reward the more active entrepreneurial or political members. A further critical component is that the distribution of revolving funds can often generate conflicts among farmers and village leaders, among rich and poor and even among the poor farmers themselves. It is for this reason that village leaders normally prefer not to become embroiled in these conflicts. And additionally, revolving funds have to be repaid by farmers at the end of the first year so that the second group of farmers can benefit. Village leaders often worry about the rate of repayment and are afraid they may not be able to repay on time, and this will affect their standing in the village. That is, they will lose reputation in the eyes of fellow villagers and township leaders. And this can undermine future opportunities for support for such development projects.

During the debate among the village leaders at the meeting called by the intervenors, Mr. Xu, the party secretary of Sanggang village, kept silent. He looked rather confident since what Ye said appealed to him. Also he knew that Ye's opinion/interpretation must reflect the township leaders' views. And in fact they had made suggestions as to the distribution of the funds. Moreover, the practitioner team was influenced by the ideas voiced by the local leaders, partly because their suggestions made some sense, but also because the practitioners' themselves needed to maintain good relations with the township leaders, since in the end they had to become partners.

Xu finally said:

> Well, from my point of view, we ourselves cannot make the decisions. No one really wants to give up on water resource systems ...

His words won immediate agreement from others:

> That's true, we cannot make decisions, it will hurt our relationships. So You can make decisions for us.

Under such circumstances, Zhang Wencheng, the Deputy Director of the County Forestry Bureau stood up and concluded the meeting with the following words:

> ... I do not think we should continue discussing the distribution of the money among the villages at this meeting, as we will never find a solution this way. The final decision will be made by the township government and CIAD.

Then, with some embarrassment, Ye declared the meeting closed. However, the village leaders did not seem to want to leave immediately. And eventually Zhao Shengli, the village party secretary from Baoshi, came to reinforce his point of view, arguing:

> Ms. Wang, we are not at all demanding: 20 to 30,000 Yuan is enough for us to build the water tower. We have collected some money for the tower, so we only lack the rest to complete the job. Please be sure we can have this amount of money!

SOME CONCLUDING REMARKS

This case highlights the importance of processes of political negotiation that take place between the various actors concerned. As highlighted above, conventional participatory methodologies are not good at resolving these kinds of conflict which almost inevitably arise, due to the existence of different (and often incompatible) social interests and meanings. It may therefore be desirable – rather than aiming at 'maximum' participation – to set one's sight on encouraging only some 'degree' of participation in decision-making. Moreover, the case also supports Cees Leeuwis' argument that decisions do not normally result from rational decision-making processes but rather they develop as part of a gradual learning process. Hence, 'decisions' in projects are shaped by a variety of negotiating processes through which compromises are struck at one level or stage, and conflict resolution at another. One such important negotiated solution came when the practitioners managed to persuade the State forestry department to provide extra money for improving the water supply, and another through allowing local leaders at the village committee level to make their own decisions regarding revolving funds.

As a matter of principle, participatory development is built upon 'bottom-up' processes and requires the involvement of local actors at various stages in the process. Decentralisation (or local governance) and transparency are stated as two important means as well as ends of this process. However, as this Chinese example indicates, participatory projects also entail negotiations and sometimes acrimony between the parties involved. In this case, after all the difficulties, the implementing agency staff simply reduced their level of participation by cutting back on the work and time they spent in the field with their 'farmer clients', while the majority of farmers showed little or no wish to challenge the existing socio-political arrangements. Yet their differences of opinion as to how to use the funds donated by the German NGO regularly resurfaced, as also did the debate about the meaning and nature of 'participation'. Hence they reverted to the usual practice of centralised control after they failed to manage the conflicts of interest generated by adopting the participatory approach. In other words, 'participation', or rather the imposition of the philosophy of participation, in such circumstances reinforces tendencies towards 'centralised' rather than 'decentralised' control.

The longstanding Chinese system of centralised government implies that the power of authority over resource allocation – including financial, physical and informational resources – remains mainly in the hands of the Party and State. Hence people who are in a position to allocate major resources are understandably reluctant to rescind their control of these. The language of decentralised governance is destined therefore to be seen as threating existing patterns of centralised decision-making over resource allocation. Seen against this, one has to bear in mind that the philosophy and practice of participation as a transparent, open and negotiated process has to date mainly been introduced in the form of 'short-term' intervention projects. Participatory projects have a foreseeable end, and people who are likely to lose power during the intervention process have a tendency to make every effort they can to retain as much influence as possible during its duration and later to reassert their claims once it is over. This raises another important dimension of development 'projects', that is they often, as I illustrated in the other cases, remain piecemeal in their impact, and may not dovetail well with larger forms of institution building that require long-term commitments and the full backing of the State and other authoritative bodies. It is normal that organisations and rules or regulations built through relatively short-term interventions become diluted or finally disappear naturally, or simply revert to previous forms once the intervention programme comes to an end.

China has been called 'a country of etiquette', where trust, reputation, reciprocity and other social norms play a more important role than other elements in decision-making. Socially and culturally, Chinese people endow 'harmonious' interpersonal relationships with the most important available social capital. This functions to realise social, economic, even political purposes. Theoretically and methodologically, participation requires the articulation of beneficiaries' needs and priorities. This is likely to create conflict and often resistance among actors. However, one should not therefore conclude that this kind of 'counter-development' will last throughout different development scenarios. The Chinese case highlights the dynamics of all this, emphasising how participatory projects are processed and endowed with different (even contradictory) meanings by those involved in them, including of course both the recipients and implementers. Thus, I argue, the critical components are best understood through identifying and analysing the specific modes and dynamics of interface that arise.

NOTES

1. Here I present activity theory as it now stands. The first formulation by Vigotsky in the 1920s and 1930s was a model of object-oriented and artifact-mediated action (Vigotsky, 1978). Later, Leont'ev, a disciple of Vigotsky, stressed

the socially mediated nature of activity and argued therefore that consciousness and meaning are always formed in joint, collective activity (Leont'ev, 1981).

2. This assessment draws upon Thierry Bardini's website collection of summary statements offered by various researchers who explore what is actor-network theory?

3. This stress on linkage and interlinked sets of activities is generally characteristic of systems models, even and those promoting 'soft' systems analysis. See, for example, Checkland (1981), Röling (1988) and Engel (1990, pp. 29–30). In contrast, my *Encounters at the Interface* (Long, 1989) emphasises the need to go beyond issues of integration and co-ordination to explore the significance of discontinuities in social relations and knowledge processes.

4. Research on 'Poverty Knowledge and Policy Processes' funded by DFID has looked closely at issues of governance and the intricacies of poverty reduction policies both within and outside government institutions in Uganda and Nigeria. The analytical framework, which draws predominately on an actor-oriented perspective, explores the links between actors, knowledge processes and the creation of socio-political spaces. It tackles a number of critical aspects relating to citizen rights, equity, institutional accountability and participation (McGee, 2004).

5. See Schatzki, Knorr-Cetina, and Von Savigny (2000) for a discussion among philosophers, sociologists and scholars of science of the centrality of human practices for re-conceptualising notions of 'structure' and 'order'. An important forerunner of this interest in everyday social practice is the work of De Certeau (1984).

6. Unni Wikan (1990) provides a convincing demonstration of the sociological importance of the personal and emotional components of social life in her Balinese ethnography. She unmasks the conventions and formalities of public cultural displays and ritual performances (the main preoccupation of much anthropological work in Bali) to reveal how individuals and families cope with crises, hardships and heartaches of daily living.

7. The idea of 'social logic' carries with it the notion of an unambiguous line of reasoning or a set of normative principles that explain the internal practices that constitute a specific social group versus other such groups. It is therefore tainted with a degree of 'essentialism' which downplays the contingent, ambivalent, heterogeneous and explorative elements of social action, especially when faced by the uncertainties of social development. Hence, from an actor-oriented perspective it projects the wrong image.

8. In Gluckman's view, an understanding of events affecting the everyday lives of people, such as the effect of rainfall, soil types, books and language differences, means that social scientists should not distinguish between exclusive domains of practice associated with the social or life sciences. He goes on to argue that 'any event which influences how men live together may thus be part of the field which an anthropologist studies' (Gluckman & Devons, 1964, p. 159). Despite Gluckman's emphasis on the impact of contingent events on individuals and how the latter respond and give meaning to these situations, in the end he resorts to a structural-functionalist equilibrium theory of social change that gives little or no space for individual innovation and room for man oeuvre (see Gluckman, 1968). It is also intriguing to note that Bourdieu recognises the influence of the Manchester School on his own thinking when he first formulates his concept of 'habitus' (1977).

9. See Baumann (1996), for further insight into these processes in a multi-ethnic area of London, see also Arce and Long (2000).

10. See Grammig (2002) for a revealing 'insider' account of knowledge exchanges between foreign and local development experts involved in 'high' and 'low' technology projects in Mexico and Chad. His study shows the usefulness of an actor-oriented interface perspective for dissecting communicative and dramaturgical acts embodied in development scenarios.

REFERENCES

Arce, A. (2003a). Re-approaching social development: A field of action between social life and policy processes. *Journal of International Development, 15*(7), 845–861.

Arce, A. (2003b). Value contestations in development interventions: Community development and sustainable livelihoods approaches. *Community Development Journal, 38*(3), 199–212.

Arce, A., & Fisher, E. (2003). Knowledge, interfaces and practices of negotiation: Cases from a woman's group in Bolivia and an oil refinery in Wales. In J. Pottier, A. Bicker, & P. Sillitoe (Eds.), *Negotiating local knowledge: Power and identity in development.* London: Pluto Press.

Arce, A., & Long, N. (2000). *Anthropology, development and modernities: Exploring discourses, counter-tendencies and violence.* London: Routledge.

Batterbury, S. P. J. (2002). Discursive review of 'courtiers en developement: Villages en quete de projects'. *Environment: Society and Space, 20*(1), 20–25.

Baumann G. (1996). *Contesting culture.* Cambridge: Cambridge University Press.

Bierschenk, T., & Olivier de Sardan, J-P. (Eds.). (1998). *Les pouvoirs au village. Le Bénin rurale entre démocratisation y décentralisation.* Paris: Karthala.

Bourdieu, P. (1977). *Outline of a theory of practice.* Cambridge: Cambridge University Press.

Callon, M., & Law, J. (1995). Agency and the hybrid collective. *South Atlantic Quarterly, 94*(2), 481–507.

Checkland, P. (1981). *Systems thinking, systems practice.* Chichester: Wiley.

Checkland, P. (1988). Soft systems methodology: An overview. *Journal of Applied Systems Analysis, 15*, 27–30.

Crewe, E., & Harrison, E. A. (1998). *Whose development? An ethnography of aid.* London: Zed Books.

De Certeau, M. (1984). *The practice of everyday life.* Berkeley, CA: University of California Press.

Engel, P. G. H. (1990). Knowledge management in agriculture: Building upon diversity, knowledge in society. *The International Journal for Knowledge Transfer, 3*(3), 28–35.

Engeström, Y. (1987). *Learning by expanding: An activity-theoretical approach to developmental research.* Helsinky: Orienta-Konsultit Oy.

Engeström, Y. (1996). Development work research as educational research: Looking ten years back and into the zone of proximal development. *Nordish Pedagogik, 3*, 131–143.

Engeström, Y. (2001) Expansive learning at work: Toward an activity theoretical conceptualisation. *Journal of Education and Work, 14*(1), 133–156.

Engeström, Y. (2009). *The future of activity theory: A rough draft.* Helsinki: University of Helsinki.

Gluckman, M. (1968). The utility of the equilibrium in the study of social change. *American Anthropologist, 70*(2), 219–237.

Gluckman, M., & Devons, E. (Eds.). (1964). *Closed systems and open minds: The limits of naivety in social anthropology.* London: Oliver and Boyd.

Golinski, J. (1998). *Making natural knowledge: Constructionism and the history of science.* Cambridge: Cambridge University Press.

Grammig, T. (2002). *Observing technical assistance.* London: Routledge.

Hilhorst, D. (2003). *Discourses, diversity and development: The real world of NGOs.* London: Zed Books.

Knorr-Cetina, K. D. (1981). *The manufacture of knowledge: Towards a constructivist and contextual theory of science.* Oxford: Pergamon Press.

Kontinen, T. (2004). Intervention negotiated? Production of shared object and power relations in the planning of a development co-operation project. In T. Kontinen (Ed.), *Development intervention. Actor and activity perspectives.* Hakapaino Oy, Helsinki: University of Helsinki. Center for Activity Theory and Developmental Work Research and Institute for Development Studies.

Latour, B. (1993). *We have never been modern.* Cambridge: Harvard University Press.

Latour, B. (1996). Do scientific objects have a history? Pasteur and whitehead in a bath oflactic acid. *Common Knowledge, 5*(1), 76–91.

Leeuwis, C. (2004). *Communication for rural innovation: Rethinking agricultural extension.* Oxford: Blackwell Science.

Leeuwis, C., & Aarts, N. (2011). Communication in innovation processes: Creating space for change in complex systems. *The Journal of Agricultural Education and Extension, 17*, 21–36.

Lektorsky, V. A. (1984). *Subject, object, cognition.* Moscow: Progress Publishers.

Leont'ev, A. N. (1978). *Activity, consciousness, and personality.* Englewood Cliffs, NJ: Prentice Hall.

Leont'ev, A. N. (1981). *Problems of the development of the mind.* Moscow: Progress Publishers.

Li, X. (1999). *Who owns development?* Beijing: China Agriculture Press.

Liu, J. (2003). Support to private and community farm forestry in China. *Unasylva, 212*(54), 57–62.

Long, N. (Ed.). (1989). *Encounters at the interface.* Wageningen: University Press.

Long, N. (2001). *Development sociology: Actor perspectives.* London: Routledge.

McGee, R. (2004). Unpacking policy, actors, knowledge and spaces. In K. Brock, R. McGee, & J. Gaventa (Eds.), *Unpacking policy: Knowledge, actors and spaces in poverty reduction in Uganda and Nigeria.* Kamala: Fountain Publishers.

Mongbo, R. L. (1995). The appropriation and dismembering of development intervention: Policy, discourse and practice in the field of rural development in Benin. PhD thesis, Wageningen University, Wageningen.

Moore, S. F. (1973). Law and social change: The semi-autonomous social field as an appropriate subject to study. *Law and Society Review, 7*(4), 719–746.

Mosse, D. (2005). *Cultivating development: An ethnography of AID policy and practice.* London: Pluto Press.

Nardi, B. A. (Ed.). (1996). *Context and consciousness: Activity theory and human-computer interaction.* Cambridge, MA: MIT Press.

Olivier de Sardan, J. P. (2005). *Anthropology and development: Understanding contemporary social change*. London: Zed Books.

Plummer, J., & Taylor, J. G. (Eds.). (2004). *Community participation in China: Issues and processes for capacity building*. London: Earthscan.

Pottier, J., Bicker, A., & Sillitoe, P. (Eds.). (2003). *Negotiating local knowledge: Power and identity in development*. London: Pluto Press.

Röling, N. (1988). *Extension science, information systems in agricultural development*. Cambridge: Cambridge University Press.

Schatzki, T. R., Knorr-Cetina, K., & Von Savigny, F. C. (2000). *The practice turn in contemporary theory*. London: Psychology Press.

Verschoor, G. (1997). *Tacos, Tiendas and Mezcal: An actor-network on small scale entrepreneurial projects in Western Mexico*, PhD thesis, Wageningen University Press, The Netherlands.

Vigotsky, L. S. (1978). *Mind in society: Development of psychological processes*. Cambridge, MA: Harvard University Press.

Wang, Y. (2003). *How discontinuities become continuities*. PhD thesis, Rural Development Sociology, Wageningen University, Wageningen.

Wikan, U. (1990). *Managing turbulent hearts: A Balinese formula for living*. Chicago, IL: University of Chicago Press.

CHAPTER 4

IS MULTIFUNCTIONALITY THE ROAD TO EMPOWERING FARMERS?

Pierluigi Milone and Flaminia Ventura

ABSTRACT

This chapter gives several explanations as to why peasant agriculture results in sturdy and sustainable growth – it also identifies the factors that undermine this capacity. Peasant agriculture entails a constructive capacity: it includes mechanisms that are used to make agriculture grow and to face adverse conditions. And when the 'normal' level of resilience does not suffice, the constructive capacity is employed to redesign and materially rebuild agriculture through the development of new products, services and markets. This capacity leads to a new farmer's empowerment that have in the multifunctionality the key to go beyond the classical agricultural system where the farming capacity is completely expressed out of the farm leaving farmers to do only mechanical operation. The chapter illustrates several examples of how farmers are reclaiming control over their own resources by defining a new level of farm autonomy and by oriented their farm towards multifunctional activities and the concept of peasants agriculture. The 'new peasantry' is consolidating itself and becoming a highly effective alternative: a viable way

Constructing a New Framework for Rural Development
Research in Rural Sociology and Development, Volume 22, 59–88

ISSN: 1057-1922/doi:10.1108/S1057-192220150000022003

of addressing the multifaceted crisis that beleaguers farmers, the increasing strictures they face and the ongoing challenges of sustainability.

Keywords: Peasants; rural development; innovation; multifunctionality; eco-economy; market

INTRODUCTION

The recent evolution of the relationship between agriculture and society reaffirms models based on farmers' know-how and practices. These models not only accept spatial and temporal heterogeneity of resources as a 'basic game rule' but use and transform these features as key factor for business success (van der Ploeg & Ventura, 2014). These models are also based on a dynamic contextualized knowledge, which is the result of farmers interacting with other economic and institutional actors within the agro-food system. This knowledge is a central asset of the farm. It is also jointly constructed and shared by several actors, creating new forms of cooperation between farmers, institutions and society. These new forms of cooperation, are important mechanisms for regaining power,[1] both in the market and in political terms. Power can be conceptualized as the 'ability to tell other people what to do with some degree of certainty that they will do it' (Dugger, 1980). In this chapter, following Bartlett (1989) we view market power as the ability to influence market variables in order to obtain a decent surplus; we view political power as the ability to influence the process of constructing institutional frameworks.

This process of regaining amplifies the potential farmers, food chains and local markets to increase their autonomy from global trends, increase territorial resilience against external shocks and have more independence in making strategic choices concerning growth and development.

People's attitudes towards food have been changing rapidly in recent years. For example, the concept of food quality has changed dramatically, moving from being purely related to the organoleptic qualities of products to a broader concept that includes the three main aspects of sustainability: economic, environmental and social. '[The] *"quality turn"... has the potential to organize linkages among various forces in agrofood systems: raising expectations among affluent discerning consumers*' (Murdoch, Marsden, & Banks, 2000). This 'quality turn' has also been recorded by other academics: FitzSimmons and Goodman (1998) and Stassart and Whatmore (2003) note the influence of food scares and consumer food safety concerns.

Goodman (1999), Murdoch et al. (2000) and Murdoch and Miele (1999) identify the importance of the presence and representation of nature in food products, while Ilbery and Kneafsy (2000) highlight the importance of producers' ambitions to wrest (back) a greater share of the food economy from other actors in the chain (Warner, 2006, p. 1).

In economic theory the assumption that the market is the most efficient place for organizing transactions is being eroded by evidence that in the reality the market assumes different forms, in time and space, depending on the existence of opportunistic behaviour, speculation and informative asymmetry (Milone & Ventura, 2014) or on institutional interventions. All these elements influence the markets' accessibility or efficiency. Basu (2011) notes that the concept of the 'perfect market' was based on the theory of the 'invisible hand', and was completely devoid of normative content, having as its main feature the freedom of individuals to make all the choices within their 'budget set': the range of available options based on one's income. In reality within this decisional autonomy individuals can engage in cheating, stealing, lying, giving false information or slandering. Such behaviour negatively affects the overall efficiency and optimality of the market and gives rise to sub-optimal solutions.

'*[The] answer is not obvious anymore: standard economics does not have any theory to guide us once we expand the range of behavior in this way. There are some actions that clearly seem to thwart optimality*' (Basu, 2011, p. 25). This leads him to propose what he calls a '*dual interpretation*' in which '*[the] Invisible Hand Theorem can be restated as follows: If we have a competitive economy, where the freedom of individuals is restricted so that they are not allowed to choose from all the alternative actions available to them, but instead are simply allowed to choose a point from their budget set, then (given a few technical conditions, as before) the resultant equilibrium will be Pareto optimal*' (Basu, 2011, p. 25).

In the real world an increasing number of restrictions on individual choice derive from the growing corpus of 'new' or 'non-traditional' commons. Scarce resources or those that are modified by their use are part of this '*corpus*', departing from natural resources and including internet or commons property. The constraints coming from uncorrected collective use are growing in number and becoming more evident (Polman, Poppe, van der Schans, & van der Ploeg, 2011).

In this new form it is evident that there is a growing need to impose restrictions on individual freedom in choices of behaviour and actions. '*[Hence], the central opinion. ... – that a complete free market is the ideal to pursue – does not have the theoretical foundation popularly assumed*' ... '*Its foundation is a myth – one that has had reverberating implications for the way we view economic policymaking in the world, and our hopes, or rather lack thereof, of a better and fairer economic order*' (Basu, 2011, p. 25).

These rapid changes have led to a profound revision of the priorities and objectives of policy strategies. The new strategy outlined in 'Europe 2020'[2] sets difficult challenges for rural areas. This new political framework involves completely rethinking the development model as a whole and outlining a new model that is radically different from that which existed up to a few years ago. For rural areas and the agricultural sectors the challenges can be synthesized as involving the reinsertion of human capital and land as central aspects of the development process. The modernization model (which previously held sway over policy) generated an over-dependence of the agricultural and food systems on external knowledge and inputs. This dependency was overseen by international lobbies that had a firm grip upon the levers of market and political power. This allowed them to exert control over two critical dimensions of farming: the supply of inputs and the market (for produce and inputs). This hegemony was supported by a scientific, technical and administrative system or to quote Benvenuti (1975, 1982), by a *Technological Administrative Task Environment* (TATE) that was greatly facilitated and supported the models promoted by these lobbies, who presented them as the optimal solutions for securing competitiveness and growth in the context of global markets and achieving economies of scale. This process contributed to the birth of what van der Ploeg terms 'food empires': '*[a] grammar or rule set comprised in the coherent complex of scientific knowledge, engineering practices, production process technologies, product characteristics, [enterprise interests, planning and control cycles, financial engineering, patterns of expansion and] ways of defining problems – all of them embedded in institutions and infrastructures*' (van der Ploeg, 2008, p. 3). There are numerous documented examples from the past 20 years or so of strategies of this ilk that have been promulgated in Europe and spectacularly failed to meet their objectives (Milone, 2009; van der Ploeg, 2008).

Within this new scenario, the 'peasant' model[3] has been reemerging in all of Europe's regions and demonstrating its relevance in meeting sustainability goals.[4] The peasant model includes several different farming styles: different strategic ways to organize and manage the farming process and the farm business as a whole. While outwardly very heterogeneous in size and focus these farmers share a common strategy: they base their core activities around the flexible and multiple use of the resources and assets that can be reproduced inside the farm or the local system. In other words, they arrange their production and marketing activities in order to distantiate themselves from the global market, thereby maximizing their autonomy. This implies not only reproducing the natural resources involved in farming, but upgrading them. It also implies maintaining and expanding agro-biodiversity through, for example, crop diversification, which provides an 'insurance policy' against unpredictable bad events (whether climatic or market generated). In this context contextualized knowledge assumes a new importance. In the 'peasant model' autonomy is not synonymous with closure, or autarchy, as there are continuous interactions between farmers, the local system and the global market. Through these interactions new knowledge, skills, technology and products are constructed. Farmers are actively and centrally involved in this process making possible for them to maintain (more) control over strategic decisions.

The 'new peasantry' is consolidating itself and becoming a highly effective alternative: a viable way of addressing the multifaceted crisis that beleaguers farmers, the increasing strictures they face and the ongoing challenges of sustainability. These new approaches are radically changing the everyday life of rural areas and go far beyond the 'normal policy' approaches designed (in far-way, almost always urban, places for these areas). Through new, and more sustainable, ways of farming, the new peasantry is reclaiming both market, and political power. As Basu (2011, p. 194) writes: '*[I] have tried to argue that there are enough cues in the present world that a better and vastly more equitable society is viable, that there is enough evidence as well as* a priori *reasons to believe that human beings are capable of not exploiting every opportunity for personal gain*'. There is strong evidence of this in the worlds of agriculture and food.

OVERCOMING SCARCITY AND RE-APPROPRIATING POWER

Modern societies are facing new scarcities and challenges: water, access to food, climate change, employment, social equality, etc. Such scarcities exist alongside two crises that have characterized the past 20 years that highlight the weaknesses of the modern agricultural marketing system. The first is related to food contamination (BSE, Botulinus, *E. coli*, etc.) that generated significant reactions from the two extremes of the food chain: consumers and producers, leading to the establishment of new alliances that shortened many food supply chains, increased consumer access to quality and niche products, and led to a rediscovery of traditional food production processes. This rediscovery has been supported by new technological solutions that guarantee food safety in artisanal processes while simultaneously safeguarding and valorizing artisanal knowledge and skills.

The second is related to the repeated failures of markets, characterized by strong fluctuations in prices (due to speculative behaviour) and a gradual increase in the cost of inputs, which have together led to a continuous reduction of the share of the shop price that is received by farmers (Horlings & Marsden, 2010; van der Ploeg, 2008; van der Ploeg et al., 2000). A survey by ISMEA (2012) on the value chain of Italian agriculture makes it clear that, during the period 2000–2009, the percentage of shop prices, and the actual amount, that goes back to farmers has been greatly reduced. The survey which is based on a retail sales of 100 euros shows that the farmer's share dropped from 25.6 euros in 2000 to 20.1 euros in 2009. Out of this share, the agricultural value added has dropped by even more: from 18.5 to 12.7 euros, since the costs of the inputs used for agriculture grew from 7.1 to 7.4 (see Fig. 1).

Two changes that have affected farmers' incomes can be seen in Fig. 1. The marketing share, rose from 68.4 to 72.9 euros between 2000 and 2009 and the imports of agricultural produce rose from 6 to 7 euros in the same

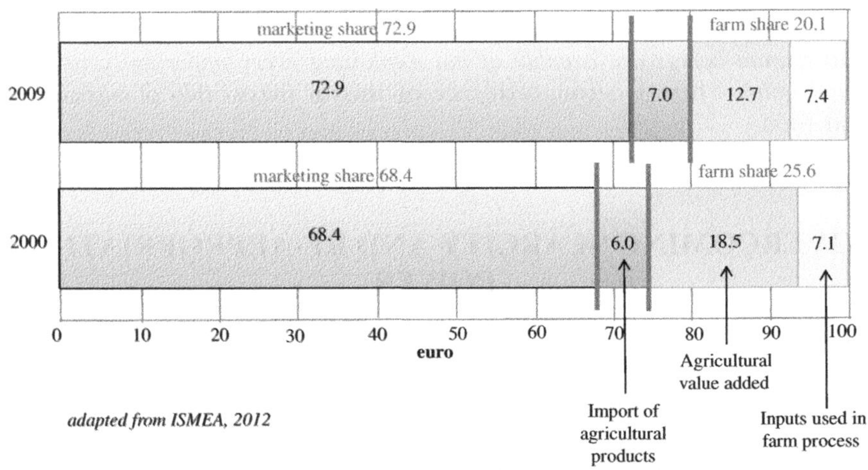

Fig. 1. Changes in the Shares within the Value Chain of Agriculture Produce.

period. The farm share decreased quite dramatically in this period from 25.6 Euro to 20.1, but the farmers' income declined much more markedly from 7.6 to 1.5 euros. There was a slight reduction in labour costs and small increase in the cost of capital and, as already said, an increase in the cost of inputs (see Fig. 2).

The survey showed that these trends are linked to several factors: the existence of structural constraints, the inefficiency of the logistics system and increased energy costs (which affected distribution costs); fragmentation within the chain and the weak market power of the farmers. As a result farmers experienced growing difficulties in maintaining their share of added value, which was constantly squeezed by a growth in costs and a stagnation in producer prices.

The main consequence of this has been growing numbers of bankruptcies among farmers and the abandonment of many farms, specifically among those considered as 'modern' farms operating intensively with a high skills base, large capital investments and a high dependency on external inputs.

Out of this scenario, that has characterized farming in Italy over the past 15 years, a new dynamic has emerged in the agricultural sector: multifunctional farming and farm businesses. The new on-farm activities that farmers adopt are closely connected with the local rural economy as well as the neighbouring urban population and respond to emerging societal demands. This dynamic suggests the need for a new paradigm for rural development, one that emphasizes the capacity of agriculture to respond to the (explicit and implicit) needs of society at large. This is leading to a

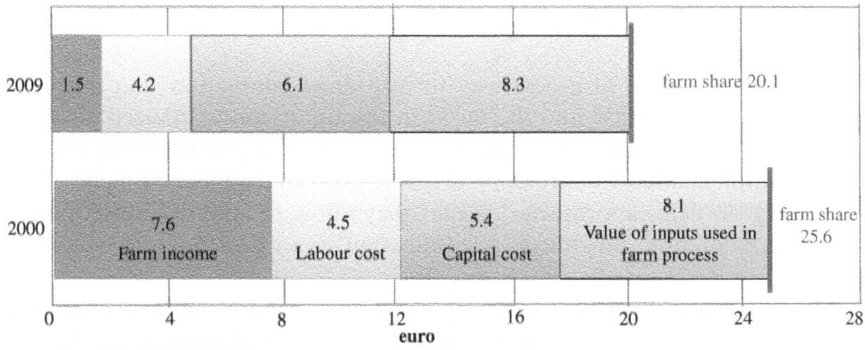

Fig. 2. Change in the Farm Share, 2000–2009.

reconnection between urban and rural societies and economies, that brings in new resources and adds new value to existing resources in rural areas and communities. But it also means the development of rural areas is increasingly dependent on the preferences of urbanites. Multifunctional farms can be found in every European region (Knickel, 2005; Marsden & Sonnino, 2005; Milone & Ventura, 2005, 2009; Scettri, 2001; Tisenkopfs & Suname, 2004; van der Ploeg, Long, & Banks, 2002) and their presence increasingly affects and involves the big and 'competitive' farms operating within the paradigm of 'modernization' (de Rooij, Ventura, Milone, & van der Ploeg, 2014). What we seek to emphasize in this chapter is how this dynamic can give back power to farmers. The multifunctional farms we examine here are family businesses and oriented to what van der Ploeg defines as a 'peasant model' (2008).[5]

The re-appropriation of power has basically occurred in two arenas: markets and institutions. It is manifest in different forms that range from the diversification of farm products, and/or agricultural activities, the implementation of more sustainable (in both environmental and economic terms) practices, innovative forms of cooperation, the use of ICTs and new technologies and the creation of new relationships and rural webs[6] (Milone & Ventura, 2010; van der Ploeg & Marsden, 2008).

The re-appropriation of power by farmers has directly generated four principal countertendencies to the dominant trajectory affecting agriculture.

1. Farmers' incomes have improved due to: better remuneration for the products they bring to market; additional revenue coming from public support for producing or maintaining public goods (positive externalities); and increased efficiency and a reduction in the costs of both capital and inputs.
2. The consolidation of a new way to introduce innovation that is driven by 'field laboratories' and the on-farm testing of contextualized environmentally friendly practices. Many of these farming practices had already been implemented by farmers but inside protected spaces or niches. The novelty of 'field laboratories' is that they allow for the full development of their potential and their 'scientification' (van der Ploeg & Marsden, 2008).
3. Improvements in product quality and a greater equity in exchange that is derived from a reduction in opportunistic behaviour (which in turn is mainly related to the need to maintain a strong reputation within the new direct sales channels).

4. The strengthening of rural economies: multifunctional farms are initiating a variety of new activities, services, crafts and tourism that contribute to reducing the isolation of farmers and strengthen employment opportunities particularly for young people, and as such are in stark contrast with the trend towards rural depopulation and the abandonment of farms.

These countertendencies are today the basis of the new strategy of growth in rural Europe and will strengthen regional and territorial resilience, help mitigate against the effects of climate change and market globalization, provide a concrete response to the new scarcities by making more sustainable use of natural resources and offer a greater and more dignified access to food for all people. The remainder of this chapter provides evidence of how farmers, through re-appropriating and exercising of power, are leading the transformation of agriculture and of the rural areas of Europe.

REGAINING MARKET POWER: THE ITALIAN EXPERIENCE

In Italy, the process of regaining power was first seen in the market place. From the 1980s onwards Italian farms started a process of diversifying their products and farm activities: improving the quality of the former and inventing new activities such as agritourism, care and bio-energy production.

The process of diversification has had three main consequences.

1. A repositioning of the produce on the market, which brings higher prices.
2. The possibility for farmers to have a 'portfolio strategy' that addresses different markets or targets different groups of consumers. The advantage of this is that it reduces the impact of price fluctuations in commodity markets.
3. The creation of new opportunities in new and different markets, through developing new activities, particularly services (i.e. care farms, agritourism, bio-energy, etc.).

Over time, the process of diversification has led to a complete reorganization of internal and external farm relationships. The consequence is a blossoming of new networks and new markets which now extend far beyond their initial niches. One highly representative phenomenon in Italy is the numerous farmers' markets initiated by the Farmers' Union, Coldiretti, and Slow Food. This exemplifies how the concept of 'the market' can change over time and space depending (according to circumstances and the economic and regulatory contexts) and how the regaining of power contributes to determining the outcome of exchanges and creates new political references.

The evolution of multifunctionality was rapid and is still very dynamic. In Italy, it began from the initiative of individual farmers driven by different motivations: their entrepreneurship, the need to rescue or re-utilize farm and family resources (and in particular, family labour). The emergence of multifunctionality resulted in changes that represented quite radical breaks from everyday local life.

Over time, the activities of these pioneering farmers were copied by an increasing number of other farmers and gave rise to new networks and alliances that went beyond territorial boundaries. The thickening of these relationships gave rise to rural webs rooted in the territory, but strongly interconnected: both in terms of market and social-political relations. It is this local–global dimension of the rural web that has made it possible for farmers to regain power. In the market this power emerged with the development of nested markets and niches and spaces for new activities. In the political arena it took the form of protected spaces (derogations of norms), quality schemes, the institutionalization of short chains and the recognition that farming practices produce public goods.

These diversification processes have allowed farmers and particularly 'peasants': those farmers who were previously considered to be marginal and uncompetitive, to regain control over the assets used in the production process (in particular land, animals and labour) and to exercise new forms of market power in their exchanges. The power consists in the possibility of defining the quality characteristics and standards of the products and services. This has allowed farmers to enter into new markets, where the attributes of services and products are increasingly socially constructed. Fig. 3 illustrates how these diversification processes have enabled the creation of strong interrelationships between farmers and consumers.

This, re-appropriation of power was made easier by the introduction of ICTs, which facilitate the creation of direct relationships/connections between producers and consumers, even in the early stages of the product cycle. This has led to strong alliances that have supported and guided the

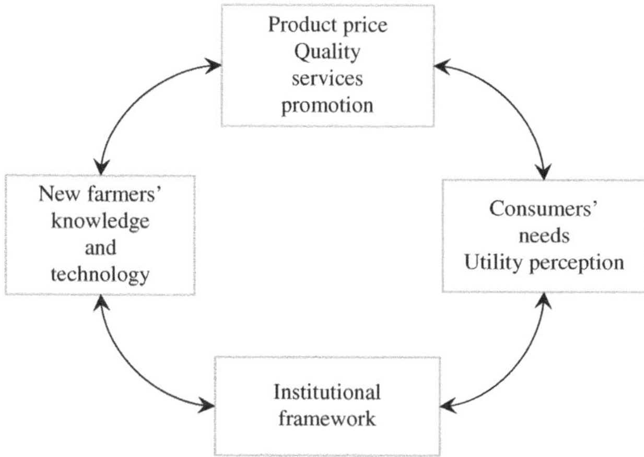

Fig. 3. Direct Interrelations between Farmers and Consumers.

new rules for food trade (food traceability systems; information and communication on food safety and animal welfare; quality schemes, etc.).

Box 1 contains some indicative stories[7] of Italian farmers, formerly marginalized by the mainstream economic regime, who have been able, within the market, to gain recognition and higher prices for their products and services and also regain decisional control over 'how, when and where' to produce and sell.

THE RE-APPROPRIATION OF POLITICAL POWER: DUTCH ENVIRONMENTAL COOPERATIVES

Dutch environmental cooperatives arose spontaneously with three main aims:

1. To overcome the constraints imposed on agricultural activities by the State with the intention of reducing nitrate run-off and maintaining the landscape.
2. To integrate local agricultural practices on a large territorial scale, with a new focus on the environment and landscape.
3. To create a new form of governance for the management of rural areas that empowered farmers and made more use of their skills.

Box 1

Gregorio and Nunzio, Shepherds from the Abruzzo Mountains

Gregorio and Nunzio are two shepherds from Abruzzo region who, in the 1990s, started to collaborate in order to improve the quality of their cheeses and the sales conditions. Over the last 20 years or so they have introduced several innovations. such as a soft 'Gregorian' cheese; a smoked ricotta and a 'black peel' ricotta – the last two being different methods of increasing the shelf life of ricotta; a 'banditry' pecorino cheese that is aged in wood chippings; a sheep salami; the 'Adopt a sheep' initiative – a new method of selling meat and cheese; and agritourism. These innovations allowed them to position their products in much more profitable market niches (the products are sold at twice the reference price of the market) and also in new markets. In effect, they have implemented a 'portfolio strategy', based on a wide range of products. Their network is well-known and popular in Italy and has been enriched with the entry of new young farmers who have taken the pair as reference models. They represent the most vibrant economic reality in agriculture in their local context: the mountainous region of central Abruzzo an area that in the logic of the modernization model is considered very marginal, with many natural constrains on competitive agriculture. It is worth noting that these farms today are not only competitive, but that they represent the main opportunity for revitalizing the area (Milone, 2009).

The Red Cows Consortium in Reggio Emilia

The Red Cows Consortium in Parmigiano Reggiano was born from the stubbornness of a breeder who in the mid-1980s initiated a personal and quite radical activity of product diversification (within the Parmigiano Reggiano quality scheme) by breeding the traditional cow breed 'Reggiana' a red cow, less productive than Friesian cows, but with a higher milk quality and better suited for the production of Parmigiano Reggiano cheese. This change in breeding strategy also necessitated the use of more natural feeding techniques that rely more on grass and hay and less on the use of concentrates. Over time, the Consortium producing Red Cow Parmigiano Reggiano cheese introduced a number of innovations. These included a differentiation based on different aging periods of the cheese (24, 28 and 36 months); the valorization of by-products, such as meat and ricotta cheese; the creation of new products containing Parmigiano Reggiano cheese, but more respondent to consumers' needs for convenience foods (such as sauces and fresh pastas). The milk is of higher quality (and thus attracts a higher price – some 20–30% more than the traditional Parmigiano Reggiano – which is already above the reference level for milk prices in the world market) and although output is lower this is more than offset by higher prices and a reduction of production costs. This experience illustrates the creation of new market niches within an already-existing quality product scheme. The Red Cow Consortium has expanded its market over time, which has been done by linking the quality characteristics of the product to the needs of the modern distribution system: an increasing standardization and reduction of aging period to reduce the price. It should also be noted that the area in question is a highly specialized agricultural area where such experiences are becoming more widespread and generating more prosperity. Currently, the Consortium has more than 40 farmers (there were only 6 initially) and over 15,000 Parmesan cheese products (from about 400 initially). (Milone & Ventura, 2014 – Interview of dairy farmer President of the Red Cows Consortium)

Agritourism Fior di Bosco

Another good example of how small farms, located in disadvantaged areas, can be drivers of important development opportunities in the local rural economy can be found in the case of Fior di Bosco Agritourism, in the Trentino Alto Adige (part of the Italian Alps). This farm has just 11 ha, plus the mountain areas of alpine pasture land (the Malga[12]) allocated by the province Yet, the farmer has been able to diversify his agricultural activities to include on-farm processing and agritourism. He began by offering accommodation services and processing milk and herbs gathered from the Alpine mountain pastures, into cheese. He also reintroduced a local dairy breed 'the Grey' which was very well adapted to high mountain pastures and good for producing high-quality meat *and* milk. He made many more innovations, particularly around energy saving and in diversifying and improving the quality of his products and services. Today, the farm employs seven people including four family members from *11 ha.* In terms of working units per hectare or per animal this is well above the average for 'modern' farms. This is an example of how such market-based solutions can, not only, ensure a satisfactory income to the farmer, but also provide job opportunities for others.

Many other farmers in Trento and Bolzano provinces have chosen to follow the example of *Fior di Bosco* and have diversified their farming activities, thereby dispelling a common myth that multifunctionality can only be adopted by a few and by a small. Today such examples can be found all over Europe.

The farmers participating in these cooperatives managed to regain control of their assets by exercising a form of political power towards local and national institutions. They have even extended their influence to European institutions – in that they have influenced the outline of the most recent EU regulations on rural development policy. This reacquisition of power occurred gradually, over time, through building extensive alliances with consumers, the scientific community and environmental movements. The phenomenon began in Friesland and now has spread across the whole territory of the Netherlands, and has even crossed national borders with similar movements now established in Belgium, Germany and Italy. These cooperatives are the response of the farmers to their marginalization by modern production and regulatory systems. The original farmers were unable or unwilling to entertain the high costs of implementing the solutions proposed by Dutch government in response to environmental pressures. These cooperatives enabled many farms not only to survive, but to increase their income and make more sustainable use of their natural resources, producing benefits for the environment, the landscape and the quality of life of its inhabitants. In the last 20 years the number of Dutch cooperatives has risen from 6 to 150 with more than 10,000 associated farms running different production systems (milk, meat, cereals, potatoes, flowers and bulbs, social educational and agritourism farms). They are grouped into five large regional associations.

Farmers involved in these environmental cooperatives share two key characteristics in their farming methods. First, they employ more sustainable and autonomous agricultural processes, reusing farm waste or wastewater, reducing costs and safeguarding their assets (land, labour and animals). One example of this is the production of 'improved manure'. This was achieved by reducing the amount of concentrates in cattle feed. In turn the use of improved manure in the fields reduces the quantity of nitrates being applied and contributes to soil fertility and biodiversity within the soil, keeping it alive. The less intensive feeding also lengthens the lactation period of cows and the animals' lives. Second, the farms have diversified their activities to include nature and landscape management, constructing and maintaining the landscape and safeguarding biodiversity. This led (after much discussion) to the emergence of agro-environmental contracts between the Dutch government and groups of farmers that stipulate the 'public goods' that the farmers will provide (but importantly do not stipulate the methods to be used to provide these goods). This can be seen as a hybrid form of market or a 'quasi-market'. These types of contracts are now permissible within and encouraged by the EU's new rural development (RD) policy (2007–2013) and in its new RD programming period (2014–2020).

Environmental cooperatives are being recognized as brokers within the institutionalized market created by agro-environmental schemes. This means that cooperatives are becoming the link between institutions and individual farmers. As such they now have to accept responsibility for devising, implementing and managing their programmes of activities as stipulated in the contracts. Five pilot projects are currently underway in order to guide the cooperatives to achieve this role by 2016. The approach is summarized in Fig. 4, which shows the 'front' (government contracts) and 'back' doors individual contracts with farmers through which these arrangements are implemented.

Through these collective actions the cooperatives have allowed farmers to regain considerable political power, but also and perhaps more importantly to regain autonomy over the use of their resources. It also gives

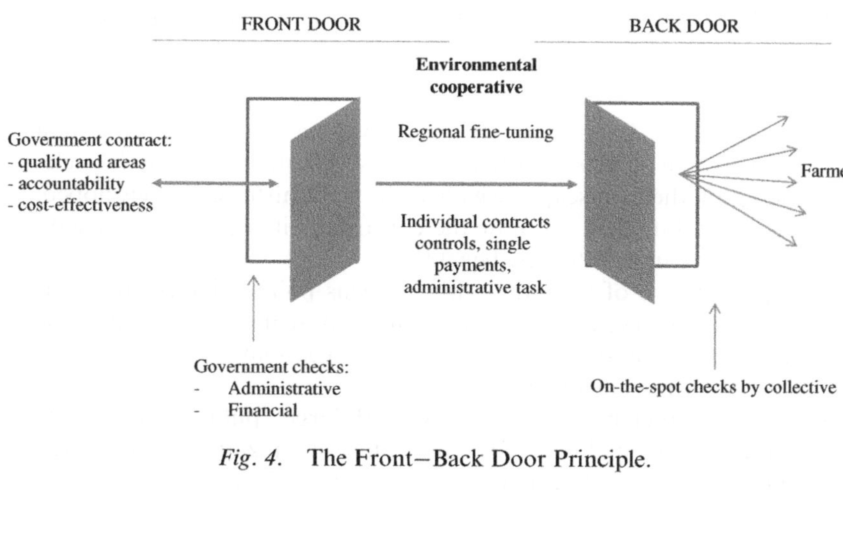

Fig. 4. The Front–Back Door Principle.

them a central role in designing the collective actions and programmes and a new role and freedom to test new farming practices within a 'protected space' based on the innovative '*field laboratory*' approach – where the farmer is and remains the main actor (Stuiver et al., 2003).

Box 2 summarizes the story of the first six environmental cooperatives in the Netherlands.

Box 2

NFW – Noardlike Fryske Walden

The Association of Northern Friesian Woodlands (NFW – Noardlike Fryske Walden) was formally established in 2002, but has operated through its associations and base cooperatives, for over 20 years. The current structure contains six environmental cooperatives and farmers' associations with over 1,100 members who farm 60,000 ha of territory. The association has three main aims: to make agriculture more sustainable; to improve the quality of the landscape; and to develop biodiversity in the area. To achieve these aims, the association has created a network of territorial cooperation involving the province, the municipalities, the water management organization, the organization for the management of natural soils, the Environmental Federation, the (former) Ministry of Economy, Agriculture and Innovation (ELI), the Ministry of Infrastructure and the Environment and the university and research sectors. The strategy of the NFW has three main elements.

1. Farmer and Landscape. It has developed a landscape vision for the area it covers which explains how the different key elements of the landscape, which have been historically developed, can be maintained and how the constraints it appears to place on farmers[13] can lead to new benefits.
2. A programme of activities with 30 focus points divided into four types of interventions: nature and landscape; agriculture, the environment and water; the regional economy; and territorial emergency management.
3. Broad partnerships involving several large, public and private bodies (municipalities, environmental organizations, ministries, universities, etc.). The activities are listed in Fig. 5.

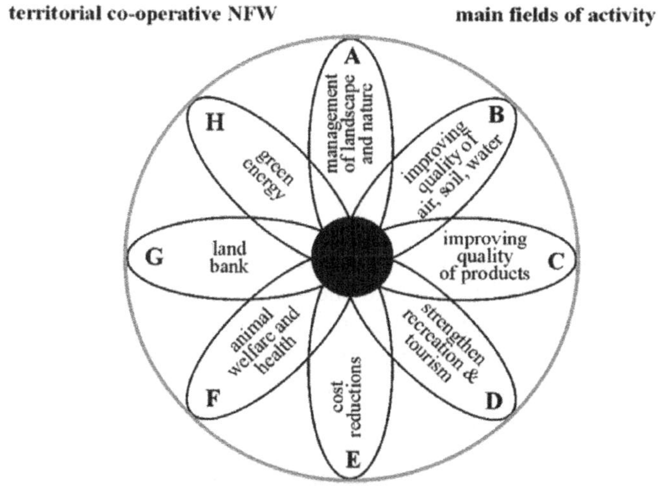

Fig. 5. The Association of Northern Friesian Woodlands' Fields of Activity.

OVERCOMING DOGMAS: RIVERFORD FARM – HOME DELIVERY VERSUS SUPERMARKETS

In the early stages of postmodern development, the agricultural sector has had to deal with a new set of dogmas.

1. That economy of scale, the enlargement of farm size and overcoming the 'limiting factors' of production are the only ways to make agricultural production, food processing and distribution competitive and capable of addressing world hunger, allowing a continuous expansion of access to food, and keeping food prices low.
2. That the competitive market is the only structure able to maximize the efficiency of exchange and all actions must be directed to its supporting its potential for ensuring growth, wealth and the territorial and individual well-being.
3. The paradigm of '*declining importance*', which envisions the inevitable long-term decline of agriculture in terms of its share of GDP and employment. This stems from the constant reduction in agricultural

prices and the ongoing effects of productivity gains from technological progress and mechanization (Johnson, 1973; Saccomandi, 1994, p. 12; Schultz, 1945).

This set of dogmas has, and is still, guiding the development and evolution of the world's agricultural systems and continue to be the foundations for the globalization of markets and the delocalization of production. They are supported by a system of power or, to paraphrase van der Ploeg (2008) and Hardt and Negri (2000), by very tangible 'food empires' or 'world orders' that have the power to continue to steer the world towards coded and linear solutions that promote the globalization of markets: solutions that also best remunerate investments in production. This set of dogmas also, at the same time, makes any other alternative seem an non-alternative, invalidating and belittling the efforts and initiatives that are increasingly evident in Europe (and over the past decade, in many other parts of the world, i.e. China, Brazil, the United States and Africa) (Hebinck, Schneider, & van der Ploeg, 2014). While there is some recognition of the existence within the mainstream discourse of 'new' markets, such as direct sales or short circuits, these are considered as just exchange spaces for very small quantities or certain types (i.e. local or artisanal) of produce and certainly not suitable for replacing the existing centralized and global distribution system. The next example sets out to describe the potential of these solutions and their ability to transcend territorial limitations. Box 3 illustrates the case of Riverford Organic Farm Box Scheme.[8]

MULTIFUNCTIONALITY: A CHOICE FOR PROTECTING AGRICULTURAL ASSETS

Is multifunctionality also the right choice for large and specialized farms? This is a legitimate question, since, as mentioned earlier, classical, neoclassical and post-modern economic theorists have expressed real doubts on the probability that the new paradigm of multifunctionality or rural development will be capable of guiding a transition from the 'modern' agricultural model to a new model, that can create growth and wealth. In short their concerns are that multifunctionality may not be appropriate for farms that conform to the competitive and productivist ethos. We will not enter a debate about the merits of the assumptions that underlie 'modernization', nor the concept of competitiveness. Instead we will confine ourselves to reporting on the results of an Italy-wide survey carried out among just under 800 farms, considered to be modern and professional. The results of this analysis have been described in an article published in the journal *Rural Sociology* by Sabine de Rooij, which was introduced thus: '*[The] research results show that larger farmers are also investing in new, multifunctional activities, alongside investments in food production; in fact, these farmers are keeping pace with, or moving ahead of, farmers who only invest in food production. They consider investments in new activities to be a "life-jacket" that strengthens their agricultural activities. The results also show that government programmes are not decisive factors for farms engaging in or further developing multifunctional activities. The main drivers are family centred, with some farmers also having "broader" motivations and seeing the wider benefits of multifunctional agriculture*' (de Rooij et al., 2014).

The central argument of this chapter is that many 'modern' and 'competitive' Italian farms are using multifunctionality as a way of saving their conventional (in the strictest sense) farming activities and giving the farmer options for the future. We would like to stress two statistics from this chapter: 27% of these farms have already started to include multifunctional activities within their 'portfolio' and another 18% intend to do so in the next 5 years. In addition, only 5% of these multifunctional farms expected to go out of business in the next 5 years, compared to 10% of farms that have not adopted multifunctionality. In contrast fewer farmers (less than 15%) are planning to continue pursuing the modernization trajectory. Forty-eight per cent of the farmers who have opted for multifunctionality see the combination with conventional farming activities as a strength and identified additional benefits in so doing:

1. more autonomy in their decision-making about when to sell their products (waiting for a better price in the market);
2. new financial resources to increase quality and to differentiate products; and
3. the ability to adopt more strategic behaviour towards the market and the capacity to better adapt to its dynamics.

The multifunctional farms in this survey were also more able to ensure the maintenance of local and conventional agricultural production. The survey shows that 34% of multifunctional farms invest in conventional agricultural production, 36% to stabilize it and 30% to decrease it. However, among the modern (non-multifunctional) farms only 16% are investing in conventional agricultural productive activities, 34% are stabilizing them and 50% are planning to reduce them (see Fig. 6).

Box 3

Riverford Organic Farm Box Scheme

This example begins with the passion of a farmer from Devon who, with only three acres (ca. 1.5 ha) of land decided to grow fresh horticultural products and deliver them directly to the homes of 30 friends. Today the Riverford Box Scheme involves a number of growers (more than 25) and small producers (more than 15) organized into four 'cooperative centres'.

> The box scheme began in Riverford on Wash Farm in Devon. Our first regional farm outside of Devon was Riverford on Sacrewell Farm in Peterborough, followed by Riverford on Home Farm in Yorkshire and then Riverford on Upper Norton Farm in Hampshire. Each regional farm grows and then delivers vegetables to local customers.

This quote, from one of the producers illustrates the modus operandi of the Riverford phenomenon: a solution that can involve new territories and new producers in order to have a production and delivery system that grows organic vegetables locally and delivers them to consumers' homes using environmentally friendly means of transport.

> As demand for our veg. boxes grew, we didn't want to grow any larger from our original Devon farm. So we joined up with organic farmers around the country who share our obsession for growing great-tasting, affordable, organic vegetables for local people. Our regional farms help us keep food miles down, support local farmers, provide local employment and help us build a strong link between growers and consumers. Back in the distant days, when we sold our veg to the supermarkets, our co-op's vegetables traveled an average of 500 miles to reach the supermarket shelves. Our frustration with this wastage and the associated cost and loss of freshness was one of the main reasons for starting our box scheme in 1993. As we dropped the supermarkets and sold more boxes the area we covered from Devon expanded from the South West across the South of the UK and the average journey by HGV grew to 150 miles; a lot less than previously but still too far. By 2004 the market had grown to a level where we thought we could sell all our vegetables locally and we hatched a plan to set up a network of regional farms that would grow some vegetables themselves and, combine them with produce from other local growers, packing boxes similar to ours for delivery to houses within 50 to 100 miles. Four years later we have four regional farms running in partnership with local farmers and are about to open a fifth.

This debunks the first dogma: the Riverford system, with free home delivery, manages to sell the veg boxes at a lower price than the same organic vegetables would cost at a supermarket.

> Every month we compare our veg box prices against the equivalent organic vegetables in Tesco, Sainsbury's and Waitrose. The good news is that our boxes tend to come out cheaper – and that's without including our free delivery.

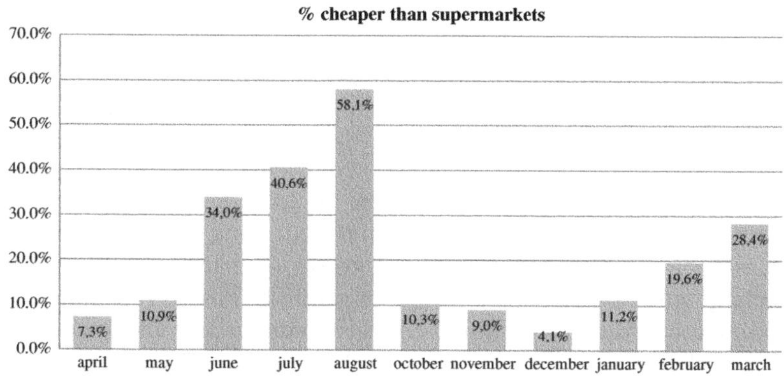

Riverford estimation

The second benefit is the efficiency of the logistics and distribution system that, through carefully organizing deliveries, are able to avoid unnecessary journeys. It is a little less flexible than a centralized logistics system but far-less polluting and less expensive.

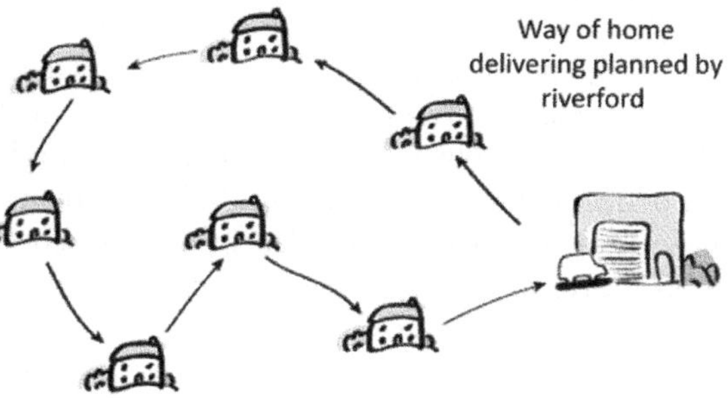

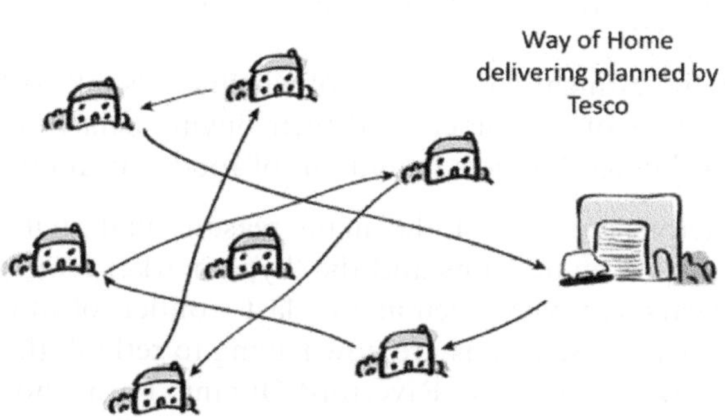

Some of our customers view us as intransigent, but by organizing rounds on a weekly basis we are able to minimize the distance travelled per drop (currently about 1 mile in urban areas and 2 miles in rural areas). Being as flexible and responsive as Tesco home delivery might win us more customers, but would increase by many times the emissions associated with, what is already, the worst stage in the vegetables' journey.

The system of home delivery is carried out by a network of autonomous and independent franchises connected with the Riverford Organic Farms organization that perform daily deliveries. More than 47,000 weekly deliveries are currently made, and this number continues to grow. The franchises have grown over the years as well as specialty store affiliates. The range of products has been significantly expanded over time in response to consumers' desires and needs. The Riverford Network now supplies fresh fruit and vegetables, cheese, milk, meat, wine, prepared or pre-cooked foods and baked goods. The network is a place of continuous experimentation, aimed at improving production techniques, transportation systems with a low environmental impact (home deliveries in towns are done with bikes or electric vans – innovations often introduced directly by the franchisee), packaging and e-commerce.

Such solutions are often ignored and underestimated but this one is so successful that it represents a major source of competition for distribution giants such as Tesco or Sainsbury's. We feel it is important to emphasize that network was built by farmers and small family producers who decided to cooperate to build a strong distributive network whose functionality is provided by franchised small carriers and now serves more than *47,000 British families per week*.

This example also illustrates that modern distribution systems have neglected some essential factors.

1. That fresh produce is susceptible to perishing and loss of quality.
2. The impact of the transport system on the environment (carbon footprint).
3. The high investment costs, many of which are 'sunk costs'.[14]
4. The fickleness of consumers and their buying behaviour who may shift their limited budgets in and out of food consumption.

These factors are one of the main reasons underlying the crisis facing the major retail chains and the 'hypermarket economy' which, just a few years ago, were seen as the 'last frontier' of modern distribution systems. These chains are now having to rethink their distribution models. By contrast the Riverford Organic Farms home delivery system not only takes into account the elements discussed above but also manages them well: the products delivered always arrive fresh and ripe; the deliveries are never farther than 100 miles (with the goal of reducing them to 50 miles); the investment costs are shared among a large number of players; consumers are at the centre of their policies; and they are continually looking for ways to improve the produce, product range and delivery service. In addition the system achieves three other important benefits: it increases the income of participating farmers; it increases the number of people employed (thereby contributing to the local economy); and it reduces the cost of, and pollution from, the distribution system. This system of exchange can be considered as a hybrid market form: a 'quasi-organization' or 'quasi-market' that reduces many of the inefficiencies and failures of the competitive market even though it provides what some would see as sub-optimal solutions. It also ensures a stability of exchange over time and a more equitable redistribution of income among the actors involved. Equally important it delivers fresh organic food to consumers at a lower price than conventional distribution systems. In conclusion, it is a system that allows an improvement in the position of both producers and consumers through an exchange that has positive social and territorial impacts.

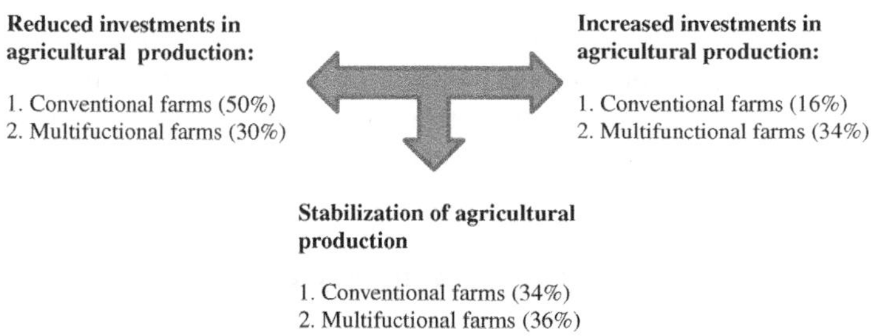

Fig. 6. Farm Strategies.

This is further proof that, far from detracting from agricultural production, in Italy and elsewhere in Europe, multifunctionality is actually enhancing it. Multifunctional farms are investing in new activities, but with the aim of enhancing, strengthening and protecting their conventional agricultural production, which is still considered as the cornerstone of the farm.

CONCLUSIONS

The multifunctionality model involves two main strategies: a market strategy and a political one. The central objective of each strategy is to regain the power to choose how, when and where, to act. Drawing on the TATE concept (Benvenuti, 1982) we can argue that multifunctionality is a response to the serious crisis facing the TATE of modernization. This TATE is being challenged by a completely new system of market and institutional relationships. Multifunctionality is a system made up of multiple 'interfaces', where the process of knowledge acquisition is central as a '... *product of interaction, dialogue, reflexivity, and contest of meaning, and involves aspects of control, authority and power*' (Long, 2015). In this sense, the process of regaining power, which emerges in the development trajectories adopted by multifunctional farmers, is '*the outcome of complex struggles and negotiations over authority, status, reputation and resources, and necessitates the enrolment of networks of actors and constituencies. Such struggles are founded upon the extent to which specific actors perceive themselves capable of maneuvering within particular situations and developing effective strategies for doing so*' (*ibid.*). This also leads to an increase in the complexity of the productive, organizational and interpersonal functions of agricultural firms that sets a new context of activities that '*implies a degree of consent, a degree of negotiation and thus a degree of power, as manifested in the possibility of exerting some control, prerogative, authority and capacity for action, be it front or backstage, for brief moments or for more sustained periods*' (*ibid.*). The interfaces that evolve over time in these new rural heterogeneous webs differ from region to region. The remoulding and consolidation of the processes of innovation and diversification, technical assistance, planning, communication, marketing, training and knowledge are ongoing.

In summary we identify the following key characteristics of the multifunctional model:

1. taking back control over the resources and farm products (leading towards greater autonomy);
2. seeking economies of scope and 'portfolio strategies';
3. the joint management of different transactional governance structures (i.e. differentiated market forms for different activities and products); and
4. dynamic adaptations to quantitative and qualitative changes in demand and to different transactional governance structures (i.e. new markets, niches or hybrid and contract forms).

New alliances with citizens and consumers are playing an important role in facilitating farmers to regain their power. According to a recent Eurobarometer survey on food security, food quality and the countryside, 81% of European citizens consider that agriculture is beneficial for the environment, 86% agree that it contributes to the beauty of the countryside, 89% believe that agriculture helps to protect rural areas and 96% claim that food quality is a factor that affects their consumption decisions.[9] According to a survey on the welfare of rural areas in Italy, 60% of Italian citizens think that being a farmer would be a good job for their children (Milone, Ventura, & van der Ploeg, 2008).[10] According to a survey on young people's perceptions of rural areas 50% agree with the statement that agriculture is an activity that achieves harmony between nature and human beings.[11]

These surveys show that the majority of European citizens today are aware of the role that agriculture plays in the preservation of natural resources and the quality of life in rural areas as well as in ensuring the autonomy in the production of high quality and healthy food. This is now the main legitimation for maintaining the EU's Common Agricultural Policy (with two increasingly integrated pillars one of which is specifically dedicated to rural development) and allocating 43% of the EU's total budget to this policy.

Another important element in the re-acquisition of power is the ability of farmers to create new relationships with markets. This is mainly due to four key factors:

1. diversification of production – based on quality, craftsmanship and the origin of the products;
2. direct contact with consumers which provides them with information about the products, processes and elements that characterize the farm and its entrepreneur, such contact has been greatly facilitated by new ICTs that have simplified the creation of new rural networks and the re-establishment of trust;
3. the development of nested markets and the complete reconstruction of relationships in the food chain; and
4. new forms of logistical organization for the transport and delivery of products.

These four elements are the basis for more solid and organized activities which are rapidly growing in Europe. Such activities are driving the transformation of European agricultural and its countryside, as places where millions of farmers and their families live and work. These factors have redefined the strategic behaviour of farmers who are no longer solely focused on productivity and profit maximization, but more on obtaining overall satisfaction from their farm activities and combining the search to make a living with personal and family well-being, the quality and vitality of the environments in which they live and the social and environmental sustainability of their farming. Fig. 7 schematically illustrates the pathways and the actors who are leading the multifunctional model and helping farmers regain power and autonomy.

The innovative aspect of this process of farmers' regaining power is that it happens with a virtual absence of conflict between the participating actors (institutions, consumers, farmers). This is because all the actors and particularly consumers, recognize the importance of the peasantry responding to, mostly unexpected, contingencies, which not only impact on farming, but also on the quality of life of citizens and consumers.

This emergent role is based on the daily interactions between farmers and the natural resource base that is available to them. Through these, rapidly changing, interactions and those with markets farmers are developing new ways and activities to safeguard the reproduction of rural resource base, the survival of the family farm and the continuity of his family and his social group (van der Ploeg et al., 2015). This goal that is not just held by farmers but is one that is shared among civil society at large. The skills and knowledge of farmers have reassumed a new value as a social resource. It is precisely this resource (as shown in the examples

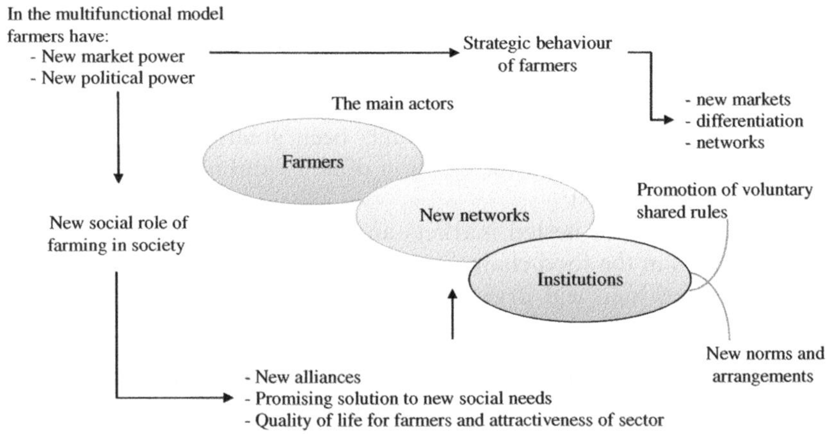

Fig. 7. Pathways and Actors Involved in Empowering Multifunctional Farmers.

given in this chapter), which increasingly characterizes processes of rural development in Europe and justifies the centrality of agriculture in the EU rural development policy.

NOTES

1. '*That some people have more power than others is one of the most palpable facts of human existence. Because of this, the concept of power is as ancient and ubiquitous as any that social theory can boast*' (Dahl, 1957, p. 201). Power can have many expressions, in both theoretical and practical ways. In the words of Max Weber '*power is the probability that one actor within a social relationship will be in a position to carry out his own will despite resistance*' (1947). If we apply this to the market and political relations we can say that the re-acquisition of power is a prerequisite for constructing a strong level of agency within a territory. The exercise of such power can strengthen the autonomy and independence of a territory from external pressures and influences.
2. The Europe 2020 Strategy has three priorities: smart growth – through more effective investments in education, research and innovation; sustainability – through promoting a low CO_2 emission economy and agricultural and agro-industrial competitiveness; and solidarity, which is focused on creating jobs and reducing poverty in rural areas. The strategy is based on five ambitious objectives that focus upon: employment, research, education, poverty reduction and climate change/energy. See http://ec.europa.eu/europe2020/index_it.htm
3. van der Ploeg (2008).
4. In the full sense of its three dimensions: economic, environmental and social.
5. Family farms and/or peasants are implementing multifunctional strategies to defend the assets they have traditionally controlled: land, labour and knowledge. It is precisely their control over these assets that allows them to make the choice to explore new paths that differ from the mainstream, and to thereby overcome the crises that have occurred over the years. As a result these farmers and peasants are today becoming the group that is leading the revitalization of rural economies.
6. The rural web is the more-or-less coherent whole of actor-networks that exist within a rural space. It is composed of the interrelations, interactions, encounters and mutualities that exist between actors, resources, activities, sectors and places. It is multi-actor, multilevel, dynamic and multidimensional. The morphology of rural webs shows a considerable variation and heterogeneity: they differ greatly from one region to another (van der Ploeg et al., 2008). A rural web has six interdependent and consistent dimensions: new institutional arrangements, social capital, governance of markets, endogeneity, novelty and sustainability (Milone & Ventura, 2010; van der Ploeg & Marsden, 2008).
7. A broad range of such experiences is documented in Scettri (2001) and Milone and Ventura (2009).
8. For more information and for those (in the United Kingdom) who would like to enjoy their fresh organic products you can visit their website: www.riverford.co.uk. The italicized sections in the box were taken from this site.

9. The survey was carried out by TNS Opinion & Social network in the 27 EU Member States between 10 and 25 March 2012; 26,593 respondents from different social and demographic groups were interviewed face-to-face, at home, in their mother tongue, on behalf of the EU's Directorate-General for Agriculture and Rural Development. The aim of the survey was to understand EU citizens' experiences and perceptions of food security and self-sufficiency. The survey also looked at consumer priorities when buying food, their awareness of quality labels and their perceptions of the link between agriculture and the preservation of nature and countryside (see European Commission, 2012).

10. The survey was carried out by Perugia University and covered every Italian municipality; 1,471 citizens of different ages (between 24 and 75 years) were interviewed by telephone using a multiple response questionnaire. The survey was part of a project funded by the Italian Ministry of Agriculture. A complete overview of the results is reported in Milone et al. (2008).

11. The survey was carried out by the Italian rural network in eight different EU member states. The main results are highlighted in Rete rurale Italia-MIPAAF (2010).

12. The Malga is a form of division of mountainous public land that exists in the provinces of Trento and Bolzano. It allows farmers to carry out their agricultural activities and for rural outbuildings (housing and infrastructures) on the land.

13. These include the division of the fields into strips with length-to-width ratios of 3:1 and 5:1; small-scale fields (ca. 2 ha) which are often broken up by dams ditches or canals. All these elements are characteristic of the Friesian landscape. They make modernization more difficult but open up new market opportunities in providing (agri) tourism or 'public goods'.

14. In economics and business decision-making, a sunk cost is a retrospective (past) cost that has already been incurred and cannot be recovered.

REFERENCES

Bartlett, R. (1989). *Economics and power (209pp.)*. Cambridge: Cambridge University Press.

Basu, K. (2011). *Beyond the invisible hand*. Princeton, NJ: Princeton University Press.

Benvenuti, B. (1975). General system theory and entrepreneurial autonomy in farming: Towards a new feudalism or towards democratic planning. *Sociologia Ruralis*, *XV*, 46–64.

Benvenuti, B. (1982). Che cos'è L'ambiente Tecnologico Amministrativo (TATE) che fissa i compiti ed a cosa serve. In *I Problemi Dell'imprenditorialità Nella Cooperazione Agricola*. Rome: AIPA.

Dahl, R. A. (1957). The concept of power. *Behavioral Science*, *2*(3), 201.

de Rooij, S. J. G., Ventura, F., Milone, P., & van der Ploeg, J. D. (2014). Sustaining food production through multifunctionality: The dynamics of large farms in Italy. *Sociologia Ruralis*, *54*(3), 303–320.

Dugger, W. (1980). Power: An institutional framework of analyses. *Journal of Economic Issues*, *14*, 897–907.

European Commission. (2012). Europeans' attitudes towards food security, food quality and the countryside. Special Eurobarometer No. 389.

FitzSimmons, M., & D. Goodman (1998). Incorporating nature: Environmental narratives and the reproduction of food. In B. Braun & N. Castree (Eds.), *Remaking reality: Nature at the millennium* (pp. 194–220). New York, NY: Routledge.

Goodman, D. (1999). Agro-food studies in the 'age of ecology': Nature, corporeality, bio-politics. *Sociologia Ruralis*, *39*(1), 18–38.

Hardt, M., & Negri, A. (2000). *Empire*. Cambridge, MA: Harvard University Press.

Hebinck, P., Schneider, S., & van der Ploeg, J. D. (Eds.). (2014). *Rural development and the construction of new markets*. London: Routledge.

Horlings, I., & Marsden, T. (2010). The new rural paradigm and redefining the rural web. In P. Milone & F. Ventura (Eds.), *Networking the rural*. Assen: Royal Van Gorcum.

Ilbery, B., & Kneafsy, M. (2000). Producer constructions of quality in regional specialty food production: A case study from south west England. *Journal of Rural Studies*, *16*, 217–230.

ISMEA. (2010). *La percezione delle aree rurali da parte dei giovani: un'indagine su otto stati membri*. Rete rurale Italia-MIPAAF.

ISMEA. (2012). *La Competitività dell'Agroalimentare Italiano: Check up 2012*. Roma: ISMEA.

Johnson, D. G. (1973). Role of agriculture in economic development revisited. *Agricultural Economics*, *8*, 421–434.

Knickel, K. (2005). New division of responsibilities in rural areas, nature management and environmental education: Some relevant experiences from Germany. Essay prepared for the Dutch Council of Rural Areas, Amersfort.

Long, N. (2015). Activities, actants and actors: Theoretical perspectives on development practice and practitioners. In P. Milone, F. Ventura, & J. Ye (Eds.), *Constructing a new framework for rural development* (Vol. 22). Research in Rural Sociology and Development. Bingley, UK: Emerald Group Publishing Limited.

Marsden, T., & Sonnino, R. (2005). Rural development and agrifood governance in Europe: Tracing the development of alternatives. In V. Higgins & G. Lawrence (Eds.), *Agricultural governance: Globalisation and the new politics of regulations*. London: Routledge.

Milone, P. (2009). *Agriculture in transition: A neo-institutional analysis* (1st ed., 256pp.). Italy: Van Gorgum.

Milone, P., & Ventura, F. (2005). *Innovatività Contadina e Sviluppo Rurale*. Milano: Franco Angeli.

Milone, P., & Ventura, F. (2009). *I contadini del Terzo Millennio*. Perugia: AMP Edizione.

Milone, P., & Ventura, F. (Eds.). (2010). *Networking the rural*. Assen: Van Gorcum.

Milone, P., & Ventura, F. (2014). The visible hand in building new markets for rural economies. In P. Hebinck, S. Schneider, & J. D. van der Ploeg (Eds.), *Rural development and the construction of new markets*. London: Routledge.

Milone, P., Ventura, F., & van der Ploeg, J. D. (2008). *La Vita Fuori Dalla Città*. Perugia: AMP.

Murdoch, J., Marsden, T., & Banks, J. (2000). Quality, nature, and embeddedness: Some theoretical considerations in the context of the food sector. *Economic Geography*, *76*(2), 107–125.

Murdoch, J., & Miele, M. (1999). 'Back to nature': Changing 'worlds of production' in the food sector. *Sociologia Ruralis*, *39*(4), 465–483.

Polman, N., Poppe, K. J., van der Schans, J. W., & van der Ploeg, J. D. (2011). Nested markets with common pool resources in multifunctional agriculture. *Rivista di Economia Agraria, LXV*(2), 295–318.

Saccomandi, V. (1994). La concentrazione produttiva dell'agricoltura italiana: alcune considerazioni. In Atti del Convegno "Giornate Tassinari sull'Economia e la Politica agraria: il sistema di agrimarketing e le reti di impresa", Assisi 14–15 luglio, CESAR.

Scettri, R. (2001). *Novità in Campagna*. Roma: IREF.

Schultz, T. W. (1945). *Agriculture in an unstable economy*. New York, NY: McGraw Hill.

Stassart, P., & Whatmore, S. (2003). Metabolising risk: Food scares and the un/re-making of Belgian beef. *Environment and Planning A, 35*, 449–462.

Stuiver, M., van der Ploeg, J. D., & Leewis, C. (2003). The VEL & VANLA environmental co-operatives as field laboratories. *NJAS, 51*(1–2), 27–39.

Tisenkopfs, T., & Suname, S. (2004). Rural community initiatives in the Latvian countryside. In A. Ilkka (Ed.), *Mapping rural problematics in the Baltic* (pp. 219–247). Aldershot: Ashgate Publishing.

van der Ploeg, J. D. (2008). *The new peasantries, Struggles for autonomy and sustainability in an era of empire and globalization*. London: Earthscan.

van der Ploeg, J. D., Long, A., & Banks, J. (Eds.). (2002). *The living countryside. Rural development processes in Europe: The state of the art*. Doetinchem: Elsevier.

van der Ploeg, J. D., & Marsden, T. (Eds.). (2008). *Unfolding webs*. Assen: Van Gorcum.

van der Ploeg, J. D., Renting, H., Brunori, G., Knickel, K., Mannion, J., Marsden, T., ... Ventura, F. (2000). Rural development: From practices and policies towards theory. *Sociologia Ruralis, 40*(4), 391–408.

van der Ploeg, J. D., Van Broekhuizen, R., Brunori, G., Sonnino, R., Knickel, K., Tisenkops, T., & Oostindie, H. (2008). Towards a framework for understanding regional rural development. In J. D. van der Ploeg & T. Marsden (Eds.), (2008), *Unfolding webs* (pp. 7–8). Assen: Van Gorcum.

van der Ploeg, J. D., & Ventura, F. (2014). Heterogeneity reconsidered, current opinion in environmental sustainability. *ScienceDirect*, 8, 23–28.

van der Ploeg, J. D., Ye, J., & Schneider, S. (2015). Rural development: Actors and practices. In P. Milone, F. Ventura, & J. Ye (Eds.), *Constructing a new framework for rural development* (Vol. 22). Research in Rural Sociology and Development. Bingley, UK: Emerald Group Publishing Limited.

Warner, K. D. (2006). The quality of sustainability: Agroecological partnerships and the geographic branding of California winegrapes. *Journal of Rural Studies*. doi:10.1016/j.jrurstud.2006.09.009

Weber, M. (1947). *The theory of social and economic organization* (p. 152). New York, NY: Oxford University Press.

CHAPTER 5

PEASANT INNOVATION AND GRASSROOTS ACTION IN CHINA

Jingzhong Ye and Huiyang Fu

ABSTRACT

In any time and space and under any circumstance, we find peasants are never passive actors in their livelihoods and rural development. Instead, they always create space for manoeuvre in order to make changes. This chapter analyses the innovative actions taken by the majority of rural inhabitants in rural areas during the overwhelming modernization process, so as to affirm that peasants are the main actors of rural development. It is they who have shaped the transformation of rural societies and the history. Through the analysis, this chapter concludes that rural development is not an objective, a blueprint nor a design. It is not the to-be-developed rear field in modernization. It is not the babysitter for cities, nor a rehearsal place for bureaucrats to testify their random thoughts. Rural development is what peasants do. The path they have chosen reveals scenery so different from modernization. If we regard development as a social change, or a cross with influential meanings, we could understand rural development as peasants' victories over their predicament. Villages accommodate not only peasants, but without peasants villages would surely vanish. In this sense, the most important part in

Constructing a New Framework for Rural Development
Research in Rural Sociology and Development, Volume 22, 89–126

ISSN: 1057-1922/doi:10.1108/S1057-192220150000022004

rural development or rural change is peasants – their conditions and their feelings.

Keywords: Peasants innovation; China agriculture; rural development; rural area; rural sociology; actors; institutions

Peasants are never completely synchronized with the state; they are just a member of their societies and the future world.

INTRODUCTION

Since the opening-up reform in China, the Chinese government has been pursuing the development strategy of modernization that encourages marketization, large-scale production and mechanization in different sectors. Such developmental preferences are distinctively reflected in the economic and social policies of contemporary China. However, the path of modernization development does not fit the traditional countryside that has complex and a different geographical, biological and social make up. Moreover, most of the benefits in modernization development can only be grasped by a few political and economic elites in rural societies. The majority of peasants are exercising their 'social instinct' to 'external changes' and constantly adjusting their ways of production and life to bridge the rifts in the two interactional factors. In other words, peasants are (continuously) exploring a different and subtle form of rural development. This new way connects to the past and leads to the future. We believe that peasants are the actors in rural development, and they form the majority of ordinary rural people except for a minor group of modernized, political and economic elites.[1]

The increasingly stronger impacts of modernization development on traditional Chinese rural society and the powerful support of government in promoting modernization in rural areas compose the current social setting of rural development in China. In this context, traditional peasants welcome many new development opportunities (e.g. the loosening of policy regulations allowing for more freedom to change livelihood activities) while at the same time encountering a series of modernization problems (e.g. the increasing pressure to have cash incomes under monetization). 'Rural development', in this context, refers to their responsive activities, regardless of degree, to the agriculture squeeze (the economic and financial crises that continuously threatens agriculture), social, economic and space inequalities, poverty, labour exploitation and the underdevelopment that this produces. These responses are creating new rural–urban relations. The responses usually take place through the production of new products and the provision of new services (which contain important values for the whole of society). In the agricultural sector, it embodies multi-functionality. In a broader level it could be understood as the creation of new markets. The new markets, new products and new services bring about many more rewards to peasants. Rural development can also be realized through the social struggles that aim to protect the required resources for new products, new services and new markets and protect the newly explored/opened spaces. In short, rural development represents a form of 'anti-development' because it differs from the capitalistic development of modern agriculture and the countryside that is induced and shaped by mainstream agriculture and food markets. Sometimes, rural development is also seen just as an adjustment to and compensation for market-led development. But it is actually more than that. It could replace market-led development through a complicated and conflicting transition without any abrupt changes.[2]

To study rural development, it is essential to recognize the agency of peasants and their subjectivity. Agency is the capacity to engender/exercise influence and to positively participate in and jointly promote development. This agency can contribute to newly created important things (e.g. new objectives, new networks and other new feasible conformations) through the activities and collaborations of actors involved. The new things can in turn provide additional opportunities for employment, more and various products and a new rural-ward flow of population. Without the positive agency of peasants, these new things are not likely to appear. They are not the outcome of self-regulation of markets, nor the result of a detailed blueprint of the state apparatus. They are the outcome of peasant agency, or the result of the active engagement of peasants in establishing new markets and dealing with the government. Innovation and pioneering spirit is one reflection of agency. The pioneering spirit of peasants is the sufficient and necessary condition to push the peasants to try and realize a feasible action. Such actions can contribute to broadening the subsistence and development space of peasants, or change their original ways of livelihood formation. Peasant initiative exists widely in all agriculture sectors and rural communities. It is the peasants and their initiatives that have fundamentally promoted regional development and social transition (van der Ploeg, Ye & Schneider, 2015).

Peasant innovation and grassroots activities reflect exactly peasant agency and capacity to act. This article reviews the associated literatures in this field to examine peasant agency and pioneering spirit, to confirm their fundamental role in rural development and further discuss their roles as actors in social transition in China. This will keep our faith in peasants while we face up to the complicated mechanism of different actors and their interwoven interests in social transition. It is intended to articulate the power, capacity and interest of a group who are usually represented as passive by others. It is an attempt to make most readers reflect, understand and have confidence in peasants when they see or hear relevant news about rural development and peasant interests, and to address the question of whether peasants really are a drag on social development.

PEASANTS' INNOVATION AND GRASSROOTS ACTION

Peasant innovation means the changes in resources, activities and goals for sustaining a livelihood. For example, this could be seen as peasants' regrouping their resources through mobilizing their own social capital. The term 'innovation' could be understood in two senses – one is abstract, referring to a kind of thoughts or methods; and the other one refers to something tangible and real (P. Yang, 2009). Peasant innovation in the view of rural development is more of an abstract meaning. It is in fact a transition of developmental ideology, but results in concrete actions. Its abstract implications could only be grasped through intentional observation and interpretation; otherwise it is no more than commonplace everyday life. As grassroots practical activities, peasant innovations are participatory. With the base of community, both the actions of individuals and community can be more influential, confident, adept and competent (Ning, 2011).

The term *caogen* stems from the English word 'grassroots', which means ordinary people and the public other than the state, government, mainstream, elites, institutions and organizations at the decision-making level. In sociology, grassroots has two kinds of meaning: one is local and public; the second is fundamental and basic (Zhang, 2008). In German 'grassroots' is '*Graswurzel*', which emphasizes organizing ordinary people together to influence and improve their living world (Deng, 2006). Studies on grassroots actions relate to governance, economy, culture, society and other aspects. Grassroots actions have broadened the substantial and developmental space for ordinary people to act in many different ways.

Peasant innovation and grassroots actions (in rural areas) are normally rooted in the countryside (van der Ploeg et al., 2015). The Chinese countryside is a network society composed of blood ties, kinship and geographical ties. The individual is the knot in the network. Families, friends and kinship connections have a high degree of trust, which can reduce operational risks and transactional costs (P. Yang, 2009). The regional characteristics of countryside are also absorbed into peasants' innovation and actions, by which the latter could be set in a horizontal and reciprocal network. In the next sections we will try to understand the actors in rural development through reviewing their actions in the fields of technology, politics (including institutions and governance), economy, society and culture.

TECHNOLOGY DOMAIN

Currently, studies on peasant technology innovation concentrate on technical innovations among folk people and practical innovations in agriculture. Among them, Tianjin University of Finance and Economics has established the Center of Popular Innovation Studies in 2006. Under the lead of Professor Liyan Zhang and Peizhong Ning, the staff members and volunteers have been searching and documenting the innovative achievements of popular technology and doing research on the promotion and commercialization of those technical innovations. The standpoint of their studies is the significant role of popular innovation in the whole process of technical innovation. They conclude that we should pay attention to popular technical innovation and actively work on its promotion and commercialization. Studies on practical technical innovation in agriculture mainly focus on the features of local technical innovation (Yang, 2009) and the mechanisms of agricultural technical innovation (Han, 2010). There is also research on practical technical innovation in agriculture in the context of participatory development projects (Lu, Wei, & Sun, 2003). The commonality in the research is that they all recognize peasants as the subjects in practical technical innovation and extension (Lu et al., 2003).

Popular innovations are innovation activities that are organized and operated by folk people and focus on scientific research, technical development and technical service (Lin, Wang, & Guan, 2009). They are innovation actions that local people spontaneously and randomly initiate. They are flashlights of popular innovation, fruits of popular wisdom (Hu, 2007; Jiang, 2010). Compared to government-led innovation, popular innovations are demand-oriented (problem solving at the farm level), and therefore have more application value and respond well to practical demands (Jiang, 2010). The characteristics of popular innovations are regional, pertinent and practical (Jiang, 2010). They are spontaneous, low-cost technical innovations, not aiming for important technological transformation, at the local level (Hu, 2007). They are non-occupational, non-mainstreaming, non-utilitarian (Lin et al., 2009), and have been summarized according to the distribution and composition of popular innovators. Jiang (2010) defined popular innovation as peasants' innovation. Peasants have not received much education and mainly initiate innovations to resolve immediate problems in their production and daily life. Zhang (2011) argues that peasant innovations are strategies and techniques whereby peasants adapt to social, cultural and environmental transformation. They are usually derived through an accumulation of experience. The process of innovation is flexible and the innovation has to fit with the demands and constraints of local politics, economy, geography society and culture. Popular innovation can provide sustainable resolution to local demands (Gupta, 1995). Besides, popular innovators take control of the techniques and knowledge suitable for local demands and understand the emergent problems for local people (Ning, 2011). They can fix the problems in a way that is more meaningful, pertinent and acceptable/suitable to local conditions.

Biological and social diversity reveals the diversity of peasant demands. Therefore technical achievements in a general sense may not be applicable for them (Zhang & Liu, 2011). L. Yang's research (2009) on features of spontaneous folk technical innovation of peasants and Lei Han's research (2010) on peasants' motivation in providing innovational technique are the outstanding research contributions on practical technical innovations in agriculture. They both recognize peasant subjectivity in practical technical innovations in agriculture and acknowledged the role of rural social networks, rural knowledge and peasants' own accumulated experience in the formation of technical innovation. Ning (2011) also analysed the features and motives of peasants' practical and technical innovation in evaluating the social effects of popular innovation.

L. Yang (2009) argues that rural technical innovation is innovation generated in certain rural cultures or societies. It derives from rural knowledge and the constant trial and error practiced by the peasants and is different from the professional technical innovation created in research institutes and the academies. The foundation of rural technical innovation is rural knowledge that has regional adaptability. Firstly, rural technical innovation derives from peasants' production practices in agriculture and is actually peasants' innovation combining local resources and rural knowledge. Secondly, rural technical innovation is low cost and more suitable for the high contradiction between people and land in China. It attempts to use the cheap resources that are abundant and save scarce resources. Thirdly, it has stronger externality because the extension and dissemination of rural technical innovation is embedded in rural social networks, which means the adopters of such techniques can use it for free or pay very little. Fourthly, it is derivable, that means a very accidental rural technical innovation could bring huge demonstration effects to local people for the same background in the social network of countryside provide the tacit knowledge for technical innovations (Yang, 2009).

Han (2010) believes that the spontaneous agricultural technical innovation of peasants is the process whereby peasants innovate on some techniques in specific production practices combining their rural knowledge and long-term experiences in production. He suggests that the motive of peasants' spontaneous innovation originates from three aspects. The first are the changes in the social and economic environment, which have broken the original balance of peasant traditional livelihood, while providing incentives in developing and trying out new means of livelihood maintenance, boosting peasants' interest to try out new things and further to initiate a multitude of peasant spontaneous innovations. Secondly, the induction and changes in demand–supply relationships in the market have prominent influences on peasant spontaneous innovation. Thirdly, peasant-led agricultural technical innovations are mostly surrounded with leading industries in the local area (Han, 2010).

Ning (2011) argued that the characteristics of peasant innovation, for example energy saving, environment friendly, low cost, strong utility, labour saving etc. have important implications for solving the difficulties in the lives of peasants and can promote the economic development of local and even regional areas. Normally, peasant innovators are not well-off. Therefore, their innovation can also be applied by other poor people (rich people can buy almost any product they need on the market). Theoretically, mutual help among the poor explains why peasant innovators are willing to provide their innovation for free. Peasant innovations are usually for resolving difficulties in everyday life instead of profit making. On the one hand, these difficulties are largely neglected by private enterprises and public authorities; on the other hand, peasants rarely consider making a profit from their innovations. Their kindness and the easy-to-learn features of their innovations allows for rapid dissemination of the innovation. Peasant innovators are generally very happy with the dissemination of their new innovation in the neighbourhood (Ning, 2011). Technical innovations in agriculture are the outcome of peasant interaction with their living environment (both natural and social). The outcome of innovation is change in the means and methods of production.[3]

Technical innovations in agriculture are the outcome of peasant interaction with their living environment (both natural and social). The outcome of innovation is change in the means and methods of production. On a smaller scale, changes in farm production could increase labour efficiency, for instance improvement in production tools can facilitate improved methods and increase production efficiency. On the bigger scale, changes in ways of production can engender changes in the ways of sustaining a livelihood. For instance, the introduction and constant innovation of winter vegetable greenhouses in Shouguang transformed most people's livelihood in the local area and nowadays peasant livelihoods mainly depend on greenhouse vegetables. From the outcome of innovation, the interaction between peasants and their environment seems occasional and random. As a matter of fact, it is not the case. Everybody cannot leave his home environment. People's interaction with their environment is a persistent process and intrinsic to people's subsistence. It is only the contingency of an innovation outcome that makes most people neglect the necessity of peasant interaction with the environment and the possible consequences. Preference for 'big event innovation' implies that the social science usually explores reasons and processes starting with the outcome and their analysis mainly works for the results as well. We should put more effort into understanding the world from the perspective of the actors themselves and their interaction with their external environment, and reflect social transformation through the accumulation of ordinary actions.

POLITICAL DOMAIN

Institutions

Ying (2008) from Central China Normal University studied the relationship between peasant spontaneous actions and institutional innovation and concluded that the former is the important impetus for institutional innovation. She defined 'spontaneous actions' as an intentional, self-designed and self-controlled practice that peasants make under objective conditions and limits based on their independent cognitive judgement and internal demands (Ying, 2009). Innovative spontaneous actions primarily refer to innovative actions of people to satisfy their demands in subsistence and interests under existing institutional arrangements and constraints. People can break the barrier of institutions while facing up to the institutional restriction. Their spontaneous innovative actions are important driving forces for institutional transformation. Such a driving force can be reflected in at least four aspects. Firstly, it constructs problem awareness that forces governments to self-reflect and make changes to formal institutions. Secondly, it imposes both pressure and motivation on those in power to govern in another way. Thirdly, it promotes the leap from quantitative change to qualitative change and incubated institutional innovation. Fourthly, it conquers authority with the total utility of actions, changes the authority's cognition and orientation for institutional choice, and facilitates the upgrading of popular innovation practices to state practice and even institutional system change (Ying, 2008).

Peasants have turned out to be the dynamic actors (neither revolutionary nor conservative as mostly described in the international literature) and the real promoters of institutional transformation in the special institutional context of rural China. A series of initiatives by peasants could hardly be explained within the framework of being revolutionary or conservative. Their actions have not been in tune with the national regulations, but usually in advance of official change. What is notable is that these actions push silently the institutional reforms even under accusations and refutations, and have often been legitimized afterwards (Ying, 2008). 'Official documents and national polices, no matter how vicious they are to the peasants, they would not dream of challenging them. Peasants know that they are so marginal and disadvantaged when facing the political apparatus. Eggs couldn't strike stones' (Zhang, 2006). The institutional innovations stimulated by peasant initiatives are in many cases a breakthrough. The basic logic is to take mild and rational strategies to conquer the institutional barriers in given conditions and to avoid direct conflict, or to apply new methods and mechanisms for the creation of space for survival and development, which may further produce pressures for institutional change. This may lead to the official integration of peasant initiatives into national practice (Ying, 2009).

Peasant initiatives may include peasant resistances in the collectivized period of China's agriculture, contracting the land to the household, doing small businesses, taking part in multiple non-agricultural activities and constructing their own towns. The sections that follow introduce three instances of peasant initiatives in institutional reforms.

Contracting the Land to the Household

In the commune period, peasants would achieve the same effect as contracting the land to the household simply by changing the forms of the production team. A typical way of doing so was to divide the production team into smaller units and reduce the scale of the production team. For instance, '*The tenth sub-production team of the Xin Wutou Production Team in Xianqiao Commune divided itself further into three production units, two of which contained six households and one of which had seven households. One with six households – Qian Zhengfu Unit – actually consisted of 2 households headed by two brothers. Now the six households are either brothers or fathers and sons*'.[4] '*Some preferred to have small units. They have reduced the team members to fewer than 10 households. Teams composed of only fathers and sons or of brothers appeared in some places*'.[5] When local governments started to criticize and tried to stop the sub-division of production teams, some commune members constructed the legitimacy of such division by resorting to the authority of the national policies. Peasants believed that '*The Sixty Articles*' forbade the contracting land to households and demarcating the farmland, but they do not stipulate against dividing the production team into smaller units.[6] In essence, this is a footnote to how peasants can utilize the loopholes in policies to legitimize their activities. Peasants are the fundamental drivers of reforms in agricultural production, which can be reflected in the change of national strategies: from complete prohibition of land contracting to tacit permission and finally to approval with laws and regulations. Later, Deng Xiaoping made this point transparently clear in his speech in South China, 'Household Responsibility System is invented by peasants' (Ying, 2008).

Being Peasants and Also Merchants

For those who were eager to do something other than work in the commune, it was difficult to earn some extra income while not breaking the rule in the commune period because of policy constraints. The members therefore adopted some 'indigenous' methods to get the permit of temporarily leaving the village, such as purchasing working points, submitting the management fee or fees for engaging in sidelines. These are 'indigenous' methods due to their limited use in particular circumstances, and were not known outside. These reflect how the people would obey the orthodoxy orders and regulations in their own ways in a specific historical context. Such methods have the following characteristics: (1) they were created by the commune members, not by law but by a group of people; this means that commune members made decisions after discussions on the standards of working points, management fees and fees for engaging in sidelines, which differ from production team to production team; (2) they follow the rule of balance and reciprocity; the members would choose carefully the time to work outside the commune so that agricultural production and the benefits of other commune members would not be affected; (3) they bring new variables into the formal arrangements without immediate collision with the existing institutions, policies and authorities. For instance, without changing the commune system, a commercial variable has been added to it in the form of a management fee, or doing business without abandoning agricultural production; (4) how far these methods can go depended on the attitude of local governments. In this way, the commune members no longer confined themselves to the village community and the production team in the face of the severe crisis of survival. Instead they actively sought survival off-the-land in order to meet the basic needs of their families, by being peasants and also merchants. Undoubtedly, peasant engagement in businesses is a sort of collective unconscious move towards a rural commercial system and against the People's Commune system. What they struggled to achieve is to adapt to the institutional framework which denies the possibilities of leaving the land and doing business, instead of changing the framework. The initial practices of peasants' involvement in commerce, under very rigid conditions, shows that peasants resort to their traditional ways of life for the sake of survival, walking on the edge of the institutions and searching for the ultimate opportunities and spaces to live (Ying, 2008).

Buying and Selling with Special Registrations

The peasant salesman had a whole set of documents to prove that he belonged to a certain enterprise when peasants were still restricted from entering the circulation/commercial domain. But the peasant salesman in fact was not a working staff member there. They merely registered in that enterprise so that they could belong to a collective or community of interest. They could avoid unfavourable institutional constraints in this way and take special advantage of belonging to state-owned enterprises in economic activities. In special institutional environments and constraints, peasants succeeded in making the informal institutions work by linking themselves to the collectives. Their strategies featured mutual benefits and reciprocity, having constructed a network of protection within the formal institutional framework and by minimizing the cost of individual economic activities. In terms of institutional transformation, registering in the enterprises means that peasants had the capacity to build alliances with the collectives, to utilize the resources in the institutions creatively and to overcome the institutional barriers in the end (Ying, 2008).

Chen (2010) reviewed the main achievements of peasant innovations since the opening-up reform: (1) household responsibility system – an innovative practice catering to the basic rural management system; developing collective economies; developing specialized collectives; and institutional reforms of collective forest rights. (2) The transfer of surplus labour in rural areas – the springing up of township enterprises; working off-the-land; and strategies of building up small towns and cities (such as 'city of peasants' in Longgang Township). (3) Self-governance of the villages – the first village committee was established in Hezhai Village, SanCha Commune of YiShan County, Guangxi Province, where 85 peasants nominated their leaders by secret ballot, agreed on village rules and realized self-governance (Chen, 2010).

Governance

In the domain of village governance, grassroots actors have guarded the power space for rural development. Their activities could be classified into three forms: rightful resistance, resistance by law and everyday resistance. Grassroots mobilization is an essential part in safeguarding rights. Ying (2007) focuses on grassroots mobilization and grassroots actors, attempting to go beyond the simple binary opposition to organized elite politics and unorganized subaltern politics and exploring more deeply the complexity of peasant politics. Ying positively appraises the role of grassroots actors in the collective activities of peasants. He defines 'grassroots mobilization' as follows: the process in which some active participants who are devoted to certain issues organize people with similar interests but less motivation to participate in expressing their interests. The activity logic of grassroots actors is to construct their own dilemma by various means into issues that local governments could not neglect so that their interests could be protected gradually. In the eyes of these grassroots actors, the differences or demarcation between rule by law or rule by men, and between judiciary and non-judiciary process do not matter that much. What counts is whether certain means are practical or not in expressing interests and solving problems. Although the majority of the grassroots actors have to gain effective control over the collective action through some organized activities, they are very unwilling to issue orders in the name of a formal (or informal) organization. The grassroots actors usually use legal or semi-legal methods (but still on the safe side) in order to make the collective action effective. They would appeal to local governments with a certain scale in the numbers of protestors, which may ring an alarm in the minds of those in government and disturb the order of everyday life to some extent. This may call for the officials to treat seriously the problems presented to them as they could threaten the present social order.

'Rightful resistance' is proposed by Lianjiang Li and Kevin O'Brian (1997), referring particularly to policy-based resistance. The main characteristic of such resistance is to use the national policies to fight against the local policies. It is an overt resistance, in pseudo-institutional or semi-institutional forms. The protestors usually would appeal to the upper level government for the support of the superior authority in order to beat down the illegal behaviours of the local cadres. Such resistance is mainly fighting for concrete interests in the context of a certain 'event' (Yu, 2004). 'Policy-based resistance' falls between political struggle and political participation. It is a fight for concrete interests within a given rights and power structure. Meanwhile, 'resistance by law' proposed by Yu (2004) is closer to pure political struggle, challenging the entire structure of rights and power. It normally has a representative with strong political beliefs as the core leader. In such resistance, a relatively stable social network for mobilization has been established by various means. The protestors appeal not to the government, but to other peasants. They believe that peasants (including themselves) should be the ones who solve the problem. They deem the county and township government as the opponents. This is a political struggle for pronouncing and establishing the abstract 'legal rights' or 'rights as citizens' for peasants as a social group (Yu, 2004).

Grassroots mobilization and actors are in a general sense provisional. Although grassroots mobilization may appear to be organized in a practical way, it is more like a de-politicization process – for it strives to control the collective actions within the limits of politics and laws while mobilizing the masses. If there are some grassroots actors in the process, the organization of collective actions can be promoted. However, it would not take the form of a formal organization. This weak organization will not last for long as it would be a threat to the political order (Ying, 2007).

Liu (2009a) believes that the protestors merely seek to meet their needs, grassroots actors or the mobilized alike. They would easily stop collective actions once their demands have been satisfied. Interests are concrete while rights are abstract. The former is easier to be achieved, but the latter needs a much longer process to be realized. Therefore, it is not difficult to understand why collective actions disappear once their appeals have been permitted if we only talk about the resistance in the sense of interests. However, in terms of abstract rights, the collective actions might continue without any limitations. If the collective actions have been endowed with political beliefs, then they will not cease before overthrowing the oppressive agency. This sort of collective action should not be viewed as simple collective action or resistance. It is more like a revolution (Liu, 2009a).

Research related to grassroots activities includes also the subaltern studies. The basic objective of the subaltern study is to explore the autonomy of peasant politics in comparison to the elite politics, as well as how the unique structure of the subaltern consciousness has shaped the subaltern politics. The initial work of this school focuses mainly on the grand events such as peasant revolution and rebels, and therefore emphasizes especially the collective power of peasants (Chatterjee, 2001). However, as criticized by Scott (1987), 'most subaltern classes have no interest in changing the grand national structure and laws. They pay more attention to what Hobsbawn describes as, "minimizing the disadvantages of the institutions"'. Scott thus proposes his everyday forms of peasant resistance. He points out that it is a luxury for the majority of the subaltern classes to take overt and organized political actions, because it is too dangerous even if not self-destructive. In order to avoid such risks, peasants usually choose everyday forms of resistance, that is to take common but continuous measures to fight against those who extort too much labour, food, tax, rent and interests from them. The forms of such resistances may include: slothfulness, pretending not to know, sneaking off, pretending to obey, stealing, pretending to be simple-minded, slandering, and arson and sabotage (Yu, 2004). Chatterjee later proposes a concept of 'political society', aiming to transfer the focus of the subaltern studies to 'policy-based resistances'. However, this school encountered another problem in this process: fragmentation. According to Chatterjee (2001), 'the subaltern history is fragmented, discrete, and incomplete. The inner world of the subaltern consciousness is split, constructed by factors from the experiences of the oppressing and the oppressed classes' (Ying, 2007).

ECONOMIC DOMAIN

Zhang (2008) explains the Zhejiang experience (the early development of a strong market economy) as the reconstruction of social space through grassroots wisdom and grassroots activities. He starts from the social actions in the regional traditional culture and shows how the social space has been recreated through the successive expansion of survival space, the fixation of developing space and the bold steps taken towards the creation of a capital space by means of 'trade by vendors', 'trade by opening factories' and 'capital expansion'. In this process, the grassroots culture (or the high mobility of Zhejiang people) nurtured in natural space has particularly significant meanings. Zhejiang Province has limited land, a dense population and frequent visits of typhoons, which means that Zhejiang people have had to step out of their hometowns, and seek the means of survival through geographical mobility. For them, this has become an accumulative grassroots culture with regional characteristics, not just an expedient. The expansion of space for survival and the restriction of space for development have combined to produce a virtuous circle between the culture of mobility and manufacturing. The potential of industrialization in Zhejiang has surpassed many extremes. The expansion of space for survival and the fixation of space for development not only change the forms of regional grassroots culture, but also trigger the 'association effects' in society. Such 'association effects' are reflected in more people choosing to work off the land and becoming vendors, among whom some vendors with foresight and entrepreneurship start to open factories and by this means the fixation of development space has been overcome. This attracts more vendors to become permanent merchants (Zhang, 2008).

Given a similar social background at the macro level, why could Zhejiang Province achieve the opportunity to develop first while other better-off areas could not grasp such chances in the opening-up period? Why could Zhejiang Province develop its private economies and almost everyone set up his or her own business? Where did such impulses come from? To answer the above questions, we need to move our eyes from the macro level to the ordinary (or grassroots) daily life and regional cultural traditions to explore the logics of their activities. We should also trace the Zhejiang phenomenon far back to the pre-opening-up era. The economic achievements of Zhejiang Province in the past three decades are clearly the result of grassroots culture and grassroots wisdom. The pioneers from the subaltern classes have continually overcome difficulties originating from the narrow natural space and limited resources by means of vending, manufacturing, trading and capital expansion. They have recreated the social space. The Zhejiang experience shows that natural conditions such as space, resources and location are not the decisive preconditions for economic development. Regional cultural traditions and related grassroots wisdom as well as related activities can be the basis of economic development for a region. Therefore, we should not change economic development into a top-down design or project imposed by outsiders. Instead, the economic development of a region could not last without grassroots culture and wisdom. The endogenous economic achievements of Zhejiang Province result from both social creativity and policy support. New development has been realized in the process of population movements that commenced with the simple pursuit of survival and later became manufacturing and product circulations. Although the impulse of setting up businesses comes from the grassroots culture and activities, we cannot understand the economic boom in Zhejiang as a result of 'letting it be so'. In fact, the local government played a central role in the process. It depended on, provoked, responded to, supported and strengthened the social creativity from the grassroots (Zhang, 2008).

Zhang (2004) analysed the evolution of state–peasant relations in Houle Village over the past 50 years. He believes that the everyday economic practice of peasants has had fundamental significance for the transfer and development of rural societies and could thereby be an important source of ideas and information for an explanatory framework. It provides the empirical feasibility for the state to respond positively to peasant autonomy and remove the social exclusions towards the peasantry. It also offers a way of identifying the indigenous factors of rural modernization in China (Zhang, 2005).

SOCIAL DOMAIN

Development Innovations

Development innovations refer to making changes happen through various activities, similar to 'management and organization innovations' proposed by Ning (2011). Peasant development innovation means peasants taking different actions to facilitate the transformation of rural households and communities. Such changes are reflected in multiple spheres, such as society, economy, culture, politics, means and legislation, human resources and gender, knowledge and technology, and environment etc. (Ye & Liu, 2000). We can always notice some kinds of development innovation in any rural community. For instance, some peasants conduct various new types of household activities including planting fruit trees, raising livestock, planting herbs, contracting barren hills, engaging in mini-processing and opening a grocery store etc., while other peasants do not, even though they live in similar natural, social, economic and cultural environments. The former peasants are vanguard farmers. They have the momentum to innovate and the consciousness of a broader strategy to develop. Compared with other ordinary peasants, they succeed in enriching their social and economic lives, given the same social, economic and cultural context. They also have great social impacts on other peasants and easily become the idols in rural communities (Ye, 2004).

Doing pioneering work is one form of peasant innovation in development. It refers to the process in which peasants expand their current business or conduct a new activity in rural communities in order to gain extra income and better development through investing a certain amount of capital in production. They usually rely on family networks (or informal organizations based on friends and kinship) for fund raising. The innovative factors in this process are not fixed, because peasants may not bring about something completely different when doing this pioneering work. We need to consider what the innovation is. Innovation may involve such aspects as technology, markets, institutions, products, and management and the like, in which ideological innovation is the core. When peasants engage in pioneering work, no matter whether they are adopting advanced technologies or doing something new, this process could be regarded as an innovation in ideology. Resources have been thereby transferred from activities with low output and low productivity to those with high output and high productivity. In some cases, resources may be reorganized to obtain higher output. As for peasants, this is an innovative activity compared to their previous production. The vanguard peasants have such entrepreneurship which engenders the integration of resources and gains added value through ideological innovation. Doing pioneering work is a process of innovation for peasants. In essence, innovation means to introduce and integrate new ways and resources into production and marketing (Guo, Zhang, & Xu, 2008).

Song and Chen (2008) believe that peasant innovativeness is the combination of innovative consciousness, innovative spirit and innovative capabilities exhibited in the construction of a new socialist countryside. Such a government project is normally led by the governments at various levels. Peasants would only follow the administrative orders in the process of constructing a new countryside, which dismisses the possibility for peasants to participate in the construction process out of their own wishes and their innovativeness is therefore handicapped. Once their innovativeness has been ignored and suppressed for so long, peasants do not keep and develop it (Song & Chen, 2008). However, peasant innovativeness will not vanish altogether. Peasants' innovative ideas and activities may be suppressed or even disappear because of environmental or political constraints, but not their innovativeness, because it is the spark that is ignited in the continuous interactions between peasants and their living environment. Some sparks may be put out, and some may keep burning. There are always new sparks produced in the process and this is endless innovativeness. Peasants have their own autonomy, which is certain. But in some circumstances, such subjectivity may not be found. This is because the outside world has some special expectations towards them, and peasants cannot be relied upon to provide exactly the same thing. For instance, the outside experts may look for responses among peasants the same as that in their minds, but peasants often present what they want. In this case, the project practitioner and the policy maker need further strategies to construct a peasant's subjectivity, or to lure them to change their ideas. The disappearance of peasant subjectivity actually means that what has been expected from others is not happening with them, which is not the real loss of peasant subjectivity.

Development Actions

The pursuit for safe production and healthy agriculture for improved food safety has been popular recently due to frequent reports of incidents of the violation of food safety in China. Such variants as community-supported agriculture (CSA), farmers' fairs in the city and the like have sprung up in China. An estimate by the first of these, Little Donkey Farm, suggests there were approximately 80 CSAs nationwide in 2011. These CSAs and farmers' fairs are mainly initiated by small farmers, citizens, NGOs, universities and institutes and have the qualities of the grassroots. The idea behind them is to build up a direct link between producers and consumers to resist the middlemen's monopolistic control over product price and quality. These movements have evident features of the nested market. The rise of the nested market could be seen as a reflection on modern agricultural against the backdrop of rural development, or as a critique of the market relationships. Farmers have not gained much status in modern agricultural development. Instead, they have been deprived of adequate choices in agricultural production and have to be subjected continuously to the market, its demands and conditions. The externalities of modern agriculture have provoked increasing concern about the prospects and the approaches of agricultural development, and even a new organization style of the market. These externalities (Tan & Du, 2010) include the destruction of the very foundations of agriculture (soil and water system), the deterioration of ecological environment, unsafe food production and unfair profit distribution in the food system, and the coexistence of starvation and overnutrition in the world. The nested market bridges producers and consumers in this context, ensuring the sustainability of multi-functional agriculture in an innovative way and becoming an essential subsidiary development of the rural market (Ye & Wang, 2011). The nested markets springing up in the rural areas of China could be regarded as a form of resistance of producers and consumers against the giant food empires and their response to the many crises in modern agriculture. It has redefined and promoted rural development with many brand-new forms (Ye, Ding, & Wang, 2012).

Peasants have been squeezed and depicted as 'losers' in the political script of the contemporary world. It is generally believed that more 'efficient' (or corporate farming) should replace the peasant way of farming. Effective agricultural production by the peasantry has thereby been hindered and at best ignored (Borras, 2008). In response to such an adverse situation, many peasants resort to an integration of non-agricultural activities with agriculture, or to ecological agriculture to lower their dependence on external market conditions. They take piecemeal actions, without even realizing these are part of political struggles (van der Ploeg, 2008). The nested market is built upon such quotidian resistance against crises of modern agriculture, '... and doing so in quiet, mundane, and subtle expressions and acts that are rarely organized or direct' (Kerkvliet, 2009). The nested market does not declare a war against the existing market, nor aims to replace it, but to expand the space for itself in forms of 'peasant' everyday politics and everyday resistance in order to have a necessary cash income' (Scott, 1987). However, this everyday resistance is changing and reshaping how the rural area develops. The establishment of the nested market, as a resistance and critique to the mainstream market, introduced to deal with the widespread crises of modern agriculture and solve, to some extent, the current problems of food safety and marketing of agricultural products. The unprompted establishment of this type of market enables trade of particular products within a normative network, which helps the peasants (producers) to sell their projects with a relatively high additional value while helping the consumers to purchase trustworthy high-quality products at an affordable price. The advent of the nested market provides another alternative to the 'farm-supermarket connection' or 'supermarket revolution'. It succeeds in finding new ways to tackle the agricultural crises through resisting the food empires and modern agriculture. At a deeper level, it offers also another alternative to rural development. It demonstrates the powerful agency and high innovative spirit of rural people (Ye, 2004), and testifies that peasants are the core of rural construction and development (Ye et al., 2012).

CULTURAL SPHERE

Peasant agency can be identified more evidently in the comparatively static cultural sphere, separate from the technical, political, economic and social spheres, which relate more closely to the existence and development of human beings. The rise of grassroots culture reveals that lowly ranked groups now have higher status and their voices are better heard. A platform of dialogue between the grassroots class and the elites has been created, in which the appeals and dreams of the grassroots can be noticed and potentially realized. Shanzhai culture (or copycat culture) is a continuity and sublimation of grassroots culture. It is rooted in the grassroots spirit of 'I can do whatever you can'. This copycat culture could be viewed as a kind of 'non-violent resistance' against the monopoly and hegemony of some industries that are continuously seeking super profits. Some sporadic copycat phenomena are more like a self-entertaining activity, or a kind of reversal, deconstruction and challenge to the elite culture in ironic forms (Liu, 2009b). It relies on the mainstream consumption culture, like a parasitic plant, but with its own creativity and irreplaceable values (Zhang, 2008). In other words, copycat culture has absorbed and learned from the merits of the mainstream culture, and created a hybrid of grassroots culture and elite culture based on grassroots particularities. This has attracted the attention of a wide range of audiences (Zhang, 2008). The CCTV News has broadcast the copycat phenomenon, and pointed out that 'with the occurrence of the copycat cell phones in 2003, the upsurge of various copycat products has changed "copycat" into more than an economic activity; it is now a social-cultural phenomenon'. 'Copycat culture' is a non-mainstream culture representing the grassroots classes. It originated from the folk people and has been branded with grassroots innovation and mass/conventional wisdom since the very day of its birth (Ye, 2010).

'Grassroots' and 'copycat' share partially the same spiritual core, which implies the bold challenge to traditional authority (Sun, 2011). The prevalence of copycat phenomena has brought into the limelight the rank differences between social classes. It can hardly be ignored that 'copycat' comes from the grassroots (Ye, 2009). Copycat culture is a grassroots culture, representing the creativity of folk. The power of folk has been developing irresistibly in social and cultural life (He, 2010). 'Copycat spirit' contains qualities of self-confidence, tenacity, perseverance and persistence, elements that resemble largely the grassroots spirit. Grassroots classes are not a bunch of uncivilized groups, but the disadvantaged people who have insufficient social resources and low social status. Copycat culture is their product, or a cultural feast under the overwhelming/dominant mainstream culture, which is related to the growing grassroots classes and the gradual deconstruction of current social norms (Zhang & Liu, 2011).

The grassroots actors are usually rich in social experience and find it difficult to be pleased with the status quo. They might easily become the leaders of the masses. The 'abnormal' activities of these actors (such as Lao Meng who organized Spring Festival Gala) could be summarized as a search for recognition of self-identity and social values. For instance, Han Jiangxue who hosted the copycat 'Lecture Room' does not have any titles or background. He recommended himself to be the lecturer in CCTV Lecture Room several times, but was denied. His self-made short documentaries are actually such a pursuit for social recognition through his 'fabulous presentations' so that his social values and existence could be proved. This mirrors somehow the bottleneck of Chinese development – institutional reforms lag behind social development, meanwhile social development fails to keep pace with the spiritual desires of the public. Members of society have desires to express themselves, but these desires have been denied in the mainstream ideologies. This is already out of the control of the national regime. When these conflicts cannot be coordinated, most people keep silent and suppress their individual or group demands. However, a few would undertake 'abnormal' activities to satisfy their needs, including parody, on-line rallies, copycat culture and so forth. Overnight, 'years of overburdened fear turn to be an explosion of hilarity' (Zhang, 2004). Such a carnival for grassroots classes could meet the people's demands of self-expression, and therefore might concentrate a huge number of participants and produce a loud public voice within a very short period of time. In some cases, network incidents have already broken out.

As for the question of what copycat culture means to society, Lao Meng (as the leader of copycat culture) explained, 'We are not fighting against authority or the official, but we are indeed fighting against monopoly'. Copycat culture always stretches its hand into the controversial TV programmes that have intimate relations with the powerful and the rich.

Copycat culture attracts numerous audiences and participants even though the powerless and moneyless organizers have to squeeze limited resources. This is a satire of the one-voice culture in the existing political context. 'In cultural sphere, the political discourse as an instrument is the only legal one, and any other voice is not allowed to exist'; and 'The only legal and institutionalized culture dominates the entire sphere and is totally submitted to the polity with the help of powerful institutional factors' (Zhou, 2007). In contrast, copycat culture has not tuned to the politics of authorities. It reflects the happiness and sadness of the folk and non-mainstream groups, rather than the national ideologies (Zhou, 2007). Chen (2009) believes that copycat culture has its characteristics as a sub-culture. It would resist the mainstream culture in terms of objects, cultural notions and cultural industries in order to establish its own cultural identity. It bears the features of multiple styles due to various conditions nationwide. It would tease the stereotype and sluggishness of the mainstream culture via destroying the present codes and creating new codes with particular popular meanings. It is an approach of the media designers and small capital possessors appeal for satisfying desires and demonstrating the folksy, as well as a way in which the lifestyle of grassroots is claimed (Chen, 2009).

In the view of Zhang & Liu (2011), the fact that copycat culture is decoded as 'resistance culture' has nothing to do with whether it intends to be so. It is shaped as a model of 'resistance' in a powerful political sphere. Copycat culture is more a massive carnival of the folk people rather than a wave of cultural resistance. Chen and Dai (2009), however, hold that the revelry represents an equal and secular life, connoting a force of resistance. It denies the authority and the existence of absolute truth, willing to open room for other possibilities (Chen, 2009). The focus in modern societies is no longer on the heroes, but on the lifestyles and living situations of the ordinary people (Ye, 2010). 'The most significant point of comic mimicking and collage lies in the fact that they deconstruct and reverse the original stereotype in mainstream culture through upgrading and degrading pairs of values in culture-power ranking systems, such as "high versus low", "noble versus humble", "grand versus tiny", "magnificent versus trivial", "deep versus shallow", and "meaningful versus meaningless"' (Tao, 2009). It is in the copycat culture that the weak banters the strong through simulation, which endows the culture with its most significant meanings (Wang, 2010). Copycat culture seeks for an aesthetic experience of hilarity. The once metaphysical idealism and futurism in communist China has been substituted by pragmatism and realism since the opening up and reform period (Zhou, 1997). People are now more accustomed to deconstruct the existing positives to have fun. 'Copycat culture' has a strong sense of carnival and pursues freedom, equality and fun. It adds seasoning to the monotony of modern life, and provides a way for stressed modern people to release their emotions. What people have gained in this aesthetic experience is happiness, a let-out of stress and feelings (Ye, 2010).

Wang and Wang (2009) explain grassroots culture with a different perspective through analysing copycat sports culture – using the mainstream culture as a reference point. Grassroots classes get to experience the meaning of Olympic Culture when copying 'the Bird's Nest', a unique cultural symbol, and express their strong appeals for being accepted by mainstream culture. 'Grassroots culture has more vitality compared to mainstream culture, because it is easier to be accepted and understood with blurry boundaries and relatively freer access. It plays a special dynamic and stimulative role in the formation of the cultural system' (Zhu, 2006). If we deem that the copycat 'bird's nest' symbolizes the sense of belonging to the Olympic moment in China (cultural icons), then other types of sports constructions exhibit people's own understanding towards and advocacy for the mainstream sports culture (Wang & Wang, 2009).

However, no matter what features they are conveying (resistance, so-called resistance or sense of yearning and belonging), copycat cultures differ from the dominant and hegemonic mainstream cultures with their own grassroots qualities. Such an orgiastic copycat culture cannot represent the entire grassroots culture. It is the product of modern information industry and network media. Freedom and equality that the grassroots culture seeks can be better represented by that part of the copycat culture which is free from the more hilarious aspects.

OTHER RELATED RESEARCH

Fang Wang (2011) argues that the community could be the foundational unit in achieving environmental improvement and low-carbon development. Bottom-up community activities can promote interactions between and integration of individual capabilities and community infrastructure, organizations and culture though based on limited power, resources and capabilities. These interactions and integration can not only change the once-unconnected individual behaviours, but also enhance the general capabilities of low-carbon development and the change of the social structure in the community. Grassroots activities have contributed greatly to the construction of a low-carbon community through their own understanding of the world in this multi-faceted society, which has had positive impacts on the ecological environment as a legalized process. This shows exactly how the ordinary citizens and community organizations could change the future (Wang, 2011).

Wang (2011) studies grassroots heroes. He believes that the grassroots heroes are a special phenomenon in the Chinese 'transformation period'. He classifies the grassroots heroes into two groups: those with instrumental rationality and those with value rationality. The grassroots heroes cease their activities when they have attained their objectives. What they are looking for is something utilitarian and that they do not have to continue indefinitely. Wang names this as instrumental activity. Another thing is that many grassroots heroes intend only to protect their own legal rights at the very beginning, which can be identified as 'instrumental activities'. However, these heroes encounter quite a few fellow citizens who are trapped in similar situations during the protest activity, and they might try their best to help these people due to a sense of social responsibility, even though their own problems have already been solved. Their actions can last for a long time, and this endows them with value rationality.

The principles of participation and empowerment in development projects provide us with another perspective for understanding grassroots actions. The community consciousness and subjectivity can be improved in the participation process, that would construct the common living space into a geographical community with social meanings as the emerging and self-transforming of community identity (Yang, 2007). In spite of this, participation is generally treated as a principle or a means to achieve project goals, rather than autonomous behaviour or the outcome of development itself.

Development projects are in-advance designs with clear objectives, procedures and activities. Rural development pushed mainly by rural actors does not seem to follow such a linear development design. Although the participation of local people has been emphasized in development projects, the primary actors are usually the outsiders who control project goals as well as the distribution and use of resources. The participation of local people can only be seen as cooperation to these outsiders in achieving costly/their development goals. However, peasants are the real actors in rural development, seldom monitored or supervised by the outsiders. They may not have an integrated design of how to develop rural areas, nor would they organize and balance their actions in order to realize a comprehensive outcome. What they are doing is to utilize various resources and opportunities to their extremes in order to expand the space of survival for themselves and their families. Although community development in development projects bears different meanings compared to rural development led by peasants, the attention given to grassroots individuals during this process could be very useful in rural development due to its focus on grassroots actions and peasant innovations. After all, peasants and the grassroots are the real promoters of rural development. They continually create and furnish some new development spaces.

We have so far argued that peasants are individuals with their own agencies and we have analysed their innovations and actions in the spheres of technology, politics, economics, society and culture. However, what mechanisms do they follow in their innovations and actions? What features do they have? We need to deepen our understanding of rural development actors through exploring their characteristics, motivations and the influencing factors that shape their behaviours.

ANALYSIS OF THE MECHANISMS OF PEASANT ACTIONS

Characteristics of Behaviours

Actors usually have rational strategies for their actions. Rationality in essence is the capability of maximizing or optimizing self-benefits within given conditions. 'Stakeholders (especially the main stakeholders) could benefit from innovations, which is not only the objective of the innovation, but also the preconditions of its sustainability'. Rational peasants do not take discretionary actions; instead, they seek for and defend their benefits through applying certain policies creatively or finding new ways and mechanisms for actions without provoking conflicts (Ying, 2009).

The Theory of Survival Rationality

Would peasants act based on morality or rationality? Chayanov, Scott and Polanyi are the main representatives of logics of survival and morality. In his famous book 'Организация крестьянского хозяйства' (*Peasant Farm Organization*), Chayanov takes the small farmers and farms before the Russian revolution as the research subject, and argues that peasants prefer to meet the consumption needs of their family. The overall objective of their economic activities is for subsistence, not for profit maximization (Ying, 2008). Scott has similar opinions and he contends in his *The Moral Economy of the Peasant* that the main motivation of peasants' economic activities is 'avoiding risks' and 'safety first'. Everyone in the same community respects other peoples' basic rights for survival, and admits there should be 'reciprocity' between the better-off and the less-better-off. Therefore, the collective actions of peasants are defensive and reparative, for resisting the external pressures on their livelihoods as well as the intrusion of capitalist market relations and state power (Huang, 1988).

The Theory of Economic Rationality

Adam Smith, Schulz and Popkin are the main representatives of the logics of economic rationality. They hold that the peasants would behave rationally and seek for profit maximization. They are nothing like 'homo economicus' in comparison to any capitalist entrepreneurs. The Nobel Economics Prize winner Schulz writes in his book *Transforming Traditional Agriculture* published in 1964, that peasants in traditional agriculture are not stupid; they could react promptly to the various changes in the market price. They stick to their inefficient ways of production only because of constraints of limited income flows and price, rather than their ignorance of maximizing profits. Likewise, Popkin states in his work *The Rational Peasant* that peasants are also confined by market rules when making economic decisions. They are individuals who could balance gains and losses before making a rational choice for the utmost benefit.

It can be concluded that scholars like Scott understand peasant behaviours at the subsistence level, while Schulz and others analyse their behaviours at the economic level. Philip Huang (1988) summarizes the three traditions in peasant studies (the above two and the Dispossession Theory of Marx) and proposes 'a comprehensive analysis of the differentiated peasant economies'. He believes that a general analysis is necessary in understanding the peasants in China. Peasants should be viewed as a trinity: as a profit-seeker, as a producer for subsistence and as a tiller vulnerable to dispossession. The three different aspects are all profiles of this trinity (Huang, 1988). Huang's research is based on the historical materials in the 1930s and his field study in 1980. His paper reveals mainly the status quo of rural peasants before open and reform policies.

His three-profile argument for a comprehensive analysis of peasants based on different classes seems to correspond to the production motivations of three groups of peasants (the rich, the poor and the tenant). Although Huang's research does not take the contemporary peasant as subjects, his 'comprehensive analysis of peasants based on different classes' can enlighten present studies of the modern peasantry, since the peasants are nowadays differentiated as well into workers, worker-peasants, peasants, merchants, merchant-peasants and so forth as consistent in the processes of urbanization and industrialization. They have definitely variable behaviour characteristics, but they constitute the peasantry in China: those registered in a rural area and with a piece of land.

The Theory of Socialized Farmers

Professor Yong Xu and his student Professor Daicai Deng found from their abundant field studies that the Chinese peasants are becoming 'smaller but more socialized' when their survival is no longer an issue and the level of socialization is relatively high. They feel that traditional peasant studies can hardly explain the motivations and behaviour patterns of contemporary peasants. They thereby propose the concept of 'socialized farmers' to summarize the behaviour characteristics and patterns of the Chinese peasantry today. They argue that socialized farmers differ greatly from traditional peasants, mechanized peasants and rational peasants. They are neither pure profit-and-utility seekers, nor producers satisfied with subsistence nor are they a depressed group. What has been confining them is no longer survival, but currency. The subsistence ethic has been replaced by a monetary ethic, and the pursuit of maximizing subsistence and utility by maximizing cash income (Xu & Deng, 2006). Apparently, they deem the peasant production to be driven by currency in the context of rural modernization. Indeed, currency (or cash) is the 'multi-pass' in a society where the industrialized production of the means of subsistence and other products dominate daily life. The pursuit for more cash income is the main characteristic of peasant behaviour in modern society. However, the concept of 'socialized farmers' is not able to fully distinguish peasants from others who have similar desires and pursuits. Rural society, the networks built upon clans and families in the rural community, the relative social positions of peasants and the rural areas in the whole society should all be taken into account when we identify peasants as peasants.

Analysis of Motivations

The innovations devised by peasants result from their rational choices. Numerous autonomous behaviours of the Chinese peasants are not individual preferences or simply tradition, nor the normalization/prescription of institutions, but their rational choices arising from deep experiences in different natural conditions, different situations of subsistence and institutions, such as contracting farmland to households, engaging in non-agricultural activities, migrating to the city and doing small businesses, and creating joint stock cooperative systems and serving on village committees etc. When an ideal life was not forthcoming or foreseeable, but a problem of subsistence was on the rise in the collective work and management of the commune system, peasants did not sit back and do nothing, but started to innovate and reform the production and management system without changing the collective ownership structure. Meanwhile, the autonomous behaviours of peasants do not neglect the benefits of the state and the collectivity, but seek a proper combination of benefits for different actors. One sentence reflects very well the rationality of peasant behaviour – ‘handing in enough to the state, saving enough for the collective, the rest of the harvest is ours’ (Ying, 2009).

Xu Yong (2006) thinks that the socialization of peasant production and ways of living places them in a highly dynamic and interregional movement. They are now facing a ‘strangers’ society’ filled with both opportunities and risks. The life experiences passed down from generation to generation seem to be inadequate. They have to obtain new knowledge, make choices and act according to their own judgement. The peasants are not dispersed and isolated anymore because of the advanced communication and transportation systems, the penetration of the market economy, highly frequent and interregional movements, the widespread basic education as well as the equal rights given by the State to the peasants etc. Peasants begin to look beyond their own piece of land and villages, exhibiting great initiative and spirit. Contracting farmland to households, township and village enterprises (TVEs), and self-governance among villagers are the three grand innovations of the Chinese peasants. All of these creations are closely related to rural households. Increasing socialization has provided new momentum and vitality to the ancient family system in China (Xu, 2006). In a word, the conventional ways of living have been changed by socialization, and peasants have to create new ways in order to adapt to these changes.

Qiaolin Chen (2009) thinks that the motivation of peasant reform comes from their own needs for survival and the policy support from the government. She groups the motivations into internal, external and combined motivations. The motivation mechanism refers to the interactions among internal factors as well as those between internal and external factors. Peasants seek to innovate because of the internal motivations for survival and the external motivation of social needs, together with the combined forces of these two groups of motivations (Chen, 2008). In addition, Chen (2010) believes that guaranteeing the needs of life and production is the key motivation for peasants to innovate, and therefore it is a kind of bottom-up innovation process.

Analysis of Influencing Factors

If viewed from the individual level, the factors influencing the innovative behaviours of peasants contain psychological factors and capabilities. The former refers to self-confidence, spirit of adventure, risk-taking capacities, persistence and abilities of understanding. The latter refers to the capabilities of identifying opportunities, self-organizing, risk-management, obtaining resources and adapting to competences and so forth. Moreover, the innovative mechanisms are also influenced by the regional social and cultural environment, including the customs of local citizens, educational levels, psychological qualities, mainstream values, social outlook and networks. These actors can somehow determine whether the people have the enthusiasm to innovate, and whether a mutual-trust and cooperative relationship could be set up (Guo, Zhang, & Xu, 2008).

Social capital is the meta-impetus of peasant innovation. Why some peasants engage in various innovative activities while others do not, even though they are living in the same rural community and in the same structural environment? Why does there exist 'vanguard peasants' and 'non-vanguard peasants'? We know that the family background and social status might have impacts on a peasant's life. However, the differences among peasants lie mainly in the innovations taken in terms of managing their resources and changing their living situations. In fact, every actor in the community has the potential to bring about change, because the human capital and human agency are there for everyone. But the practices of rural development have shown that in any given community there are always some peasants who succeed in innovating new ways of living, while others do not. It is generally accepted that the differences between these peasants, or the meta-impetus of innovations, is related to tangible resources and capitals as well as the actors' technological abilities. These are usually classified into four capitals, namely, natural, physical, human and financial capital. However, case studies show that the meta-impetus for peasants to innovate is not necessarily these four groups of capitals. Instead, some other factors are more influential, such as social networks, information, mutual enlightenment, trust, prestige, respect, credit, experiences, lessons from others, self-help and cooperation, interests, beliefs, curiosity and pressures etc. Most of these factors can be classified as social capital. Therefore, social capital is the meta-impetus of innovation. Development innovations and social capital are also not static, but produced and evolved in certain or multiple social conditions. The actors in the social network would act consciously according to certain values and social rules so as to maintain the existence and operation of the social network. It is via this operation that the actors in the network can obtain the necessary social resources (and other resources) to act. The interactions of these interwoven factors thereby produce social capital. In other words, the combination of these factors and their interactions come together, inspiring peasants to innovate (Ye, 2004).

From the regional level, Ying (2008) studies 'peasants' autonomous actions and institutional change' and finds that natural conditions, customs in industries and commerce, and indigenous knowledge such as pragmatic theory as well as the willingness and orientations of the local government are the main factors influencing peasant behaviours. Her study is based on a series of autonomous innovations of peasants in Zhejiang Province (especially the central and south parts of the area) since 1952. To be specific, some natural conditions like the low land–tillage ratio could barely be correlated with the collective farming system, resulting in evident conflicts. Moreover, conflicts could be found between the traditional preferences of individual operation or family farming among peasants in Zhejiang Province and the institutions that clearly dispel such traditions. Thirdly, the innate customs and cultures for industries and trades among the grassroots have direct impacts on peasant behaviours, which can create opportunities for them to break through some institutional barriers. Fourthly, the utility culture from the East Zhejiang School[7] endows peasants with qualities of pragmatism and an innovative spirit. Lastly, the values and orientations of the local government is the key variable that influences the peasant choices in those areas.

From above, Fu (2011) analyses the factors that restrain the improvement of peasants' innovative capabilities. For instance, historical factors from feudal times may hinder the formation of peasants' innovative capabilities. The planned economy of the New China and the urban–rural dual system both constrain peasant agency. Social factors also have negative impacts on peasant innovative capabilities, such as weak rural economic development, backward rural education, the not fully established rural education systems, inadequate scientific and technological training and expansion, and defective education laws. Other factors, including individual factors, may exert some inhibitive influences. The deeply rooted feudal ideologies may prevent some peasants from taking initiatives. The educational level of peasants influences the formation of new ideas as well (Fu, 2011). However, we argue against this view. Peasants' innovative behaviours and grassroots activities are indeed produced in this social context and development structure. We would contend that these factors are not confining peasant innovative capabilities. Rather, the peasant innovative spirit is exactly the result of the breakthrough/overcoming of these constraints. The constraints become causes of innovation.

CONCLUSION: WHO RULES DEVELOPMENT?

Rural development is not simply an objective, a slogan, a plan or a design. It is not the rear battlefield of modernization. Rural areas are not babysitters for the urban, nor should they be used as a drill ground for bureaucrats. Rural areas should not be dumping grounds for urban wastes, nor be hidden locations for high-risk industries. Rural development refers to what peasants do. The path peasants choose to take has been experiencing different scenarios. If development is seen as a social change, or a significant and critical crossroads, rural development can be understood as a series of victories of peasants against/over their predicaments. Not all the people living in rural areas are peasants, but rural areas cannot exist without peasants. What matters most in rural development or rural social transfers are peasants, their situations and their feelings. History is what happened in the past. Peasants have been creating history in their own space and time. The peasant innovations and grassroots activities are the models of such creative behaviours. They are the rational choices of peasant social instincts and external changes. We can understand this 'social instinct' as the notions, capabilities and eagerness of peasants under the influences of the social environment. 'External changes' refer to the new institutions, policies or other powers of control in comparison to the traditional environment that peasants live in. Peasant innovations and grassroots activities are the reactions to these external changes based on their social instinct.

Most development innovations are autonomous strategies taken by peasants in order to fight against economic exclusion and the vulnerability of their rural lives (Schneider, 2012). Peasants have a low reliance on the old institutions. They have been marginalized by these institutions and sometimes are even their victims. Therefore, peasants have internal needs and impulses to change. They are eager to break through the fetters of the systems in the planned economy that strictly control their lives. Just as American scholar Coser points out, 'marginalized groups are less bounded by customary institutions'. These customs usually have a tight grasp on the lives of the insiders. But the marginalized can see the possible choices unnoticed by insiders, and they are more sensitive to the structural defects (Su & Liu, 2005). The peasants at the bottom level of society naturally become the initiators of innovations. Historical materialism suggests that people are the subject and the creators of social practices and history. Peasants are the subject of rural reforms and development. They have tremendous creativity. As long as the spirit of initiative persists and the benefits can be protected and respected, their enthusiasm will be stimulated under the necessary conditions and supports, and the rural reforms and development in China could be sustained with incessant innovations (Chen, 2010).

However, before the 1980s, peasant studies have focused more on how the state has normalized and shaped rural societies. Such research is from a theoretical perspective: the formal institutions have strong control over social life; there is no autonomous social life; there is no independent social power and mass culture; the masses are passive; the resistance of the populace is weak if not non-existent; social life is tidy and integrated under the overwhelming control of the party and the state; and the power of reform is from the party and the apparatus of the state (Sun, 2000). But in recent research, the autonomous behaviours of peasants, their initiative and spirit, and their influences on institutional innovations and social change have attracted more attention from the academy. Apart from the research mentioned above, the most systematic studies on peasants and the grassroots are the 'subaltern studies' by historians specialized in modern south Asia.

A series of works by historians on modern south Asia was published in 1982, entitled 'Subaltern Studies'. The well-known 'subaltern historiography' comes from this. 'Subaltern' is borrowed from Italian Marxist

Antonio Gramsci who used this word in at least two senses. For one thing, the subaltern refers to the proletariats. For another, it is used to discuss the subaltern classes in pre-capitalist societies. 'Subaltern history' brings to light the forgotten history of the masses that has already been buried under the western capitalistic civilizations. This could undoubtedly make the narratives about the western modernity more detailed and comprehensive. However, there is no such 'bottom-up' history that is able to challenge the existence, stability or legalized history of capitalist modernity. 'Bottom-up' history, unsurprisingly, is always written as a tragedy (or as an apology). Almost every historical document leads to the 'fact' that the subaltern is a 'deviation from the ideal'. Gayatri Spivak argues in his two influential articles that the subaltern history shows that the 'people' or 'citizens' in capitalist history could only be the elites. Why should the subaltern class be disguised as the ruler and pretend to be the creator of the history? The subaltern history itself challenges the idea that there exists a ruler who has an integrated volition and controls everything. Why would this idea be transplanted into subaltern history? It is a myth that the subaltern class could voice their thoughts through the scripts of the historians. In fact, Spivak states that it is the historians who are expressing between lines the thoughts on behalf of the subaltern. The subaltern cannot speak (Chatterjee, 2001).

Anthony Giddens uses his systematic structuralized theory to explore the interactions between social structure and human agency. He discards the perspectives of viewing society as the subject or the object. Instead, he defends the study of society from the social practices. His structuralized theory is featured with the duality of structure, or the circularity of social practices. The duality of structure means that structure is the mediator of behaviours continually self-organizing, and it is also the result of such behaviours. In his view, social structure is not the pure result of individual actions, but the production and reproduction of constantly involved behaviours. He defines structure as 'rules and resources', which are the preconditions of human agency and unexpected outcomes. He starts his analysis from actions and actors. Both have vivid agency. He also emphasizes that social actors exhibit skills and qualities in their everyday activities. They reflect the processes of their activities. Such a reflective monitoring refers to the intentions or objectives of the behaviours of human beings. As for the practices that comprise social systems, the structure is both its mediator and a result of its own dynamic. Structuralizing therefore means that social relations continue to be solidified as social structure through the duality of structure across time and space. Social interactions reveal their qualities of circularity and creativity at any time. Meanwhile, social actors with cognitive capabilities exhibit their skills and achievements during the interactions, and social systems are reproduced unceasingly across time and space. The duality of structure combines these two processes (Deng, 2006).

If we examine society through the lens of peasant social practices, we might notice that it is constrained by the structure on the one hand, and pushes the reforms of the structure on the other. However, we cannot thereby conclude that the peasant dominates social development, because any given actor might contribute more or less to social reform. So how should we deal with this? The study of any subject or phenomenon does not mean that the researcher needs to appreciate or despise it. The aim is more to understand it. To understand something is a continuous process of deconstruction. Why do we need deconstruction after all? Just as in the subaltern studies, the subaltern could not speak because of the scripts of historians. They would not be shaped into something just because of others' expectations or constructions. They lead a life with their social instincts and in view of external changes. This may dismiss any kind of grand narrative, or even the researchers' meaningful construction of their existence. Such a life is a deconstruction. The meaning of deconstruction is as transparent as life itself.

NOTES

1. NB: The differentiation could be observed in conventional rural areas as well, such as the gentry and the ordinary peasants. They are the counterparts of elites and peasants today. The gentry had an important role to play, which was to maintain order in the villages. They had to be from the local area. In contrast, the elites nowadays seek to break up the old order in the villages and bring in new activities. They are not necessarily from the villages. The actors we are discussing in this paper are the majority of the rural population except for the elites. These people would interact with the elites in four ways: cooperation, neutrality, objection or resistance.
2. Ye, van der Ploeg, and Schneider (2012).
3. Taken from Yang (2009).
4. Archive 6-2-62-8, Office of Rural Work, On the scale of production team and related suggestions, 4 May 1963, p. 48. Jinhua: Jinhua Archives Bureau.
5. Archive 94-7-12-17, Rural Work Department of Prefectural Party Committee in Wenzhou, CPC, On the two paths of management of contemporary People's Commune and corrections, 14 October 1959. Wenzhou: Wenzhou Archives Bureau.
6. Archive 1-29-45, The County Party Committee's investigation on the current rural work and the subdivision of production team and summaries of the ban of such practices, 1979, p. 76. Yi Wu Archives Bureau.
7. The thoughts of this academic school emphasize practical utility. It was developed by the scholars in Shaoxing, Ningbo and Taizhou, which are located in east

Zhejiang Provence, China, that the school flourished during Ming and Qing dynasty, while the source can be traced back to Song dynasty. The academic thoughts emphasize practical utility.

ACKNOWLEDGEMENTS

We would like to extend our thanks to Dr. Chunyu Wang and Dr. Lu Pan for their contributions in the finalization of this chapter. Appreciations also go to Professor Jan Douwe van der Ploeg for his guidance, and to Professor Tony Fuller for his English language editing work.

REFERENCES

Borras, S. M., Jr. (2008). La Via Campesina and its global campaign for agrarian reform. *Journal of Agrarian Change*, *8*(2–3), 258–289.

Chatterjee. (2001). Focusing on the subaltern. *Dushu*, *8*, 13–20.

Chen, D. (2009). Imitation subculture: Resistance and ridicule. *Academic Exploration*, *1*, 107–110.

Chen, M. (2010). Review on farmers' initiative spirits. *Theory Research*, *27*, 64–65.

Chen, Q. (2008). Analysis for driving force of innovation of the farmers in China's rural reform. *Journal of Chang'an University (Social Science Edition)*, *10*(3), 101–106.

Chen, X., & Dai, Y. (2009). Analysis of 'copycat culture'. *News World*, *9*, 117–118.

Deng, D. (2006). The socialized farmers: Motivation and behavior. *Journal of Huazhong Normal University (Humanities and Social Sciences)*, *3*.

Deng, R. (2006). *Voluntary behaviors and institutional constraints: The case of a grassroots environmental protection organization*. Master's thesis, Minzu University of China, Beijing, China.

Fu, H. (2011). *Suburban farmers' innovation ability training method research*. Master's thesis, Agricultural University of Hebei, Hebei, China.

Guo, J., Zhang, Y., & Xu, Q. (2008). Impact studies of innovation mechanism on farmers' entrepreneurship. *Shaanxi Journal of Agricultural Sciences*, *3*, 185–187.

Gupta, A. K. (1995). Knowledge centre: Building upon what people know. Presented at IFAD's International Conference on Hunger & Poverty in Brussels during November 16–23, 1995.

Han, L. (2010). *Study on mechanism of agricultural technology innovation in which farmers are assumed as the main body*. Master's thesis, Shandong Agricultural University, Shandong, China.

He, B. (2010). A reflection on "Shanzhai culture". *News Fan (Xinwen Aihaozhe)*, October (2nd ed.).

Hu, M. (2007). On the folk innovation's "do" and "not do". *Journal of Changshu Institute of Technology (Philosophy & Social Science)*, *11*, 34–38.

Huang, P. C. (1988). *The peasant economy and social change in North China*. Stanford, CA: Stanford University Press.

Jiang, L. (2010). Research of spread of grassroots innovations. Master's thesis, Tianjin University of Finance and Economics, Tianjin, China.

Kerkvliet, B. (2009). Everyday politics in peasant societies (and ours). *Journal of Peasant Studies*, *36*(1), 227–243.

Li, L., & O'Brian, K. (1997). Rightful resistance of peasants in contemporary China. In W. Guoguang (Ed.), *The effects of return of HK*. Pacific Ocean Research Institute.

Lin, H., Wang, F., & Guan, M. (2009). A research on the private innovation and support system in China. *Economic Management*, *1*, 133–139.

Liu, Y. (2009a). Mobilization confined in structures – An explanatory framework of mobilizing peasants' collective actions. *Journal of the Party School of CPC Changchun Municipal Committee*, *6*, 24–28.

Liu, Y. (2009b). The analysis of the Shanzhai culture. *Journal of Chinese People's Armed Police Force Academy*, *25*(3).

Lu, M., Wei, X., & Sun, C. (2003). On peasants' role in the process of practical technique innovation: Case study of water saving rice engineering in Shuangyang District. *China Agricultural University (Social Science Edition)*, *4*, 20–26.

Ning, P. (2011). Views on the patent rights of peasants' innovations – Based on investigations on peasant innovators. *Modern Finance and Economics*, *31*(1), 66–71.

Scott, J. (1987). *Weapons of the weak: Everyday forms of peasant resistance*. Yale, CT: Yale University Press.

Schneider, S. (2012). *Pathways of rural development in emerging economies: The case of Brazil*. Retrieved from http://cohd.cau.edu.cn/main/html/xueshuhuodong/2012/1119/4886.html

Song, G., & Chen, X. (2008). Paths of constructing new types of peasants' subjectivity. *Journal of the Party School of CPC Jinan Municipal Committee*, *3*, 98–99.

Su, G. & Liu, X. (Eds.). (2005). *Theories in social theory* (p. 619). Beijing: SDX Joint Publishing Company.

Sun, H. (2011). The so-called Shanzhai, Shanzhai products, Shanzhai culture and others. *Journal of Changsha Railway University*, *12*(1), 68–70.

Sun, L. (2000). Process-event analysis and the forms of state-peasant relations in contemporary China. *Tsinghua Sociological Review* (Special Issue), 17. Fujian: Lujiang Press.

Tan, X., & Du, Z. (2010). *Postmodern agriculture: From an approach of sustainable food supply Chain* (Vol. 1, Social Science edition). Beijing: China Agricultural University.

Tao, D. (2009). My view on "Shanzhai Culture". *The Beijing News*. Retrieved from www.the-bei-jingnews.com/omment/1108/2009/03-28/008@021524.htm

van der Ploeg, J. D. (2008). *The new peasantries: Struggles for autonomy and sustainability in an era of empire and globalization*. London: Earthscan.

van der Ploeg, J. D., Ye, J., & Schneider, S. (2015). Rural development: Actors and practices. In P. Milone, F. Ventura, & J. Ye (Eds.), *Constructing a new framework for rural development* (Vol. 22). Research in Rural Sociology and Development. Bingley, UK: Emerald Group Publishing Limited.

Wang, R., & Wang, Q. (2009). On Shanzhai sports culture. *Sports Culture Guide*, *9*, 137–139.

Wang, Y. (2010). The tension of metaphor and irony in Shanzhai culture: A symbolist perspective? *Social Scientists*, *161*(9), 151–154.

Wang, F. (2011). Ecological responsibility, grassroots action and building capacity for low-carbon communities: Cases in Britain and America and inspirations. *Journal of Jiangsu Administration Institute*, *6*, 61–66.

Xu, Y. (2006). Farmer household re-cognition and socialized small agricultural economy construction. *Journal of Huazhong Normal University (Humanities and Social Sciences)*, *3*, 2–8.

Yang, L. (2009). Research on characteristics of indigenous technological innovations. *Science and Technology Management Research*, *7*, 27–30.

Yang, M. (2007). Community as state governance unit: A case study on residents: Community participation and cognition in the process of community building campaign. *Sociological Studies*, *4*, 137–164.

Yang, P. (2009). *Commercialization of grassroots innovations: Challenges and solutions.* Master's thesis, Tianjin University of Finance and Economics, Tianjin, China.

Ye, J. (2004). Creating space for change. *China Rural Survey*, *4*, 37–45.

Ye, J., Ding, B., & Wang, W. (2012). Opening a new road: The autonomous nested-market and rural development. *Chinese Rural Economy*, *10*, 4–12.

Ye, J., & Liu, X. (2000). Meaning of the modern development and its applications in the international development. *Rural Economic Problem*, *11*, 39–44.

Ye, J., van der Ploeg, J. D., Schneider, S. (2012). Rural development: Actors and practices. Position paper for the 3rd seminar on the comparative analysis of rural development processes in China, Brazil and the EU.

Ye, J., & Wang, W. (2011). The rise of the nested market: A resistance to the infinite market and modern agriculture. *Guizhou Social Sciences*, *2*, 48–54.

Ye, Y. (2009). Rise from the grassroots, coexist with the mainstream in harmony. *Journal of Chongqing Institute of Technology (Social Science)*, *23*(7), 125–128.

Ye, Y. (2010). An aesthetic analysis of 'copycat culture'. *News Fan* (Xinwen Aihaozhe), March (2nd ed.), pp. 144–145.

Ying, X. (2007). Grassroots mobilization and the mechanism of interest expression of the peasants group: A comparative study of four cases. *Sociological Studies*, *22*(2), 1–23.

Ying, X. (2008). *Farmers' autonomous actions and institutional change: Taking Zhejiang province from 1952 to 1992 for example.* PhD. dissertation, Central China Normal University, Hubei, China.

Ying, X. (2009). Farmers' autonomous actions and institutional innovations. *CASS Journal of Political Science*, *2*, 75–82.

Yu, J. (2004). An explanatory framework of peasants' rights protection activities. *Sociological Studies*, *2*, 49–55.

Zhang, J. (2006). *What happens in Zhe Jiang: The democracy in transformation periods.* Beijing: The Eastern Publishing Co. Ltd.

Zhang, L., & Liu, R. (2011). Case studies on the interactions between peasants and formal departments in rural innovations. *Journal of Henan Agricultural University*, *45*(5), 595–599.

Zhang, N. (2004). *Cultural symptoms* (p. 282). Shanghai: Shanghai Literature and Art Publishing House.

Zhang, W. (2011). *Dislocation and fracture of concept interpretation: Research of production and conception of Shanzhai.* Master's thesis, Nanjing University, Jiangsu, China.

Zhang, Y. (2008). *Vitality and limit of 'Faux Pas'.* Retrieved from http://blog.sina.com.cn/zhangyw. Accessed on 14 December 2008.

Zhang, Z. (2005). Fifty years of rural villages: The state and the peasant in daily economic practice – An empirical study in Houle Village, Yiwu City. *Open Times*, *4*, 71–83.

Zhang, Z. (2008). "Grass-roots" wisdom and the reconstruction of social space – An explanation of "Zhejiang Experience" from the perspective of sociology of space. *Zhejiang Social Sciences*, *4*, 2–6.

Zhou, X. (1997). *Aesthetic culture studies in contemporary China* (p. 30). Beijing: Peking University Press.

Zhou, X. (2007). *Cultural representation and cultural studies* (pp. 12–13). Beijing: Peking University Press.

Zhu, X. (2006). *A philosophical analysis of contemporary culture* (p. 139). Shanghai: East China Normal University Press.

CHAPTER 6

SEEDS AND SPROUTS OF RURAL DEVELOPMENT: INNOVATIONS AND NESTED MARKETS IN SMALL SCALE ON-FARM PROCESSING BY FAMILY FARMERS IN SOUTH BRAZIL

Sergio Schneider and Marcio Gazolla

ABSTRACT

In this chapter we examine how the small scale agro-industries located in Southern Brazil, specifically in the North of the State of Rio Grande do Sul, started to deal with changes in their production processes, how they created and adapted technologies, and devised new products. Among the main outcomes of the study we highlight the novelties observed during the field research, especially regarding the family situation and the agro-manufacturing activities, in which we observed (i) a relative raise in autonomy; (ii) improvement in both the income level and the quality of life of household members; (iii) creation of new nested markets and marketing channels; (iv) development of more environmentally sustainable

Constructing a New Framework for Rural Development
Research in Rural Sociology and Development, Volume 22, 127–156

ISSN: 1057-1922/doi:10.1108/S1057-192220150000022005

products; (v) improvement of the value added to food products; and (vi) development of new interfaces between families and other social actors.

Keywords: Food production; on farm processing activities; innovations; food markets; rural development

INTRODUCTION

The paths and the trajectories trodden by farmers to facilitate their productive activities and ensure social and economic reproduction are neither linear nor predictable. Similarly, the aspects that contribute to decision making in any case are not teleological and even less structurally dependent. The initiatives, practices, capabilities, and resources mobilized by farmers and their families enable a multiplicity of activities and processes to be undertaken for tackling everyday problems or particular limitations they face. These determinants produce the contingencies that impel farmers to look for and mobilize resources, knowledge, social relations, and even political support. This is what leads farmers and rural families to become social actors. It is the actor condition that allows farmers to give *differential responses to similar structural circumstances, even if the conditions appear relatively homogeneous* (Long, 2007, p. 43).

The power and capacity of social actors stem from their "agency," a concept defined by Long as the ability of an actor *to process social experience and to devise ways of coping with life, even under the most extreme forms of coercion* (Long, 2001, p. 16; Long & van der Ploeg, 1994). This is also connected with what van der Ploeg, Ye, and Schneider (see Chapter 2[1]) claim in the position paper of the Third Seminar on the comparative analysis of rural development processes in China, Brazil, and the EU. In that position paper it is assumed that "(a) *these practices have certain traits in common* and (b) *that there are important and intrinsic relations between the actors and practices*" (chapter 1, p. 9).

The consolidation and the strengthening of family farming in Brazil in recent years have enabled an enormous variety of initiatives and practices, historically developed at the grassroots, to gain room and prominence. This is the case, for instance, of the processing of agricultural products and food stuffs that used to serve only the consumption needs of the farm unit and later became merchandise for exchange or sale. Such initiatives gave rise to small scale on-farm processing, organized around farm household units, which process raw agricultural products into diverse value-added agri-food products.[2] Most of the work as well as the business management in these on-farm processing activities is done by family members, who provide these entrepreneurial initiatives with their knowledge and expertise. These on-farm processing units constitute enterprises characterized by a small scale of production, that enjoy economies of scope and operate through strong linkages with local and regional markets, often without registration (Gazolla, Niederle, & Waquil, 2012).

In this chapter, we aim to analyze small scale on-farm processing located in Southern Brazil, specifically in the North of the State of Rio Grande do Sul in a region called Alto Uruguai (High Uruguay) (named after the river of the same name that flows into Brazil's neighboring country).[3] We intend to examine how these small scale on-farm processors bring about changes in production, how they create and adapt technologies, and devise new products. Our goal is to explain the process of transition toward these novelties and their integration into the existing socio-technical food regime. We also discuss marketing channels and flows set by these on-farm processors using the concept of *nested markets*, as formulated by van der Ploeg, Ye, and Schneider (2010).

The small scale on-farm processing activities are analyzed here from the perspective of rural development practices, since they may as much arise from contingent and spontaneous innovations as be responses to exclusion or marginalization endured by many farmers who are unable or who are not sufficiently efficient to meet the requirements of the dominant agri-food system. Therefore, on-farm processing emerges both as initiatives – expression of farmers' creativity and entrepreneurial skills – and as responses and reactions from those who cannot afford to follow the hegemonic production model. Many of the featured initiatives are new and others are adapted from previous such enterprises, but they all emerge as strategies devised by farmers and their families to seek ways of working and producing that allow for their permanence/continuance in rural areas.

The analogy of such practices with "seeds" and "sprouts" is a metaphor for examining the socio-technical production processes within agriculture and agri-food production. This analytical approach allows us to go beyond the current productivist rationality that prescribes widespread use and incorporation of external technologies (mechanical, chemical, and genetic) and the pursuit of productivity gains through economies of scale.

In such terms, these practices can be characterized as "seeds" that are yet to be put in fertile soil for germinating and producing something more, and as "sprouts" when they are already sown and emerge, starting to reveal their configuration and potential. Hence, seeds and sprouts are perceived as both tools and strategies developed by farmers as means and mechanisms for doing things differently and thus creating and developing the groundwork for more substantial changes.

Accordingly, the rural on-farm processing activities described in this chapter express the power of agency of farmers as social actors. According to Long, the agency "attributes to the individual actor the capacity to process social experience and devise ways of coping with life, even under the most extreme forms of coercion. Within the limits of information, uncertainty and other constraints (e.g., physical, normative or politico-economic) that exist, social actors possess knowledgeability and capability" (Long, 2007, p. 48). Farmers who have power of agency seek to solve problems, learn how to intervene in the flow of social events, and continuously monitor their own actions, observing how others react to their behavior and noting various unexpected circumstances. This is the case of small scale rural on-farm processing studied in this research work.

In spite of being small-scale, the importance of family on-farm processing has grown in recent years in Brazil. Estimates by the Ministry of Agrarian Development (MDA) indicate that there were approximately 35,000 on-farm processors in 2008. Gazolla et al. (2012) refer to data from the Agricultural Census (IBGE, 2006) pointing out that 16.7% of farms in Brazil either process or manufacture some raw agricultural product. In Rio Grande do Sul (RS), data from the State Program of Family On-farm Processing (Programa de Agroindústria Familiar – PAF/RS) for the year 2011 indicate the existence of 7,700 on-farm processing units, most of them still unregistered. The micro region of Frederico Westphalen, our research field, encompasses 14.12% of all existing on-farm processing units in RS, thus being the leading region in the state regarding the number of experiences.

This chapter is organized into five sections besides the introduction and final remarks. In the first one, we briefly discuss what is meant by production of novelties and innovations, based on some relevant literature. In the second part, we describe the Medio Alto Uruguai/RS region, where the research was conducted. In the third, the two studies of on-farm processing – Agroindústria Biorga and Ludke – are presented. The fourth part analyzes the main novel products and production processes as well as some of their repercussions for families. The fifth part discusses/examines the main marketing channels, the *nested markets*, and the new collective and network organizations that have emerged, as for instance RECOSOL – the cooperative marketing network of family on-farm processing.

INNOVATIONS AND NOVELTIES BY SOCIAL ACTORS

By discussing the new ways of practicing agriculture and producing food, we are entering the field of studies on innovation, knowledge generation and transfer, and technological change. These studies have gained prominence in recent decades within the fields of sociology, geography, and economics. We do not intend here either to do a literature review or to enter the debates on the state of the art of this subject. Our purpose is simply to present some selected references and make clear the perspectives that guide our understanding of the concept of innovation and the way it was used in this research.

Generally, an overview of the literature shows that innovations have, almost always, two dimensions, which repeatedly appear in the various definitions (Wiskerke & van der Ploeg, 2004). The first one is the creative or ingenious dimension that can be verified in the effect of its use, insofar as, for something to be deemed an innovation, it must improve some existing artifact, technique, medium, or resource that used to operate in a similar, though less effective way. There are, however, many good and effective ideas and creations that, even so, do not become innovations. What they lack is precisely the social approval granted to those innovations that turn out to be recognized and legitimated as ideas or inventions that make a difference and become effectively as a social practice.

There seems to be a consensus among scholars that changes resulting from innovations do not occur "in jumps," but rather gradually and continuously through small changes within society, which may be identified overall as transitions (Marques, 2009; Rotmans, Kemp, & van Asselt, 2001). The transition is the result of developments in distinct domains, such as socio-technical systems, networks, organizations or social groups, or even norms and institutions (Geels, 2004). In rural studies, transition leads to the constitution of a new form of organization in agriculture and food production, which is identified with rural development, this latter can be regarded as a multilevel, multifaceted, and multi-actor process embedded in historical traditions (van der Ploeg et al., 2000).

Recent studies on innovation have highlighted the social dimension of the process. Amin and Cohendet (2004) show that the processes of innovation and technological development are embedded in social contexts and that invention and creativity are results of an intense process of interaction and exchange of experiences based on practical and contingent circumstances. For the authors, although novelty generation on the factory floor can happen through learning-by-doing, it is necessary to comprehend both the social and the institutional environments within which the interactions and exchanges that give rise to creative and innovative solutions to complex problems occur.

At the core of this new way of understanding innovation and learning processes, lies an epistemological shift grounded in the works of Cetina (2005), who suggests that, in the knowledge society, we must recognize that the production of knowledge is not limited to science and the experts. Cetina develops the concept of innovative epistemic practice defined as the practice focused on knowledge produced when problems arise within a particular routine or in the course of a new work.

The interest in farmers' modes of innovation and in the creation of experiments and tools aimed at *doing things in a different way* is embedded in such a perspective – one that comprises the sphere in which individuals change, modify, and confer new functions to a particular resource or device. Farmers are very inventive and ingenious in the art of modifying, adapting labor tools, and/or adapting resources for production. These processes of creation and inventiveness are what we call novelties.

Forms of innovation comprise the repertory of practices and initiatives created and developed by farmers to cope with the unexpected structural and contingent situations that diminishes their autonomy, thus weakening their situation as producers. In a context where agriculture is increasingly embedded in market circuits, within which farmers mobilize production resources (inputs, seeds, etc.) mostly through purchases, thus becoming dependent on external demand for selling their produce, the innovative capacity, creativity, inventiveness, and the creation of room for maneuver grant farmers their flexibility, learning opportunities, and knowledge – elements that become essential for their interaction with the economy and broader society (van der Ploeg, 2008; van der Ploeg, 2003b).

These so described practices and initiatives by family farmers are consistent with what Stuiver and Wiskerke (2004) have described as novelties, which are distinct from incremental innovations. These authors claim that innovations are linear and incremental because they are created within a particular environment (laboratory, university, etc.) and then transferred to other spaces where they are replicated, adapted, and possibly improved. Van der Ploeg et al. (2004), furthermore, states that incrementalism is characterized by the addition of the next small step along a predefined route, producing small changes and adjustments in the pattern or in the direction of the adopted technological development. Novelties, in contrast, represent frequent ruptures in a discontinuous and unpredictable process, which undergoes recurrent adjustments, feedbacks, and alterations (Knickel, Brunori, Rand, & Proost, 2008).

In this sense, we agree with Gaglio (2011), who points out the need of distinguishing innovation from invention (which he associates with the cognitive capacity of creating), from novelty (that is something different, not yet existent), from fashion (that is a trend), and from creativity (that refers to talent, capacity, and ingenuity). He emphasizes that an innovation can be recognized and identified by the following characteristics: (a) processual conception that presupposes a route from an initial project or idea to a final product; (b) integration into the market, which implies that a creation must face and be subjected to public evaluation and judgment; and (c) the commercial success that is the positive sanction of public preferences.

Novelty production constitutes a reference framework where novelty is understood as continued activities by farmers for seeking viable solutions to the everyday problems they face and for which they try to create and devise new and better ways for optimizing the use of production factors (Oostindie & van Broekhuozen, 2008; Stuiver, 2008). According to Oliveira, Gazolla, and Schneider (2011), innovation does not result only from the introduction of technologies or exogenous knowledge. In our view, innovation also stems from a continuous and daily round of adjustments to the conditions that farmers face and tackle.

For Gazolla (2012), novelties are characterized by being based on farmers' knowledge (particularly, tacit and contextualized knowledge), by showing a rather radical nature, being internal to the institutional context in which they emerge and rooted in the socio-spatial territory where they are created. Novelties also have the potential to generate relevant transformations in established social practices by adding greater degrees of autonomy and sustainability to production and economic activities of their creators. Relying on European literature about novelties, Gazolla points out another characteristic, namely that novelties often emerge outside of formally established norms and regulations.

Authors like Hebinck (2001), Wiskerke (2003), Wiskerke et al. (2004), and Moors and Wiskerke (2004) call attention to the fact that the creation of novelties in agriculture is a highly localized process dependent on time, local ecosystems, and cultural repertories surrounding the organization of work. A novelty can be understood as a change in, and sometimes a break from, existing routines. Hence, a novelty can either imply a change in an existing practice or comprise a novel practice. It can also be a novel way of thinking or doing things, presumably able to bring about improvements in existing routines (van der Ploeg et al., 2004).

The general analysis of novelties comprises, however, one level that is not referred to as the use of artifacts, techniques, or resources. Such a level involves the creative processes that bear a collective nature, since they are characterized by new forms of social and political organization realized in the form of cooperatives, associations, and other joint activities that lead to social cohesion (Schneider et al., 2014). These are processes that some authors refer to as social and institutional innovation (Piraux & Bonnal, 2011). Such innovations imply a convergence of interests toward a common goal or cause, whose implementation occurs by means of a grouping mechanism that requires organization, governance, and distribution of incumbencies and power.

In this sense, our purpose here is to demonstrate that, whenever farmers try *to do things in a different way*, it involves both the technical practices of production and the processes (creating marketing channels and new markets), as well as of particular forms of social organization. The experiences of family on-farm processing are emblematic. The start-up lies always in the creation of some novelty, either in the field of production processes or in the development and improvement of technologies applied to convert raw materials into merchandise and food. It is also manifest in the creation of marketing channels and sales outlets for the products. Finally, these novelties reach the ambit/level of collective organization when they unfold into mechanisms that lead to the creation of cooperatives and other forms of association – political organizations aimed at consolidating this process and guaranteeing its broader reproduction.

TRADITIONAL "COLONIAL" FARMING AND THE MODERN AGRICULTURAL *SQUEEZE*

The social, economic, and cultural context, in which such innovation practices of family farming in Rio Grande do Sul emerge and develop, is marked by an historical trajectory referred to as the process of immigration and colonization of the State by Europeans. The region called Medio Alto Uruguai/RS was occupied by descendants of European immigrants, mainly Italian, German, Polish, among other ethnic groups, that settled colonies in the region as of 1925, when the State Government established the Land Commission in the city of Palmeira das Missões. As a result of this process, the Northern part of the state has historically developed production systems predominantly characterized by the production and labor[4] of the family unit.

To a certain extent, Medio Alto Uruguai region shares many characteristics with the region of Missões, already portrayed by Schneider and Niederle (2010, p. 388). Once settled in the areas of the Atlantic Forest, using a practice of cutting, burning, and planting, the colonists developed an agricultural system known as the Colonial Agricultural System (CAS). This system consisted of growing some crops for sale (potatoes, cassava, and beans) and in the occupation of new neighboring areas by grown-up children, as soon as new family units were created. This constituted a way of life, since it involved both a mode of producing and working that was peculiar to those farmers and which had particular forms of sociality, cultural traits, and social values (Schneider, 1999). Regarding the mode of production, CAS, was characterized by the diversity of crops and food products primarily intended to supply households (own/self-consumption), holding few connections with existing markets, and selling only some surplus. As to the forms of neighborhood sociality, much importance was attributed to symbolic exchanges of food products, the practice of mutual aid between families, kinship and neighborhood relationships, and also to community celebrations.

This system started to collapse due to soil and native flora degradation as a result of the farming practices that consisted of cutting, burning, and planting, and that led to subsequent abandonment of the area. From the 1960s on, family farming in Medio Alto Uruguai region entered a new stage characterized by the abandonment of polyculture and the introduction of soybeans as the main monoculture. Family farmers left behind other crops and started growing soybeans that, between the mid-1960s and the 1980s, garnered attractive prices in view of the huge export demand for this commodity. With the practice of monoculture, the tradition of cultivating varied crops along with animal raising was gradually abandoned and farmers become dependent on the purchase of external inputs, especially fertilizers and seeds, but also on agrochemicals for the control of infestations and diseases that had started to appear.

As a result of this process, an increasing appropriation of external knowledge and technologies by family farmers took place. Large soybean fields spread throughout the region are the major indicator of such a socioeconomic and productivist process. The agriculture also becomes increasingly integrated with agro-technologies, and input and commodity markets, thus becoming dependent on these latter for its own reproduction. Accordingly, we observe a phenomenon called by authors such as van der

Ploeg et al. (2000) the "agricultural squeeze." On the one hand, production costs of rural establishments rise due to the acquisition of external inputs and technologies and, on the other hand, such establishments get low prices for their products in the markets, which implies very small margins and ultimately decreased incomes.

The agricultural squeeze led Medio Alto Uruguai region into the second major socioeconomic crisis in its short history. This crisis impelled farmers to mobilize for confronting the negative effects of this productive pattern as well as looking for alternative ways to get out of it. As a result, new agricultural activities and added value strategies began to be developed by families, such as fruit growing, milk production from pasture-fed cows, agri-food manufacturing, diversification of agricultural produce, and sales to institutional markets under the Food Procurement Program (FPP) and the National School Feeding Program (NSFP). It is in this context that the family on-farm processing (food products manufacturing units organized within rural establishments and households) emerges, giving birth to innovative farming activities (new products, new ways of processing food, marketing channels, and organizations), as we will show in the following sections.

Thus, a third phase in family farming development was initiated in Medio Alto Uruguai region – one that is characterized by the creation of technological alternatives and a search for new ways of integrating family farmers into the various food markets. This phase occurs concurrently and coexists with the hegemonic pattern of production of export commodities such as soybeans. In a sense, one may claim that this is an attempt to resume or return to the farming of earlier modes practiced in the region prior to soybean monoculture. Certainly, the context has changed, bringing about both opportunities and new challenges, which will be further analyzed on the basis of the trajectory of two small scale on-farm processing cases.

THE TRAJECTORIES OF TWO SMALL SCALE ON-FARM PROCESSING ACTIVITIES – THE CASES OF BIORGA AND LUDKE[5]

In order to analyze the social process of emergence of small scale on-farm processing activities we chose the cases of Cooperativa Biorga in the municipality of Erval Seco and Agroindustria Ludke in Constantina. As it is shown in Table 1, both enterprises were established in the 2000s and present a wide variety of products and processed foods. Biorga stands out for working with small alternative grains cultivated in family farms, such as flaxseed, wheat, beans, popcorn, peanuts, sesame, linseed and sesame oils, as well as hominy corn, and flours made of corn, sesame, linseed, and wheat, all of them organic foods. The small scale agro-industry Ludke is distinguished for producing milk from pasture-fed cows and for manufacturing parmesan and seasoned cheeses from the raw material (Table 1).

Cooperativa Biorga is a rural small scale agro-industry that operates through a networking association, and is formed by 32 associated family farmers from the neighboring municipalities of Cristal do Sul and Erval Seco. Its labor force is mostly comprised of the associated families, and its center of operations counts on one employee, who develops all food processing activities, and one manager, responsible for the marketing and accounting operations.

The creation of Biorga was impelled by two main factors (Table 2). On the one hand, the appropriation by local farmers of new knowledge on agroecological production, acquired during training courses and visits to enterprises of other organizations and farms. In this respect, the Lutheran Church, the Support Center for Small Farmers (Centro de Apoio ao Pequeno Agricultor – CAPA), and the NGO Terra Nova Mondai/SC were instrumental in supporting these families. On the other hand, the emergence of "awareness" of alternatives to conventional farming, especially because of the harm and damage caused to associated families by pesticides and monocultures.

Agro-industry Ludke stems from the family farming traditional production of milk and cheese that had never been sold in the market and served only to supply a family's own consumption needs. Production surpluses were sold only in small quantities, without playing an economic role in

Table 1. Small Scale On-Farm Processing in Biorga and Ludke.

Small Scale Agro-Industry and Locality	Year of Constitution	Food Produced and Processed
Cooperativa Biorga (Erval Seco)	2001	Flaxseed, wheat, beans, popcorn, peanuts, sesame, linseed and sesame oils, hominy corn; flours made of corn, sesame, linseed, and wheat
Agroindústria Ludke (Constantina)	2002	Farmhouse natural parmesan and seasoned cheeses

Source: Gazolla (2012).

Table 2. Main Reasons for Family Farmers Setting up Small Scale On-Farm Processing on Their Farms.

N	On-Farm Processing	Reason for Its Creation/Emergence
1	Cooperativa Biorga – Erval Seco Subsidiary	• Course of agroecology promoted by the Lutheran Church, providing basic knowledge on the organic farming of alternative grain crops. The course was developed in partnership with the NGO Terra Nova from Mondai/SC; • Visit to a factory of conventional seed oils in Panambi, where visitors acquired some information on the processing of vegetable oils; • Technical agroecology advice by the Support Center for Small Farmers (Centro de Apoio aos Pequenos Agricultores (CAPA) – Mondai/SC);
2	Agroindústria Ludke (Constantina)	• Families had traditional knowledge of the production of dairy products, especially cheeses for home consumption; • Visits to other agro-manufacturing initiatives, in the States of Rio Grande do Sul and Santa Catarina, for learning how food products were organized and manufactured; • Incentives by the municipal government and other local institutions (the rural extension and technical advisory agency – EMATER, the rural workers union – STR, and the Municipal Department of Agriculture) for the establishment of small scale on-farm processing in the municipality, and the implementation of a municipal program for family farming agro-manufacturing.

Source: Gazolla (2012).

household income. The agro-industry is currently fully run by the couple, Mr. and Mrs. Ludke, and their married son. All activities in the enterprise are carried out by family members, from the dairy farming stages to marketing.

The agro-industry derived from traditional knowledge about cheese making that has been passed down through generations in the family (Table 2). Before starting up the small scale agro-industry, the family visited other initiatives in RS (Guaporé, Erechim, and Sananduva) and in the state of Santa Catarina (Chapecó), to learn about production processes, social organization, and marketing of food products. With the support of the municipal administration of Constantina, the rural extension, and technical advisory agency – EMATER, the Municipal Department of Agriculture, and the Rural Workers Union, the Ludke family succeeded in structuring their agro-enterprise and enhancing their farming activities to a higher economic level than that of just supplying their own consumption needs.

NOVELTIES AND AUTONOMY: HOW DO THEY EVOLVE?

Fig. 1 presents an overview of the novelties developed by the small scale on-farm processing activities in Biorga and Ludke, and aims at explaining the main factors, either internal or external to the manufacturing units, involved in the creation of novelties. These factors are characterized as essentially multidimensional, multi-actor, and multi-institutional. The factors that generate novelties can be understood as knowledge that combines lores (contextual, scientific, tacit), available resources, and the labor

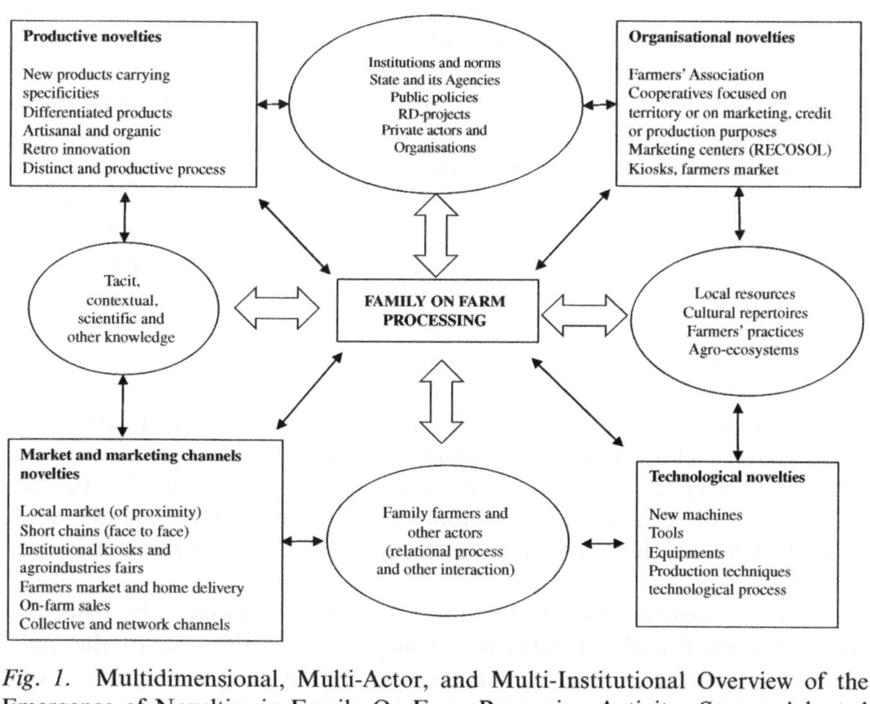

Fig. 1. Multidimensional, Multi-Actor, and Multi-Institutional Overview of the Emergence of Novelties in Family On-Farm Processing Activity. *Source*: Adapted from Gazolla (2012).

practices developed by farmers. The interactions of farmers with other social actors are also relevant. Although in many small scale on-farm processing units, it is the farmers' knowledge that comprises the basis for the creation of novelties, the interaction with other farmers and agents such as extension technicians also play a role.

In Fig. 1, it is shown how the creation of novelties is influenced by institutions, public policies, private organizations, and social actors that share interfaces with farmers and their activities. In many cases, the institutional environment strengthens the production of novelties as, for instance, the existence of rural credit programs like the national program for strengthening family farming (PRONAF Agroindústria). Conversely, such an environment may hinder novelties, by means of restrictions to the operation of the small scale on-farm processing unit as, for instance, restrictions on informal activities in view of the agri-food legislation. The production of novelties in the small scale on-farm processing environment stems from these determinants.

The novelties can be categorized according to four main types: productive novelties – new agro-ecological differentiated products that imply specific productive processes such as rotation; technological novelties – those that involve the invention or adaptation of technologies by farmers for producing either inputs or processed food products, such as new machines, equipment, tools; marketing novelties – these comprise the New Circuits for sales built by small scale on-farm processing, such as direct selling, kiosks, on-farm sales, networks and collective marketing channels, public events, among others; organizational novelties – these comprised of new social organizations which originate in on-farm processing activity, as for instance RECOSOL and its partner and networking social organizations (cooperatives, associations, farmers groups, sales outlets). We focus, here, on productive novelties and novelties in markets and marketing channels, as well as on the case of a collective social networking organization (RECOSOL) as novelties derived from the two studied on-farm processing cases. To some extent, these novelties can also be contrasted with the established hegemonic socio-technical food regime, so as to verify whether they generate transitions and/or incrementalism in such a regime.[6]

Table 3 presents the productive novelties developed by the two researched small scale on-farm processing cases. In the case of the agro-industry Cooperativa Biorga, the innovative products are organic virgin sesame and linseed oils. As to agro-industry Ludke, the novelties introduced were three kinds of seasoned cheeses. In the first case, there was an

Table 3. Types and Characteristics of Productive Novelties Produced by On-Farm Processing.

Types of Novelties	What was Made?	Characteristics of the Novelties
Sesame and linseed oils	New organic products	Organic virgin and artisan oils; products that do not undergo industrial chemical refining; participative certification by Agroecology Network Ecovida (ECOVIDA); recontextualization of external knowledge.
Cheeses seasoned with salamis, oregano, and bell peppers	Change in one stage of the cheese maturation process	New process for production of seasoned cheeses; recontextualization of external knowledge; product manufactured from raw milk.

Source: Gazolla (2012).

invention of new products and, in the second, a change in the production process.

Agroindustry Biorga stands out in the design of new technical production methods as shown in Table 3. This initiative produces differentiated products like organic linseed and sesame oils, which are innovative in the local context of family farming, because they are the only manufacturers of such products in the region. The oils from these seeds are deemed as agroecological, since farmers develop all stages of the production in compliance with the principles of organic food production and processing. They are also bound by the official regulations of the federal government for organic production, and hold the participatory certification of Ecovida Agroecology Network (Radomsky, 2011).

The oils are manufactured by cold pressing, filtration, and airtight packing. It results in unrefined virgin oils without addition of any of the chemicals common in industrial manufacturing. Such artisan result in integral virgin oils that carry the essential elements of the grain. In this agroindustry, farmers' traditional knowledge on manufacturing of food products interacted with external knowledge for making these new products. Biorga Cooperative mobilized a wide range of social networks and alliances to be able to obtain the required knowledge to develop these new food products Members sought information about organic production of grains and other inputs in courses developed by the NGO Terra Nova Mondai/SC, with the intermediation of the Lutheran Church, a major institutional actor in supporting this initiative. Encouragement for the production of novelties came also from the Support Center for Small Farmers (CAPA), the Rural Extension and Technical Advisory Agency (EMATER/RS), Erval Seco Municipal Department of Agriculture, Ecirtek, the company that supplied equipment, and Ecovida Agroecology Network, with which Biorga is also associated (Table 3).

Agro-industry Ludke has also introduced new products, which are considered productive novelties (Table 3). This agro-industry produces cheeses that are typical of the region as those seasoned with salamis, oregano (a medicinal aromatic herb), and bell peppers. The family changed one of the crucial stages of the maturing process of the so-called "colonial cheeses" that are traditionally produced in RS.

The change consisted of adding condiments and herbs to the curd together with the salt before the molding stage, and leaving it at rest for few days (maturation process of the cheese) to allow ingredients to interact. For each flavor of cheese, different ingredients are added to the curd, resulting in the distinctive seasoned "colonial cheeses" produced by the Ludke family. This provides exclusive food products that are distinct in taste, flavor, and palatability.

The basis for the production of these cheeses was the family's traditional knowledge on the technology for manufacturing colonial cheeses (Stuiver, 2008). This knowledge interacted with that of the other social actors and institutions that supported the agro-industry. A family member, Mrs. Ludke, attended a course at the Farmer's Training Centre of EMATER associated with the Family Agro-industry Program (PAF/RS), in the city of Montenegro/RS, where she learned techniques for producing seasoned cheeses. These two kinds of knowledge were integrated, being locally recontextualized and producing the novelties, as already demonstrated by studies in this area (Brunori et al., 2009; Milone, 2009; van der Ploeg et al., 2004).

As to the main characteristics of the productive novelties developed by small scale on-farm processing, they stem from the recontextualization of knowledge of both farmers and other social actors and institutions. The productive novelties emerge from ecological/organic/agroecological processes for food production and manufacturing. Furthermore, they are based on artisanal processes, as opposed to industrial ones that use preservatives and other chemical additives. The farmers' ingenuity is a central element for the generation of differentiated and specific products (Table 3).

NEW SOCIAL ORGANIZATIONS AND NESTED MARKETS

In addition to the generation of novelties, such as new products and specific changes in production processes, the small scale on-farm processing phenomenon also produces two other kinds of novelties. On the one hand, the initiatives succeed in building new marketing channels and new markets, which are seen as marketing novelties. On the other hand, they also make room for the creation of new collective and networking social organizations such as, RECOSOL, a case discussed in this section as an organizational novelty arising from family on-farm processing.

The markets created by family on-farm processing bear the characteristics portrayed by the concept of *nested markets* as described by van der Ploeg, Schneider, and Ye (2012; see also van der Ploeg, Ye, & Schneider, 2015). Nested markets are grounded on social relations among actors who exchange food and products. These relations are historically constituted with a basis on mutual recognition (consumers recognize the distinctive features of the food products and farmers recognize those who purchase their products). The negotiated food products have qualitative specificities such as being organic, stemming from agroecological cultivation and artisanal processes, being consistent with fair trade principles, etc. These specificities endow them with attributes that define their quality on the basis of distinction and social recognition. The resources applied by farmers in the constitution of nested markets come from common resources mobilized by families either on their own or on their associations and cooperatives. Therefore, we may claim that the nested markets are locally and territorially embedded, in what represents a major element providing for its own reproduction and maintenance.

One of the outstanding characteristics of nested markets is that they create reciprocity and interknown relations among participants, either between producers and consumers (between supply and demand) or among the producers themselves. Such relations end up entailing the formation of social networks that help these nested markets to expand their scope and occupy new spaces, a crucial factor for them to scale-up. Another relevant aspect of such relations is related to price formation. In nested markets, prices are not a direct result or expression of production costs, related expenses and depreciations added to expected return rates. Price formation here also takes into account attributes embedded in existing relations of proximity between producers of the same product, who often are in contact with each other or seek information on prices. It is a resource for an equalization of prices that reflects less the relationship between demand and supply than the interknowing relations among producers. This is also reflected in the status of food products sold, which are more valued for their known origin or the trust in the producer and less for its price. Similarly, nested markets present a coevolution both in time and space and are susceptible to trade (of goods, services, resources, social networks, etc.) showing some degree of flexibility and innovation that distinguishes them from "market niches" (Milone & Ventura, 2014; van der Ploeg, 2014). Some of these characteristics of nested markets are clearly identified in the family on-farm processing cases, presented here.

The new nested markets[7] comprised/supported by family on-farm processing can be seen in Table 4, which shows both the marketing channels built by the two studied initiatives and their respective situation with regard to food regulatory institutions. Both are formally registered with food

Table 4. The New Marketing Channels Built by On-Farm Processing at Biorga and Ludke and Their Respective Institutional Situations.

Agro-Industry	Situation Regarding Food Regulation	Types of Marketing Channels
Biorga	Formal: Certification Ecovida, CNPJ, Regional Health Department (MS), and FEPAM (environmental regulation).	Long chains (supermarkets in SP and RJ), RECOSOL kiosks (Erval Seco and Frederico Westphalen), local supermarkets, on-farm sales, municipal and local fairs, Fair of Palm Heart Producers (SC), institutional markets (Food Procurement Program – FPP), CORAC (FPP) and FPP purchases for provision (National Company of Food Supplies – CONAB), cooperatives COOLMÉIA and COOPERBIORGA.
Ludke	Formal: Municipal Inspection Service (Serviço Municipal de Inspeção – SIM)	Family farming fairs (Porto Alegre, Distrito Federal, Rio de Janeiro, and some regional ones), on-farm sales, RECOSOL kiosks, supermarkets, direct sales at consumers' homes and workplaces, restaurants and canteens, other fairs, institutional markets (PAA), COOPERAC.

Source: Gazolla (2012).

regulatory agencies. Biorga is registered with the National Register of Legal Entities (CNPJ), the Regional Department of Health (MS), and the State Foundation of Environmental Protection (FEPAM), besides holding a "participatory certificate" from the Agroecology Network Ecovida. The second agro-industry (Ludke) holds a license from the Municipal Food Inspection Service (SIM) and can sell food products only in the municipal area of Constantina. This restricts both its socioeconomic viability and its integration into larger markets.

The second noteworthy aspect observed in Table 4 is the wide diversity of marketing channels used by the small scale on-farm processor. These built nested markets most often depend on the family's history, local context, type of product manufactured, regulatory norms on food products, personal relationships, knowledge, among other aspects. This strategy of market diversification provides farmers with the necessary autonomy in transactions, since, if some markets do not operate properly, they can focus on others, thus avoiding crises, deception, or other unexpected events. This is what happens, for instance, in fairs and with on-farm sales. These sales are seasonal, occurring only in some periods of the year, and farmers cannot rely exclusively on these channels to survive, because their sales are uneven and uncertain.

We organized the analysis of these marketing channels into groups, so that they could be described according to their key characteristics and dynamics. The channels were grouped into six similar sets, which are: (a) institutional markets (NSFP and FPP); (b) short chains or direct sales from farmers to consumers (farmers markets, work/home delivery, on-farm sales); (c) marketing events (family farming fairs, festivals, and expo fairs); (d) long chains (sales to supermarkets, wholesalers, and distant middlemen); (e) formal outlets (supermarkets, "*bodegas*" (grocers' stores), restaurants, bars, and canteens); and (f) new marketing channels of collective and networking social organizations (cooperatives, RECOSOL, kiosks, farmers' associations).

These different marketing channels can be understood as kinds of nested markets fostered by the small scale on-farm processing ventures, as is shown in Fig. 2, which is based on the CAAF[8] survey (Pelegrini & Gazolla, 2006). The first set of marketing channels is comprised of institutional markets which, in 2006, accounted for 4.7% of the sales from on-farm processing activity (Fig. 2). The institutional channels are those in which family farm products are purchased by the State for supplying social programs. The programs created by the Brazilian State are FPP and NSFP. These markets are characterized especially by approaching and reconnecting farmers and local consumers, enabling family incomes to rise, allowing diversification of production, and institutional strengthening of on-farm processing. A major problem identified in this channel was that informal on-farm processing cannot access such markets because of existing food regulatory requirements.

The short chain or farmer–consumer direct sales comprise the main nested markets built by on-farm processing, accounting for 51% of total sales (Fig. 2). The main features of these chains are: direct relationships between farmers and local consumers, autonomy of the social actors involved in transactions (contracts, pricing, negotiation possibilities/flexibilities), facilitation of exchanges due to social and geographical proximity, established social relationships and mutual knowledge among actors (Wilkinson, 2008). The high institutional informality of on-farm processing is the main explanation for the dynamics of these markets of social proximity (Gazolla & Pelegrini, 2011).

Such marketing channels operate based on prices and the "highest qualities" assigned to products in the perception of consumers. Prices in these markets are usually lower than those in traditional outlets like supermarkets and grocery stores, which works as an appeal to consumers.

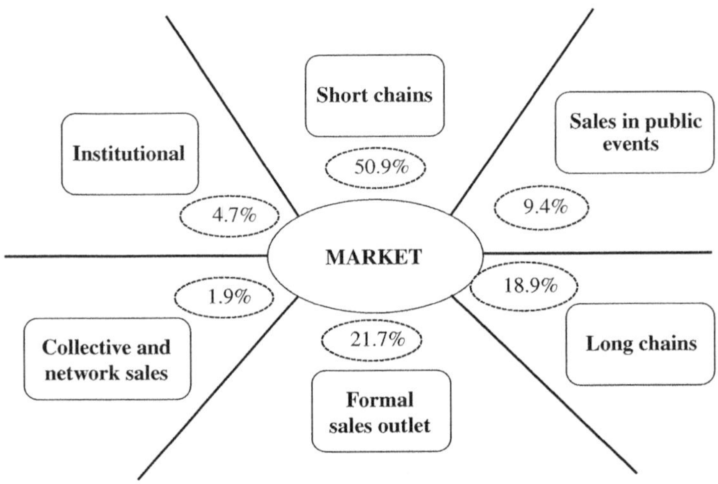

Fig. 2. Market Channels Built by Family On-Farm Processing and Respective Percentages of Sales. *Source*: CAAF Survey (Pelegrini & Gazolla, 2006) and fieldwork (2011). *Note*: The collective and network were considered within the percentages that CAFF Survey named "other markets."

These prices are also negotiable, rather than set a priori by farmers, insofar as the transacting agents already know each other (Brunori et al., 2009). Moreover, consumers see these food products as having "higher qualities" and assign them attributes such as "natural," "without preservatives," "organic," "nutritive," "ecological," "fair trade," among others (Brunori, Rossi, & Malandrin, 2011). Such special qualities of food items produced by on-farm processing activities comprise an appreciable dimension in the creation of nested markets, since all these products bear some degree of productive specificities and are differentiated (van der Ploeg et al., 2010).

Sales at events like farm expositions are also characterized by the proximity and connectivity between farmers and consumers in transactions, although sometimes it occurs far from the farm base (Fig. 2). These channels are comprised of sales at fairs, events, festivals, and exhibitions. Although some sales are made through these channels, their main characteristic is advertising the products by means of tastings, attractive food displays, and conversation with the visiting public. Such marketing channels account for 9.4% of total sales. They are also distinguished for comprising both formal and informal channels, a mixed situation with respect to food regulatory requirements.

On-farm processing also accesses long chains (Fig. 2). Through these channels, the products reach long distance markets, being transported from the area of production to markets and consumers located in other cities or states. In this case, the food products will supply supermarket chains, jobbers, wholesalers, and industries that resell and redistribute this produce. The long chains represent 19% of sales, being relevant from the point of view of social reproduction of on-farm processing, as they account for almost one-fifth of the volume of production. Among the main characteristics of these channels that is worth highlighting is the long distances traveled by food products, the high economic and environmental costs of these trips (food miles), the dominance of big agribusiness players, and the restricted autonomy of farmers (in setting contract conditions, prices, and dynamics of these chains) (Pretty, Ball, Lang, & Morison, 2005).

Such research findings ratify the conclusions of Marsden and Sonnino (2006) that alternative agri-food networks develop interfaces with the conventional agri-food system so that there is no clear-cut distinction between them. This fact reveals the potentiality of these initiatives and channels in that, under favorable conditions, they can expand their room for maneuver and broaden their scope. Therefore, apart from the competition, we perceive an imbrication of these processes, which involves the coexistence of conventional marketing channels and alternative networks.

The formal marketing outlets are local supermarkets, bars, "bodegas" (grocery shops), restaurants, and canteens (Fig. 2). Many of them are restricted to informal enterprises due to hygiene and sanitary certification requirements. These channels account for a significant part of the on-farm processing sales (21.7%), being second only to short chains as the largest marketing channel. These channels are characterized by the demand for a regular supply of food products throughout the year, for quality standards, transportation, and placement of products on supermarket shelves, as well as, in some cases, fees charged to farmers for the shelving units in supermarkets.

The sixth type of marketing channel used by family on-farm processors is comprised of networks and other collective arrangements, and is represented here by the experience of RECOSOL as illustrated in Fig. 3. RECOSOL can be defined as a solidarity network set up by the on-farm processors, which aims to promote associative culture and the social organization of the enterprises, cooperatives, and associations, as well as to consolidate new marketing channels by means of networks and collective efforts. RECOSOL develops nested markets that are comprised of

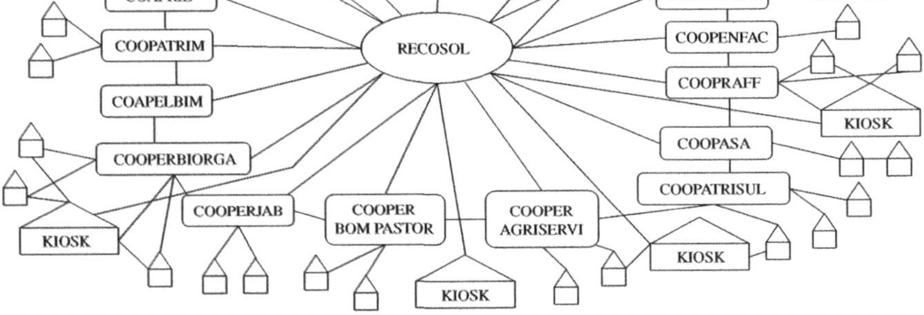

Fig. 3. Social Organization of the Network of Family On-farm Processing Cooperatives (RECOSOL). *Source*: Gazolla (2012).

cooperatives, associations, farmers markets, kiosks for selling the products from on-farm processing activities, formal groups of farmers, among others. In 2006, previous to the creation of RECOSOL in 2007, these channels accounted for 1.9% of the total annual sales of small scale on-farm processing. Current figures are believed to be much higher in view of the large number of social organizations associated with RECOSOL, although data have not been updated since then.

As can be observed from Fig. 3, RECOSOL represents about 70 family on-farm processing activities involving diverse production chains. As to the number of participant cooperatives and associations, by the time of the 2011 survey, there were 17. All of them were related to agriculture and family on-farm processing, and were distributed within a range of 34 municipalities. The spatial distribution matches that set by the territorial policies of the MDA, which granted many of these organizations and enterprises with public resources. Six kiosks and one farmer's market complement the territorial network of collective sales. Both the studied cases of on-farm processors participate in the social organization of RECOSOL and sell their products through the social network.

The small scale on-farm processors, which comprise the nucleus of the network, form the basis of RECOSOL (Fig. 3). These on-farm processing units are connected to regional cooperatives or associations involving family farming and/or on-farm processing. Such cooperatives and associations, in turn, are the link between individual or collective initiatives and RECOSOL. In addition, kiosks and a farmers market complement this regional structure, by constituting sales outlets gradually established by RECOSOL and that are located in strategic high pedestrian traffic places, such as downtown zones, areas near to bus stations or public squares, and on the side of roads where other kiosks are usually found.

Both single and collective on-farm processors can freely sell their food products through the previously described marketing channels, and the cooperatives, and other means which RECOSOL makes available to them. Cooperatives count on supermarkets and other sales outlets where the on-farm processors place their products. The cooperatives also sell other products that do not come from on-farm processing, since it has to meet the interests of all its associate members. Kiosks and farmers markets offer a commercial structure scattered over the territory and are a further option for on-farm processing to sell their produce. Such kiosks usually serve a region, comprising several municipalities, and exchange food products among all localities within the region, since each of them produces certain kinds of food products and not others. The exchange of food products among social organizations allows communities in the region to access the whole range of existing products and helps to increase sales from small scale on-farm processing.

The formation of RECOSOL can be understood as a novel entity, in view of the creativity of social actors and organizations that constitute it. The collective and network arrangement is a typical characteristic of both organizational novelties and nested markets. Another specificity of RECOSOL is that it was the first solidarity network in the State of Rio Grande do Sul to focus on marketing the produce of family on-farm processing, thus revealing the pioneer and inventive/innovative character of the experience.[9] The new market spaces created by RECOSOL also represent a novelty, because they provide small scale on-farm processors with a wide range of unprecedented marketing channels for selling their produce.

The new market spaces built by RECOSOL represent the major novelty created, that is, the social construction of marketing channels and also of a new form of collective and networking social organization, developed by social actors in recent years in the research region. RECOSOL reflects the effort of farmers and their organizations to build nested markets. In sum, this effort is directed toward three purposes: (a) to increase production and sales by acting collectively, so that to survive in a context of adversities, food crises, and an increasingly globalized economy; (b) to reduce transaction and production costs, by sharing these costs among the various on-farm processing units and social organizations (e.g., a single brand, label, registration, barcode, team of technicians, etc.); (c) to gain political strength for bargaining with the State for appropriate resources related to public policies and agri-food legislation.

SOME FINAL REMARKS

Among the main outcomes that can be pointed out from the analysis of the trajectory of the two small scale on-farm processors, it is worth noting that the novelties generated – either productive, organizational, or related to marketing channels – contribute to the propagation of continuous transitions in the established socio-technical food regime, transitions that can be described according to four main directions:

(a) the first transition refers to the production of food products that carry some specificities (artisanal, "colonial" features, typical, agroecological, ethnic, etc.), which distinguishes them from highly industrialized products. The transitions take place when these foods with specific qualities and values compete in the market with the food products of the established economic and technical food regime;

(b) the second source of transition is related to the new marketing channels created by farmers, as in the case of local outlets, short chains, and collective markets that are alternative to the long chains, which comprise supermarkets, wholesalers, middlemen, and the conventional sales outlets for food products;

(c) other transitions are in connection to newly emerging organizations such as RECOSOL and its member associations and cooperatives. These new organizations become spaces where new practices, organizational processes, routines, rules, and norms can be conceived, which will gradually change the institutional environment in which they are embedded;

(d) a fourth example of a relevant transition is the existing governmental programs, at federal and State levels, created as a result of the emergence of on-farm processing. In this respect, it is worth mentioning the National Program for Strengthening Family Farming (PRONAF – Agroindústria) and the Program for Family Agro-industry (PAF/RS) of the State government of Rio Grande do Sul, as two examples. The creation of these programs suggests a transition in the traditional regime, since a possibility (a window of opportunity) was opened to the small scale on-farm processor for influencing such regimes, albeit to a still limited degree.

In addition to these transitions introduced in the socio-technical food regime, other effects of the novelties were observed during the field research, especially regarding the family situation and agro-manufacturing activities: (i) a relative rise in family autonomy in relation to other social actors, institutions, and markets in which the on-farm processors are embedded; (ii) improvement in both the income level and the quality of life of household members; (iii) creation of new nested markets and marketing channels, such as RECOSOL, and the set-up of short chains; (iv) development of more environmentally sustainable products, such as the organic food of Agroindustry Biorga; (v) value added food products as a result of their innovation and differentiation; (vi) development of new interfaces between families and other social actors, institutions, and organizations, especially with regard to the processes of co-construction of the knowledge required to generate novelties and nested markets.

NOTES

1. The position paper presented in November 2012 in China is shown in Chapter 2 of this book.

2. Wilkinson, Durigon, & Mior (2012) adopt the concept of "small and medium-sized agro-industries" for describing what herein we call "small scale on-farm processing." The article by Wilkinson, Mior, and Dorigon deals with the context of formation of these small enterprises in the Western region of Santa Catarina State, a region that shows many characteristics similar to those described in the present work.

3. Empirical data used here are drawn from Marcio Gazolla's doctoral thesis presented in 2012 to the Graduate Program of Rural Development, Federal University of Rio Grande do Sul (PGDR/UFRGS). We also made use of data drawn from a CAAF survey (Pelegrini & Gazolla, 2006) that researched 106 family agro-industries as well as of secondary data from the 2006 Agricultural Census conducted by Instituto Brasileiro de Geografia e Estatística (IBGE, 2006).

4. The term *colônia* (colony) does not refer to a region that is colonized by another country and/or people, as we usually understand it. The term is referred to the notion of colonization in the sense that outsider immigrants enter into a new area of land to start up economic activities. In the case of RS, the "new" colonies of the Northern region descend from the "old" ones, as the first European immigrant colonies such as Serra Gaucha (the Mountain Region) (Italian colony) and São Leopoldo (German colony) are called. See Schneider (1999) for further elaboration on this topic.

5. The information on the two cases study described in this section were taken from the PhD thesis made by Gazolla (2012) to which the reader is recommended for further details.

6. The socio-technical regime is understood to be set of norms and regulations governing the production, distribution, marketing, and consumption of food. The current socio-technical food regime is characterized by standardization of food products, monopoly of big retail and production chains, mergers and acquisitions of large firms, predominance of long chains, growing industrialization of food, nutritionally unbalanced diets, centralization of agribusiness capital and, occasionally, by severe economic crises and food related illnesses (see, e.g., Roep & Wiskerke, 2004; Moors, Rip, & Wiskerke, 2004).

7. According to van der Ploeg et al. (2010) and Hebink, Schneider and Ploeg (2014), the *nested markets* are defined as real places where concrete transactions occur, involving producers, consumers, and reference frameworks that help to understand the emergence of new markets.

8. CAAF – acronym for *Caracterização e Análise das Agroindústrias Familiares* – a survey project for characterization and analysis of family agro industries.

9. The formation of RECOSOL was inspired by the Support Center for Rural Family Agro-industries of Santa Catarina West Region (Unidade Central de Apoio às Agroindústrias Familiares Rurais do Oeste Catarinense – UCAF), which is similarly organized, although much stronger and more advanced in terms of length of existence, resources, and structure for providing support to farmers. For further

details, see: http://www.ucaf.org.br/Site/index.html. This experience (of UCAF) is also analyzed by Wilkinson, Durigon, and Mior (2011).

REFERENCES

Amin, A., & Cohendet, P. (2004). *Architectures of knowledge: Firms, capabilities, and communities*. New York, NY: Oxford.

Brunori, G., Rand, S., Proost, J., Barjolle, D., Granberg, L., & Dockes, A. C. (2009). *Towards a conceptual framework for agricultural and rural innovation policies*. Insight Project, 27pp.

Brunori, G., Rossi, A., & Malandrin, V. (2011). Co-producing transition: Innovation processes in farms adhering solidarity-based purchase groups (GAS) in Tuscany, Italy. *International Journal of Sociology of Agriculture and Food, 18*(1), 28–53.

Cetina, K. K. (2005). *La Fabricación del conocimiento. Un ensayo sobre el carácter constructivista y contextual de la ciencia*. Argentina: Universidad Nacional de Quilmes.

Gaglio, G. (2011). *Sociologie de l'Innovation*. Paris: PUF.

Gazolla, M. (2012). *Conhecimentos, produção de novidades e ações institucionais: cadeias curtas das agroindústrias familiares*. Porto Alegre, Tese (Doutorado em Desenvolvimento Rural). Programa de Pós-Graduação em Desenvolvimento Rural, UFRGS, 302f.

Gazolla, M., Niederle, P., & Waquil, P. (2012). Agregação de valor nas agroindústrias rurais: uma análise com base nos dados do Censo Agropecuário. *Revista Paranaense de Desenvolvimento*, (122), 241–262.

Gazolla, M., & Pelegrini, G. (2011). Novos mercados da agricultura familiar: o caso das pequenas unidades agroindustriais produtoras de alimentos. In S. Schneider & M. Gazolla (Eds.), *Os atores do desenvolvimento rural: perspectivas teóricas e práticas sociais* (pp. 133–150). Porto Alegre: Editora da UFRGS.

Geels, F. W. (2004). Understanding system innovations: A critical literature review and a conceptual synthesis. In B. Elzen, F. W. Geels, & K. Green (Eds.), *System innovation and the transition to sustainability: Theory, evidence and policy*. Cheltenham, UK: Edward Elgar.

Hebinck, P. (2001). Maize and socio-technical regimes. In P. Hebinck & G. Verschor (Eds.), *Resonances and dissonances in development* (pp. 119–138). Assen: Royal Van Gorcum.

Hebinck, P., Schneider, S., & Van der Ploeg, J. D. (2014). *Rural development and the construction of new markets* (1st ed., p. 212). London: Routledge.

IBGE. (2006). Instituto Brasileiro de Geografia e Estatística. Censo Agropecuário.

Knickel, K., Brunori, G., Rand, S., & Proost, J. (2008). *Towards a better conceptual framework for innovation processes in agriculture and rural development*. 8th European IFSA symposium, Clermont-Ferrand, France, July 6–10, 11pp.

Long, N. (2001). *Development sociology: Actor perspectives* (1st ed., 285pp.). London: Routledge.

Long, N. (2007). *Sociologia del Desarollo: una perspectiva centrada en el actor* (1st ed., 504 pp.). México: Colección Investigaciones.

Long, N., & van der Ploeg, J. D. (1994). Heterogeneity, actor and structure: Towards a reconstitution of the concept of structure. In D. Booth (Ed.), *Rethinking social development: Theory, research and practice*. Harlow: Longman.

Marques, F. C. (2009). Velhos conhecimentos, novos desenvolvimentos: transições no regime sociotécnico da agricultura. A produção de novidades entre agricultores produtores de plantas medicinais no Sul do Brasil. (Tese de Doutorado). Programa de Pós-Graduação em Desenvolvimento Rural, UFRGS, Porto Alegre, 220f.

Marsden, T., & Sonnino, R. (2006). Beyond the divide: Rethinking relationships between alternative and conventional food networks in Europe. *Journal of Economic Geography*, *6*, 181–199.

Milone, P. (2009). *Agriculture in transition: A neo-institutional analysis* (1st ed., 256pp.). Assen: Van Gorgum.

Milone, P., & Ventura, F. (2014). The visible hand in building new markets for rural economies. In P. Hebinck, S. Schneider, & J. D. van der Ploeg (Eds.), *Rural development and the construction of new markets*. London: Routledge.

Moors, E., Rip, A., & Wiskerke, J. S. C. (2004). The dynamics of innovation: A multi-level coevolutionary perspective. In J. S. C. Wiskerke & J. D. van der Ploeg (Eds.), *Seeds of transition* (pp. 31–56). Assen: Van Gorcun.

Moors, E., & Wiskerke, J. S. C. (2004). The dynamics of innovation: A multilevel coevolutionary perspective. In J. S. C. Wiskerke & J. D. van der Ploeg (Eds.), *Seeds of transition: Essays on novelty production, niches and regimes in agriculture* (356pp.). Assen: Royal Van Gorcum.

Oliveira, D., Gazolla, M., & Schneider, S. (2011). Produzindo novidades na agricultura familiar: agregação de valor e agroecologia para o desenvolvimento rural. *Cadernos de Ciência & Tecnologia*, *28*(1), 17–49.

Oostindie, H., & van Broekhuozen, R. (2008). The dynamic of novelty production. In J. D. van der Ploeg & T. Marsden (Eds.), *Unfolding webs: The dynamics of regional rural development* (262pp.). Assen: Van Gorgum.

Pelegrini, G., & Gazolla, M. (2006). Caracterização e análise das agroindústrias familiares da Região do Médio Alto Uruguai (CAAF). Projeto de pesquisa. Edital FAPERGS 001/2005 – PROCOREDES, Frederico Westphalen, 10pp.

Piraux, M., & Bonnal, P. (2011). Ações públicas territoriais e inovações sociais e institucionais. O caso do território da Borborema e da Articulação do Semiárido. *Revista Estudos Sociedade e Agricultura*, *19*(1), 62–88.

Pretty, J. N., Ball, A. S., Lang, T., & Morison, J. I. L. (2005). Farm costs and food miles: An assessment of the full cost UK weekly food basket. *Food Policy*, 30, 1–19.

Radomsky, G. F. W. (2011). Certificação participativa e agricultura ecológica: rede, processos de inovação e conhecimentos locais. In S. Schneider & M. Gazolla (Eds.), *Os atores do desenvolvimento rural: perspectivas teóricas e práticas sociais* (pp. 235–251). Porto Alegre: Editora da UFRGS.

Roep, D., & Wiskerke, J. S. C. (2004). Reflecting on novelty production and niches management in agriculture. In J. S. C. Wiskerke & J. D. van der Ploeg (Eds.), *Seeds of transition: Essays on novelty production, niches and regimes in agriculture* (356pp.). Assen: Royal Van Gorcum.

Rossi, A., Brunori, G., & Guidi, F. (2008). I mercati contadini: un' esperienza di innovazione di fronte ai dilemma dela crescita. *Rivista di Diritto Alimentare*, Anno II, n°3, Luglio-Settembre.

Rotmans, J., Kemp, R., & van Asselt, M. (2001). More evolution than revolution: Transition management in public policy. *The Journal of Futures Studies, Strategic Thinking and Policy*, *3*(1), 1–17.

Schneider, S. (1999). *Agricultura familiar e industrialização: pluriatividade e descentralização industrial no Rio Grande do Sul* (205pp.). Porto Alegre: Editora da UFRGS. Série Estudos Rurais.

Schneider, S., Menezes, M. A., da Silva, A. G., & Bezerra, I. (2014). *Sementes e Brotos da Transição* (1st ed., p. 240). Porto Alegre: UFRGS Publisher.

Schneider, S., & Niederle, P. A. (2010). Resistance strategies and diversification of rural livelihoods: The construction of autonomy among Brazilian family farmers. *Journal of Peasant Studies*, *37*(2), 379–405.

Stuiver, M. (2008). *Regime, change and storylines: A sociological analysis of manure practices in contemporary Dutch farming* (175pp.). Wageningen University.

Stuiver, M., & Wiskerke, J. S. C. (2004). The VEL and VANLA environmental co-operatives as a niche for sustainable development. In J. S. C. Wiskerke & J. D. van der Ploeg (Eds.), *Seeds of transition: Essays on novelty production, niches and regimes in agriculture* (pp. 119–148). Assen: Van Gorcum.

van der Ploeg, J. D. (2003a). The virtual farmer: Past, present and future of the Dutch peasantry (1st ed., 432pp.). Assen: Van Gorcum.

van der Ploeg, J. D. (2003b). Structure and agency. In D. A. Clark (Ed.), *The Elgar companion to development studies*. London: Edward Elgar.

van der Ploeg, J. D. (2008). *Camponeses e impérios alimentares: lutas por autonomia e sustentabilidade na era da globalização*. Porto Alegre: Editora da UFRGS.

van der Ploeg, J. D. (2014). Newly emerging, nested markets: A theoretical introduction. In P. Hebinck, S. Schneider, & J. D. van der Ploeg (Eds.), *Rural development and the construction of new markets*. London: Routledge.

van der Ploeg, J. D., Bouma, J., Rip, A., Rijkenberg, F. H. J., Ventura, F., & Wiskerke, J. S. C. (2004). On regimes, novelties, niches and co-production. In J. S. C. Wiskerke & J. D. van der Ploeg (Eds.), *Seeds of transition: Essays on novelty production, niches and regimes in agriculture* (pp. 1–28). Assen: Royal Van Gorcum.

van der Ploeg, J. D., Renting, H., Brunori, G., Knickel, K., Mannion, J., Marsden, T., … Ventura, F. (2000). Rural development: From practices and policies towards theory. *Sociologia Ruralis*, *40*(4), 391–408.

van der Ploeg, J. D., Schneider, S., & Ye, J. (2012). Rural development through the construction of new, nested markets: Comparative perspectives from China, Brazil and the European Union. *Journal of Peasant Studies*, *39*(1), 133–173.

van der Ploeg, J. D., Ye, J., & Schneider, S. (2010). Rural development reconsidered: On comparative perspectives from China, Brazil and the European Union. *Rivista di Economia Agraria*, *65*(2), 1–28.

van der Ploeg, J. D., Ye, J., & Schneider, S. (2015). Rural development: Actors and practices. In P. Milone, F. Ventura, & J. Ye (Eds.), *Constructing a new framework for rural development* (Vol. 22). Research in Rural Sociology and Development. Bingley, UK: Emerald Group Publishing Limited.

Wilkinson, J., Durigon, C., & Mior, L. C. (2011). The emergence of SME agro-industry networks in the shadow of agribusiness contract farming: A case study from the South of Brazil. In C. A. Silva & N. Mhlanga (Eds.), *Agribusiness economist innovative policies and institutions to support on-farm processing development* (pp. 87–118). Rome: FAO.

Wilkinson, J., Durigon, C., & Mior, L. C. (2012). The emergence of SME agro-industry networks in the shadow of agribusiness contract farming: A case study from the South of

Brazil. In C. A. Silva & N. Mhlanga (Eds.), *Agribusiness economist innovative policies and institutions to support on-farm processing development* (pp. 87–118). Rome: FAO.

Wilkinson, J. M. (2008). *redes e valores: o novo mundo da agricultura familiar* (p. 213). Porto Alegre: Editora da UFRGS.

Wiskerke, J. S. C. (2003). On promising and constraining sociotechnical regimes: The case of Dutch wheat and bread. *Environment and Planning*, *35*, 429–448.

Wiskerke, J. S. C. & van der Ploeg, J. D. (Eds.). (2004). *Seeds of transition: Essays on novelty production, niches and regimes in agriculture* (256pp.). Assen: Royal Van Gorcum.

CHAPTER 7

HIDDEN TREASURES: RECONNECTING CULTURE AND NATURE IN RURAL DEVELOPMENT DYNAMICS

Paulo F. Petersen

ABSTRACT

Fighting the drought. Based on this idea, for almost two centuries now the Brazilian State has elaborated policies and programmes intended to stimulate rural development in the semiarid region of the country. It is this idea which has nourished the illusion that immense infrastructures need to be built to capture, store and transport large volumes of water in order to supply production activities in the region. Associated with this proposal is the attempt to reproduce the same pattern of development adopted in other Brazilian biomes, the main characteristic of which is the use of monoculture practices on large properties managed according to entrepreneurial modes of production. However the rich social experience promoted by rural worker organizations in the region has challenged this model by proposing living with the semiarid (Convivência com o Semiárido) as the guiding principle for alternative trajectories of development. Inspired by the experience of territorial development under

Constructing a New Framework for Rural Development
Research in Rural Sociology and Development, Volume 22, 157–194

ISSN: 1057-1922/doi:10.1108/S1057-192220150000022006

way in the Agreste da Borborema region of Paraíba state, the chapter shows that the evolution of these new paths of development depends on revitalizing and mobilizing locally available resources, such as ecological potentials, social mechanisms for organizing labour and for producing and sharing knowledge, local forms of connecting food production to consumption and so on. The text concludes by emphasizing the need to design and implant institutional frameworks that enable a more balanced distribution of power between the State and civil society organizations, thereby allowing the latter to assume a more substantial role in identifying and managing endogenous resources that underpin self-centred development strategies.

Keywords: Rural development; agroecology; peasants innovation; Brazil agriculture; semi-arid region; new institutional arrangements

> The role of our unions is to discover the treasures hidden in our municipalities
>
> Zé Pequeno (family farmer from the Agreste region of Paraíba)

A HIDDEN TREASURE

Manoel Apolônio de Carvalho, better known as Nel, is a family farmer from Sergipe state in the Northeast of Brazil. His life trajectory is similar to those of tens of thousands of rural inhabitants from the Brazilian semi-arid region who 'tried their luck in the South', in most cases with the intention of eventually returning to their land of origin to pursue a living as farmers. This veritable saga of migration of Northeastern peasant farmers to the main dynamo of the Brazilian economy, the Southeast region, was beautifully described and analysed by Afrânio Garcia Jr. in his book '*O Sul: o caminho do roçado*' – '*The South: The Path of the Swidden*' (1990). Opposing the interpretations then in vogue, which associated this ceaseless migratory flow with the supposedly inevitable depopulation of the rural Northeast, Garcia Jr. perceived that *the return to the rural world, to the place of origin, could constitute the motive for leaving for the South* (*ibid.*, p. 13).

The *return to the swidden* was also the path taken by Nel after a brief period spent working as a bricklayer in São Paulo. During his time as a migrant, he learned to make pre-moulded slabs of cement for use in the construction of swimming pools, a technique that he later tested back home in the Northeast to build cisterns for storing rainwater. Since it resulted in a cheaper and more resistant final product than the traditional brick cisterns, the technique soon attracted the interest of his neighbours.[1] Nel was subsequently asked to build cisterns all across the region, opportunities that proved valuable in training of other farmer-bricklayers and in the gradual perfecting of his innovation.

For Nel, the social acceptance of slab cisterns was proof of his invention's success. However he could not know at the time that his intellectual enterprise of adapting a swimming pool construction technique, learnt by himself in the country's biggest and wealthiest city, to his home community would contribute, years later, to meeting a vital need of millions of people in the Brazilian semi-arid region. This impressive increase in scale was enabled by the implementation of the *One Million Rural Cisterns Programme* (P1MC),[2] an initiative conceived and executed by the Brazilian Semi-Arid Alliance (ASA),[3] a civil society network composed of more than 1,000 organizations active in the region's 11 states.[4]

As well as allowing widespread dissemination of equipment capable of storing water and maintaining its quality for human consumption during dry periods of the year,[5] P1MC reproduces at a larger scale some of the procedures adopted by Nel and his companions during the first phases of disseminating the novelty: (1) capacity building for local bricklayers so that the knowledge is independently put into practice and adapted by the communities; (2) by stimulating the practice of peasant reciprocity, community work is mobilized to perform manual activities, such as digging a hole in the soil to hold the cistern; and (3) the construction materials needed to make the cisterns (cement, sand, etc.) are purchased from local markets. The combined application of these three elements in the localities covered by the programme has afforded a series of positive effects that extend far beyond the direct (and more visible) impacts on the food security and health of rural families.

Analytically speaking, P1MC reproduces practices and perspectives consistent with the notion of *endogenous rural development*, a pattern of development founded on the activation and revitalization of resources locally available in rural territories (Long & van der Ploeg, 1994). These local resources span both ecological and socio-cultural potentialities, the latter including the capacities for local innovation needed for the constant adjustment of technical and socio-organizational systems to the contextual alterations that affect ways of life in the rural world.

OMNIPRESENT AND INVISIBLE

This succinct description of Nel's trajectory and his invention is presented here as an illustration of a reality that is at once commonplace as well as extraordinary in the rural world. Commonplace because farmers and their organizations do not simply remain passive in the face of realities that for them are very often oppressive. They are *social actors*: in other words, they possess *the capacity to process social experience and delineate forms of confronting life, even under the most extreme forms of coercion* (Long & van der Ploeg, 2011, p. 25). Although omnipresent in the universe of peasant life, this capacity for social agency is widely neglected and, thus, concealed by the paradigm of agricultural modernization that since the 1960s has dominated the public policy frameworks for rural development in Brazil (Petersen, 2013). In the wise and beautiful words of Zé Pequeno, the Paraiban farmer cited in the epigraphy, these actors are the *hidden treasures* of peasant farmer communities.

The extraordinary side of Nel's story is that he and his innovation emerge as *discovered treasures*, widely recognized and valued through a public programme conceived and executed by a civil society network with an extensive grassroots presence in Brazil's semi-arid region. Additionally, this programme was designed in a way that combined the two aspects of Nel's innovation: the slab cisterns (the hardware) and the social organization to construct the cisterns (the software).

The combined dissemination of hardware and software through P1MC distinguishes ASA's initiative from the current official interventions directed towards rural development. In this case the central distinction is that the software programming government initiatives obeys a linear model of innovation, according to which some actors assume the function of managing the innovations (the hardware), others are involved in transferring the innovations (or disseminating them) while the farmers themselves assume the role of receivers (or adopters). In this linear and top-down conception of innovation processes, the farmers are individually and collectively envisaged as passive recipients of the interventions of public programmes, thereby downplaying their own creative capacities to recombine locally accessible and controlled material and non-material resources in order to solve locally defined problems.

As well as exacerbating dependency on exogenous solutions, the imposition of diffusionist schemes by the rural development programmes atrophies the potential of the kind of social agency responsible for the emergence of slab cisterns and a myriad of other peasant farmer innovations that, unlike Nel's invention, remain hidden as treasures that could be revealed and incorporated into the dynamics of rural development.

Taking as its reference point the reality of Brazil's semi-arid region and, more particularly, the Agreste region of Paraíba state, this chapter examines the theme of peasant farmer innovation by seeking to relate it to the emergent dynamics of rural development observable in the region. By contrasting the *paradigm of combatting the drought* historically responsible for orientating government programmes and policies in the region with the *paradigm of living with the semi-arid*, which has become consolidated through the initiative of civil society organizations and networks linked to ASA, the text explores aspects related to institutional design[6] in the field of rural development, looking to show that the recognition and redynamization of the role of social actors at the territorial level emerges as a central challenge in moving beyond the paradigm of modernization.

THE BRAZILIAN SEMI-ARID REGION AND THE IMAGINARY OF THE DROUGHTS

In both territorial and demographic terms, the Brazilian semi-arid region is one of the largest of its kind on the planet. Covering a geographic area of 980,000 km^2, concentrated in states located in Brazil's Northeast, the region contains a population of 22.5 million inhabitants – 12% of the national population – with 44% living in rural areas, making it the least urbanized region of the country (IBGE, 2010) (Fig. 1). Containing more than half of the Brazilian population living in poverty (58%), this semi-arid region is still considered in some intellectual and political circles to be a *problem region.*

This kind of interpretation is grounded in a deterministic bias that associates, as two sides of the same coin, the low social indicators with the recurrent droughts typical of semi-arid conditions. The narratives produced as a result of this bias have imposed themselves on the national collective and political imaginary, creating an environment that tacitly accepts the supposed historical destiny of the region to be poor and *backward* relative to Brazil's other regions. Just as this discursive recourse to geographic determinism (or divine will) has the power to induce passivity in face of a theoretically pre-ordained fate, it also functions as a powerful ideological lever for legitimizing public interventions informed by the notion of *combatting the drought.*

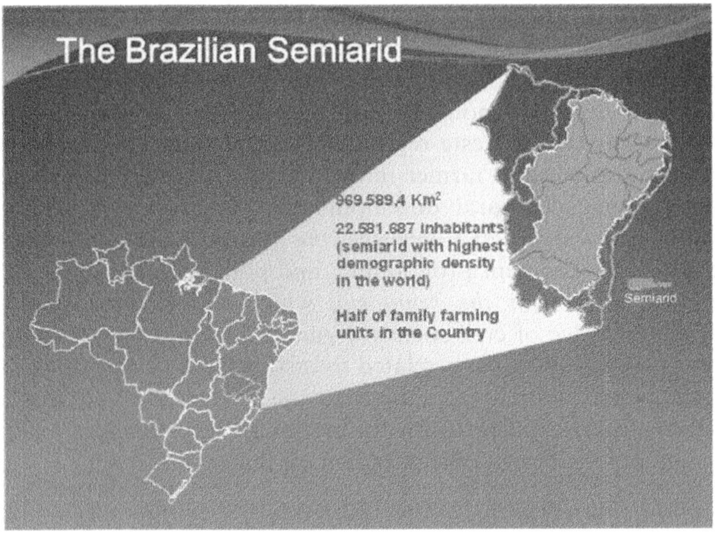

Fig. 1. The Brazilian Semi-Arid Region. *Source*: AS-PTA (www.aspta.org.br).

The government initiatives framed by this conception can be traced back to Brazil's imperial period in the nineteenth century. Since the Old Republic at the start of the twentieth century, these initiatives have been orchestrated by the National Department of Works to Combat Drought (DNOCS), an entity today linked to the Ministry of National Integration. The very name of the institution leaves no room for doubt that the official strategy for fighting droughts is founded essentially on the implementation of hydraulic works designed to capture, store and transport huge volumes of water. As well as concentrating water resources in just a few localities, thereby failing to meet the demands of rural communities for geographically diffuse and functionally diverse sources of water, the so-called *hydraulic solution* consolidates old systems of power dominated by the agrarian oligarchies. This is because the water sources are frequently located on large farm estates, thereby reinforcing the high concentration of land ownership in the region, a characteristic common to rural Brazil whose roots extend back to the very beginning of European colonization. This double concentration of environmental assets decisive to the economic and social life of the rural world makes the poorer populations of the semi-arid region highly vulnerable to the unpredictability of the climate, thereby entrenching the unequal social structures seen in the region.

An examination of this structural setting reveals that, although the natural and social worlds are closely interconnected and to an extent coproduced in the semi-arid region, they possess distinct causalities, a fact that challenges the rhetoric used to justify extreme poverty, as well as continuation of the so-called *drought industry*.[7]

FULL OF OPPORTUNITIES, RICH IN LIFE[8]

Contradicting the fatalist perspectives cultivated by geographic determinism, peasant families and rural communities from the semi-arid region, over the generations, have been able to develop sophisticated and unique strategies for managing agroecosystems and organizing social life. Founded on what is today identified as the paradigm of *living with the semi-arid* (Conti & Pontel, 2013; da Silva, 2006; Galindo, 2013), these strategies have been shaped around building analogies between the technical reasoning that structures and organizes the functioning of agroecosystems and the ecology of natural ecosystems (Petersen et al., 2002). Within this dynamic of agriculture–nature coproduction, farmers have been induced to *exercise their creativity with the aim of improving and innovating their forms of management [...] based on living intimately with the unwritten codes of nature* (*ibid.*, p. 23).

Close conviviality with the environment is, indeed, the precondition for the ecological opportunities to be continually revealed in a natural environment which, at first sight, appears hostile to obtaining acceptable levels of social welfare (Box 1).

The socially constructed analogies only become visible when the practices of living with the unpredictable climate fluctuations are examined as a whole in a systemic approach. By developing patterns of occupying

Box 1. Seasonal Contrasts in the Semiarid Region. *Source*: Petersen et al. (2002).

Rapidly examined by the casual observer during the dry part of the year, the natural landscape of the semi-arid region may suggest conditions unsuited to any kind of productive activity. A more careful inquiry, however, one which contemplates the seasonally marked climate, will instead perceive the enormous biological production potential of the ecosystems. A veritable *resurrection* takes place in the surroundings with the arrival of the first rains after the dry season. In the sequence of more or less lengthy periods of biological latency, these rains stimulate the rapid mobilization and translocation of nutritional and energy reserves stored in special organs of plants, bringing vivid colours to the landscape in contrast to its washed out appearance during the dry spells.

agricultural space that form mosaics of biodiversity, farming families create ecological infrastructures analogous to those of natural ecosystems, thereby reproducing the environmental services essential to the continuous regeneration of the fertility of the agroecosystem. Consequently the practices of conviviality become spatially and temporally integrated, forming strategies for multiple and sustainable use of the resources of ecological capital (this aspect will be illustrated later with examples from the Agreste region of Paraíba).

THE EMERGENCE OF THE BRAZILIAN SEMI-ARID ALLIANCE

Although this movement of peasant innovation has been responsible for the development of an extensive array of technologies and processes for managing production and for social organization adapted to the particular conditions of the semi-arid region, this knowledge for a long time passed unnoticed and/or under-valued by public programmes focused on regional development.

Without doubt, the approach of combating drought plays a decisive role, at the intuitive level of public administrators and intellectuals, in concealing this empirical reality linked to active popular creativity in search of better adapted means and ways of life. Reinforcing this tendency, the implantation of the agricultural modernization project in Brazil accentuated the ideological load responsible for de-legitimizing the important role played by farmers and their organizations in producing and sharing knowledge on agricultural management of the natural world.[9]

It was only from the 1980s onwards and the gradual return to democracy in Brazil that civil society institutions became structured to provide systematic advice to peasant organizations, seeking to associate the critique of the historical pattern of the agricultural occupation and the conservative modernization project with the construction of alternative styles of rural development. Initially associated with the idea of *alternative agriculture*, these organizations soon recognized that new patterns of development would emerge *as the result of a social construction* rooted *in the huge range of productive practices and economic survival strategies expressed in the farmers' resistance to the modernizing policies, productive forces and markets that tend to expel them from the rural world* (Gomes de Almeida, 1991).

Today, identified with the Brazilian agroecological field, these civil organizations (basically NGOs) work in rural territories dispersed throughout the country. In the context of the semi-arid region, at the end of the 1990s, after almost two decades of activity, the organizations persuaded the federal government to implement the creation of the P1MC programme (followed later by the P1+2 programme), an initiative that provided the political and financial conditions for the constitution of the Brazilian Semi-Arid Alliance.[10]

By conceiving the promotion of water security in rural communities of the semi-arid region as a process of social mobilization, ASA created unique conditions for promoting the visibility and recognition of peasant innovation as the source and motor of autonomous dynamics focused on endogenous development in the region. In its founding document, ASA highlighted that *men and women from the region are entirely capable of taking their destiny into their own hands, overthrowing the structures of political, hydrological and agrarian domination.*[11] In a later public manifestation, the entity stated its belief *in the diversity of the experiences developed by farmers in Brazil's semi-arid region and its conviction that these experiences produce knowledge that, once inter-related with academically systemized knowledge, will be transformed into knowledge capable of driving forward the sustainable development of the semi-arid region.*[12]

Through these manifestations, ASA highlights its view of the role played by farmers and their organizations as actors in rural development – in other words, as agents propelling territorialized dynamics of technical and socio-organizational innovation that are strengthened by the support of its own public programmes directed towards the provision of infrastructures for supplying water to rural families and communities.

By working to promote social mobilization in this way, the ASA programmes function as *seeds* for creating the endogenous dynamics of rural development.[13] The conditions for the germination, development and maturation of these seeds in the different territories vary significantly according to the specific socio-ecological contexts involved, resulting in very different outcomes in terms of the dynamics of rural development. However these structural conditions did not emerge with the *Genesis*: rather they are social constructions directly related to the institutional configurations established in the specific context of the territories with the objective of strategically managing niches of socio-technical innovation.[14] The experience under way in the Agreste region of Paraíba state is presented here as an illustration of these endogenous dynamics of innovation, embedded in the valorization of the territorial specificities and based on the idea of living with the semi-arid.

PEASANT INNOVATION IN THE AGRESTE REGION OF PARAÍBA

Characterized by the dense presence of family farming, the Agreste region of Paraíba historically became established as the main food-supply region for Paraiban society. Situated between the coast occupied by sugar cane monocropping and the cattle ranching *sertão*,[15] (Fig. 2) the history

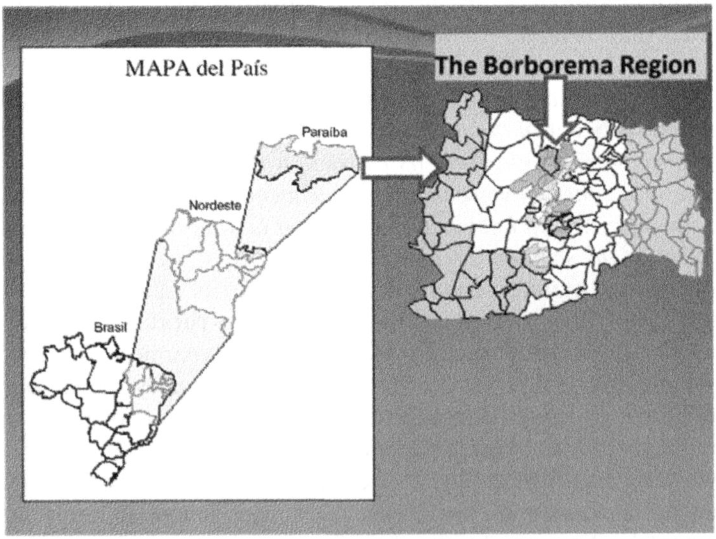

Fig. 2. The Borborema Region. *Source*: AS-PTA (www.aspta.org.br).

of the region's occupation was marked by cycles of repeasantization and depeasantization that alternated as a function of the equally cyclical interests of agrarian elites in occupying portions of the territory in response to the rise or decline in the scale production of agricultural products destined for the big markets (Silveira, Freire, & Diniz, 2010). Conditioned by the ebb and flow of the interests of rural businesses, these cyclical processes did not unfold historically without various forms of resistance being organized by local populations.[16] Though less visible, the forms of economic and technical organization of the systems of production, today understood to be an essential mechanism of peasant resistance and struggles (Scott, 1986; van der Ploeg, 2007), played a decisive role in sustaining the open struggles marking the social history of peasantry in the region (Moreira & Targino, 1997). In the interstices of the large properties and running counter to the dominant model of occupying large tracts of agrarian space for monoculture systems run according to an entrepreneurial logic, the peasant farmers developed economic strategies based on the diversification of food crops, sale to local markets and pluriactivity.

Because of the endless dispute over the possession of agricultural land with the large estate owners, as well as the constant fragmentation of family properties due to the intergenerational fragmenting processes of land inheritance, the physical space available to assure the social and economic reproduction of family farming became more and more restricted over the decades. As a result of the declining availability of land in the region, transformations took place in how the fertility of agroecosystems was managed, including the gradual reduction and eventually complete abandonment of the practice of slash and burn fallow vegetation, and the adoption of management strategies focused on agricultural intensification.

As Boserup (1981) showed, this pattern of technological transition was repeated in other regions of the world based on *triggering local innovation*,[17] a process of highly endogenous cultural production directed towards identifying, activating and dynamizing sources of ecological capital. In these transition processes, van der Ploeg (2008) identifies the peasant strategy of continuous development and improvement of the base of locally available and controlled resources.

In its studies of family farming agroecosystems in the region, AS-PTA[18] identified three basic principles that interconnect and lend strategic coherence to the practices of intensifying the use and management of agricultural lands (Petersen et al., 2002): (1) the maintenance of high functional biodiversity in agroecosystems; (2) the constitution and management of stocks of productive resources; and (3) the productive valorization of limited spaces of high biological productivity (Box 2).

Technically speaking, the practices connected by these principles converge towards the optimization and regulation of the ecological processes

Box 2. Principles of Strategy in the Multiple Uses of Resources of Ecological Capital by Peasant Farming in the Agreste Region of Paraíba. *Source*: Petersen et al. (2002).

(1) *Maintenance of high functional biodiversity in agroecosystems*: In the agroecosystems managed by family farmers, exotic and native plant species are combined in time and space through production practices deliberately designed to optimize the ecological–economic efficiency of the system. Through the occupation of different ecological niches, these species perform different functions in the agroecosystem (functional diversity), increasing its stability and productivity. The biomass produced is circulated in the agroecosystem using labour practices strategically defined to synchronize management operations and reinforce synergy and complementarity between the animal and vegetal subsystems.
(2) *Constitution and management of stocks of productive resources*: In order to reconcile the irregular and uncertain supply of rainwater in the region with the regular demands of farmers there is only one way: store water to stabilize supply. That's exactly what nature does since the native vegetation has developed biological–evolutionary mechanisms to reserve water, nutrients and energy in a form that traverses dry periods. Likewise the peasant farmer systems in the Paraiban Agreste combine a set of resource-storing practices (water, seeds, animal fodder, food, capital, etc.)
(3) *Productive valorization of limited spaces of high biological productivity*: The huge environmental diversity in the semi-arid region creates landscapes in the form of mosaics in which environments with striking differences in biological productivity are located side-by-side. Since water availability for plants is the critical factor in the region's ecosystems, this diversity is essentially determined by this ecological attribute. The lower areas of the landscape (the lowlands) are generally those in which water is available for most of the year since the soils are deeper and more

permeable, as well as receiving the water draining from the higher areas of the landscape. Through management practices, the farmers create areas of high biological productivity, such as domestic yards and reservoir shores. Despite their small territorial dimension, these areas play a decisive role in the economic strategies employed by family farming, whether in producing food for self-consumption or sale, or in producing animal feed.

that convert the basic abiotic resources of agroecosystems (water, solar radiation and nutrients) into biotic resources (plant and animal biomass) without the need for large quantities of external inputs that are chemical based, expensive and which generate dependency on markets. By integrating with each other, the management practices constitute a complex and organic whole, each of them assuming a multifunctional character insofar as they engender positive knock-on (systemic) effects on the ecological and economic functioning of agroecosystems. They are, therefore, coherent with the peasant perspective of *intensifying economic production without simplifying ecological reproduction* (Petersen et al., 2013).[19]

In a longitudinal study of the transformations in the technical management of agroecosystems in the Agreste region of Paraíba over a 70-year period, Sabourin (2002) identified and described the endogenous process of innovation rooted in socio-technical networks constituted by relations of interknowledge and proximity and by reciprocal aid in the production or redistribution of produce and knowledge. In his studies of the Brazilian rural world, the author also observed that the more peasant farmer communities are closed off and/or dominated and marginalized, the more isolated, discrete or even invisible innovation becomes (Sabourin, 2009). These observations highlight the importance of territorially embedded collective action for the establishment of fertile socio-cultural environments for the emergence, development and intensification of social networks of farmer innovation.[20]

In the Agreste region of Paraíba, the *cultural warming* that enabled the dynamization and densification of networks of preexisting socio-technical innovation occurred as a result of the emergence of a collective actor at the regional level: the Borborema Union and Family Farmer Organization Pole (or simply Pole).

THE BORBOREMA POLE: A CONTEMPORARY ACTOR OF HISTORICAL PEASANT STRUGGLES

During the movements of resistance and struggle of family farmers in the Agreste region of Paraíba in the early 1990s, a period coinciding with a decline in the union movement among rural workers, the Solânea, Remígio and Lagoa Seca unions took on the challenge of implementing a strategy of innovative action explicitly directed towards the management of socio-organizational dynamics focused on the core of the specific set of problems faced by family farmers in the region. The aim was to connect their traditional political agenda, until then generic and heavily influenced by the union movement at national level, with the reality and concrete motivations of the numerous and diverse family farming perspectives in the territory (Silveira, Victor, & Anacleto, 2007).

This change in the focus of union activity was largely stimulated by the beginning of the partnership with AS-PTA, an NGO that began working in the region in 1993 with the goal of providing assistance to family farming organizations, based on an agroecological approach to rural development. In order to kick-start the work in this field, the unions undertook a joint effort to produce knowledge on the reality of family farming and to mobilize their social bases through experimentation with technical and political-organizational innovations.

The first participative agroecosystem appraisals led to the emergence of new perceptions of the distinct agrarian landscapes in the municipalities concerned and the corresponding diversity of their productive systems. Stimulated by the appraisals, as well as the contacts with new experiences provided by exchange visits held inside and outside the territory, a growing number of farmers engaged in experiments on their own properties and in their own communities. The interactive flows and initiatives that resulted from this process elicited new questions and demands for knowledge that reflected the breadth of the motivations and problems to be confronted. The questions raised in the process stimulated a series of later studies and diagnoses concerning specific aspects suggested by the social dynamics of innovation.

These joint exercises in producing knowledge focused both on themes related to production strategies – such as the diversity of cultivated beans, livestock breeding systems, water resource management strategies, the use of native fruits and medicinal plants, the productive management of house yards – and to methodological and political aspects, including the participation of poor families in the innovation networks and the impact of public policies on the sustainability of regional family farming as a whole.

The evolution of the knowledge processes concerning the lived reality and the experimentations resulted in the configuration of an integrated cycle of radiating and mutually productive actions. The undertaking of the appraisals enabled the union leaders not only to understand better the structure and functioning of the agroecosystems in their municipalities, but above all to visualize them in all their diversity as an expression of the peculiar strategies of technical and economic reproduction adopted by the family farmers.

The exchange activities enabled the intensification of the interactions among farmers and became an important mechanism for projecting their technical, socio-organizational and political capacities. Likewise, the direct participation of farmers conferred a new meaning to the production of knowledge, altering the nature of their contribution to local development processes. Simultaneously it generated a new identity associated with the social and political presence of farmers in the organized community spaces and in union life as they became known and recognized themselves as *farmer-experimenters*, integrating with the emerging movement of agroecological innovation (Petersen & Silveira, 2007).[21]

Institutionally coordinated by the unions, the dynamic of experimentation mobilized the growing interaction with academic institutions, which began to formulate research projects based on issues of interest to thematic networks of farmer-experimenters organized through specific commissions – on water, local seeds, livestock breeding, yard production, market access and so on.

In a few years, a large range of innovative practices had been developed and/or adapted and incorporated in local agroecosystems. Taking as a reference point the three strategic principles of valorizing ecological capital presented in Box 2, Table 1 presents the relations between practices traditionally adopted by the region's farming families and the innovative practices developed and/or improved through the establishment of networks of agroecological experimentation.

The advance of the experimentations gradually spread and stirred the interest of unions and other family farming organizations present in other municipalities of the Paraiban Agreste. The successful experiences in managing water resources and community seed banks gained special visibility during the 1998–1999 drought, precisely because they assured family smallholdings of greater stability and capacity to resist the adverse climatic conditions.

Table 1. Relations between Agroecosystem Management Principles and Traditional and Innovative Practices.

Management Principles	Practices	
	Traditional	Innovative
Maintenance of high functional biodiversity	• Consortia and polycultures • Use of fodder or native species • Use of local varieties • Hedge planting	• Recuperation, improvement and multiplication of local varieties • Evaluation and introduction of new varieties and races • Reforestation of farms • Cultivation in rows • Agroforestry systems • Green manure • Vegetable contour lines
Constitution and management of stocks	• Capital investment in the form of cattle • Claypits, cisterns, stone tanks, etc. • Domestic storage of seeds • Storage of crop leftovers as a source of fodder	• Community seed banks • Underground dams • Stone tanks • Slab cisterns and paved cisterns • Silage and haymaking practices
Valorization of limited spaces with high biological production potential	• House yards • Intensive planting in low-lying wetlands	• Improved house yards • Underground dams • Stone barriers

Source: Petersen et al. (2002).

This fact persuaded the region's unions, then associated with a preexisting space of institutional coordination, the Borborema Union Pole, to mobilize their social bases in the communities in order to share their innovative experiences under way in the three pioneer municipalities. Through this evolution, the Borborema Pole began to present itself not only as an actor of political representation in dealings with the State but, fundamentally, as a political-organizational space unifying the set of family farming organizations around the conception and execution of a shared project of rural development for the territory.

The bases of this project were established at the start of the 2000s, formed by the formulation of an action strategy centred on two interrelated axes: the first, dedicated to stimulating dynamics of local innovation through networks of farmers-experimenters; the second, directed towards elaborating and defending public policy proposals adapted to the socio-ecological particularities of the territory.

THE POLE AS A NICHE OF PEASANT INNOVATION

As a territorially referenced collective actor, the Pole plays a decisive role in enhancing the strategic coherence of the territory's actors, activities and resources, looking to identify, mobilize and interconnect them in specific socio-productive configurations. By adopting this approach, the Pole helps boost the autonomy of local social dynamics from the hierarchical and centralized logic typical of the interventionist actions of the State and agri-business companies in the rural world. In this sense, the Pole functions as a *strategic niche of peasant innovation* – that is a space relatively protected from the dominant socio-technical regime, enabling the creation of a socio-cultural environment favourable to innovation, based on the activation of ecological, social and human capital and oriented towards ensuring that the territory's farming is founded on the same capitals.[22]

The legitimization and intensification of farmer experimentation associated with the affirmation of the 'farmer-experimenter' identity was a key element in increasing the levels of cohesion between the organizations making up the Pole. By coordinating and providing a strategic direction to the networks of farmer-experimenters in the territory, the Pole helps them acquire independence from institutionalized systems of knowledge and presents itself to the State and market actors alike as an agent capable of inducing endogenous forms of rural development. Hence farmer innovation is a key process in the promotion of higher levels of self-determination at different geographic and social spheres – from family farms units to the territory as a whole.

However this distancing from institutionalized science is not absolute. Through partnerships established with research groups linked to official scientific-academic institutions, the network of farmer-experimenters coordinated by the Pole counts on the input of academically systemized knowledge, as well as the methodological resources of objective science to advance the process of local innovation. To this end it elaborates and participates actively in pursuing a research agenda aligned with the themes that mobilize farmer experimentation in the territory. As well as helping to advance knowledge on the technical and economic management of agroecosystems, these partnerships play the important role of legitimizing farmer innovation in the eyes of the State. The case of participatory research on local varieties of maize illustrates various aspects of this question (see Box 3).

Box 3. Seeds or Grains? Research with Local Maize Varieties.

Seen by conventional Agronomy as less productive compared to so-called *improved varieties* – which are only accessible via the markets or public programmes – local varieties, locally known as *sementes da paixão* (passion seeds), have not even been officially recognized as seeds, but as grains. To demonstrate the opposite, a team of researchers from EMBRAPA (Brazilian Agricultural Research Corporation) was invited to support the network of farmers-experimenters to conduct trials to compare the varieties distributed by public programmes and the passion seeds. The trials were repeated over a three-year period, in three environmentally different regions and in the crop growing conditions commonly employed by the communities responsible for carrying out the trials. The results are unequivocal in demonstrating the systematic agronomic superiority of the local varieties, both in relation to the production of grains, and in relation to the production of fodder biomass (hay), an essential input for feeding cattle during the dry periods of the year.[23]

The research proved what we already knew, one farmer stated in a seminar organized for the presentation and debate of the results with public officials from federal and state spheres. Indeed this shared process of building knowledge concerning an important component of the ecological capital of the territory largely ignored by the State exerted an important role in the fight against the invisibility of the passion seeds and their farmer stewards. Based on the feeling of empowerment provided by the research results, farmer-experimenters told the public officials that they would no longer accept government bodies reducing passion seeds to the status of grains[24] (Petersen et al., 2013).

In the form conducted, with the network of farmer-experimenters actively involved from its conception to the evaluation of the results, the research with passion seeds was able to disclose traditional strategies of valorizing agrobiodiversity capable of inspiring the reformulation of public policies in the area. Firstly because it showed that the use of 'improved' varieties is not the best option for a mode of farming conducted in highly unpredictable environmental conditions like those found in the semi-arid. As genotypes dependent on the presence of optimal environmental conditions, generally provided by the input of irrigation and chemical fertilizers, the improved varieties display productive performances lower than the local varieties, the latter improved through processes of local selection carried out by generations of farmers.[25] Secondly because the research findings throw into question the 'seeds versus grains' dichotomy that underlies the design of public agricultural support and credit programmes. This questioning affirms that the seeds produced by farmers deserve official support. Thirdly because it shows how the farmers compare the varieties grown by themselves according to a range of different criteria and not only in terms of their physical productivity levels. The practical implication of this multi-criteria evaluation is that the farmers do not seek 'the best variety' but the best *pool* of varieties that meets their many productive and reproductive expectations.[26] Fourthly, and finally, because this pool of varieties varies from region to region as an outcome of particular environmental factors and cultural preferences. This necessity for local adaptation of plant varieties to the socio-ecological and cultural specificities of rural territories undermines the execution of public programmes conceived in a centralized form, based on a universalist distributive logic. The practical implication of this fact is that the supply of seeds used by family farming should be ensured through the action of territorialized networks dedicated to the use, management and conservation of local varieties, emphasizing the active role of farmers as *stewards of agrobiodiversity*.

Another important aspect of the dynamics of farmer experimentation incubated by the Pole in the Borborema territory is that the latter favours the systemic coordination between the innovations and creates the objective (material) and subjective (symbolic) conditions for other novelties to be created and included in the agroecosystems in a coherent form. This leads, therefore, to the development of networks of interconnected innovations that remodel the socio-material reality of family farms.

By being coordinated in systematic networks inside and outside family farms, the farmer innovations reconfigure the structure and functioning of agroecosystems, generating positive effects on the economic productivity and resilience of family farming vis-à-vis the environmental unpredictability of the semi-arid region. A clear example of this was observed in the 2012–2013 period when the family farming of Paraíba's Agreste region demonstrated a high capacity of resistance and response to the harshest drought of the last 50 years, showing a clear contrast with the devastating effects of the less severe droughts seen in previous periods.

THE POLE AS A POLITICAL ACTOR

The territorialized focus adopted by the Borborema Pole set it apart from the union movement's tradition, whose political agendas very frequently involved the pursuit of a generalizing approach disconnected from the real-world situation and thus distant from the specific demands, potentialities and perspectives present in its diversified social base. In this sense, the Pole emerges as an institutional innovation focused on building increased levels of governance over the dynamics of rural development in the territory.

To perform this role, the Pole establishes an interface between the grassroots social dynamics activated by farmer experimentation and the different levels and operational sectors of the State. This interface involves the establishment of connections between the issue-based networks of farmer innovation dispersed horizontally across the territory and the political pressure work applied to official bodies, whose actions, implemented on larger scales, interfere vertically on the local dynamics of rural development. The dynamics of these networks are coordinated by theme-based commissions constituted by farmer-experimenters and linked to the political coordination of the Pole. Consequently the continual updating of the Pole's capacity to propose policies to the State is directly connected to the everyday life experiences of farming families in their different forms of resistance and their daily struggle to improve their strategies for social and economic reproduction.

Given the predominance of a political culture that combines the authority of leaders from social movements and from organizations representing family farmers, the form in which the Pole relates to the State emerges as a political-institutional novelty of extreme importance in terms of mobilizing public resources in support of endogenous development. This is because the traditional methods informing the action of the union movement tend to be fairly insensitive to the social experimentation and the strategies that implicitly rise from it. By employing generalizing approaches to their understanding of reality, the leaders of these movements become professionalized in their posts and, little-by-little, are disconnected from grassroots social processes. Consequently they gradually become incapable of incorporating into their political strategies the lessons contained in the diverse ways in which farming families work to address their problems.

The federating role played by the Pole in constructing a critical and active political awareness of the reality faced by family farming in the Borborema territory occurs at two interdependent levels: at one level, by promoting better cohesion between the formal and informal family farming organizations present in the geographic areas covered by the Pole's work; at another level, through the intermediation of community and municipal grassroots organizations, by stimulating farming families to join the networks of agroecological innovation established at a territorial level – while also enabling them to benefit from exchanges held outside the territory.

The interaction between these two levels occurs through collective dynamics of knowledge production that feed the experiences undertaken in the spheres of private action – that is in the family farms – and collective action – that is in the community, municipality and territory as a whole. Through this multiscalar and multithematic political-pedagogical approach, the networks of farmer-experimenters create an environment for social learning about the territory's reality, identifying its internal diversity – expressed in the different configurations of the agroecosystems – the range of different social actors involved and their corresponding development projects.

These learning processes combine knowledge concerning the technical and economic management of agroecosystems with knowledge concerning the governance of common assets in a community/territorial context (see the next section on innovation in institutional arrangements). Additionally they enable a critical reading of the power relations underlying the different *farming styles*[27] found in the territory.

This close connection between lessons learned in the technical management of agroecosystems and the political economy of farming styles creates favourable conditions for the farmer-experimenters linked to the Pole's theme-based commissions to also work as activists in defence of public policies congruent with the development trajectories in which they are embedded. By constructing its strategies for political action through a critical reading of the local reality, the Pole establishes relations with the State in order to mobilize public resources for augmenting the resource base controlled by farming families and their communities, thereby strengthening the technical autonomy, economic efficiency and environmental sustainability of the region's agroecosystems.[28] Some examples of this kind of work are presented in Box 4.

Box 4. Political Actions Undertaken by the Pole on Various Issues Related to the Processes of Farmer Innovation in the Agreste Region of Paraíba.

(a) The Pole's water resource commission criticized the major hydraulic works that have historically typified the State's intervention in this area. It argues instead for a conception of water management based on the decentralization of the water supply through the development of a network of small infrastructures to meet the water demands of families and communities. By working alongside other organizations from the semi-arid region, the Pole contributed to the conception of and political campaigning for the P1MC and P1 + 2 programmes to be implemented by the federal government. (b) The seed commission criticized the policies for distributing improved seeds and releasing transgenic varieties in the semi-arid region. As an alternative, it formulated and campaigned for programmes in defence of local seeds and the valorization of farmers as stewards of agrobiodiversity.[29] (c) The livestock breeding commission argued for the allocation of public funds for the purchase of machines capable of processing the biomass potentially usable as fodder on family farms, valorizing the construction of silos and thereby ensuring a stable source of animal feed during dry periods of the year. (d) The ecological crops commission declared its opposition to the state government's initiative of compulsory spraying insecticides to combat the new pest attacking the region's *Citrus* plantations. As an alternative, it proposed conducting experiments with non-toxic products.

One of the strategic dimensions of the Pole's work involves converting these public resources into common assets to be continually mobilized by families in the operation of their farms. Since the behaviours and strategic decisions of farming families depend directly on the economic, socio-cultural, institutional and environmental contexts in which their farms operate, the expansion and diversification of the base of locally available common assets considerably amplifies the room for manoeuvre of the families when it comes to conceiving and putting into practice strategies of endogenous development.

Analytically, the territory functions as a socio-ecological system in which family agroecosystems are structurally coupled. The increase in the self-controlled base of common assets in the territory strengthens these links of structural coupling between the agroecosystems and the territorial supra-system, enabling permanent flows of goods and services between the spheres of collective and private action, without creating the need for monetarized transactions, or the growth of dependency on externally defined market rules. In this sense, the input of public resources through negotiations established between the Pole and the State plays an important role in the densification and intensification of the ecological, economic and social flows regulating the labour and other processes involved in the production and distribution of wealth in the territory.

At the same time that it positions itself vis-à-vis the State as a political actor defending territorialized farming styles, the Pole (and its organizations) act to create and lend political-institutional support to decentralizing collective processes aimed at improving the governance and sustainable use of common assets indispensable to the agroecological intensification of agroecosystems. In this sense, the Pole functions as an incubator of local institutions intended to regulate the production and use of common assets and services by rural families and communities.

THE POLE AS AN INCUBATOR OF INSTITUTIONS[30]

A particularly decisive factor in the Pole's action as a driving force in rural development dynamics resides in the fact that its work focuses on supporting the creation and/or improvement of devices for collective action designed to manage common assets. These new devices, or institutional arrangements, can be seen to be an emergence from the networks of farmer-experimenters activated by the pole: that is as outcomes of the combined action of the social processes of local innovation and the mobilization of public resources through political action. Box 5 presents some of these devices for collective action.

Box 5. New Institutional Arrangements for Managing Common Assets. *Source*: Petersen et al. (2013).

(1) Shared management of equipment: unions and associations belonging to the Pole have worked to organize the collective management of 10 mobile silage machines funded by the Territorial Development Programme of the Ministry of Agrarian Development (MDA). These machines are used to produce silage, allowing the storage of cattle feed for use during dry periods of the year. The system for circulating the machinery is regulated by locally defined rules, associated with community work rallies that process the large volumes of fodder biomass produced by various plant species grown on family smallholdings. As well as allowing many families to make stockpiles of fodder in a short period of time, the system stimulates the planting of fodder species with the potential to be used as silage. This institutional arrangement benefits around 150 families with an average annual output of 10 tons of fodder. As well as the silage machines, a set of fruit pulpers is also managed by community work groups. These machines allow large volumes of native and exotic fruits to be processed for sale during the inter-harvest season, playing an important role in stimulating the planting of fruit species. (2) Collective practices for preserving and reproducing biodiversity: a network of 65 community seed banks ensures that the substantial agrobiodiversity heritage is conserved and made available for planting as soon as the rains start. As well as being adapted to local environmental conditions and crop systems, the passion seeds afford families greater autonomy and security in developing their crops. The network of nurseries used to produce tree saplings (forest and fruit species) is another initiative that has provided hundreds of families with access to a genetically diverse and high-quality material. Managed by unions and community associations, this network formed by six nurseries was developed as a system to reforest the farming landscape with multiple-use species. A network of forest seed-collecting farmers was subsequently linked to the network of nurseries, stimulating the creation of a social group with knowledge and practical knowhow concerning the propagation of native tree species. To ensure the production of saplings, the organization of work in the nurseries very often makes use of work rallies (mutirão).

(3) Community work rallies: as we have seen in the previous items, this practice is very widespread in peasant farming regions, and is also used to construct small works for capturing, transporting and storing rainwater, which have been essential in terms of structuring a vast and interconnected water supply to meet the multiple demands of farming families. (4) Community savings and loans: a set of 90 Solidarity Revolving Funds (FRS) has been employed to enable the purchase of a variety of equipment and inputs needed to intensify the productivity of agroecosystems: water supply infrastructures, ecological ovens, screens for use in yards, manure, zinc silos, small livestock, etc. (5) Organization for accessing markets: a network of eight agroecological fairs in the region's municipalities, as well as collective sales in institutional markets, especially via the Food Purchase Programme (PAA) and the National School Meals Programme (PNAE), enables the outflow of the diverse produce typical of family farming and an improved financial return for the work of the families involved.

The emergence of these innovative devices for collective action created a new institutional environment in the territory, establishing a positive feedback mechanism with the dynamics of agroecological innovation by encouraging the circulation of goods and services between families and communities independent of market rules. A virtuous circle was generated, mutually strengthening human, social and institutional capital.[31]

From the analytic viewpoint, the core function of these new institutional arrangements is to stimulate beneficial connections and help produce synergies between different activities and actors in the territory, as well as between different levels in the multilevel system of territorial governance (Knickel et al., 2008). In this sense, these territorially rooted institutions perform the role of catalyzing agents among actors on the same level – like the networks of farmer-experimenters – and as mediators between higher and lower levels – like the agroecological fairs or the seed banks in relation to government policies and to farming families.

The intensification of social practices founded on reciprocity and mutual trust is another key element afforded by the emergence of these institutions. The transactions taking place through these practices are institutionally regulated at territorial level, mobilizing social and natural resources for economic production and reproduction independently of the commercial markets for inputs and services. Interpreted through the prism of the neo-institutional economy, these practices enable a drastic reduction in the transaction costs involved in sustaining regional economic dynamics. In addition, they enable improvements in terms of the scale and quality of these economic activities.[32] The case of the revolving funds used in the construction of slab cisterns is presented in Box 6 as an illustration of this phenomenon.

Box 6. The Multiplication of Effects by Self-Regulated Institutions: The Case of the Dissemination of Slab Cisterns. *Source*: Petersen and Rocha (2003).

The Solidarity Revolving Funds (FRS) are financing systems administrated by informal groups and/or community associations. Instead of directly funding the families, as occurs in the official banking system, the FRSs are composed of small groups that assume shared responsibility for managing financial capital. The revolving nature of the funds refers to the chain funding mechanisms through which each family benefits from the funds coming from the devolution of loans taken out earlier by other families. During the initial period of operation of the One Million Cisterns Programme in Paraíba's Agreste region, the public funds allocated towards the building of the cisterns were used to set up the FRSs. In 2003 some 1,380 cisterns had been funded via this system, 656 of which had been built using financial resources repaid to the FRSs by the first families to receive the credit. This meant that the FRS mechanism enabled a 90% increase in the number of families benefitting from the funds originally allocated to the territory by the programme. Taking into account, too, that the unit costs for the construction of the cisterns was reduced by an average of 30% due to the use of cooperative work by community members, we can calculate that the initial funds invested in the territory were multiplied by 172% due to the activities of institutions founded on reciprocity and cooperation. In other words: had the P1MC Programme been implanted by a private company, the resources invested would have been sufficient for the construction of only 506 cisterns at most.

THE TREASURE MAP

The experiments being conducted in Brazil's semi-arid region reveals the importance of local actors as protagonists of rural development. A number of core ideas are essential to understanding the role of these actors and how they work, as well as the development trajectories driven by them. The first and most relevant of these ideas is that of *immobilized local resources*. These are the *hidden treasures*, as metaphorically described by one farmer from the Paraíban Agreste. They correspond to locally available environmental and social potentials that can be activated and developed by the processes of generating social wealth, but which more often remain concealed by the dominant forms of interpreting and intervening in the local reality. Consequently they fail to become integrated into the flows of economic production, rendering them superfluous insofar as they become squandered in the socio-ecological metabolism.[33]

The second key idea is that of *peasant innovation*, a social process defined here as the identification, experimentation, evaluation and interconnection of locally available resources within the territory's economic systems. Farmer innovation unfolds through the continual learning of practices capable of altering preexisting work routines, responding to problems and obstacles experienced locally by rural families and communities. In the experience described here, the agents of farmer innovation are farmer-experimenters. Setting out from the identification of a problem, a farmer-experimenter is someone who has an idea about the cause of this problem and decides to test a way of solving it through the use of locally available resources. It is, therefore, a process of experimentation just as formal as the most systematic scientific research (Hocdé, 1999).

The dynamics of peasant innovation evolve through the continuous learning enabled by consistently connecting the lessons learnt through the action of the farmer-experimenters. In the present case, this horizontal interconnection between the actors involved in farmer innovation is expressed through the notion of a *network of farmer-experimenters*, the third key idea.

The networks of producing and sharing knowledge founded on farmer innovation are structured and dispersed through specific socio-physical realities in which local resources are identified, mobilized, interconnected and developed. These realities are expressed at various geographic scales, which correspond to distinct levels of socio-organizational aggregation. The upper scale is the space delimited by the reach of the farmer-experimenter networks. This space corresponds to the *rural territory* – the fourth key idea – a scale where local resources are present in the form of common assets, both material and immaterial. The new institutional arrangements – that is devices for collective action – designed to regulate socially the management of common assets are the main products of farmer innovation at this scale.

The lower scale corresponds to the family farm, the private space of farmer innovation. This space is that of the *agroecosystem* – the fifth key idea – a scale economically managed by the farming families themselves. In this sphere of activity, local resources are identified, mobilized and recombined on the basis of productive strategies experimented at the initiative of individuals and/or families. At this scale, the novelties at a technical level are the main products of farmer innovation. These are essentially designed to valorize the ecosystem's abiotic resources – water, nutrients and solar radiation – by integrating them into ecological cycles through biodiversity management. By employing this strategy of valorizing ecological capital, peasant innovation promotes *economic intensification without ecological simplification*, in the process developing more productive agroecosystems that are less dependent on external inputs.

The private and collective contexts in which peasant innovation occurs are not particularly clearly defined given that a mutual interdependence exists between the socio-physical transformations occurring in both spheres. As family management units, the agroecosystems are conditioned by the transformations in the institutional arrangements that occur at higher spheres, just as the evolution of the territory as a socio-ecological system is a direct outcome of the transformations taking place at the level of the agroecosystems run by farming families. Analytically speaking, the agroecosystems and the territory establish an autopoietic relation – that is a relation of coproduction between systems interconnected at distinct hierarchical levels.[34] Taking concepts from the theory of autopoiesis, we can say that the *operational closure* of agroecosystems depends on their *structural coupling* with the territory.

The grammar of peasant innovation is structured, therefore, through the release, use and development of the *immobilized local resources*, configuring a strategy geared towards the continuous expansion of the room for autonomy from market-based rules imposed from outside. In place of the growing dependence on financial capital generated by the trajectories of agricultural modernization, farmer innovation is based on the mutual valorization and strengthening of the forms of human, social, institutional and ecological capital present in rural territories. These are the *hidden treasures* that, when seen in an integrated form, make up *territorial capital* (Ventura et al., 2008).[35]

The comprehension of the multifaceted, multidimensional and multilevel nature of territorial capital implies understanding the agricultural reality through a systemic approach focused on the rural territories and the agroecosystems structurally coupled to them. In other words: territorial capital is the outcome of a specific complex reality and can only be discerned and valorized in trajectories of endogenous development when comprehended in the context of the socio-ecological system that produced them. Groucho Marx expressed this idea with these simple words: 'Shall we discover some treasure in that house? – But there isn't any house ... – So let's build one!'

The study (*logos*) of the house (*oikos*) forms the object of Ecology, which, applied to the study of agrarian systems, can be specifically termed Agroecology. This emphasizes the central importance of the use of an *agroecological perspective* – the sixth key idea – as part of the process of building knowledge of the agricultural reality of Paraíba's Agreste region. With the contribution of AS-PTA, the reality of the territory and the diverse forms in which its agroecosystems are shaped have been studied through participatory appraisals and the systemization of the results of farmer experimentations in the context of farmer-experimenter networks. AS-PTA also plays a decisive role in the mediation between the Pole and academic institutions, mobilizing knowledge from many scientific disciplines as a way of enriching the *cognitive capital* (Dowbor, 2011) that circulates in farmer-experimenter networks.

The agroecological approach employed in the process of producing and sharing knowledge also generates a *strategic coherence* to the forms in which the farmer-experimenter networks conceive reality and intervene in it. This coherence is produced through the interrelation between lived, perceived and conceived spaces (Halfacree, 1993, quoted in Ventura et al., 2008). Lived space corresponds here to the realm of practices, perceived space to the realm of knowledge and conceived space to the system of values, or ideology, that frames the visions and divisions of reality (*ibid.*).[36]

In this sense the shift from the notion of *combatting the drought* to *living with the semi-arid* is a manifestation of the construction of a new strategic coherence that favors the repositioning of local actors vis-à-vis their reality. In turn, this repositioning impacts on the construction of the *political capital* of the Pole (and ASA) through the promotion of a rural development project based on the *paradigm of living with the semi-arid* – the seventh key idea.

This indeed is how the Pole has presented itself in different spheres of political negotiation with public bodies. Its action at this level can be defined as the fight to increase territorial capital. From this viewpoint, the public funds allocated by State policies and programmes reach the territory to increase the self-controlled base of resources, thereby amplifying the degree of autonomy involved in the unfolding trajectories of endogenous development.

In a context dominated by the modernization paradigm, this shift in perspective concerning the role of the State vis-à-vis civil society organizations manifests itself as an enormous political challenge. This challenge is expressed both in the design of the public policies executed by governments, and in the legal frameworks that regulate the access to and use of public funding by civil organizations.

The position of the Brazilian State concerning the experience of disseminating the slab cisterns described in this chapter provides a clear indication of the challenge to be met in order for the paradigm of agricultural modernization to be superseded in theory and practice, so that the State includes the *treasure map* within its strategies for promoting rural development.

A NEW CONFRONTATION

Despite the unequivocal demonstration of the efficiency and effectiveness of the software developed for the implantation of the slab cisterns for the P1MC Programme, the State has demonstrated a failure to assimilate the multifaceted nature and its systemic implications for the dynamics of rural development.

At first sight this is somewhat incomprehensible. The federal government proposed a massive programme offering tens of thousands of new water cisterns to the semi-arid region. This was presented as an 'acceleration' of the civil society initiatives discussed in this chapter.

In order to understand this confrontation it is important to go back to the cistern hardware and software developed by the bricklayer Nel and later widely disseminated under the aegis of the ASA. The 'Nel' type of cistern is made of concrete and iron. It is constructed by local bricklayers and built with materials bought in local and regional markets. Thus the cistern was indeed able to function as a seed of change. It strengthened the local economy and increased employment. It also allowed for flexibility. The cistern could be designed and scaled according to local conditions, needs and possibilities. The installation required excavation (a laborious task given the rocky subsoil found in the semi-arid region). This was resolved with voluntary labour based on reciprocity. Here again the cistern functioned as a 'seed' (a catalyst). It strengthened the social capital in the area. Likewise new institutional arrangements were introduced, like the 'revolving funds'. The implantation of the P1MC Programme through revolving funds, in turn, was prohibited due to the absence of an appropriate legal framework. The funds were considered an irregularity subject to legal penalties.

Above all the cistern and the associated method (or 'software') generated the conviction among the local population that they themselves could contribute strongly to the development of the region. Development was not necessarily a 'gift' that came from elsewhere (i.e. from the benevolent state or from regional governors operating a system of clientelism) – it could be constructed, instead, very adequately by local actors themselves. Thus a new 'political field' was opened and established.

Compared to the 'Nel type' of cistern, the government proposal was very different. The new cistern was not made in situ, but industrially and out of plastic (polyethylene). Thus the flexibility of adapting the cistern to local conditions was lost, just as the additional employment for local bricklayers was eliminated. Needless to say, the raw materials needed for the new cisterns cannot be acquired in the region itself. The 'software' also changes. Everything is paid for by the State. Voluntary labour, revolving funds and so on are all features that become redundant. Ironically this makes the 'new' cisterns more expensive than the former 'Nel-type' ones. Thus the 'seed' nature of the initial novelty is completely lost. The 'new' cisterns are an artefact introduced from the outside (typically it is an expression of exogenous development). They no longer translate into new, additional activities and effects that together constitute a process of self-driven and self-controlled development. The 'new' cistern again turned 'development' into a blessing coming from elsewhere.

Among the social movements participating in the ASA framework, the 'new' cistern and the associated programme were immediately understood as an expropriation – not only of 'their' cistern but above all of the political space that had been constructed in such a well-balanced way. Instead of functioning as a seed, it acted on the social process like an herbicide.

This was the reason why ASA organized a large-scale protest against the imminent deconstruction of P1MC announced by the federal government. As the most visible expression of this resistance, 15,000 farmers from all parts of the semi-arid region travelled to the town of Juazeiro, Bahia, in December 2011 to demonstrate in the streets and express their dissatisfaction. This demonstration of collective strength led the government to negotiate its position. Since then we have seen the coexistence of P1MC, a programme that seeds new horizons for living with the semi-arid conditions, with the programme implanted exclusively by governments, responsible for reinforcing practices that lead to social demobilization.

NOTES

1. As well as reducing the unit cost of a 16,000 litre cistern from US$ 690 to US $ 240, the equipment invented by Nel has a cylindrical form, eliminating the corners of the vertical walls that formed weak points where the cracks and infiltrations frequently occurring in brick cisterns would appear (Petersen & Rocha, 2003).

2. Training and Mobilization Programme for Living with the Semi-Arid Region – One Million Rural Cisterns – P1MC. Years later, ASA inaugurated the One Land and Two Waters Programme (P1 + 2), focusing on the implantation of small rainwater capture and storage infrastructures for use in food production.

3. To mobilize the resources needed for this enterprise, ASA established partnerships with the federal government, private companies and international agencies.

4. See www.asabrasil.org.br

5. From 2003 to March 2014, P1MC built more than 523,000 cisterns, benefitting over 2,250,000 people. The programme won national and international awards recognizing its impact on improving the quality of life in Brazil's semi-arid region. These awards included the 2010 Human Rights Award, given by the Presidency of the Republic, and the 2014 Seeds Award, given by the United Nations (UN) (ASA, 2014).

6. Institutional design is a proposal developed by the neo-institutionalist school of thought, which argues that social action is the outcome of the interaction between individuals through the intermediation of their institutions and between institutions themselves.

7. The drought industry is a term used to designate the strategy employed by certain social groups to benefit from the large volumes of resources and advantages offered by the drought fighting policies in the Brazilian semi-arid region.

8. This subtitle is the slogan adopted by the Brazilian Semi-Arid Alliance (ASA) and reflects its strategy of deconstructing the collective imaginary related to the determinist rhetoric that ideologically sustains the idea of combatting the drought.

9. The modernization project was only implanted in small areas of the semi-arid region that possessed the appropriate environmental conditions for reproducing intensive styles of farming, based on an economy of scale and regulated by globalized markets, led by the tropical fruit market. The access to water springs for the installation of large intensive irrigation projects is the main precondition for establishing this style of production. To render the system viable, the State invests huge financial resources in the installation of the infrastructure required to capture, store and transport the water.

10. The constitution of regional and/or state networks is a feature of the organizational process of the Brazilian NGOs identified with the agroecological field. The

regional networks (which includes the ASA) are connected to social movements (also national and regional in scope) to form the National Agroecological Alliance (ANA), a national-level network of networks.

11. Excerpt from the *Declaração do Semiárido*, a document elaborated by the civil society organizations assembled in 1999 during the Parallel Forum to the 3rd Conference of Parties to the United Nations Convention to Combat Desertification, held in Recife.

12. Excerpt from the *Political Charter of the 4th National Encounter of ASA* (2003), held in Campina Grande.

13. *Seeds of transition* is the apt metaphor coined by Wiskerke and van der Ploeg (2004) to characterize the emergence and consolidation of novelties among the endogenous dynamics of rural development.

14. The notion of *strategic niche management* derives from a multilevel theoretical perspective. According to this approach, technological transitions are explained by the interrelation of processes at three different heuristic levels: the analytic concepts of innovation niches, technological regimes and socio-technical landscapes. Niches represent the local level of innovation processes and are commonly referred to as protected or incubatory spaces in which new technologies or socio-technical practices emerge and develop in isolation from the normal market pressures or systems. The technological regime is characterized by stabilized products and widely accepted technologies, stores of knowledge, use practices, protocols, techniques, expectations, norms and regulations (Geels, 2005; Kemp et al., 1998 quoted in Marques, 2009).

15. The term *sertão* originates from the word *desertão* (i.e. big desert) and was used by Portuguese colonizers to describe their perception of the physiography of the interior region, marked by the presence of Caatinga vegetation (*white forest* in the Tupi language) typical of Brazilian semi-arid conditions in contrast to the coastal region, occupied by dense tropical rainforest.

16. Indeed the region has been the setting for peasant struggles that date back to the colonial period. The current processes of resistance cannot be understood, therefore, without taking into account the history of these struggles (Silveira et al., 2010).

17. In her classic work, Boserup (1981) showed that changes to the technological base of farming were frequently induced by a reduction in the environmental resources available to sustain the local population, especially arable land. Increases in population density leading to land scarcity functioned as triggers unleashing dynamics of socio-technical innovation towards agricultural intensification. One of the main conclusions of Boserup's work is that there is no agrarian ceiling or natural support capacity within any particular region. Productivity levels depend not only on ecological capital, but also on the social and human capital capable of continually improving technical systems through investment in local experimentation.

18. AS-PTA – Family Farming and Agroecology (www.aspta.org.br) is a national-level NGO that since 1993 has maintained a programme providing advice and assistance to family farming organizations in the Agreste region of Paraíba with the goal of supporting their role as collective actors central to the dynamics of rural development.

19. The understanding of the role of peasant rationality in agricultural intensification opened up new perspectives for the development of the science of Agroecology from the 1980s onwards (Gliessman, 1998). Since then Latin America

has seen an upsurge in the creation of NGOs dedicated to the dynamics of rural development driven by peasant organizations through the employment of the agroecological approach.

20. The social process of constructing structured coherences between the natural and social environments with the aim of capturing flows of resources has been called *territorialization*. The idea of a network is a metaphor increasingly used to describe and explain these processes of territorialization (Ventura et al., 2008).

21. The notion of the farmer-experimenter was assimilated following an exchange trip to Central America held in 1996, in which technicians from AS-PTA and union leaders were able to learn about the *Movimiento Campesino a Campesino* in Nicaragua. In particular, they became acquainted with the mechanisms for institutionalizing collective dynamics of agricultural innovation via the proactive engagement of farmers and their organizations. The Regional Programme for Reinforcing Agronomic Research on Basic Grains (PRIAG in the Spanish acronym), linked to the Inter-American Institute for Cooperation on Agriculture (IICA), was also visited during the same trip. Coordinated at the time by the French agronomist Henri Hocdé, PRIAG was attempting to shift beyond the farmer-to-farmer dynamic by stimulating interaction with official research institutes from the six Central American countries. The notion of the farmer-experimenter was used by Hocdé (1999) to redefine roles and identities of the farmer vis-à-vis those of the technical researchers and extensionists working in the official systems.

22. A similar situation is described by Ploeg (2008) in the case of territorial cooperatives in the north of Holland, which, the author proposes, function as *field laboratories*.

23. The findings are available at www.cpatc.embrapa.br/publicacoes_2012/doc_179.pdf (accessed on 12 February 2014).

24. The results of this process were decisive in ensuring the federal government's commitment to back the creation of a support programme for community seed banks in the semi-arid region, executed by the Brazilian Semi-Arid Alliance. This programme, started at the end of 2014, forms part of the National Plan for Agroecology and Organic Production and aims to build hundreds of seed banks in the rural territories where ASA runs its programmes to promote water security.

25. In this sense the genotypes of local varieties are carriers of biological and cultural messages, making them products of human–nature coproduction (Petersen et al., 2013).

26. The production of maize straw for cattle feed, for example, is a criterion highly valued by farmers from Brazil's semi-arid region. Varieties that produce little straw, such as the *Catingueiro* maize distributed by government programmes across the entire semi-arid region of Brazil, due to its extreme precocity (and higher chance of production in low rainfall), have been questioned by farmers. Varieties with dual purposes (used to produce both grain and straw) tend to be more valued in these production conditions. This example reveals the lack of a systemic perspective in the implementation of conventional agronomic research and the importance of the dialogue between knowledge practices for research to be adequately contextualized and conducted, with the aim of reinforcing the complex and singular strategies of production and reproduction pursued in family farming.

27. The concept of farming styles proposed by van der Ploeg (1994) derives from a theoretical-methodological approach that has proven to be extremely useful and versatile in describing and interpreting the diversity of contemporary farming. One of the central elements in this proposal is distinguishing between different styles on the basis of the degree of autonomy (or dependence) in relation to the market and access to technologies. The construction of styles as a tool for representing agricultural diversity involves the identification of varied forms of organizing the social and material resources used in the context of production units, without losing sight of the relations established with outside agents (financial institutions, input suppliers and product buyers, technical advisory services, etc.).

28. The Pole acts as an institutional mediator with public bodies operating at different federal levels and managing different resources: municipal, state and national governments, the Territorial Development Committee (a body linked to the territorial development policy of the Ministry of Agrarian Development). It also works to mobilize resources from international cooperation.

29. The experience developed by the Pole inspired the creation of a state network in defence of passion seeds, institutionally coordinated by the Paraíba Semi-Arid Alliance (ASA-PB), the branch of ASA Brazil in Paraíba state. The state seed network holds annual meetings, bringing together thousands of farmers in defence of public policies aimed at promoting and conserving agrobiodiversity. A state law supporting community seed banks was created in 2002 as a result of the political campaigning of ASA-PB. This experience in turn inspired the formulation of a programme for the entire Brazilian semi-arid region, set to be implemented in 2015 as one of the measures of the National Plan for Agroecology and Organic Production (Planapo).

30. Institutions can be understood as structures and mechanisms of social configuration and cooperation that govern individual behaviour. They can also be comprehended as sets of regulations, laws, norms and traditions shaped through social interactions (North, 1990, quoted in Knickel, Shiller, Münchhausen, von Vihinen, & Weber, 2008).

31. As Knickel et al. (2008) point out in reference to the dynamics of rural development in Europe, the interaction between the institutional dimension and social capital is significant since regions with higher levels of social capital are better prepared to create and adapt new forms of organization.

32. Van der Ploeg (2008, p. 67) calls attention to the fact that even when money is no impediment to the realization of economic exchanges, 'reciprocity is extremely advantageous when compared with the market alternative, especially because it functions as a mechanism for maintaining the quality' of the work. This applies to the process of cistern building through community work rallies compared to their construction by private companies contracted by the government.

33. The original idea of a metabolism in the relation between nature and society came from an insight first made by Karl Marx (Foster, 2000) and subsequently developed by ecological economists. Seen through the notion of socio-ecological metabolism, the economy is envisaged as an organism that collects resources from outside and later discards residues.

34. Developed by the Chilean biologists Humberto Maturana and Francisco Varela, the Theory of Autopoiesis, or New Systems Theory, postulates that the

living system is structurally connected to its environment through recurrent interactions, each of which unleashes structural changes in the system (Maturana & Varela, 1995, 1997). I have argued elsewhere that the agroecosystem, as a basic management unit in peasant farming, can be comprehended as the expression of a technical-economic strategy focused on valorizing the resource base that the farming family can deploy to attain its objectives, using specific patterns of operational closure and structural coupling with the rural territory (Petersen, 2011).

35. The meaning of the term capital has gradually expanded in the social sciences as part of the attempt to explain growing differentials between regions that, in theory, possess the same capital when measured in a conventional form. In this expansion of the concept, capital took on various forms: human, social, economic, cultural, symbolic and natural (Bourdieu, 1995, quoted in Ventura et al., 2008). Territorial capital is composed of a stock of resources specific to the territory (both material and immaterial) that are available to be mobilized by those living and working in the territory in the realization of their projects (Ventura et al., 2008).

36. 'These three dimensions, lived, perceived and conceived spaces, are strongly interrelated. Practices connect social representations with material components of space and are affected by the cognitive frameworks of the actors. A plant can be thought of as a weed or as a useful plant, not only because of its characteristics, but also because of the knowledge of its uses by users. In turn, knowledge is strongly affected, and more often distorted, by ideology. At the same time, reflecting on practices may cause adjustments of cognitive schemes and systems of values' (Ventura et al., 2008, p. 155).

ACKNOWLEDGEMENT

My thanks to Jan Douwe van der Ploeg for collaborating in the development of the section 'A New Confrontation'.

REFERENCES

ASA. (2014). *P1MC; resultados*. Recife. Retrieved from http://www.asabrasil.org.br/Portal/Informacoes.asp?COD_MENU=1558

Boserup, E. (1981). *Population and technological change: A study of long-term trends*. Chicago, IL: University of Chicago.

Bourdieu, P. (1995). *Ragioni Pratiche*. Bologna: Il Mulino.

Conti, L. I., & Pontel, E. (2013). Transição paradigmática na convivência com o semiárido. In L. I. Conti & E. O. Schoroeder (Eds.), *Convivência com o semiárido Brasileiro; autonomia e protagonismo social* (pp. 21–30). Brasília: Ed. IABS.

da Silva, R. A. M. (2006). *Entre o combate à seca e a convivência com o Semi-Árido: Transições paradigmáticas e sustentabilidade do desenvolvimento*. Brasília – DF. Doctoral thesis – UNB. Retrieved from http://repositorio.unb.br/bitstream/10482/2309/1/2006_Roberto%20Marinho%20Alves%20da%20Silva.pdf. Accessed in January 2014.

Dowbor, L. (2011). A economia da criatividade, Le Monde Diplomatique, em 01/6/2011. Retrieved from http://diplomatique.uol.com.br/artigo.php?id = 947

Foster, J. B. (2000). *Marx's ecology. Materialism and nature*. New York, NY: Monthly Review Press.

Galindo, W. (Ed.). (2013). *Vozes da convivência com o semiárido*. Recife: Centro Sabiá.

Garcia, A. R., Jr. (1990). *O Sul: O caminho do roçado; estratégias de reprodução camponesa e de transformação do capital*. Brasília: Editora da UNB.

Geels, F. W. (2005). *Technological transitions and system innovations: A co-evolutionary and socio-technical analysis*. Cheltenham: Edward Elgar.

Gliessman, S. (1998). *Agroecology: Ecological processes in sustainable agriculture*. Ann Arbor, MI: Sleeping Bear Press.

Gomes De Almeida, S. (1991). *A agricultura alternativa em construção. Alternativas – Cadernos de Agroecologia* (pp. 1–6). Rio de Janeiro: AS-PTA.

Halfacree, K. (1993). Locality and social representation: Space, discourse and alternative definitions of the rural. *Journal of Rural Studies*, *9*, 23–37.

Hocdé, H. (1999). *A lógica dos agricultores-experimentadores; o caso da América central*. Rio de Janeiro: AS-PTA.

IBGE. (2010). *Censo Demográfico Brasileiro*. Brasília: IBGE.

Knickel, K., Shiller, S., Münchhausen, S., von Vihinen, H., Weber, A. (2008). New institutional frameworks in rural development. In J. D. van der Ploeg & T. Marsden (Eds.), *Unfolding webs: The dynamics of regional rural development* (pp. 111–128). Assen: Van Gorcum.

Long, A. e., & van der Ploeg, J. D. (1994). Endogenous development: Practices and perspectives. In *Born from within: Practices and perspectives of endogenous rural development*. Assen: Van Gorcum.

Long, N. e., & van der Ploeg, J. D. (2011). Heterogeneidade, ator e estrutura: Para a reconstituição do conceito de estrutura. In S. e. Schneider & Gazolla, M. (Eds.), *Os atores do Desenvolvimento Rural: perspectivas teóricas e práticas sociais* (pp. 21–48). Porto Alegre: Editora da UFRGS.

Marques, F. C. (2009). *Velhos conhecimentos, novos desenvolvimentos: Transições no regime sociotécnico da agricultura; a produção de novidades entre agricultores produtores de plantas medicinais no Sul do Brasil*. Porto Alegre: PGDR/UFRGS. (tese de doutorado).

Maturana, H. R., & Varela, F. (1995). *A árvore do conhecimento: As bases biológicas do entendimento humano*. Campinas, SP: Psy II.

Maturana, H. R., & Varela, F. (1997). *Machines and living things. Autopoiese to do Organização Vivo*. Brazil: Medical Arts, Porto Alegre.

Moreira, E., & Targino, I. (1997). *Capítulos de geografia agrária da Paraíba*. João Pessoa: EDUFPB.

North, D. C. (1990). *Institutions, institutional change and economic performance*. New York, NY: Cambridge University Press.

Petersen, P., & Rocha, J. C. (2003). *Manejo ecológico de recursos hídricos enel semiárido brasileño; lecciones del agreste paraibano*. In Leisa Revista de agroecologia (pp. 16–18). Lima: ETC-Andes.

Petersen, P., & Silveira, L. (2007). Construção do conhecimento agroecológico em redes de agricultores-experimentadores: A experiência de assessoria ao Pólo Sindical da Borborema. In P. Petersen & A. Dias (Eds.), *Construção do conhecimento agroecológico; novos papeis, novas identidades*. Rio de Janeiro: ANA.

Petersen, P., Silveira, L., & Freire, A. G. (2013). Intensificação sem simplificação; estratégia de combate à desertificação. *RevistaAgriculturas: experiênciasemagroecologia, 9*(3) pp-1-10, AS-PTA & ILEIA, Botafogo, Rio de Janeiro, Brazil. Retrieved from http://aspta.org.br/revista-agriculturas

Petersen, P., Silveira, L. M., & Almeida, P. (2002). Ecossistemas naturais e agroecossistemas tradicionais no agreste da Paraíba: Uma analogia socialmente construída e uma oportunidade para a conversão agroecológica. In L. M. Silveira, P. Petersen, & E. Sabourin (Eds.), *Agricultura familiar e agroecologia no Semiárido Brasileiro; avanços a partir do agreste da Paraíba* (pp. 13–122). Rio de Janeiro: AS-PTA.

Sabourin, E. (2002). Manejo da inovação na agricultura familiar do Agreste da Paraíba; o sistema local de conhecimento. In P. Petersen, L. Silveira, & E. Sabourin (Eds.), *Agricultura familiar e Agroecologia no Semiárido; avanços a partir do agreste da Paraíba* (pp. 177–199). Rio de Janeiro: AS-PTA.

Sabourin, E. (2009). *Camponeses do Brasil; entre a troca mercantile e a reciprocidade.* Porto Alegre: Garamond. (Col. Terra Mater).

Scott, J. (1986). Everyday forms of peasants resistance. *The Journal of Peasants Studies, 13*(2), 5–35.

Silveira, L., Freire, A., & Diniz, P. (2010). Polo da Borborema; ator contemporâneo das lutas camponesas pelo território. *Agriculturas, 7*(1), 13–19.

Silveira, L., Victor, R., & Anacleto, N. (2007). Saindo de trás do birô; a reconstrução do movimento sindical no agreste da Paraíba. *Agriculturas, 4*(2), 10.

van der Ploeg, J. D. (1994). Styles of farming: An introductory note on concepts and methodology, In J. D. van der Ploeg & A. Long (Eds.), *Born from within-practice and perspective of endogenous rural development.* Assen, The Netherlands: Van Gorcum.

van der Ploeg, J. D. (2007). Resistance of the third kind and the construction of sustainability. Presented to the XXII ESRS Conference Plenary Session on sustainabilities, Wageningen, 23 August. Published online. Retrieved from http://www.jandouwevanderploeg.com/EN/publications/articles/resistance-of-the-third-kind. Accessed on 12 March 2014.

van der Ploeg, J. D. (2008). *Camponeses e impérios alimentares; lutas por autonomia e sustentabilidade na era da globalização.* Porto Alegre: UFRGS.

Ventura, F., Brunori, G., Milone, P., & Berti, G. (2008). The rural web: A synthesis. In J. D. van der Ploeg & T. Marsden (Eds.) *Born from within: The dynamics of regional rural development* (pp. 149–174). Assen: Van Gorcum.

Wiskerke, J. S. & van der Ploeg, J. D. (2004). *Seeds of transition: Essays on novelty production, niches and regimes in agriculture.* Assen: Van Gorcum.

CHAPTER 8

RURAL DEVELOPMENT FROM THE GRASSROOTS: TWENTY YEARS OF THE EU "LEADER APPROACH"

Laurent Van de Poele

ABSTRACT

Today a large majority of European citizens feels very uncomfortable about the lack of solutions for the ongoing economic-financial crisis. The EU institutions and the member states are engaged in intensive dialogues with each other while ignoring the necessity to translate the crisis into clear political terms understandable for public opinion. This may be one of the explanations of the disconnection of public opinion from the integration process which is often leading to a support for populist and nationalist movements. At the same time this crisis has made Europe more important than ever before for the daily lives of citizens. It is therefore important to support projects that allow citizens and civil society at large to become involved in EU affairs. Apart from the "Europe for Citizens program" (2014–2020) there are, although very few, examples in EU policy making where the sphere of public debate has been widened up, allowing citizens to participate more intensively in the democratic life

Constructing a New Framework for Rural Development
Research in Rural Sociology and Development, Volume 22, 195–207

ISSN: 1057-1922/doi:10.1108/S1057-192220150000022007

of the Union. In the rural development pillar of the Common Agricultural Policy (CAP) a "participatory democracy" tool has been created in order to stimulate from the grassroots the economic growth of rural areas: the Leader initiative.

Keywords: Rural development; leader approach; cooperation; rural area; collective action; local actors

THE LEADER[1] INITIATIVE: THE EU APPROACH TO RURAL DEVELOPMENT

The Leader initiative represents a bottom-up approach based on the selection of the best local development plans devised and designed by *Local Action Groups* (called hereafter LAGs) representing public–private partnerships. The EU supports financially a range of actions, such as the operating costs of LAGs; projects for inter-LAG co-operation; experimental and pilot projects; and capacity-building and animation which is necessary to prepare local development strategies (Commission of the European Communities [CEC], 2004). The Leader initiative is designed to help rural actors, as stakeholders, and to improve the long-term potential for the economic development of their local region. It aims to encourage LAGs to implement integrated, high-quality and original strategies for the sustainable development of their localities. It strongly emphasizes partnership and networks for the exchange of good practice and experience.

The Leader initiative is now in its fourth generation. LEADER I (1991–1993) marked the beginning of the new approach to rural development policy, making it territorially based, integrative and participative (CEC, 1988). The experience of this first phase suggested that area-based programs involving partnerships between the local community and other agencies and interests could play a meaningful role in promoting socio-economic development in rural areas, but also elsewhere. LEADER II (1994–1999) saw the approach put to more widespread use, with a greater emphasis on its experimental nature in terms of the innovative aspects of projects. The third phase, called LEADER+ (2000–2006), as well as the initiative's present form as a special priority in EU rural policy's mainstream development programs (2007–2013) continues its role as a laboratory. It aims to promote the emergence and testing of new approaches to integrated and sustainable development and, in this way, to influence, complete and reinforce EU rural development policy. A distinctive feature of the Leader initiative is the broadly based nature of the local partnerships (LAGs) which draw up and implement the integrated development programs for their local rural areas.

The Leader initiative and its distinctive "Leader approach" in many ways epitomizes the EU's approach to rural development policy. It involves:

- a broad policy framework, which comprises strategic aims;
- common rules and financing established at EU level by the member states and the European Commission;
- a bottom-up approach with rural stakeholders designing, at their local level, rural development measures which best suit their requirements; and
- regional and national selection and approval processes for LAGs (CEC, 2003a).

LAGs are selected under an open procedure based on the criteria laid down in the programs. The number of LAGs selected by EU25 member states for LEADER+ (2000–2006) was close to 900, while today (EU 27) it may be more than 1,400. National networks were created in a number of member states with the double objective of (a) sharing and disseminating information from the national level to the LAGs and (b) of acting as a forum for the exchange of information, experience and know-how between LAGs. They also deliver assistance for local and transnational co-operation between LAGs, an important element in disseminating and sharing good practice.

CHARACTERISTICS OF THE LEADER INITIATIVE

The approach embodied in the Leader initiative rests on a number of principles:

- elaborating and implementing a "local action plan" in rural areas of between 10,000 (exceptionally 5,000) and 100,000 inhabitants[2];
- the local action plan will have a number of characteristics: it will
  (1) define a limited number of strategic priorities for development (frequently known as development axes) and corresponding measures, which will be put into action during the period covered by the rural development plan;
  (2) be designed and implemented by a local partnership (LAG), which will be the final beneficiary of the initiative;

(3) it will be multi-sectorial and involve the systematic interlinking of development actions embedded in the overall vision and strategy.

One further factor became embedded in the approach – innovation. The implementation of "innovative actions" by rural public and/or private actors – not just any actions but "innovative" actions – became an explicit aim embodied in the Leader initiative. The European Commission interpreted the concept of "innovation" in a broad sense. It did not confine "innovation" to the method by which a project was implemented. It interpreted it to pertain to the technical content of the project, whether in the product, the production process, the market or some other aspect. And the concept of innovation could be concerned purely with economic aspects or with cultural and environmental aspects if they were closely linked to rural development.

In the method of the Leader initiative, the "Leader approach," LAGs consist of a combination of public and private partners jointly devising a strategy and innovative measures for the development – or for an aspect of the development – of a rural area on the scale of a community of, roughly, less than 100,000 inhabitants. These partners are allocated an administrative and financial lead agency which has the capacity to manage grants from public funds. The lead agency ensures full participation of all of the local partners who are concerned with the strategy, including leading figures in the economic and social life of the various sectors and in the associations concerned with the environment, culture and social integration.

In 1994 the European Commission adopted a decentralized approach towards the initiative's implementation, which works through the national or regional level but which does not change its local nature. Accordingly, at regional or national level, a planning and decision-making partnership is established, including all those who provide part-finance at national level, such as the state or region. These partners draw up a Leader-initiative program at regional level, the program being a synthesis of specific operations already submitted by potential local beneficiaries. These regional programs are submitted to the European Commission, studied and then negotiated in partnership with the member state, taking into account the degree of innovation reflected in the program, the rural character of the projects being put forward and the degree of involvement of the rural population. When the program is approved, the regional level partners are then allocated a budget by the Commission.

In 2004, the European Commission spelt out the fundamental aspects of its "Leader approach" in its blueprint document "New Perspectives for EU

Rural Development." The decentralized approach is essential, permitting the "multi-level" character of policy implementation (Bryden & Hart, 2001). Authorities at European, national, regional and local levels need to co-operate to identify needs within a pre-set overall concept for rural development, to define appropriate measures and to manage EU instruments and programs (CEC, 2004). Rural development policy aims to respond to national as well as regional and local needs. It is member states which know best what national needs are and they are, thus, given a central role in drawing up rural development programs and in their implementation. The programming phase begins with each member state presenting its plan which has to take account of the overall EU strategy for rural development. It ends with the Commission approving them, after having assessed their consistency with the rural development regulation. The national or regional strategies must contain quantified objectives and result indicators. More than €5 billion was spent in the framework of the LEADER+ initiative (2000–2006) of which about €2 billion was paid from the EU budget. For the past period (2007–2013) more than €9 billion is foreseen of which some €6 billion from the EU budget (see Table 1). In order to maximize the benefits of potential synergy and avoid losses, the New Perspectives blueprint calls for a better co-ordination between development programs and other European or national support schemes. The viability of rural areas is best maintained and enhanced through territorial approaches, which target multiple sectors in the rural economy. The key element of policy is that they should be based on strengthened local-and-regional co-ordination and management structures and be open to the bottom-up participation of local actors, beginning from the programming phase.

Table 1. The Extent of Leader Initiative Programs, 1991–2013.

LEADER Initiative	No. of LAGs	Area Covered (1,000 km^2)	EU Funding (Billion Euro)
Leader I (1991–1993)	217	367	0.442
Leader II (1994–1999)	906	1375	1,775
Leader (2000–2006)	893	1,577[a]	2,105[b]
Axis 4 – Leader (2007–2013)	1,400	3,500[c]	5,800[d]

[a]Equal to 75% of the total territory of EU-15 and covering some 50 million people.
[b]Plus 1.5 billion euro by private contribution and some 1.5 billion euro by member states of EU-15.
[c]Covering 88 million people in EU-27.
[d]Plus 3.4 billion euro by EU-27 Members States and private contribution.

Networking and exchange of good practice, both nationally and cross-border, increase the effectiveness of programs. This requires support already from the programming stage from both EU and national levels.

The Leader initiative and its "the Leader approach" are marked by their high adaptability to different governance contexts – not only within the EU but also outside – and specific challenges for different rural areas (CEC, 2001). It is highly responsive to small-scale activities and it changes the social fabric in rural areas (Borraz & John, 2004). It mobilizes a high degree of voluntary efforts and fosters equal opportunities between women and men and social groups in rural areas of the EU.

The method of the Leader initiative has eight specific features, which can be classified into local, trans-local and vertical categories (CEC, 2003b) (see Table 2). The following paragraphs enlarge the points listed in the table.

Local features include an area-based approach, a bottom-up approach, partnership approach, innovation and multi-sectoral integration.

The area-based approach (see Fig. 1) as opposed to a sectoral approach, means that:

1. development is focused on a specific territory, which is small, homogenous and socially cohesive;
2. local activities are horizontally integrated; and
3. there are common identities and a shared vision.

Table 2. Features of Leader.

The local features	Area-based approach Bottom-up approach Partnership approach Innovation Multi-sectoral approach	Represented by the local group and by the local development strategy
The trans-local features	Networking Trans-national co-operation	Emerge from interaction between local groups and their respective strategies
The vertical feature	Decentralized management and financing	Represented and implemented by the programming authority. It provides the governance frame in which the local groups carry out their activities. However, the local partnership represents an important element of this feature, which can be considered as management's "terminal" at local level

Source: CEC (2003b, p. 66).

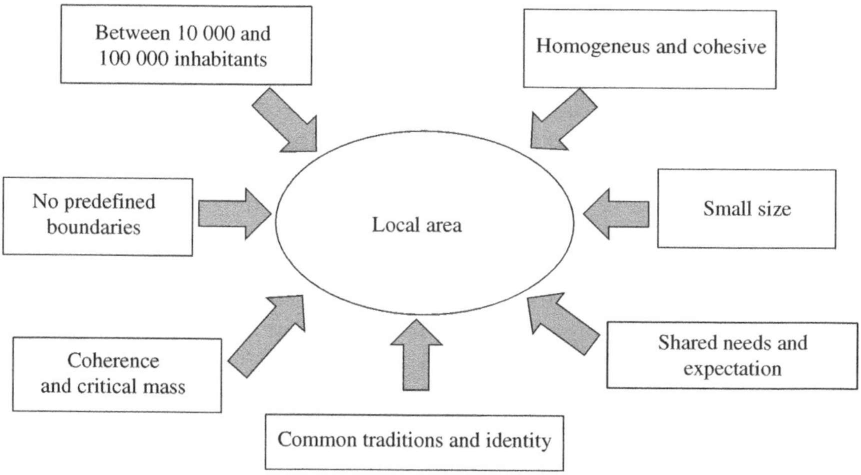

Fig. 1. Area-Based Local Development. The Main Features of Leader Approach to Rural Development – July 2008.

It contributes to a more effective use of endogenous resources due to the closeness of program delivery to the local community and the creation of new links between partners. These new links allow natural, cultural, technological and human resources to be mobilized and secured from oblivion and thus turn them into an economic value for the area (van der Ploeg and Long, 1994). An area-based approach also fosters strategic thinking.

The bottom-up approach refers to the active participation of all interested people and organizations in planning, decision-making and implementation of social and economic development (Terluin, 2001). By bringing the program close to people new opportunities are created for the inclusion of new beneficiaries and weaker members of the population. It is an approach which allows the local community and local players to express their views and to help to define the course of development for their area in line with their own views, expectations and plans. The bottom-up approach has four levels of participation:

1. information through public meetings for the entire community (farmers, non-farmers, residents, etc.);
2. consultation or a kind of "village audit" of active community groups;
3. joint development of projects by the LAG; and
4. collective decision-making of the actions and strategies.

The advantages of the bottom-up approach include the clearer identification of local problems and needs, better organization of development players, better understanding of local decisions by the community, greater acceptance of local decisions by the higher authorities and stimulation of ideas and project leading to innovative local actions.

The partnership approach refers to the temporary coalition of individual persons or collective bodies, based on a contract binding all partners under the same conditions and for the same purpose. In this way new partnerships such as local development agencies and co-operation structures emerge and contribute to the diversification and dynamism of rural territories. Many partnerships evolve into permanent development agencies and, even where they cease to exist, a consciousness of the importance of local partnership as a place for negotiation and the concentration of divergent local interests remains. The effect of the local groups in creating links between activities is strongly influenced by the composition of the partnership. Despite the existence of good examples of both exclusively public and exclusively private partnerships, local groups showing a balanced representation of the private, profit-making and non-profit sector most likely achieve the best results.

Innovative actions give new answers to the existing problems of rural development, and therefore provide added value and an increased territorial competitiveness. One innovation path could be to discover and upgrade local resources and potential. Another could be related to the reshaping of local organizations and networks and to the methodological support for implementing participatory practices in local development. The "Leader approach," in itself, constitutes an innovation when it leads to the creation of trust and confidence and makes people believe in change. The consequent awareness of local people of their own creative potential is the main source of innovation, which leads to an interest in learning and the quest for knowledge transfer.

Multi-sectoral integration refers to both (a) the combination of activities of different economic sectors or of public and private activities in one project and (b) the strategic coherence between different projects in accordance with a common vision. Integration requires that the actions are linked so that the rural innovations program becomes more coherent. One example of the horizontal integration approach is when local restaurants include in their menus typical food products from local producers, thereby stimulating local tourism as well as sales of local products.

As to *the trans-local features* of the experience of the Leader initiative, networking and trans-national co-operation are the most important.

- Networking emerges from interactions between local groups and between their strategies. It is the capacity and readiness for collective action with other independent actors for a common purpose. It is instrumental in strengthening the economic links of local players to the outside world, bringing in expertise and establishing commercial links at long distance. Networking facilitates the dissemination of information, as well as the dissemination and transfer of know-how and good practice.
- Transnational co-operation refers to the co-operation of LEADER groups located in at least two member states for jointly designing, producing and marketing goods or services. It brings a European dimension to the essentially local dimension of the Leader initiative and for many local groups constitutes the first step to networking across borders. It facilitates the dissemination of information and the transfer of know-how and good practice.

The vertical features relate to the multi-level character of program – implementation and to decentralized management and financing.

The priority themes laid down by the Commission for 900 LAGs under LEADER+ (2000–2006) were:

- making the best use of natural and cultural resources, including enhancing the value of sites (selected by 34% of the total number of LAGs);
- improving the quality of life in rural areas (24%);
- adding value to local products, in particular by facilitating access to markets for small production units via collective actions (20%); and
- the use of new know-how and new technologies to make products and services in rural areas more competitive (12%) (CEC, 2003a).
- The remaining 10% of LAGs selected more than one priority theme.

Ever since 2007, the Leader initiative has been more closely embedded in the mainstream development programs of EU rural development policy. In this way, it has lost some of its independence but it has gained in other ways. It has access to a larger amount of EU co-finance and, by being more closely related with the mainstream of development policy, its ideas and innovations can have a wider and more long-lasting impact. It has been embedded by declaring it as one of four priorities for rural development policy 2007–2013, which is designed to pursue three major objectives. The first is *to increase the competitiveness of the agricultural sector* through support for restructuring, which would be built on measures relating to human and physical capital and to quality aspects. The second is *to enhance the environment and countryside* through support for land management and complies with certain standards in the field of environmental protection, public health, animal and plant health and animal welfare. And the third objective is *to strengthen the quality of life in rural areas and to promote diversification of economic activities* through measures targeting the farm sector and other rural actors. Some examples of projects related to these objectives and realized in different member states are mentioned here (Leader European Observatory, 2000):

- assistance types for start-up enterprises and the expansion of existing enterprises including the adoption of new technologies;
- measures increasing the visual appearance of farm and farmyard;
- adding value to local products, including support for business networks, collective marketing, local branding initiatives, the development of artisan processing facilities;
- actions to foster rural entrepreneurship;
- support to enhance the economic and social attractiveness of villages, small towns and the surrounding countryside;
- development of the use of the internet and e-commerce facilities in general for the provision of booking and information services to tourists;
- measures providing appropriate cultural and leisure facilities to local communities.

In realizing the above mentioned objectives, the implementation method has always been based on encouraging local involvement, a bottom-up approach or a policy from the grassroots, i.e. the "Leader initiative."

SOME CONCLUSIONS

There is a strong similarity between the EU's experience with its Leader initiative and the present form of policies for rural development and poverty reduction in some other countries such as China and Brazil. Two similarities which are noteworthy are the benefits to be gained from a grassroots approach to economic development, operated within a centrally determined set of development priorities and objectives, and from higher levels of education for farmers and other rural residents. Put another way, governments may decide the direction and objectives of its rural development policy at a macro-level and implement it at a micro-level.

The Leader initiative and its distinctive "Leader approach" has the same properties and it has generated results which have gone far beyond those which could have been achieved by central policy-makers acting alone. It has shown the importance for rural development of a territorial approach, of the participation of local actors and of the formation of networks between them (OECD, 2006, 2009). It has been instrumental in bringing a local and territorial identity, or dimension, to local development strategies, thus reinforcing the coherence of development projects and magnifying the effects of synergy. Areas which were formerly anonymous have become "unique" with their own strong identity.

Placing an element of "local identity" at the core of a territorial strategy has made it possible for unused, neglected or even forgotten resources to regain their economic and social value. This has given rise to unique products resulting from unusual combinations of different elements and sectors. Good examples are the "Village of Bread" in Belgium and the "route du vin" in France, but there are many more.

Participation has enabled local actors to "imagine" a future for their rural area – to build a consensus around a "vision" for their socio-economic development – and this, in turn, has created opportunities for previously under-represented groups to play a role. For example, it is remarkable to note the strong participation of women in LAGs. Also, it has become clear that the decline of certain areas, even where it is well-advanced, is never terminal because local players make it possible to explore new avenues of development. In some cases visionary players came forward to present a totally new product or service which then has a multiplier effect. In addition, new technologies have been introduced, such as "télé-medecine" in France, establishing a telemonitoring system to support and improve the care of patients.

Networking has similarly led to exchanges of experience, to mutual willingness to learn from each other and to the possibility of co-operation between rural areas by establishing vital European Leader-initiative networks of local groups. Cross-border co-operation has allowed the planning and implementation of joint projects and, even more importantly, has provided a concrete demonstration of the possibilities for the development of rural Europe.

The "Leader approach," incorporated into integrated rural development strategies, has allowed experiments with local (territorially based) small scale actions (pilot projects) using the endogenous potential of the locality. The underlying assumption is that development processes involve a different mix of relevant factors that are unique and typical of a particular geographical space and time and, therefore, development programs need to be conceived at local level.

Experience of the Leader initiative clearly illustrates that the success of the projects also depends on good management. There is an absolute need for young and intelligent people to be in the driver's seat and the optimum arrangement is that the best people should be on duty in the most fragile areas. The mainstreaming of all features of the Leader methodology (bottom-up, territorial, partnership, integrated approach ...) strengthens rural development policy by making it more adequate to deal with the increased diversity of EU28 but it should be handled in such a way that it does not lead to the loss of the many excellent and extremely motivated animators and managers of local Leader projects.

EU rural development policy continues to aim at the maintenance of a lively and healthy countryside. Rural development interests have sought to encourage the diversification of local economies away from their former dependence on primary production. This led to the use of a set of simple transparent instruments for job creation, growth, the development of the quality of life and of a countryside as a recreational resource for all, but equally for the environment, renewable energy and new forms of sustainable agriculture.

This allows the valorization of the Union's immense territorial diversity and, at the same time, helps to preserve the Union's cohesion. These essential objectives are achieved on the basis of the involvement of the local stakeholders, which serves as a Europe-wide example of participative democracy.

NOTES

1. French abbreviation "Liaison entre Actions pour le Developpement de l'Economie Rurale"=links between actions for developing the rural economy.
2. This population size would be larger than most of China's administrative villages.

REFERENCES

Borraz, O., & John, P. (2004). The transformation of urban political leadership in Western Europe. *International Journal of Urban and Regional Research*, *28*(1), 107–120.

Bryden, J., & Hart, K. (2001). *Dynamics of Rural Areas (DORA): The international comparison*. Aberdeen: The Arkleton Centre for Rural Development.

CEC. (1988). *The future of rural society*. Brussels. Com (88) 501 final.

CEC. (2001, July 25). *European governance. A White Paper*. Com (2001) 428 final. Brussels.

CEC. (2003a). *Fact sheet. Rural development in the European Union*. Luxembourg: Office for Official Publications of the European Communities.

CEC. (2003b). *Ex-post evaluation of the Community Initiative Leader II*. Final report. Vienna: Austrian Institute for Regional Studies and Spatial Planning.

CEC. (2004). *New perspectives for EU rural development*. Luxembourg: Office for Official Publications of the European Communities.

LEADER European Observatory. (2000). *Territorial competitiveness. Creating a territorial development strategy in the light of the LEADER experience*. Dossier no 6, part 1.

OECD. (2006). *Rural policy reviews: The new rural paradigm: Policies and governance*. Paris: OECD.

OECD. (2009). *Rural policy reviews*. Paris: OECD.

Terluin, I. J. (2001). *Rural regions in the EU. Exploring differences in economic development*. Utrecht: Nederlandse Geografische Studies.

van der Ploeg, J. D., & Long, A. (1994). *Born from within: Practice and perspectives of endogenous rural development*. Assen: Van Gorcum.

CHAPTER 9

THE DISTINCTIVENESS OF RURAL DEVELOPMENT PRACTICES IN NORTH WEST EUROPE

Rudolf van Broekhuizen, Bart Soldaat,
Henk Oostindie and Jan Douwe van der Ploeg

ABSTRACT

Comparing rural development with agricultural modernisation, there are fundamental differences. Industrial development of agriculture more and more segregates agriculture from other functions and is based on an 'individualised transaction model' *in which the world consists of loose particles that are linked by markets (atomistic world view). Conversely rural development can be perceived as a form of re-socialisation of agriculture and is based on a* 'relational cooperation model' *in which new relations characterise business development.*

This chapter is a second level type of analysis of many research findings of these common traits or features and gives a picture of the distinctiveness of rural development practices. Nine different features that characterize rural development practices are described and discussed: (1) novelty production, (2) relative autonomy, (3) synergy, (4) clashes and

Constructing a New Framework for Rural Development
Research in Rural Sociology and Development, Volume 22, 209–238

ISSN: 1057-1922/doi:10.1108/S1057-192220150000022008

competing claims, (5) coalitions and new relations; the construction of rural webs, (6) common pool resources, (7) new division of labour, (8) the distinctive different impact and (9) resilience. The more these features are present and intertwined, the better the specific practice can face and withstand adverse conditions. These features and the associated practices have to be understood as part of a wider transitional process that might co-evolve with or run counter to competing transitional processes.

Keywords: Rural development; local practices; novelty; autonomy; regional development; rural actors

INTRODUCTION

There are many examples of rural development like on-farm processing, agro-tourism, new cooperative forms of commercialisation or agricultural nature and landscape management, agro-ecological production, etc. These practices have certain traits in common. This chapter is a second level type of analysis of many research findings of these common traits or features and gives a picture of the distinctiveness of rural development practices. Nine different features that characterize rural development practices are described and discussed: (1) novelty production, (2) relative autonomy, (3) synergy, (4) clashes and competing claims, (5) coalitions and new relations; the construction of rural webs, (6) common pool resources, (7) new division of labour, (8) the distinctive different impact and (9) resilience. The more these features are present and intertwined, the better the specific practice can face and withstand adverse conditions. These features and the associated practices have to be understood as part of a wider transitional process that might co-evolve with or run counter to competing transitional processes.

Comparing rural development with agricultural modernisation, there are fundamental differences. Industrial development of agriculture more and more segregates agriculture from other functions and is based on an '*individualised transaction model*' in which the world consists of loose particles that are linked by markets (atomistic world view). Conversely rural development can be perceived as a form of re-socialisation of agriculture and is based on a '*relational cooperation model*' in which new relations characterise business development.

NOVELTY PRODUCTION

Rural development practices often are the outcome of novelty production.[1] As compared to conventional agriculture, rural development practices are distinctively different. In the beginning they were new, representing deviations from the rule. Novelties, although often difficult to notice and detect, are crucial for rural development. Novelty production refers to the capacity, within a region, to continuously renovate and improve processes of production, products, patterns of cooperation, mechanisms for distribution and marketing. Many at first sight are minor changes in the process of production, cooperation or combination of resources, introduced on purpose or unintentionally, which can result in increased competitiveness of the local economy and of quality of the countryside. These changes may consist of, and result in, new insights, practices, artefacts, and/or combinations (of resources, of technological procedures, of different bodies of knowledge) that enable specific constellations (a process of production, a network, the integration of two different activities) to function better (van der Ploeg et al., 2008). They make the economy perform better: they drive the 'frontier function' in an upward direction (Timmer, 1970). In short, a novelty is 'a new configuration that promises to work' (Rip & Kemp, 1998). Once created, rural development practices continue to be the cradle for further novelty production.

Novelties are, as yet, unelaborated in terms of codified (scientific) knowledge:

> Novelties are located on the borderline that separates the known from the unknown. A novelty is something new [...]. At the same time, [they] are, as yet, not fully understood. They are deviations from the rule. They do not correspond to knowledge accumulated so far – they defy, as it were, conventional understanding. Novelties go beyond existing and explained regularities. (Wiskerke & van der Ploeg, 2004)

Novelty production is highly bound to and rooted in the local context and therefore is unique to a specific region. Thus it might give a particular region a competitive advantage. However, novelties are part of a system of tacit knowledge and cannot easily be transported from the specific context from which they have emerged towards other settings. Repetition elsewhere seldom is a matter of simple copying. The newly created patterns and activities are to be adapted to new situations. This is a major difference between a novelty and an innovation.

An innovation is an expression of codified knowledge that is embodied into an artefact and which can travel from one place to another (Oostindie & Van Broekhuizen, 2008). In Box 1 some differences between novelties and innovations are summarised.

Analytically speaking it might be argued that novelty production is intrinsic to agriculture as a result of co-production, that is the on-going encounter, interaction and mutual transformation of the social and the natural (Rip & Kemp, 1998; Roep, 2000; Toledo, 1990; van der Ploeg et al., 2004). Peasant innovativeness (Ventura & Milone, 2005) unfolds along different trajectories that are all grounded, in one way or another, in co-production. These trajectories centre on: (a) improving resources, (b) fine tuning of growth factors, (c) boundary shifts, and (d) re-patterning resource use.[2]

Box 1. Differences between Novelties and Innovations.
Source: Taken from Oostindie and Van Broekhuizen (2008).

The figure below summarises some of the crucial differences between the learning processes underlying novelties and innovations. It shows that novelties are primarily 'grass-root' driven, grounded in the worlds and processes of production and labour and spurred by learning process that occur through contextualisation, territorialisation and socialisation. By contrast, innovations primarily stem from worlds that are external to the sphere of production: expert-driven learning processes that are characterised by standardisation, externalisation and globalisation. These processes can also translate novelties into innovations and the opposite might also occur: with innovations being translated at the grass-root levels into novelties through contextualisation, territorialisation and internalisation.

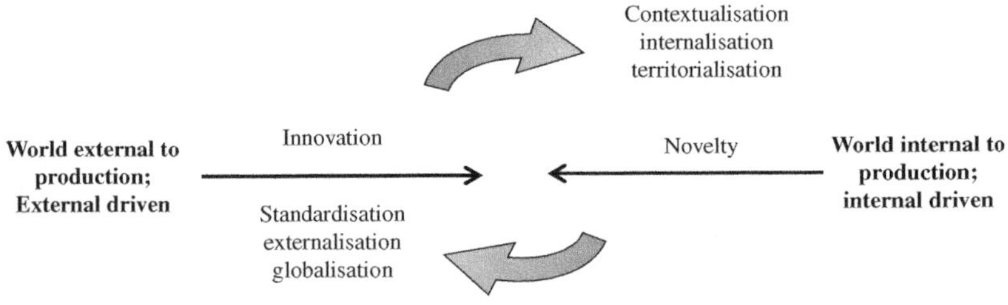

RELATIVE AUTONOMY

Many rural development practices explicitly tend to enlarge the autonomy of the involved rural enterprises (mostly multifunctional farms). At regional level there equally are attempts to construct higher degrees of autonomy (this relates sometimes to the struggle for self-governance). Autonomy is not something isolated or singular, it is always related to something else. The concept of autonomy only has meaning within a social context in which there also is dependency (i.e. not-autonomy). Relations with others limit autonomy insofar as they imply forms of dependency. At the same time they are also an essential prerequisite for autonomy; relations with others can enlarge someone's room for manoeuvre. Autonomy regards the degree in which dependency-relations are self-chosen and self-controlled. Hence it is quite understandable that 'development of new relations with citizens and consumers' is a very important motive of the involved actors (van der Ploeg et al., 2015). The creation of a new 'nested market' by a network of farm-shops, for instance, requires new mutual relations between farmers and new relations with consumers and thus new forms of (self-chosen and self-controlled) dependency, but simultaneously reduces the dependency of chains of supermarkets (van der Ploeg, Ye, & Schneider, 2012). So it always is about *relative* autonomy; rural development processes refer to a search for a new specific balance of control of social relations. Rural development initiatives and practices, and the related struggle for autonomy, often emerge as a response to and mirror image of the processes of globalisation and the connected uniformisation and standardisation of production (although different for regions and countries). Globalisation tends to be a development process that is out of balance: the networks and social relations often are geared to the interests and prospects of the powerful actors, the control of food being concentrated in the hands of fewer and fewer multinational actors. The spatial consequences include marginal and sparsely populated rural societies that are reduced to being the producers of raw materials or where agriculture even disappears from the scene (Oostindie, van Broekhuizen, Brunori, & van der Ploeg, 2008). In this process the position of primary producers tends to become weaker and smaller, as expressed by their decreasing share of the total value added and the reduced control of the farm development process.

However, forces that tend towards global integration and reduction of autonomy also generate counter tendencies. Gouldner speaks about the 'iron law' of opposition to oligarchy:

> Tendencies toward system integration [....] are always interpreted and implemented by some system part which has its own distinct drive toward functional autonomy. Correspondingly, [...] oligarchic tendencies that threaten the autonomy of the other parts of the system, generate opposition to oligarchy, polarize the system around an internal conflict, and, in effect, constitute an 'iron law' of opposition to oligarchy. (1970, p. 216)

The more globalisation and standardisation proceed, the more meaning locality and singularity gets and the more opportunities for distinction and local exceptions with their own logics arise. Rural development initiatives can be understood as reactions to the 'externalisation' of control and as attempts to develop a new own development-logic and thus autonomy. In many regions actors are actively looking for mechanisms and instruments to create new *balances* between exogenous and endogenous resources that better fit the local situation and the related interests and prospects. They try to maintain, utilise, reproduce and renew the specific local characteristics and, by doing so, create some distance and distinction from 'the global' or to use and control global relations according to their own 'local logic' (i.e. relative autonomy). These practices are grounded in the economic interest of (groups of) farmers, local history, passion of civilians and consumers or policy and are *initiated and controlled*, at least partly, by local society (Oostindie et al., 2008).

Creating autonomy is not the same as avoiding external influences as much as possible. On the contrary, as stated by Long (1988, pp. 121–122):

> All forms of external intervention necessarily enter the life-worlds of the individuals and groups affected and thus, as it were, comes to form part of the resources and constraints of the social strategies they develop. In this way so-called external factors are internalised and may come to mean quite different things to different interest groups or actors. Externally-originating factors are therefore mediated, incorporated, and often substantially transformed by local organisational and cognitive structures.

External factors don't determine 'the optimal solution' but can be translated and utilised in a way that strengthens the specific local development and *local control* (see e.g. Box 2). So autonomy implies the construction of a self-controlled *interaction* between the local and the extra-local/global and does not mean absolute autonomy, but always *relative* autonomy.

A related concept is 'endogenous development'.[3] This is an operationalization of 'relative autonomy' at regional level. In endogenous development

Box 2. New Form of Globalisation of Relations that Strengthens Local Autonomy and Endogenous Development: Hotel De Boerenkamer in the Laag Holland Area (NL).

Laag Holland is an attractive rural area that is the 'backyard of Amsterdam'. The Hotel De Boerenkamer (Farmers-room) is a cooperation of farmers who offer high quality accommodation for tourists in individual farm houses. The quality standards, branding and marketing are organised collectively. Especially successful is the marketing by means of a collective website. Internet offers the opportunity for this 'group of individuals' to develop their own global marketing strategy and for tourists from all over the world to discover and book these hotel rooms on attractive farms in an attractive rural area and in the immediate vicinity of Amsterdam (e.g. 10–15 minutes by bike to the city centre). Indeed many tourists from, for example, Italy, The United States and Japan are able to find Hotel de Boerenkamer.

the notions of local *resources* and local *control* are central. The 'endogeneity' of rural economies refers to the *degree* to which local and regional rural economies are:

- built on local resources,[4]
- organised according to local models for resource combination and which equally imply local control over the use of these resources,
- strengthened through the distribution and reinvestment of the produced wealth within the local or regional constellation.

The degree of endogeneity is to be understood as the outcome of particular development trajectories within and through which the balance of local and external resources is continuously being redefined and reshuffled. Some rural economies are more endogenous than others. A high degree of endogeneity might entail a range of specific advantages.

SYNERGY

Many rural development practices combine different activities. Out of this emerges synergy which on its turn enlarges autonomy, and increases regional rural competiveness and quality of life in rural areas. The rural development practices encountered in the North West of Europe show that many rural development processes (1) start with *new activities* on individual farms, (2) that such new activities often induce other new activities on the farm and thus generates a new *multifunctional business-model* (see Box 3) and (3) cooperation among farmers and with others actors strengthens the activities of individual farmers, creates new conditions that enable new activities, and results in rural development as a model for *regional rural development* (see, e.g. Box 4). Synergy implies that one activity has a surplus value for another and the other way around.[5] The same goes for different involved sectors and actors: the total is more than the sum of the parts.

Agrarian-based rural development practices are no longer limited to individual projects, as they were some decades ago. They increasingly depart from, and unfold through, wider networks that link many activities on individual farms and of different actors, several different levels (the local, the regional, the national, the EU) and articulate in different dimensions (Ventura, Milone, & van der Ploeg, 2010). So the impact of rural development initiatives is not only relevant at the level of individual enterprises, but is increasingly significant at the regional level as well[6] (quality of life, employment levels, increased value added, synergy effects, etc.).

At the same time, it is within the regional context that rural development emerges as a concrete interest to be defended and strengthened by regional institutions and through regional policies. For a long time, rural areas have

Box 3. Gradual Development of Multifunctional Agriculture as a Business-Model.

In the beginning of the 1990s, a Dutch farm-family started with a mini-camping enterprise. When more and more campers asked for sailing boats they decided to add a small marina to the farm and to start renting out small boats. Recently bad-weather accommodation and meeting rooms have been built, especially because of the growing demand from local organisations such as the agricultural nature organisation, the church and regional NGO's. Right now new plans are under construction to enlarge the marina, to increase the number of rental boats and to realise a new agricultural nature area around the marina (Oostindie, Seuneke, van Broekhuizen, Hegger, & Wiskerke, 2011, p. 13).

> ***Box 4.*** Rural Development as a Model for Regional Rural Development: Tuscany.
>
> Tuscany is an attractive region in the middle of Italy. Why does it attract tourists? It is not because of several multifunctional farms or the like. The farmers together produce an attractive landscape. The many high quality and region-specific products according to a collective standard and brand, like Chianti wine and the connected wine-routes etc., create an attractive gastronomy. The many farms with a high quality 'agri-tourism' create a good tourism infrastructure. The regional policies that reserve the rights to start agro-touristic activities for, indeed, 'real farms', support the further development of regional specific products, and protect the quality of the area by means of their spatial policy and planning. Altogether an attractive region or 'district' is created that results in extra regional income that in its turn stimulates new rural development investments. The different activities are geared to one another and 'the total' has added value for the individual actors.

been – and to a certain degree still are – characterised by cleavages between different sectors. Agriculture, forestry, small- and medium-scale industry, recreation and tourism, nature conservation and housing all operated as sectors that were isolated from each other. Agricultural modernisation was and is one of the driving forces of this segregation of functions. Currently there are rural development activities, processes and policies that together cross these lines of demarcation. District formation, economies of scope, multifunctionality and positive externalities are important keywords here. Different sectors are being 'bridged' and are tied together at the local level.[7] Bringing together economic sectors and activities that have previously been separated, their active entwinement and the creation and use of synergy are becoming important activities that might become self-propelling. The 'bridges' that are constructed in this way are essentially local (Ventura et al., 2010).

It is further important to underline the significance of the time and scale dimension here. It takes time to (re-)construct synergies at farm and, particularly, the territorial level as for example is demonstrated by research-outcomes regarding the dynamics of multifunctional farm enterprises (Oostindie et al., 2011) and rural-web analysis (Milone & Ventura, 2010; van der Ploeg & Marsden, 2008a, 2008b). Combining activities and linking sectors are time consuming processes that imply continuous and mutual re-balancing of resources and interests. For example, the process of developing a 'model for regional rural development' in the Laag Holland area in the Netherlands (as described in van Broekhuizen and Oostindie (2010) and illustrated hereafter in this chapter) took about 30 years, is grounded in 'blood, sweat and tears' and still contains vulnerabilities, pitfalls and challenges. It is very important to distinguish this process of creating synergy in practice from 'theoretical' blue-print synergy drawn up on the drawing board of planners or authorities and that subsequently has to be implemented in practice. It can then often result in new conflicts of interest, new struggles, resistance and/or barriers for renewal instead of 'new bridges'.

CLASHES AND COMPETING CLAIMS

In many policy papers rural development is represented as constituting a harmonious process (the use of words like dialogue, cooperation, new coalitions and shared visions). Nonetheless, the practice of rural development is characterised as much by conflicts as by cooperation. Alongside coalitions there are as many cleavages and divisions (between e.g. 'locals' and 'newcomers') – several of them not simply prior to but indeed stemming from the processes of rural development themselves (Marsden & van der Ploeg, 2008). Since many rural development practices start as deviations from the rule and can be understood as counter-movement (counter to modernisation), they are accompanied by clashes with those who defend and/or stick to the rules or follow other perspectives. Such clashes do not diminish with the further dissemination of particular practices – on the contrary, when particular practices tend to become stronger (just as the claims that are inherent to it) the 'counter-claims' will grow as well.

Rural development processes, most certainly at regional level, mostly develop stepwise and every step invokes a kind of struggle. Many of these processes started as struggles against the state (e.g. against spatial planning practices in which nature reserves were designated or against other claims on agricultural land), against vested farmers unions, against large food supply chains, etc.[8] A crucial step often is that 'protest' is combined with the idea 'we can do it better'. This, subsequently, leads to concrete action. All this might be summarised as 'constructive dissatisfaction', a notion used in innovation and management theories (see e.g. Brewster & Dalzell, 2007). The value of 'constructive dissatisfaction' is that it goes beyond 'just being unhappy' but that it moves involved actors into action mode in which the objectives of 'the opponents' are taken seriously as well. An integral ingredient of many rural development practices is the capacity to engage in clashes and quarrels without making definitive enemies, to redirect conflicts into meaningful resolutions, to transform the competing claims that indeed often accompany rural development practices into more constructive learning and negotiation settings. This could be illustrated by on-going searches for experimental space within agri-environmental policy frameworks in the EU to further explore the potential benefits (as well as limitations) of self-regulation initiatives (see e.g. Box 5). First small concrete constructive initiatives and first small 'successes' in practice are needed to deserve a certain trust that in its turn is needed to develop the next step. Rural development relies upon building trust relationships, management of individualism in ways which create new collective gains, and forging new alliances and coalitions (through new networks) (Marsden & van der Ploeg, 2008).

Box 5. Laag Holland, 30 Years of Step-by-Step Development of a Rural Web (van Broekhuizen & Oostindie, 2010).

The first nuclei of a functioning model for regional rural development in Laag Holland can be traced back 30 years. At that time, a group of farmers founded the Working Group Young Farmers Waterland in an area that is currently at the heart of the National Landscape. Their ideas and initiatives indicated an important change of approach to agricultural development in the region. It represented the beginning of a farmers' movement that in many respects represented an alternative to the logic of agricultural modernisation. Some elements of this approach were as follows:

- In contrast to prevailing and dominant ideas, the future of farming in Waterland was seen as being dependent on the integration of nature and landscape management into farming practices.
- The tendency towards further de-localisation, uniformity and standardisation in agriculture was replaced by an approach in which local conditions and ecology formed the starting points of agricultural development.

- Local self-organisation and self-regulation as opposed to the centralisation tendencies of the traditional and powerful agricultural organisations developed as a pro-active strategy. Instead of a reactive, defensive attitude towards national policy changes, alternative and locally developed ideas and proposals were pro-actively elaborated starting from the conviction that 'We can do it better' and that farmers could contribute effectively and efficiently to landscape and nature management.
- New forms of territory-based cooperation with other groups were initiated.

In the 1970s, during the early stages of this new farmers movement, the 'conventional' policy for 'less favoured rural areas' still implied large-scale land consolidation projects. Holdings were enlarged by filling in ditches, new roads were constructed, water levels were lowered, ditches were straightened and drainage patterns changed. This approach ran counter to the growing concern for landscape and nature preservation. Government solutions to this problem included a spatial segregation of areas reserved for further agricultural modernisation from those 'nature function' areas where agriculture would have to disappear in time. Waterland was identified as a nature development area. The local farmers' movement played an important role in the shift from a policy oriented towards a segregation of functions to the current policy of an increased integration of functions.

What started as a small group that protested against a nature reserve is 30 years later a professional organisation that expanded its field of work to cover the entire Laag Holland area: the professional agri-environmental cooperative Association for Agricultural Nature and Landscape Management, now known as Water, Land and Dikes. This Association has about 430 farmer members and 10 employees. Many new projects and activities have been organised and new partnerships with other farmers' initiatives, nature organisations as well as municipalities continue to be developed. Gradually the Association is recognised by many stakeholders and authorities as a capable and crucial organisation and fulfils an important role in the region. The farmers' movement initiated a process characterised by territory-based cooperation between multifunctional rural enterprises. In addition to – and partly related to this Association – many other territory-based networks of rural enterprises have been established focusing on region-specific food, rural tourism and the provision of on-farm care. The growing synergy between these new rural activities has led to the construction of a specific *territorial model*, one that re-links agricultural production to rural services and urban consumers.

This also illustrates how the ideas and proposals of the *Young Farmers Working Group* that were initially classified as 'unacceptable' or 'infeasible' by public authorities, the established powerful nature preservation organisations and conventional agricultural interest groups, are now being put into practice. Many of the Group's activities have built upon as well as strengthened available social capital by developing shared visions and the construction of coherence and many-sided cooperation between grass-root initiatives. Taken as a whole this has induced new institutional arrangements as well as new linkages with urban markets.

'Successful' regional rural development certainly not only depends on grass-roots initiatives. They can function as 'seeds of transition' (see Wiskerke & Van der Ploeg, 2004), but these seeds need a well-prepared seedbed as well. It also requires connection of initiatives at the grass-root level with the positive opinions of 'others' at regional level (NGO's, citizen groups, etc.), and the policy level. Indeed, an integral ingredient of regional rural development is the art to protest and engage in clashes and quarrels in such a way that later on initial opponents become allies. Clashes and quarrels indeed can be 'constructive'; initially disputed or even 'unacceptable' new rural development initiatives in retrospect can be identified as the first building blocks and starting points for the design of new policies. Effective new policies mostly are, at least partially, 'induced policies'. Interaction with practices is needed to design effective policies and policy instruments. In the analysis of rural development processes and the related process of policymaking the time-dimension also plays an important role. The unfolding of a rural web in Laag Holland (see Box 5), for instance, covered a period of 30 years: the step-by-step process of rural development in this period of time often needed new momentum; 'small successes' were followed by new clashes and quarrels, etc. The current policy is not designed at one time, but the result of a succession of adaptations, of many different steps among other things grounded in 'constructive dissatisfaction'. To put it somewhat simply, the 'management of quarrelling', that is the capability of splitting the process up into 'manageable quarrels', is an important element of rural development.

COALITIONS AND NEW RELATIONS; ABOUT THE CONSTRUCTION OF RURAL WEBS

Simultaneously, the making of coalitions and the entering into new relations are essential ingredients for rural development as well. This applies to coalitions and relations between farmers; between (groups of) farmers and consumers, citizens, regional nature organisations and rural dwellers; between local initiatives and authorities at different levels. The main finding of the ETUDE research programme[9] is that successful rural development in practice is rooted in a myriad of encounters, transactions, interactions, mutualities and networks that link people, resources, activities (be they social, economic, political or cultural), sectors and markets. This loosely structured constellation is referred to as a 'rural web'. To put it differently, the 'rural web' is the more or less coherent whole of actor-networks that exist within the rural (van der Ploeg et al., 2008).[10] The web, that is the conglomerate of actor-networks, is multilevel: it covers the local and the regional and this, in turn, influences the inter-linkages with higher levels of aggregation. Rural webs involve many actors, institutions, enterprises, state agencies and social movements. They are, in short, also multi-actor. When comparing these networks, one finds large heterogeneity: they differ considerably from one region to another. The ETUDE-project shows that in regions where there are real 'gaps', conflicts or tensions in the rural web rural development are less successful than in areas with a more unfolded web (see a.o. van Broekhuizen & Oostindie, 2010). Rural development proceeds as an unfolding and further strengthening of the rural web.

Such an approach is in line with the characterisation of 'territory' by Camagni (2007). Territory, he argues, is:

> 'a system of localized proximity relationships which constitute a 'capital' – of a social, psychological and political nature – in that they enhance the static and dynamic productivity of local factors' [and also function as] 'a system of rules and practices defining a local governance model'.

Rural development can also be understood as a process of re-connecting and re-balancing the rural and the urban; in the end rural development is about the construction of new relations between the rural and the urban. The simple rural – urban dichotomy, that is the rural and the urban are mutually exclusive, is not satisfactory. This simple divide no longer fits with the spatial, cultural, economic and social characteristics of 21st Century Europe. Town and countryside are intimately linked and interdependent; urbanisation is currently creating the need for more rurality in order to maintain a balanced society and an acceptable quality of life (as argued by, e.g. the Dutch Council for the Rural Areas – Raad voor het Landelijke Gebied [RLG], 1997). Rural development can be seen as the interlinking of many expressions of new societal demands with new forms of rural supply.

These new societal demands require the existence of an agriculture that actively articulates with the new needs that are emerging from the cities: for example high quality products, regional products that carry an identity, care facilities, energy production, attractive landscapes, attractive expressions of nature and biodiversity, possibilities for housing, recreational facilities. In 'new rural areas', as described by van der Ploeg et al. (2008), considerable parts of agriculture are developing into new forms of multifunctional farming (Knickel et al., 2004) that respond to this broad range of new needs. Multifunctional agriculture in these 'new rural areas' increasingly is intertwined with the regional economy and society, thereby contributing to regional qualities (as biodiversity, landscape, the supply of services, quality of life, energy production). The multi-product enterprise is a distinctive feature of these regions. Through its new activities value added is increased and new meeting points between urban consumers and citizens and rural producers are created. At the same time these activities are coordinated through networks that allow for the inclusion of more actors. Tuscany (see Box 4) is a telling example here. In these new rural areas, new urban needs and new rural supplies are interacting and simultaneously shaping and reshaping each other and resulting in new markets.[11] Here, most of all we find that the 'rural' is being made to blossom again. In this respect it might be argued that rural areas as Laag Holland (see Box 2 and Box 5) as part of a large metropolitan area are far more rural than for example the sparsely populated Finnish Woodlands, precisely because it is valued by many inhabitants of Amsterdam and other cities who like to take their leisure there (Broekhuizen & Oostindie, 2010).

COMMON POOL RESOURCES

Many rural development practices contribute to, and increasingly depend on, the construction of new common pool resources (CPRs). A nested market (e.g. Chianina beef or Texels lamb) typically is a CPR, just as an attractive landscape; *through a commonly shared set of rules joint common/mutual benefits are produced.* The capacity to produce distinctive products or services (a high quality product, an attractive landscape) that are hard to copy or imitate is based on underlying common pool resources (e.g. see Box 6). Such a capacity is a resource that is open to an increasing number of producers and, thus, to a potentially growing number of consumers (Polman, Poppe, van der Schans, & van der Ploeg, 2010). There is an extensive debate on CPRs in general and on the relation between rural development, nested markets and CPRs. Regarding these debates we limit ourselves to referring to van der Ploeg et al. (2012) and Polman et al. (2010). What we want to emphasise here is the role of CPRs as self-governing institutions (organised and governed by the resource users

Box 6. CPR in Laag Holland.

There are rather successful rural development practices in the area in which the landscape quality is a crucial element; the rural economy to a large extent is landscape-based (see also Box 2 and Box 5). Can the landscape of Laag Holland be understood as a CPR? However the landscape itself is not a CPR. It could be understood as a barrier or as 'anti-resource' for agricultural development as well. It has to be made a CPR. A resource has to be recognised and defined as a potential resource (instead of as a barrier). Only specific rules, networks, self-organisation and local knowledge make it a CPR and indeed a resource for several activities that together strengthen the rural economy.

Landscape management cannot be organised by individual farmers; farmers need specific knowledge for example on the relation between farm-management and the meadow-bird population; collectives of farmers need cooperation with relevant authorities and nature organisations to alter regulation and spatial planning in a way they will be involved in the management of nature and landscape; interfaces with consumers and citizens with specific preferences are required. The specific knowledge, the shared visions, the set of rules, the social networks, the needed organisational capacity, together with the material characteristics of the landscape create a CPR as a self-governed institution that (a) protects vulnerable landscape and ecological values in a sustainable way, (b) requires adapted agricultural management (see also Box 5) and (c) allows new multifunctional activities (e.g. Hotel de Boerenkamer, see Box 2).

themselves) that produce joint benefits, function as a kind of 'lines of defence' against loss of autonomy and (hostile) take-over by large food companies and create a distance from the logic of globalisation and of capital. Common Pool Resources cannot be sold or expropriated, because they are intrinsically tied to the collective that is its main carrier. The set of rules reflect, in contrast with capital, the interests and perspectives of the involved producers, ecological cycles, and/or principles such as social justice and solidarity (van der Ploeg et al., 2012). Unfolding rural webs become a kind of CPR. In 'working on rural development', for example, designing support-programmes or new rural development polices, it is important to be aware that the typical construction and governance of CPRs can be of great importance.

NEW DIVISIONS OF LABOUR

Rural development practices often imply new patterns of the social division of labour. The development of new activities, of multifunctional agriculture and of new forms of cooperation and networks and the reclaiming of autonomy and control goes together with a process of redefining the content, role and divisions of labour. The new divisions of labour often are both the beginning and outcome of clashes and/or competing claims. Some examples will be described briefly, with the common denominator the search for increased self-control and autonomy, at both individual and collective (regional) levels.

A first example is the re-patterning of the division of labour between agriculture and retail, or agriculture and the food industry. New short food chains, self-processing of raw products into final products and the construction of new nested markets are examples of 'forward integration' that imply a redistribution of tasks, responsibilities and power. This is a reversal of the modernisation process in which the position, role and tasks of farmers has been narrowed down and reduced, such that in differentiating food chains, their task and role is more and more (re-)defined and designed by other more powerful parties in the food supply chain and is reduced to the production of raw materials processed and marketed by others. Of course this reversal requires new relations between for example cooperating farmers (new arrangements and appointments), between groups of producers and shops, as well as new competences, skills and learning processes.[12]

Another example, more typical of the Netherlands, concerns the shifting responsibilities between farmers engaged in nature conservation and the nature conservation organisations. The monopoly on the management of large areas of land with a nature and/or landscape function has been broken and farmers, under specific conditions, now get the opportunity to manage (a part of) these areas (see Box 5). This type of division of labour is a source of many clashes and counter-claims referred to before.

A third example is the strong growth in the number of 'care farms' in the Netherlands (to more than a thousand in 2012), the result of a comparable process of de-monopolisation. The funding system of care initially was focused on care-institutes. This system partially has been replaced by a system in which the individual care recipients have at their disposal an individual personal budget that can be used to purchase the needed care. As a result many people buy the care provided by a care-farm. By now many care farms are organised in an association that organises training, provides quality certificates and the like. More and more large care assurance companies are willing to make contracts with care farms.

A fourth example deserves special attention regards gender relations. Frequently new rural development activities and processes are initiated by (farm) women: for example care farms, child care, recreation and self-processing of products. Crucial elements are the 'broader view' that women have on society and social relations (less preoccupation with technical production), and the wish for an independent domain in the agricultural enterprise (Bock, 2002, 2010; de Rooij, Brouwer en, van Broekhuizen, 1995). Whereas, to put it strongly, modernisation of agriculture often has been accompanied by an erosion of the role and position of women in agriculture, whilst rural development, by contrast, goes together with re-gaining the integral position of women within farm-businesses.

A fifth example is the increased flexibility in farm business development. A Dutch research project (Oostindie et al., 2011) reveals the importance of voluntary transfer of room for manoeuvre and decision-making to the next generation. The parents consciously and purposefully create flexibility in the farm organisation (both in terms of activities and finances) in order to allow the next generation to make own choices and to choose their own position in the prevailing conditions. Investments that determine and fixate the long term organisation of the farm are avoided. Different from what often can be observed in conventional agriculture (where farmers often have a firm idea and picture of 'the farm of the future', e.g. with respect to size, activities), multifunctional farmers follow a more strategic way of thinking in which there is always some room to integrate new activities and to anticipate new developments and conditions.

A DISTINCTIVELY DIFFERENT IMPACT

Outcomes of rural development practices are in many ways different from conventional practices. For example, rural development practices tend to provide more employment opportunities and more income generation capacity. They also tend to enlarge the resilience of farm enterprises and thus sustain the investments in food production *sensu stricto*. So rural development is definitely not to be seen as a farewell to food production. It is precisely the other way around.[13] The most interesting and important feature, however, is that the impact of rural development activities cannot be captured with a single indicator nor with a limited set of such indicators. The point is that the impact of rural development activities is *multiple* and *mouldable*. Hence, the way in which the impact materialises is not fixed, but might be re-shaped when conditions change and/or when the process of rural development proceeds further.

Rural development activities often generate extra value added. This might result in improved incomes at farm enterprise level. However, the extra value added might be used as well to create additional employment (e.g. contract a shop assistant for the farm shop) – then there will be no extra income in the farm enterprise as such. But let us assume that extra value is translated into extra income. Now, this might be used for consumption, it might also be saved in order to be used for investments in: (1) the already created rural development activities, (2) new, additional rural development activities, (3) in the conventional part of the farm, (4) new territory-based networks, (5) preservation of rural amenities, etc. In turn, some of such activities might strengthen the competitiveness of the area and thus feedback positively on the creation of value added at the farm level. This refers to a third characteristic that is important when talking about the impact of rural development. That is that the processes become increasingly *self-propelling*.

Besides direct positive material impact as described above, rural development practices can have many indirect effects. The positive contribution to the attractiveness of the area and the resulting quality of life of citizens in and around the area often has to be understood as the main positive impact (see e.g. in Box 7). This especially applies to the many densely populated regions in Europe and tourism areas (that often have difficult

Box 7. Attractiveness of the Area as Main Impact of Rural Development, the Example of Laag Holland (NL) (van Broekhuizen & Oostindie, 2010).

The Dutch Laag Holland area (see Box 5) is an important nature and recreation area for urban dwellers from the northern wing of the Randstad, a metropolitan area with more than one million inhabitants. Laag Holland's cultural landscape is a factor that attracts urban dwellers and most of them can reach the area less than 15 minutes. This is increasingly seen as an important competitive advantage both in relation to the southern wing of the Randstad – the industrial Rotterdam region – and in terms of the international competitiveness of the area (Provincie Noord Holland, 2006a, 2006b). The attractiveness of the area is illustrated by the relatively high rural estate prices in the Laag Holland area (this could be an opportunity to generate extra financial flows for the sustainable management of the area – the so-called 'red for green' mechanism).

The economic significance of rural development (agricultural nature and landscape management, agri-tourism, recreational activities, etc.) is primarily determined by its contribution to the attractiveness of the northern Randstad as a place to live and as a centre for international business. From an urban perspective the countryside is no longer perceived as a kind of superfluous space available for city and motorway expansion, but is increasingly appreciated and seen as an indispensable, valuable man-made landscape worthy of protection in the interests of the northern wing of the urbanised Randstad. So the quality of the area rather than the size and direct profitability of rural development economic activities is the most important economic factor. Because of this, the National Landscape organisation and other policy programmes promote the idea of a 'landscape-based economy' with a multifunctional agriculture that is able to maintain cultural landscape values (Provincie Noord Holland, 2006b).

production circumstances; e.g. Tuscany, the Alpes, the Dutch Wadden isles). This quality offers opportunities for new economic rural development activities that in turn can maintain or improve the overall quality of the area.[14]

Alongside extra added value and attractiveness, the impact of rural development also may include rural employment, new territorial identity, multiple natural resource management, rural distinctiveness, increased quality of care, preservation of rural amenities, mutual beneficial rural – urban interrelations, and new forms of territorial cooperation and networks.

Therefore rural development can also be described as a development '*towards polyvalency*' or towards a polyvalent countryside; practices entail several meanings and values for different persons and parties involved. Rural development practices will attract people to the countryside and create a so-called 'living countryside', because there is extra work or something to see, to experience, to eat or to buy. On the other hand conventional modernising agriculture 'chases people away', because: (a) business development more or less is synonymous with labour-saving technologies, (b) visitors become troublesome because they can disturb the production process, (c) business development has negative consequences for the accessibility and attractiveness of the environment. Following this line of reasoning it could be hypothesised that, from a broad societal perspective, rural development practices are superior to conventional activities (and so they must be in order to be able to 'compete') because they deliver a more polyvalent impact. For instance, they deliver besides agricultural products an attractive landscape, more biodiversity for the same amount of money, more biodiversity per hectare, more employment etc.

RESILIENCE

The concept of resilience refers to the ability of a system or community to bounce back from and to withstand external stress or shocks. For example, the increased volatility of conventional agricultural markets can be seen as a growing vulnerability for such external shocks. The relevant question here is whether and how rural development practices increase this resilience both at farm level and at the level of rural regions. In our opinion conventional agricultural development increases vulnerability (price squeeze, exchangeable regions, decrease of the share of value added by farmers) and rural development is one of the responses that tries to increase resilience.

Flexibility and adaptability, two important conditions for resilience, often are the outcome of rural development practices. Many rural development practices are designed (or evolve) in such a way that they entail considerable flexibility, they allow for adaptations, for learning by doing. They allow for resilience. They 'add' as well resilience to the involved farm enterprises and make farms attractive for the next generation. We already explained that, at the level of the individual farm enterprise, (a) parents often create flexibility in the farm organisation (both in terms of activities and finances) in order to allow the next generation to make their own choices, (b) investments that cement the long term organisation of the farm are avoided and (c) a strategic way of thinking is followed in which there is always room to integrate new activities in the farm and to enter into new forms of cooperation (Oostindie et al., 2015). Additional to this, research shows that many multifunctional activities cannot be understood independently of agricultural production, they are inextricably linked with it, and that they also result in extra investments in agricultural production.[15]

In general terms, the combination and intertwinement of the features of rural development practices as novelty production, autonomy, synergy, distinctive impact (value added) and new coalitions creates a relative strong own rural ability to 'translate' and 'transform' changing external conditions by means of an own self-controlled logic in such a way that rural distinctiveness and competiveness are maintained, preserved and strengthened. New forms of cooperation and the construction of new (nested) markets result in a certain distance and independency with regard to anonymous (world) markets. Thus the sensitivity and vulnerability regarding external conditions (shocks, volatility) is reduced in comparison with conventional agricultural development in the context of modernisation, specialisation and industrialisation.

An important element in rural resilience is co-production. In large parts of the European countryside, there is a search for the preservation, maintenance and management of 'cultural landscapes'.[16] In conventional development, the ecological, social and economic dimensions of regional development often become more and more separated. This can be noticed for example in spatial separation of areas for nature, for agriculture and for living and recreation. Such spatial segregation of functions often is at the disadvantage of cultural landscapes that require a certain type of maintenance and management (e.g. Tuscany, the Alpes, Dutch polder-landscapes like Laag Holland). The integration of the social and economic dimension with the ecological/physical dimension (i.e. co-production), characteristics of rural development practices, increases 'rural' resilience. Co-production refers to the importance of the management of the immobile natural and physical environment in rural development, and thus legitimises the use of the concept 'rural' development (and not regional development).

BY WAY OF CONCLUSION; RURAL DEVELOPMENT AS A RELATIONAL COOPERATION MODEL

Several features that characterise rural development practices in North West Europe have been described and discussed. Some parts of our analyses are largely grounded on observations in rather densely populated parts of Europe. We assume our analysis holds for other types of regions as well, but to which extent is, as yet, an open and unanswered question.

As mentioned in Chapter 1, in the different practices these features are not always present in their totality, mostly there is a specific combination, but we think that the more features are present and the more they are intertwined, the stronger the specific practice is. At that point a strategic question (also raised in Chapter 2 by Jan Douwe van der Ploeg, Jingzhong Ye, Sergio Schneider) comes to the fore: do these interrelated practices constitute a (partial) process of transition, or are they 'only complementary' to mainstream development? Being in the midst of dynamic rural development processes that often still show weaknesses and imperfections, answering this question requires some caution. As is already stated in Chapter 2:

> on the whole rural development represents a 'counter development': it differs from the development of agriculture and the countryside (and, consequently, the development of food processing, distribution and consumption) as induced and shaped by the main agricultural and food markets. Rural development may well go beyond market-induced development and can replace market-induced development – not in and through a sudden change – but through a complex and contradictory process of transition.

When comparing rural development processes in some rural areas (e.g. see the boxes 4 and 5 on Tuscany and Laag Holland) to the situation in the countryside during the previous decades, it could be claimed that they indeed represent a transition. Rural development is a specific mode of (re-)patterning the countryside and the many activities entailed in it. The morphology and dynamics of rural regions and its agriculture are changed and agriculture re-invents itself as a crucial actor for rural and regional development. However, in several rural regions in Europe, contrasting processes can be observed as well, such as: spurred specialisation and scale-enlargement; conversion into new 'spaces of consumption', in which leisure, nature and second homes become dominant; marginalisation and/or depopulation; and suburbanisation (Marsden & Van der Ploeg, 2008). The features and the associated rural development practices as described in this text have to be understood as part of a wider transitional process. However, it is not a generic process. In some areas the rural development process might dominate whereas in other regions it runs counter to or co-exist with competing transitional processes; new quarrels and questions will emerge. Furthermore, development has to be understood as a relative concept; development of one region often implies the relative under-development of another, so a relevant question is: what are the potential consequences of regional rural development for other regions? As yet questions regarding domination, competition, co-existence and 'relative' development are unanswered.

Comparing rural development with the conventional agricultural model (modernisation and industrialisation of agriculture), there are some differences that can be traced back to fundamentally different underlying principles and logic. The shift in practice from one logic to the other can be interpreted as a transition.

Agro-industrial development of agriculture is based on an *'individualised transaction model'* in which the world consists of loose particles that are linked by markets (atomistic world view).[17] This is expressed by the following elements:

- Specialised chains are increasingly divided in many specialised parts that are related to each other by means of markets and contracts;
- There is competition within the chain instead of between chains;
- Within the chain there is a price-asymmetry to the disadvantage of primary producers;
- Food has become an anonymous product, there is no direct contact between farmers and consumers;
- Calculating behaviour of the involved actors becomes dominant at the expense of cooperation;
- The bond with each other (social cohesion and social capital) decreases and individual interest dominates public and group interest;
- Transaction costs increase.

Conversely rural development is based on a *'relational cooperation model'* in which the search for (new) relations characterises business development and logic (relational world view). Some key characteristics are:

- Cooperation (especially at local and regional level) between farmers, between sectors, etc., replaces negotiations and competitive relationships;

- Forward integration replaces externalisation of tasks;
- Individual interest and group interest increasingly run parallel;
- Rural entrepreneurs do more with their resources than only produce specialised food.

Multifunctional agriculture is part of the broader rural development process that in its turn is part of broader societal changes in which integration and sense of belonging are important elements. It is telling that rural development initiatives, impulses, engagement and participation come from different sides; for example from care assurance companies, care recipients, city dwellers, rural dwellers, rural estates, consumers, municipalities, and local nature organisations. So, rural development can be perceived as a form of re-socialisation of agriculture.

These two contrasting models illustrate that rural development responses to changing circumstances and the (economic, social and ecological) crises are decisively different from the conventional ones. By way of conclusion we present some topics where rural development 'makes a difference':

- It provides a specific answer to globalisation without denying or avoiding global relations and falling back into isolationism through an own self-controlled logic to select, translate, utilise and control (both global and local) relations;
- It provides an answer to the debt-crisis: it creates robustness through the re-discovery of added value, new flexibility and reduced market-dependency;
- It re-connects agriculture with citizens, consumers, the city, other sectors and varied societal demands and thus generates extra support and potential flows of money;
- Agriculture is again tuned to and re-connected to natural processes (instead of further disconnection from nature by reducing the living part as much as possible);
- It concerns a strategic approach, that is, there is built-in flexibility and it is open for the integration of new activities and relations. So it offers potentials and opportunities for continuous further expansion of activities, cooperation, integration of other 'new elements': for example development of low carbon economies, new water management models, etc.

A general conclusion is that in rural development, 'success' more and more becomes the result of the quality of the actions of the direct involved actors instead of being determined by external conditions and prescriptions and, thus, that rural development indeed can go beyond market-induced development through a complex and contradictory process of transition.

NOTES

1. In Europe we undertook the AGRINOVIM programme on novelty production (see Wiskerke & Van der Ploeg, 2004). This was followed by several additional studies (a.o. Stuiver & Wiskerke, 2004; Swagemakers, 2002, 2008). The IPODE programme in Brazil also studied novelty production. The thesis of Jinghzhong (2002) equally is about novelty production. Thus, interesting comparisons between Europe, Brazil and China can be made.

2. For an elaboration of these trajectories, see Oostindie and Van Broekhuizen (2008, pp. 71–81).

3. In recent literature, this notion of endogenous development often is denominated as 'neo endogenous development' (e.g. Ray, 2002). The prefix 'neo' is used to distinguish it from one-sided bottom-up perceptions of endogeneity.

4. The concept of resource is a relational one. In order to be considered as a resource, something has to be recognised by someone as potentially useful and able to fulfil his/her objectives. Endogeneity starts from this process of recognition of *local* resources (see also Oostindie et al., 2008).

5. For example Care Farms: care is not only a simple extra activity that can be judged and evaluated independently from agriculture. It provides some extra income that strengthens the economy of the farm as a whole and delivers some extra financial means to invest in agricultural development. In turn, the presence of agriculture can increase some specific qualities and 'healing properties' of care.

6. As is amply documented and quantified in van der Ploeg, Long, and Banks (2002, especially Chapter 13).

7. It is interesting that in international literature the essence of entrepreneurship has often been linked to the capacity to link sectors and value circuits previously separated from each other. Long (1977), gives an overview.

8. Of course 'the opponents' are not a monolithic block. Besides opponents there are allies. Sometimes an institutional setting is partially perceived as an ally and partially as an opponent. An extensive survey in six EU-countries ($N = 3{,}264$) showed that the general perception of farmers is that national governments are the most important barriers and hindrances for rural development. Another important authority, the EU and its Rural Development Programmes are assessed as one of the most important stimuli and catalysts for rural development (Oostindie, van der Ploeg, & Renting, 2002).

9. See the two ETUDE books van der Ploeg and Marsden (2008a, 2008b) and Milone and Ventura (2010).

10. Theoretically the web refers to six dimensions: government of markets, institutional arrangements, social capital, sustainability, novelty production and endogeneity.

11. This particular type of rural development evidently requires specific conditions in terms of farm size, the size, composition and educational level of the

farming family, the quality of the landscape and the proximity of large urban centres. However, research also demonstrates that the involved actors are able to go beyond the immediacies of such conditions through novel arrangements (like the use of the internet to link with distant consumers, cooperation to go beyond limited farm or family size, new patterns for the division of labour in order to reduce entrance barriers). This illustrates how new institutional arrangements and new forms of governance are crucial dimensions of the rural web.

12. For development of new skills, competences and learning processes, see Oostindie et al. (2015).

13. See van der Ploeg et al. (2002), Oostindie et al. (2011), and De Rooij et al. (2014).

14. In practice such a process will encounter many barriers, problems.

15. See references in note 13.

16. A large percentage of the land is not suitable for so-called 'optimal' agricultural production for the world market, is less favoured area. See for example Wetenschappelijke Raad voor het Regeringsbeleid (1992), in which it is stated that about two third of the used cultural land is not needed for agricultural production if the 'best land' is used in an 'optimal way'.

17. Such a model is not exclusive for agriculture, but can be detected in many places in society. For example, in Wageningen University more and more functions are organised according to this model in which 'cooperation' is replaced by 'paid services', that is the researchers are not 'colleagues' from persons working at the ICT-service, cleaners, the HRM-department, Facility Services etc., but 'internal clients' that are related by means of internal contracts (so-called Service Level Agreements). The contacts between persons more and more are depersonalised, objectified and commoditised.

REFERENCES

Bock, B. (2002). *Tegelijkertijd en tussendoor, gender, plattelandsontwikkeling en interactief beleid.* Wageningen: Wageningen Universiteit.

Bock, B. (2010). *Personal and social development of women in rural areas of Europe.* Brussels: European Parliament.

Brewster, M., & Dalzell, F. (2007). *Driving change, the UPS approach to business.* New York, NY: Hyperion.

Camagni, R. (2007). Towards a concept of territorial capital. Joint Congress of the European Regional Science Association (47th Congress) and ASRDLF (Association de Science Régionale de Langue Française, 44th Congress), Paris, August 29–September 2.

de Rooij, S., Brouwer en, E., & van Broekhuizen, R. (1995). *Agrarische vrouwen en bedrijfsontwikkeling* (Wageningen: Circle for Rural European Studies/Wetenschapswinkel; Haarlem: WLTO), Studies van landbouw en platteland no. 18, 113 pp.

de Rooij, S. J. G., Ventura, F., Milone, P., & van der Ploeg, J. D. (2014). Sustaining food production through multifunctionality: The dynamics of large farms in Italy. *Sociologia Ruralis, 54*(3), 303–320.

Gouldner, A. W. (1970). *The coming crisis of western sociology*. London: Heinemann.

Jinghzhong, Y. (2002). *Processes of enlightment: Farmer initiatives in rural development in China*. Ph.D. thesis, Wageningen University, Wageningen.

Knickel, K., Siebert, R., Ganzert, C., Dosch, A., Peter, S., & Derichs, S. (2004). Wissenschaftliche Begleitforschung des Pilotprojektes Regionen Aktiv – Land gestaltet Zu-kunft. Ergebnisse der Begleitforschung 2002–2003. IfLS, Frankfurt/M.

Long, N. (1977). *An introduction to the sociology of rural development*. London: Tavistock.

Long, N. (1988). Sociological perspectives on agrarian development and state intervention. In A. Hall & J. Midgleg (Eds.), *Development policies: Sociological perspectives* (pp. 108–148). Manchester: University Press.

Marsden, T., & Van der Ploeg, J. D. (2008). Some final reflections on rural social and spatial theory. In J. D. van der Ploeg & T. Marsden (Eds.), *Unfolding webs, the dynamics of regional rural development*. Assen, The Netherlands: Van Gorcum.

Milone, P., & Ventura, F. (Eds.). (2010). *Networking the rural; the future of green regions in Europe*. Assen, The Netherlands: Van Gorcum.

Oostindie, H., Seuneke, P., van Broekhuizen, R., Hegger, E., & Wiskerke, H. (2011). *Dynamiek en robuustheid van multifunctionele landbouw; rapportage onderzoeksfase 2: Empirisch onderzoek onder 120 multifunctionele landbouwbedrijven*. Wageningen: Leerstoelgroep Rurale Sociologie WU.

Oostindie, H., van der Ploeg, J. D., & Renting, H. (2002). Farmers' experiences with and views on rural development practices and processes: Outcomes of a transnational European survey. In J. D. van der Ploeg, A. Long, & J. Banks (Eds.), *Living countrysides* (pp. 214–230). Doetinchem: Elsevier.

Oostindie, H. A., & van Broekhuizen, R. E. (2008). The dynamics of novelty production. In J. D. van der Ploeg & T. Marsden (Eds.), *Unfolding webs, the dynamics of regional rural development* (pp. 68–86). Assen: Koninklijke Van Gorcum.

Oostindie, H. A., van Broekhuizen, R. E., Brunori, G., & van der Ploeg, J. D. (2008). The endogeneity of rural economics. In J. D. van der Ploeg & T. Marsden (Eds.), *Unfolding webs, the dynamics of regional rural development* (pp. 53–67). Assen: Koninklijke Van Gorcum.

Oostindie, H., van Broekhuizen, R., Soldaat, B., & van der Ploeg, J. D. (2015). Towards the characterization of actors engaged in rural development processes in the north west of Europe. Introduction. In P. Milone, F. Ventura, & J. Ye (Eds.), *Constructing a new framework for rural development* (Vol. 22). Research in Rural Sociology and Development. Bingley, UK: Emerald Group Publishing Limited.

Polman, N., Poppe, K., van der Schans, J. W., & van der Ploeg, J. D. (2010, June). Nested markets with common pool resources in multifunctional agriculture. In Rivista di economia agraria, a comparative analysis of rural development processes in China, Brazil and the European Union, Anno LXV, N.2, pp. 295–318.

Provincie Noord Holland. (2006a). *Uitvoeringsprogramma nationaal landschap Laag Holland 2007–2013*. Haarlem, The Netherlands: Province Noord Holland.

Ray, C. (2002). *Endogenous socio-economic development and trustful relationships: Partnerships*. Working Paper 45. Social capital and individual agency, Centre for rural economy, University of Newcastle Upon Tyne.

Rip, A., & Kemp, R. (1998). Technological change. In S. Rayner, & E. L. Malone (Eds.), *Human choice and climate change* (Vol. 2, pp. 327–399). Columbus, OH: Battele.

RLG (Raad voor het Landelijke Gebied). (1997). *Tien voor de Toekomst; advies ten behoeve van de beleidsagenda voor het landelijk gebied in de 21ste eeuw*. Publicatie RLG 97/2, RLG Amersfoort (also published as *Ten points for the future: Advice on the policy agenda for the rural areas in the 21st century*. RLG 97/2a, RLG, Amersfoort).

Roep, D. (2000). *Vernieuwend werken: Sporen van vermogen en onvermogen; een socio-materiele studie over vernieuwing in de landbouw uitgewerkt voor de westelijke veenweidegebieden*. Ph.D. thesis, Wageningen University, Wageningen.

Rooij, S., Ventura, F., Milone, P., & van der Ploeg, J. D. (forthcoming). Sustaining food production through multifunctionality: The dynamics of large farmers in Italy. *Sociologia Ruralis*. First published online 4 November 2013.

Stuiver, M., & Wiskerke, J. S. C. (2004). The development of VEL and VANLA as a niche. In J. S. C. Wiskerke, & J. D. van der Ploeg (Eds.), *Seeds of transition: Essays on novelty creation, niches and regimes in agriculture*. Assen: Van Gorcum.

Swagemakers, P. (2002). *Verschil maken: Novelty productie en de contouren van een streekcooperatie*. Wageningen: Circle for Rural European Studies.

Swagemakers, P. (2008). Ecologisch kapitaal: Over het belang van aanpassingsvermogen, flexibiliteit en oordeelkundigheid. Ph.D. thesis, Wageningen University, Wageningen.

Timmer, C. P. (1970). On measuring technical efficiency. In *Food research institute studies in agricultural economics* (Vol. 9, No. 2, pp. 99–171). Trade and Development.

Toledo, V. M. (1990). The ecological rationality of peasant production. In M. Altieri & S. Hecht (Eds.), *Agroecology and small farm development*. CRC Press.

Van Broekhuizen, R., & Oostindie, H. (2010). National landscape Laag-Holland: Rural web dynamics in a metropolitan landscape. In P. Milone & F. Ventura (Eds.), *Networking the rural; the future of green regions in Europe* (pp. 92–108). Assen, The Netherlands: Van Gorcum.

van der Ploeg, J. D., Bouma, J., Rip, A., Rijkenberg, F. H. J., Ventura, F., & Wiskerke, J. S. C. (2004). On regimes, novelties, niches and co-production. In J. S. C. Wiskerke & J. D. van der Ploeg (Eds.), *Seeds of transition* (pp. 1–27). Assen: Van Gorcum.

van der Ploeg, J. D., Long, A., & Banks, J. (Eds.). (2002). *Living countrysides: Rural development processes in Europe: The state of the art*. Doetinchem, The Netherlands: Elsevier.

van der Ploeg, J. D., & Marsden, T. (Eds.). (2008a). *Unfolding webs*. Assen: Van Gorcum.

van der Ploeg, J. D., & Marsden, T. (2008b). Some final reflections. In J. D. van der Ploeg & T. Marsden (Eds.), *Unfolding webs, the dynamics of regional rural development* (pp. 225–234). Assen: Koninklijke Van Gorcum.

van der Ploeg, J. D., van Broekhuizen, R., Brunori, G., Sonnino, R., Knickel, K., & Oostindie, H. (2008). Towards a framework for understanding regional rural development. In J. D. van der Ploeg & T. Marsden (Eds.), *Unfolding webs*. Assen: Van Gorcum.

van der Ploeg, J. D., Ye, J., & Schneider, S. (2012). Rural development through the construction of new, nested, markets: Comparative perspectives from China, Brazil and the European Union. *Journal of Peasant Studies*.

Van der Ploeg, J. D., Ye, J., & Schneider, S. (2015). Rural development: Actors and practices. Introduction. In P. Milone, F. Ventura, & J. Ye (Eds.), *Constructing a new framework for rural development* (Vol. 22). Research in Rural Sociology and Development. Bingley, UK: Emerald Group Publishing Limited.

Ventura, F., & Milone, P. (2005). *Innovatività Contadina e Sviluppo Rurale: Un'analisi neo-istitutionale del cambiamento in agricoltura in tre regioni del Sud Italia.* Milano: Franco Angeli.

Ventura, F., Milone, P., & van der Ploeg, J. D. (2010). Understanding rural development dynamics. In P. Milone & F. Ventura (Eds.), *Networking the rural; the future of green regions in Europe* (pp. 1–29). Assen: Koninklijke Van Gorcum.

Wetenschappelijke Raad voor het Regeringsbeleid. (1992). Grond voor keuzen: Vier perspectieven voor de landelijke gebieden in de Europese Gemeenschap. Rapporten aan de Regering/Wetenschappelijke Raad voor het Regeringsbeleid, SDU, 's-Gravenhage.

Wiskerke, J. S. C., & van der Ploeg, J. D. (2004). *Seeds of transition: Essays on novelty production, niches and regimes in agriculture.* Assen: Royal van Gorcum.

CHAPTER 10

TOWARDS THE CHARACTERIZATION OF ACTORS ENGAGED IN RURAL DEVELOPMENT PROCESSES IN THE NORTH WEST OF EUROPE

Henk Oostindie, Rudolf van Broekhuizen, Bart Soldaat and Jan Douwe van der Ploeg

ABSTRACT

Rural development is, above all, constructed by actors operating at grass-root level. These actors are increasingly facilitated by specific policy programmes, but these programmes often follow *the initiatives and practices already developed by the grass-root actors themselves. Policies follow, they do not trigger nor drive. This chapter is a second-level analysis of available European and national research material and focuses on the role of agricultural actors as crucial co-constitutors of RD processes. Some distinctive elements and characteristics of RD-practitioners are identified, described and discussed. Taken together these characteristics underscore that RD-actors may reflect distinctive features. It is finally argued that RD-actors will develop especially*

Constructing a New Framework for Rural Development
Research in Rural Sociology and Development, Volume 22, 239–254

ISSN: 1057-1922/doi:10.1108/S1057-192220150000022009

distinctive personal attributes through iterative learning by doing processes and unfolding agency. Both are thought to be key components of the resilience of RD-actors to withstand adverse conditions and to grasp new opportunities for alternative, more promising agricultural pathways.

Keywords: Common Agricultural Policy; rural development; actors; family farm; agency; agrarian modernization

INTRODUCTION

As compared to the process of *agrarian* development, one could hypothesize that the process of *rural* development is far more actor-dependent, at least in the NW of Europe. Whilst for a long time the CAP (Common Agricultural Policy) guided and shaped the process of agrarian development (through price regulation, subsidies, long term security and a clear image that specified the way ahead) and agro-industries, banks, extension services and research institutes (delivering new technologies) provided the required tools – the process of rural development, although increasingly being facilitated by the RD regulation of the EU, lacks the clear and fixed parameters and the amount of resources that characterized and spurred agrarian development during the last decades. There is less imprint of the state (and the supra-national state) on rural development. There is also less imprint of social movements (or no imprint at all) as is the case in Brazil.[1] In North West Europe it applies that rural development is, above all, constructed by actors operating at grass-root level, although the further unfolding of these grass-roots initiatives may increasingly occur through cooperation and the creation of new institutional arrangements. This underlines the centrality of actors in rural development. These actors are increasingly facilitated (at least in some respects) by specific policy programmes, but these programmes often *follow* the initiatives and practices already developed by the grass-root actors themselves. Policies follow, they do not trigger nor drive. At best they are facilitating – which is alright of course, but it also generates some important questions. Here we will focus on the role of agricultural actors as crucial co-constitutors of RD processes. Who are these actors? Are they different from others not engaged in RD? If so, in what respects? Are the actors engaged in RD practices changed by their active engagement and if so, in what respects?

In this chapter we try to formulate at least some answers for these emerging questions. In doing so we consult and synthesize a range of studies in which we have been involved over the last two decades, covering European Research Projects as: *Mult-Agri* (Theoretical understanding of multifunctional agriculture); *IMPACT* (socio-economic impact of rural development activities); *Sus-Chain* (Sustaining food chains); COFAMI (New Collective Farmers Marketing Initiatives); *ETUDE* (Enlarging theoretical understanding of rural development); *RUDI* (assessing impact of rural policies); *DERREG* (Developing European Regions in the Era of Globalization). Additionally to this exploration of European and national research projects we will further draw upon relevant other personal work experiences through advisory work, consultancy and LEADER coordination activities.

The method underlying this text is in itself simple. What we try to do is to make a secondary-level analysis of research findings and personal experiences in the last decades which, in the following paragraphs, is being used to characterize actors actively engaged[2] in RD processes and that are driven by a broad spectrum of underlying forces.

It is important to have in mind that RD-engagement may have many drivers. Available research materials reveal a broad spectrum of relevant push and pull factors representing specific balances between resistance and renewal, between change and continuity. Table 1 gives an impression of the more specific driving forces that may be witnessed in the Dutch context.

Table 1. Drivers of RD-Engagement in the Netherlands.

N = 120	% (Highly) Important
More contacts between citizens and the agricultural sector	72
More contact with consumers/citizens	63
Need for additional income	59
Risk-spreading	52
Farm-internal surplus labour	43
More influence on farm-development	43
Wish for own income activity by partner	40
Logical step after earlier new RD-activities	39
'Pulling' new rural markets	33
More influence on product marketing	32
Enlargement of succession opportunities	29
Inspiring examples in vicinity	23
Active institutional support	22
Interesting subsidy opportunities	18

Source: Oostindie, Van Broekhuizen, Seuneke, and Wiskerke (2011).

It shows how RD-engagement traces back to specific combinations of more personal-and farm-internal as well as external driving forces. It further confirms that rural policy and broader institutional settings indeed are clearly of less importance than more personal drivers as wishes for more direct contact with consumers and citizens and more influence on farm-development. Later we will return in more detail to the different socio-cultural backgrounds of this wish to '*farm differently*' and its implications for changing professional identities in agriculture. The same goes for the significance of typical family-farm drivers as '*availability of surplus labour*', '*wish for own income activity by partner*' and '*enlargement of succession opportunities*'.

Here we restrict ourselves to the conclusion that European farm families may, for many reasons, opt for other farm-development trajectories than further specialization, intensification and scale-enlargement that characterize the agricultural modernization model (Oostindie, van der Ploeg, & Renting, 2002; van der Ploeg et al., 2002). The same variety of relevant driving forces in Table 1 simultaneously demonstrates that it is impossible to understand RD-engagement in isolation from the situational aspects of rural settings.

CAPACITY TO RELATE TO OTHERS

Even if we can state, in general terms, that rural development is strongly actor-dependent and many initiatives start as individual ones, we realize that rural development is a multi-actor process characterized by complex interplays between (1) farmers and other rural actors (SME's, rural dwellers, newcomers, commuters, etc.); (2) rural and urban actors (consumers, leisure seekers, visitors, etc.); (3) nearby and distant actors (food empires, flows of labour migration, information, images, etc.); (4) human and non-human actors (physical and material settings) and (5) public and private actors (new forms of governance, new expressions of self-regulation, etc.). As actors actively engaged in RD processes, farmers will have to create new social networks. *At the level of single actors this is reflected in their capacity to relate to others*. That is, the capacity to convince and mobilize others, to create and/or join new networks and to establish new interlinkages. The significance of this capacity has been emphasized from multiple perspectives in European research programmes (see Table 2).

Drawing on the overall outcomes of these European Research Programmes, it may be concluded more generally that this capacity is strongly interwoven with the following co-constituting components:

Table 2. Farmers' Capacity to Relate to Others in European Research Programmes.

MULT-AGRI	Farmers as Providers of Multiple Rural Functions
IMPACT	Farmers as initiators of new RD-activities with significant socio-economic impact at different scale levels
SUS-CHAIN	Farmers as co-constitutors of multiple transition trajectories towards sustainable food chains
COFAMI	Farmers as collective actors with positive impacts on different types of rural capital assets (social, cultural, ecological, institutional)
RUDI	Farmers as drivers of self-regulation initiatives and more community-led rural policy delivery systems that create new policy-practice relations
ETUDE	Farmers as co-designers of rural webs that preserve rural distinctiveness, competitiveness and quality of rural life
DERREG	Farmers as participants in capacity building, governance and knowledge systems that mediate, transform and reshape global-local interaction patterns

- Step-by-step approaches.
- A certain belief in 'we can do better'.
- Trust-based relationships.
- Glimmers of hope.
- Simultaneity.
- The art of balancing and coordination.

This could be further explained with the help of Fig. 1. It synthesizes how Dutch RD-initiatives (farmers-driven as well as initiated by other rural stakeholders) have to cope with different '*fields of attention*' to realize their specific objectives.

The figure makes a distinction between (1) internal and (2) external relations, (3) the mutual linkages between the internal and the external, (4) the need for integration and (5) collaborative learning as specific fields of attention that co-shape overall ability to realize the objectives of RD-initiators. It further aims to underscore that these different fields of attention need to be actively attuned, aligned and coordinated in a '*working whole*' (Roep, 2000). As such it points to the importance of '*the art of balancing and coordination*' and '*simultaneity*' in relation to RD-engagement. Both will emerge particularly through step-by-step approaches that start from a certain belief in '*better ways of doing*' and '*glimmers of hope*'. After all, 'no one likes to flog a dead horse', to invest time and energy without hope on potential improvements or future benefits. These elements, in their turn, will especially flourish in settings characterized by trust-based relationships, not just among involved RD-practitioners (the internal relationships), but also with

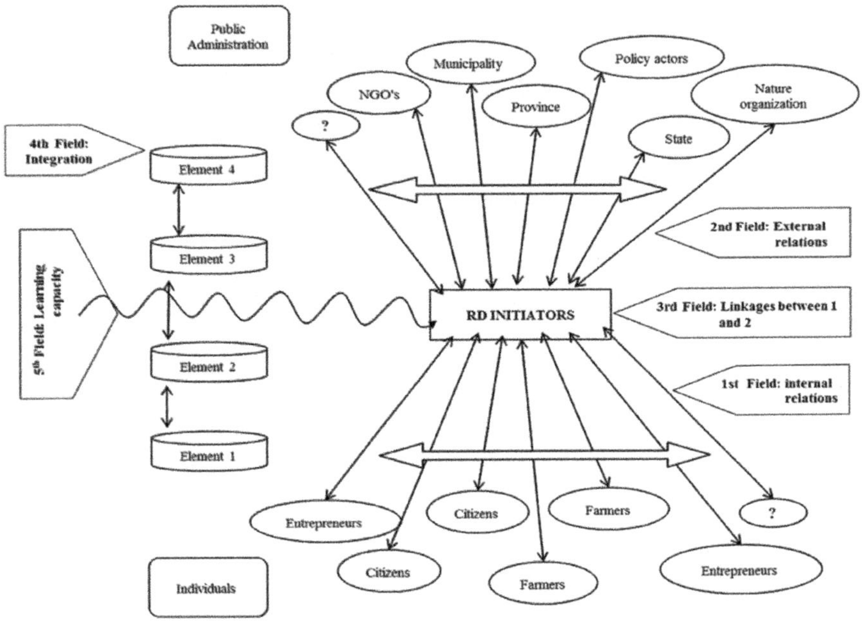

Fig. 1. RD-Engagement as the Art of Balancing and Coordination.
Source: Remmers, van Broekhuizen, and van der Ploeg (2000, p. 24).

their broader institutional environment (the external relationships). It explains how different fields of activity and their co-constituting elements, especially through mutually re-enforcing interrelations, are thought to contribute to the '*capacity to relate to others*' as another characterizing feature of those actively engaged in RD-activities.

PARTICULARLY ROOTED IN FAMILY-FARM RESILIENCE

Apart from being intrinsically situational and relational, it needs to be further emphasized that features shared by RD-practitioners are not just 'social'. They will also be mostly 'material', that is rooted in the places where agricultural activity is located and implying many of the 'things' embedded in this activity. In this respect the importance of the family farm comes to the fore. The family farm represents a resource base that allows for a certain autonomy, not by itself, but as an *emerging* feature whenever and wherever this resource base is aptly used by the related actors. It is a resource base that produces a certain resilience to 'bounce back' and to 'bounce forward'. That is to say, the ability to resist the negative externalities of globalization and modernization forces as losses of autonomy as well as to transform and to reshape those same forces in more beneficial ways. This relevance of the family-farm specificities already appears in a variety of driving forces of RD-engagement, covering, amongst others, specific responses to price squeeze tendencies and new rural market opportunities (see Table 1).

Farming differently in this respect is really a key word. Increasingly farm-households want to farm differently because the established routine does not offer any way forward, or any satisfaction. *Farming differently* represents resistance. It triggers at the same time processes of *redesign*: people are looking for alternatives, they experiment, and effectively change the way of farming. Also, they do so in a way that *resilience* is one of the outcomes of these processes. It makes that resilience will be grounded in combinations of the following specificities of family-farm recourse management:

- Strong interlinkages between economic and socio-cultural values as integrating forces for productive as well as consumptive rural functions.
- Newly emerging gender relations that result in new patterns of labour division and distribution of responsibilities.
- Newly emerging professional identities with alternative strategic meanings of agricultural activity (multifunctional rural enterprises, life-style-farming, etc.).
- Flexibility in resource use, including the organization of inter-generational succession.

Later we will return to some of these specificities. Here it is important to underline that RD-engagement is certainly not an exclusive domain of family farms. In Central and Eastern EU Member States, for instance, involvement in new RD-activities may be for historical reasons dominated by other farm organizational models. Family-farm resilience, therefore, is thought to be particularly a key feature of RD-practitioners in North west Europe.

DISTINCTIVE 'EARLY-ADOPTER' CHARACTERISTICS

We believe that RD-engagement may be further characterized by specific '*early-adopter*' features. In the 1960s and 1970s a good deal of research was done on the '*diffusion of innovations*'. This resulted in extended lists that summarized the 'properties' or socio-psychological characteristics of the 'early adopters', 'adopters' and 'laggards', etc. Starting from the premise that there are basic differences between agrarian and rural development (readymade solutions to be *implemented* versus actively *designing* new solutions) it may be hypothesized that associated personal traits will be different as well. Table 3 gives an impression of such differences, building upon a comparison of well-known cross-cultural early-adopter generalizations of agrarian modernization (Rogers, 1962; Rogers & Shoemaker, 1971) and more recent insights into the specificities of RD-practitioners.

We realize that classifications on the basis of 'diffusion of innovation approaches' have been sharply criticized since their heyday. Indeed, the crucial role of practices, interfaces and dissimilarities all have been neglected. What might be a promising innovation in one practice could very well be something quite awkward in another. Also, interactions at different interfaces (between e.g. bankers, extensionists, farmers and traders) probably explain more than individual attributes of involved farmers. Those who were early adopters in one respect could very well be laggards in other respects.[3] Notwithstanding all these limitations, we would argue that different actors play active roles, farmers included and that it should not be excluded, a priori, that particular personal features were – and are – relevant with respect to RD-engagement.

Especially grounded in our common experience, we share the opinion that 'early RD adopters', those who design and try out new practices for

Table 3. Early-Adopter Characteristics of Agrarian versus Rural Development.

Agrarian Development	Rural Development
Early adopters are more highly integrated with the social system than laggards	Early adopters are often relative outsiders
Early adopters have a higher social status	Early adopters have more differentiated social statuses
Early adopters are more likely to have a commercial orientation than laggards	Early adopters have more ambiguous orientations
Early adopters have a more favourable attitude toward credit than laggards	Early adopters focus on the valorization of farm-internal resources
Early adopters have a more favourable attitude towards risk than laggards	Early adopters focus on risk-spreading
Early adopters have a more favourable attitude toward science than laggards	Early adopters focus on 'learning by doing' and 'novelty production'

the first time, are frequently relative 'outsiders'. They are more often farmers located at the periphery of the mainstream approaches, routines and identities. As *relative* outsiders these farmers may know the routines, etc., but they deviate from it on purpose. They link to standard routines and discourses, but do so in a *critical* way. More than '*outsiders*', they are peripheral – and they often look for the periphery in a conscious and well thought-out way. As one of them (an estate owner) said: '*I did not want to farm in the Wageningen way*' (!).

In overviewing the '*early adopters*' that we are familiar with, we think we can distinguish at least five categories (albeit far from being clearly outlined at this point):

1. Many have an urban background. Farming according to the rules' has never been attractive for them or it was increasingly impossible. Farmers from the mainstream typically perceived them as 'the alternative ones', as 'open sandals and woolly socks types'. Later on the ranks of the 'alternative ones' grew with newcomers that came from the agricultural sector itself, often with (temporary) professional experience outside agriculture and often, initially, equally classifiable in terms of open sandals and woolly socks by mainstream farmers.
2. This first subgroup is complemented by a second one that is at first sight radically different. It concerns the larger farmers, with vested names, who also started quite early to integrate new RD-activities in their farm enterprises. Often these farmers had official positions in the boards of the farmers' unions. It is telling that they mostly behaved in a low-key way when it came to their new RD-activities (not seldom classified as just being a hobby without income motivations) not clear (probably to avoid any classification in terms of sandals and socks). However, they share one key feature with the first subgroup: they are both peripheral (although on different sides of the average), both deviate from the rule. Probably, there is some historical continuity in all this as well. As Hofstee (1985) described: in the past large farmers were the ones that had, according to local cultural repertoire, not only the right, but also the duty to experiment, to try out new things – precisely because they could *afford* to do so.
3. A third subgroup that gets involved quite early in the design and development of RD-activities consists of specific landowners as for example, rural estate owners (not all of them of course, but many). Rural estates allow for experiments, new development can be tried out relatively easily. Rural estate owners are, like the other subgroups, at

the periphery of the hegemonic 'agricultural world'. They do not feel much pressure to follow dominant trends and well-trodden pathways. On the contrary, their position obliges them (there is a 'moral economy' element to this) to do it differently.

4. A fourth, quite different, but nonetheless highly important subgroup is composed of farm women. They were equally peripheral to, and within, the dominant discourse of agriculture as a 'men's world'. However, women increasingly became unhappy with this and several of them try to construct *their own domain* within the farm enterprise as a whole (this could be a mini-camping, a set of apartments, a small shop, a cheese-making facility, a space to teach other women the art of making bouquets, etc.). Thus another cradle for the development of new RD-activities was born (see also Bock, 1998; de Rooij, Brouwer, & Van Broekhuizen, 1995).
5. A fifth group concerns farmers in rural areas with unfavourable ecological settings for agricultural modernization and with an early awareness for the prospects of new, more multifunctional farm-development pathways. These often relatively younger farmers often become early involved in new forms of territory-based cooperation to facilitate the uptake and further development of new RD-activities (see van Broekhuizen & Oostindie, 2010).

Just as RD arose as an alternative to the dominant modernization trajectory, these first architects are people who are somewhat peripheral to the average farmer (and especially to the role model of the 'vanguard farmer' of the agricultural modernization project). In this respect there is probably more continuity than discontinuities. When the modernization project was initiated (the early 1950s) and the first empirical studies on the diffusion on innovations were realized, modernization was itself a deviation from the rules (i.e. the ones differing from the dominant peasant agriculture). Typically, the '*early adopters*' were seen as *modern*, as having more contacts with the cities and urban culture, being closer to extensionists and willing to take more risks than others. In short: they were, to a degree, defined as well in terms of a deviation (see again Table 3). Equally the '*deviators*' that triggered current RD processes may have more in common than the foregoing classification into distinguishable subgroups suggests. We feel that these communalities particularly reside in the following points:

(a) The actors initiating RD processes had, on the whole, a far wider overview of the world.

(b) Due to their peripheral positions overviews of the wider world are less limited than many mainstream farmers. They are, as it were, able to look well beyond the horizon. Equally, they are less convinced of being right.
(c) This evidently links with their involvement in wider social networks. Typically, subgroups 1 and 5 related to peasants and peasant organizations in the 3rd World, subgroup 2 have been to visit other farming areas, and subgroup 4 is linked to the upcoming feminist movement. Subgroup 3 always had its own particular networks.
(d) They share the capacity to mobilize, sooner or later, other actors.
(e) They are equally capable of organizing support.
(f) The foregoing points imply that they were able to constitute (together with others) a 'multi-actor' function in RD.
(g) They create a certain 'room for manoeuvre' for RD-engagement that starts from positive socio-cultural driving forces.

DISTINCTIVE PERSONAL ATTRIBUTES THROUGH UNFOLDING AGENCY

So far we gave a sketch of the distinctive features of the '*early adopters*', the RD-pioneers. When it comes to the larger group of '*followers*' (in time as well as activities) it turns out, according to our studies (both at European level[4] and within the Netherlands[5]) that those involved in RD-activities (of whatever kind) are, as compared to those not involved, on average:

- have larger farms (which allows for more room for new RD-activities);
- are younger;
- are better educated;
- are more satisfied with total incomes;
- are more optimistic when it comes to future farming prospects.

These averages tell a rather optimistic story, although the same averages may hide, especially when it comes to farm size and income, considerable standard deviations. The question that remains to be answered is again as follows: *do these features refer, in one way or another, to distinctively different personal attributes?*

Thus far this question has been approached from the situational (underlying drivers) and relational characteristics (network building, creating coalitions, mobilizing support, etc.) of RD-engagement. The importance of socio-cultural aspects has been emphasized by pointing to issues such as a growing desire among the farm population to '*farm differently*' and the specific features of *early adopters*. Here we want to add especially that those actively involved in RD often succeed to go beyond the narrow boundaries of agriculture, farmers' union, the village, etc. They develop wider views and learn more about society generally than those without active engagement. Our common work experience further suggests that these farmers (and others) are better able to guide their own farm-development. '*I think we moved from experiencing ourselves as victims towards feeling that we can adjust, negotiate, and create our own solutions and ways forward*'. Others argue: '*we now have the feeling that we can make a difference and together with that there is now more joy, more spirit here in our area, and this is a big difference with the frustrations that dominate elsewhere ... Of course, we know the problems very well, maybe even better than others, the difference is that we feel that we can face them and maybe resolve them*'.

These quotes refer, in short, to the relevance of emerging agency. It is through their practices and experiences that RD-practitioners develop more agency than others. This agency, as further concluded by available RD-survey material, may reshape professional identities. It is through the new experiences, the new meetings, the new networks and the new skills that accompany the uptake of RD-activities that ideas about farming and its future start to change. What emerges is a reshaping of professional identities that subsequently opens new horizons, transforms into new ways of doing things and induces new coalitions and partnerships. In short, RD-engagement should not be perceived as something static that permits for a priori or rigid distinctions between those engaged and those that are not. Contrastingly, it is much more something that is dynamic and that will transform RD-actors, albeit to different degrees, indeed into people with also increasingly distinctive personal attributes.

The relevance of unfolding agency may express itself also in farm-dynamics. It turns out that RD-engagement in the Netherlands frequently goes along with the uptake of other new RD-activities in time, which may be understood as a reflection of a growing ability to (1) recognize and create synergies between different RD-activities and (2) to increase overall socio-economic performance of RD-engagement. The co-existence of differentiating farm-level pathways reveals at the same time how unfolding agency may manifest itself in many different ways (Oostindie et al., 2011). This may be further illustrated by involved learning processes. Fig. 1 already referred to collaborative learning as a field of activity of specific importance for

RD-initiatives and emphasized as such the need to take the social embeddedness of learning processes into account. Together with changing professional identities that '*cross traditional boundaries of agriculture*' this social embeddedness has been identified as crucial aspects of promising '*learning work environments*' that may facilitate and strengthen RD-engagement. Seuneke and Wiskerke (2013) refer, in this respect, to the importance of strategic-, social-, communicative- and commercial competences. It is further emphasized that this requires learning by doing through:

- A fundamental re-orientation on the farm economy based on a rediscovery of value added production and extra '*grip*' on farm management through less dependency on conventional agricultural markets.
- A less detailed and more strategic way of planning that acknowledges the significance of contingency and flexibility in contrast with the 'recipe' ways of planning typical of the agricultural modernization model.
- A preference for informal learning circuits with, for example, study-groups instead of formal learning settings as extension services and official courses.
- An iterative development of capacities, capabilities, contacts and views.

Fig. 2 visualizes how this learning by doing indeed fundamentally differs from more linear ways of thinking that incorrectly suggest that it might be possible to make strict and rigid distinctions between (1) vision formulation; (2) strategic planning; (3) plan elaboration and (4) practical plan implementation. This explicit recognition and acknowledgement of the iterative nature of involved learning processes implies again that RD-engagement should be much more perceived as a vehicle that induces the development of distinctive personal attributes than driven by already a priori present distinctive attributes.

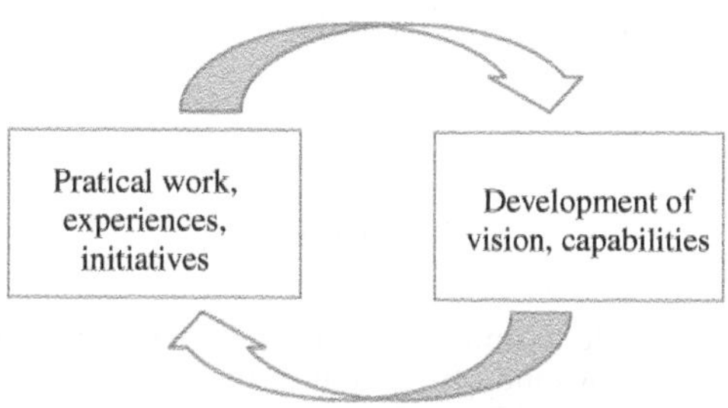

Fig. 2. RD-Engagement as an Iterative Learning Process. *Source*: Remmers et al. (2000, p. 22).

CONCLUSIONS

Particularly based on second-level analysis of available European and national research material, complemented with our personal work experiences, we approached the characteristics of actors engaged in RD-activities from different angles and perspectives. It forms a methodological approach that enables to identify the following distinctive elements of RD-practitioners:

- A key role for the desire to '*farm differently*' within a wider set of driving forces of RD-engagement.
- An outspoken capacity '*to relate to others*'.
- Materially strongly rooted in the '*resilience*' of family farms.
- Clearly different '*early-adopter*' features compared to the agrarian modernization model.
- Multiple 'early-adopter' categories.
- Distinctive personal attributes that are especially obtained through '*unfolding agency*' and *iterative learning processes*.

Taken together, these characteristics underscore that RD-actors may reflect historically rooted (e.g. family-based farming) as well as more recently emerging distinctive features (e.g. changing ideas about farming). Underlying expressions of resistance and redesign of RD-engagement may be found particularly among '*relative outsiders*'. These may differ in terms of socio-cultural backgrounds, gender positions and agro-ecological conditions, but share deviations from dominant agricultural thinking. Apart from these 'early-adopter' features, it is finally argued that RD-actors will develop distinctive personal attributes through iterative learning by doing processes and unfolding their agency. Both are thought to be key components of the resilience of RD-actors to withstand adverse conditions and to grasp new opportunities for alternative, more promising agricultural pathways.

NOTES

1. It is, of course, possible to understand the many people engaged in rural development as constituting a *new* kind of social movement.
2. We realize that there are different ways to 'engage' in RD. Our analysis starts with a more general characterization of RD-practitioners. This is followed by a more classical innovation theory inspired approach that enables us to make a

distinction between the characteristics of 'early adopters' and 'followers' (see especially paragraphs 5 and 6).

3. See for an extensive summary of this critique Albrecht (1969).

4. See for example the results of the IMPACT survey (Oostindie & Parrot, 2002).

5. De Vernieuwing (Ettema, Nooij, Van der Ploeg, & Van Broekhuizen, 1994); De Toekomst (Ettema, Nooij, van Dijk, van der Ploeg, & Van Broekhuizen, 1995), Oostindie et al. (2011).

REFERENCES

Albrecht, H. (1969). *Innovationsprozesse in der Landwirtschaft, eine kritische Analyse der agrarsoziologischen 'adoption' and 'diffusion'.* Forschung in Bezug auf Probleme der landwirtschaftlichen Beratung. Saarbruecken.

Bock, B. B. (1998). *Tegelijkertijd en tussendoor: Gender, plattelandsontwikkeling en interactief beleid.* Wageningen: Wageningen University.

de Rooij, S., Brouwer, E., & Van Broekhuizen, R. (1995). *Agrarische vrouwen en bedrijfsontwikkeling.* Circle for European Studies, Wetenschapswinkel Landbouwuniversiteit Wageningen en Westelijke Land- en Tuinbouw Organisatie, Wageningen.

Ettema, M., Nooij, A. T. J., Van der Ploeg, J. D., & Van Broekhuizen, R. (1994). *De Vernieuwing: een bespreking van de tweede Boerderij enquête voor het nationaal Landbouwdebat.* Doetinchem: Misset.

Ettema, M., Nooij, A. T. J., van Dijk, G., van der Ploeg, J. D., & Van Broekhuizen, R. (1995). De Toekomst: een bespreking van de derde Boerderij enquête voor het nationaal landbouwdebat. Doetinchem: Misset.

Hofstee, E. W. (1985). *Groningen van grasland naar bouwland, 1750–1930.* Wageningen: Pudoc.

Oostindie, H., & Parrot, N. (2002). *Farmers' attitudes towards rural development: Results of a transnational survey in six European Union countries.* Wageningen, The Netherlands: Department of Social Sciences, Wageningen University.

Oostindie, H., Van Broekhuizen, R., Seuneke, P., & Wiskerke, J. S. C. (2011). *Dynamiek en Roep D. (2000). Vernieuwend Werken: Sporen van vermogen en onvermogen.* Wageningen, The Netherlands: Wageningen University Press.

Oostindie, H., van der Ploeg, J. D., & Renting, H. (2002). Farmers' experiences with and views on rural development practices and processes: Outcomes of a transnational European survey. In J. D. van der Ploeg, A. Long, & J. Banks (Eds.), *Living countrysides: Rural development processes in Europe: The state of the art* (pp. 213–230). Doetinchem, The Netherlands: Elsevier.

Remmers, G., van Broekhuizen, R., & van der Ploeg, J. D. (2000). *Initiatiefgroepen op het platteland: naar het creëren van koppelingen tussen praktijk en beleid, Hoofdrapport,* leerstoelgroep Rurale Sociologie Wageningen Universiteit, Wageningen.

Roep, D. (2000). *Vernieuwend Werken: sporen van vermogen en onvermogen.* Wageningen: Wageningen University Press.

Rogers, E. M. (1962). *Diffusion of innovations.* New York, NY: The Free Press.

Rogers, E. M., & Shoemaker, F. F. (1971). *Communication of innovations: A cross-cultural approach.* New York, NY: The Free Press.

Seuneke, P., Lans, T., & Wiskerke, J. S. C. (2013). Moving beyond entrepreneurial skills: Key factors driving entrepreneurial learning in multifunctional agriculture. *Journal of Rural Studies*, *32*, 208–219.

van Broekhuizen, R., & Oostindie, H. (2010). National landscape laag-Holland; rural web dynamics in a metropolitan landscape. In P. Milone & F. Ventura (Eds.), *Networking the rural; the future of green regions in Europe* (pp. 92–108). Assen: Koninklijke Van Gorcum.

van der Ploeg, J. D., Roep, D., Renting, H., Banks, J., Alonso Mielgo, A., Gorman, M., … Ventura, F. (2002). The socio-economic impact of rural development processes within Europe. In J. D. van der Ploeg, A. Long, & J. Banks (Eds.), *Living countrysides: Rural development processes in Europe: The state of the art* (pp. 179–191). Doetinchem, The Netherlands: Elsevier.

CHAPTER 11

WEAVING THE INSTITUTIONAL MARKET: THE POLITICS OF FOOD PRODUCTION IN LAND REFORM SETTLEMENTS IN BRAZIL

Claudia Job Schmitt

ABSTRACT

The chapter seeks to reflect on the dynamics of the reconstruction of family farming and peasant agriculture in agrarian reform settlements ("assentamentos") in Brazil, exploring the limits and potential of government food purchases from family farming, particularly the Food Acquisition Program (Programa de Aquisição de Alimentos – PAA), in the creation of alternative paths of rural development. The work analyzes the different strategies through which farmers and their organizations mobilize public policy instruments and market connections, expanding their room for maneuver and agency capacity. Research was conducted in the Baixo Sul Territory of the state of Bahia, focusing the heterogeneous web of social organizations involved in the implementation of the Food Acquisition Program in this setting.

Keywords: Food market; land reform; Brazil agriculture; public policies; peasant strategy; family farm

Constructing a New Framework for Rural Development
Research in Rural Sociology and Development, Volume 22, 255–299

ISSN: 1057-1922/doi:10.1108/S1057-192220150000022010

INTRODUCTION

This chapter focuses on the limits and potential of government food purchases from family farming,[1] particularly the Food Acquisition Program (*Programa de Aquisição de Alimentos – PAA*). The program is an instrument capable of building new linkages between actors, resources, and activities, reinforcing farmers' control of their resource base and strengthening repeasantization processes,[2] as the result of land struggles.

The focus adopted here draws inspiration from a set of approaches which seek to address contemporary rural change as a result of a conflictual, complex, and multilinear processes, through which the material and symbolic orderings which constitute social reality are instituted, reproduced, contested, or transformed in the interactions established between social agents. These new readings of rural development are distanced from linear models of interpretation which analyze the transformations of agriculture and the rural space as a unified phenomenon, capable of being explained en masse by capitalist logics or by the "inexorable" process of differentiation and modernization of national societies,[3] emphasizing the heterogeneous and multilinear nature of social change and the role of social actors – whether they are individuals, groups, or networks – in the construction of rural development. The idea here is that the standards of development which become hegemonic or which, as Law (1994) suggests, manage to stabilize themselves materially and socially, and at times are perpetuated for long periods, are always the result of plural and incomplete processes through which order is permanently constructed and reconstructed. From this focus, development can be looked at from two distinct perspectives. On the one hand, as an enacting discourse, temporarily and spatially referenced, which was able to affirm itself, especially after the Second World War, as a device ("dispositive") of knowledge and power, capable of forging subjectivities and imposing itself on other forms of knowledge (Escobar, 1995, 2005; Hobart, 1993). From another perspective, it is a contingent and discontinuous process, in which specific models and "forms of organizing the world" are maintained, contested, negotiated, rejected, or reappropriated in different contexts. This produces a heterogeneous set of arrangements which emerge as a result of the distinct modes through which the dominant processes associated with development and modernity are repositioned in local life worlds (Arce & Long, 2000; Long, 2007).

This chapter seeks to understand the conflictual, multiple, and contradictory nature of the dynamics of rural development in Brazil, taking as an object of investigation, the relations established by Brazilian farmers, settled by agrarian reform policies, with markets and public policies. It is intended to recognize the distinct strategies through which farmers and their organizations mobilize public policy instruments and market connections, expanding their room for maneuver and agency capacity (van der Ploeg, 1990), as they seek to respond to the challenge of working and living off the land in the agrarian reform settlements. The participation of land reform settlers and their associative organizations in the so-called institutional markets[4] for food products was chosen as the guiding thread in this research.

The social processes analyzed here presume the structuration in rural areas of a segment composed of around one million smallholdings, most of them family based,[5] which emerged as a result of settlement policies implemented by the Federal Government, from the end of the 1970s onward, and, in a more limited manner, by state governments and even municipalities. This sector coexists, on the one hand, with business agriculture, based on large properties, with the intensive use of mechanization and chemical inputs, and strongly connected to global commodity chains, and, on the other, with a highly heterogeneous family farm sector,[6] marked by much differentiated forms of linkage with markets and agro-industrial chains. From the middle of the 1990s onward, this second type of family farming became the object of differentiated public policies, which sought to deal with the specificities of this category of producers, including, here, family farmers settled by agrarian reform policies.[7]

The 2006 Agricultural Census (IBGE, 2009) identified the existence in Brazil of approximately 4.3 million family farming units, occupying a total area of around 80 million hectares, 24.3% of the total area occupied by agricultural units in Brazil.[8] In this period, this segment was responsible for 74.4% of people with agricultural employment. In regards to the production of foodstuffs, family farms were responsible for 83.3% of the Gross Production Value (GPV) of manioc, 68.7% of beans GPV, 56.4% cow milk GPV, and 47% of corn GPV (França, Del Grossi, & de Marques, 2009). Nonfamily agricultural farm units, in turn, encompassed, according to the 2006 Agricultural Census, a universe of approximately 809,369 farm units, occupying an area of more than 253 million hectares, equivalent to 75.7% of land occupied by agricultural units in Brazil. They provided an important share of the production of grains (particularly soybeans), sugarcane, meat, raw materials for industrial use (such as timber), amongst other commodities.[9] In 2006, nonfamily agriculture employed 25.6% of people working in agriculture.

Based on research carried out using the results of the 2006 Agricultural Census, Kageyama, Bergamasco, and Oliveira (2010) found, comparing data related to farm units located in land reform settlements (without definitive land deeds) with the general information referring to family farm units, that the agrarian reform settlements "were not a 'category apart'. These settlements were not 'enclaves' in the productive structure, or 'pockets of poverty': to the contrary, according to the majority of indicators of land distribution, forms of production, technology, commodification, and productivity, the settlements were similar to the general average of farm units" (Kageyama et al., 2010, p. 31). The study called attention to the fact that the settlements tended to reproduce the productivist model of agriculture, based on the mechanization and use of chemical fertilizers and pesticides. The incorporation of alternative practices of agricultural production is still very restricted/limited and few settlements practice ecologically based farming. Despite presenting[10] a very similar profile to family farming as a whole, the land reform settlements had indices of productivity of land and labor inferior to family farming in practically all regions, which, according to the authors, could be a consequence of the fact that a large number of the settlements were set up on land with lower agricultural productivity, distributed by the State through agrarian reform policies.

This brief reference to the data produced by the last Agricultural Census, carried out in 2006, helps to illustrate the contradictory tendencies that mark Brazilian agriculture and rural development at the beginning of the twenty-first century. From the end of the 1990s onward, the strengthening of the agribusiness economy in Brazil (Delgado, 2012)[11] was accompanied, as Leonard, Bonnal, Foyer, and Leite (2009) and Sabourin (2007) have observed, by the institutionalization of a dualist public policy approach to agriculture, based on segmentation between business agriculture and family farming. This duality materialized in the actual political and institutional organization of the Brazilian state, through the existence of two ministries: the Ministry of Agricultural, Livestock, and Supply (*Ministério da Agricultura, Pecuária e Abastecimento* – MAPA), whose mission is "to promote sustainable development and the competitiveness of agribusiness for the benefit of Brazilian society"[12] and the Ministry of Agrarian Development (*Ministério do Desenvolvimento Agrário* – MDA),[13] responsible for agrarian reform policies, the sustainable development of family farming, and the identification, recognition, delimitation, demarcation, and entitlement of land occupied by remnants of *quilombo* communities.[14]

The meanings associated with family farming are currently subject of intense dispute in Brazilian society, often involving the image of a subsistence, backward, and unproductive agriculture, which demands, according to the representatives of agro-industrial interests, "expensive social compensations from taxpayers" (Sabourin, 2007, p. 718), or also the vision of a very productive and environmentally sound agriculture, highly important for food security. It is important to note that the volume of funds allocated to family farming has grown significantly in Brazil in recent years, rising from R$ 2.17 billion in 2000–2001 (approximately US$ 1.1 billion), basically used for credit operations of the National Program for Strengthening Family Farming (*Programa Nacional de Fortalecimento da Agricultura Familiar* – PRONAF), to R$ 39 billion (US$ 17.7 billion), announced by the Federal Government at the release of the 2013–2014 Harvest Plan for Family Farming (*Plano Safra da Agricultura Familiar 2013–2014*). These funds are used in a wide range of actions and programs concerned with family farming. During this period the Brazilian State also provided important support for business agriculture, expanding significantly the volume of funds invested in this sector. By way of illustration, it is worth noting that according to the information provided by MAPA, the provision of rural credit for business farming increased more than fivefold in the last 10 years, raising from R$ 27 billion in 2003–2004 (approximately US$ 12.3 billion) to R$ 136 billion (US$ 61.8 billion) in the 2013–2014 harvest (Brasil, 2013).

Specifically in relation to family farming, the total amount of resources allocated to this category of producers increased importantly after 2003, the year Luís Inácio Lula da Silva began his first mandate as President, leading a coalition of forces under the *Partido dos Trabalhadores* (PT – Workers' Party), and whose election counted on widespread support from the land movements and family farming organizations. During the last 10 years, especially in the first four years of the Lula administration, various public policy instruments were created, including the Food Acquisition Program (PAA).

The aim of this program, a part of the broader set of policies initially created under the *Fome Zero*[15] (Zero Hunger) strategy, was to link support for family farming, the formation of strategic stocks, and access to food to people experiencing food insecurity. In practical terms, the program makes available, through different mechanisms, food acqired by the Federal government, for consumption by people legally eligible, through different social programs, some of them implemented by the government and others by civil society organizations, in partnership with the State. On the production side, the beneficiaries of the PAA are family farmers, as defined by Law 11.326/2006, a definition which covers a very diversified universe of producers, including, family farmers, people settled by agrarian reform policies, people working in forestry or aquaculture, *agroextrativistas* (workers who extract natural resources, such as rubber tappers), small fishermen, indigenous people, and members of rural communities that are remnants of *quilombos*, as well as other traditional communities or peoples. In the consumption side the beneficiaries of the program are individuals facing food and nutritional insecurity, as well as people covered by the public social assistance network and by food and nutrition policies and programs, which can include, in a complementary manner, the National School Meals Program (Programa Nacional de Alimentação Escolar – PNAE). The PAA is an intersectorial program whose actions are coordinated by the Ministry of Social Development and Fight Against Hunger (Ministério do Desenvolvimento Social e Combate à Fome – MDS), but in whose administrative body, various ministries participate.[16]

In 2012, the PAA, which commenced in 2003 with a relatively restricted public of 42,000 families, reached the mark of 185,000 farming families, in other words, 4.3% of the total universe of family farming establishments in the country, estimated at 4.3 million productive units (IBGE, 2009). The total amount of funds invested in food purchases from family farming through the PAA also increased significantly in this period, involving an investment of R$ 838 million in 2012 (Soares et al., 2013) and which is forecast to expand for the 2013–2014 harvest, according to MDA, to R$ 1.2 billion. In relation to the people covered by the distribution networks for the food supplied by PAA, data released by the program administration for 2003–2010, point to an annual average of 9.2 million food beneficiaries.

It is important to highlight that our object of study is the political and associated dynamics related to the implementation of PAA in the context of the agrarian reform settlements. We do not intend to provide, therefore, a general evaluation of the effects of this policy, but rather to understand, in a more wide-ranging way, the impacts caused by PAA on repeasantization processes underway in agrarian reform settlements. The analysis aims to identify the possible contributions of the program to the construction of against-the-grain trajectories of rural development which seek to distance themselves from hegemonic models based on the incorporation of the technological package of the Green Revolution (mechanization, chemical fertilizers, pesticides, commercial seed varieties developed by research) and on the integration of markets controlled by large agro-industrial enterprises.

We have chosen as a case study agrarian reform settlements in the *Baixo Sul* of Bahia, an area whose economic history was closely tied to the production of cacao (*Theobroma cacao* L.) – in crisis since the first half of the 1990s – and where landholding is marked by a quite significant presence of agrarian reform settlements and remnants of *quilombo*.[17]

In the next section, we seek to trace the struggle for land in Brazil and the establishment of agrarian reform settlements. Afterward, conditioning factors influencing the relations established by land reform settlers with markets and public policies are discussed. The section "The Implementation of the PAA in Land Reform Areas" presents a brief evaluation of the implementation of the Food Acquisition Program in agrarian reform settlements in different regions of Brazil, seeking to highlight some factors which influence the implementation of the program among this specific segment of farmers. In the section "Weaving the Institutional Market: Access to Markets and Repeasantization Strategies in the Baixo Sul of Bahia," the experience of the implementation of PAA in land reform settlements located in the *Baixo Sul* Territory of Bahia is discussed. The analysis seeks to understand how farmers settled by agrarian reform policies, in a specific economic, social, and ecological context, mobilized different public policy instruments and market connections, seeking to expand their margins for maneuver and their agency capacity in the construction of strategic alternatives for rural development. Access to institutional markets through PAA is therefore perceived as part of a broader set of social dynamics related to the reconstruction of family farming and peasant agriculture in agrarian reform settlements. The final considerations seek to highlight some central points of the argument.

THE STRUGGLE FOR LAND AND THE ESTABLISHMENT OF AGRARIAN REFORM SETTLEMENTS IN BRAZIL

The structure of land property/holding in Brazil has been historically marked by high levels of concentration. Hoffman and Ney (2010), in a meticulous research effort, faced the methodological challenges inherent in comparing official Brazilian statistics over the last few decades, working with the results of the Agricultural Censuses (from 1975 to 2006) and the National Household Sample (*Pesquisa Nacional por Amostra de Domicílios* – PNAD) from 1992 to 2008. The analysis of the Agricultural Census data points to a strong stability of landholding inequality, measured by the Gini index, which maintained values equivalent to 0.855, 0.858, 0.857, and 0.856 in 1975, 1985, 1995–1996, and 2006, respectively. Similar results were obtained by comparing PNAD data, based on a sample of rural households. What attracts attention in this period is the large decline in the number of small land tenants (*arrendatários* and *parceiros*) and the increase in the number of farmers with less than 10 ha of land. In 2006 small farms in Brazilian standards (up to four fiscal modules)[18] represented 93.3% of the total number of agricultural production units, but only occupied 28.2% of the area covered by farm units (DIEESE/MDA, 2011).

The landholding profile described above, which goes back to the colonial period, was reproduced throughout the industrialization cycle of the country, without any great changes in the subsequent period. It is worth noticing, however, that Brazilian history is strongly marked by the economic, social, and political presence of peasants in all their distinctive expressions. Referring to the constitutive historic experiences of this social category, Wanderley (2009) calls attention to the secondary and subordinate place of family production in Brazilian society: "*the history of the peasantry in Brazil can be defined as the history of struggles to achieve their own space in the economy and society.*" These struggles are often expressed in collective actions fighting for land, gaining social rights, or empowering farmers in their relations with market agents. Migration to the agricultural frontier in search of "free land" (*terra liberta*) (Velho, 1979; Martins, 1996) and employment in cities or on large plantations at specific times of the year or stages in the family life cycle (Garcia Jr., 1990) were strategies used by thousands of families in the reproduction of their ties with the land as a space of work and livelihood.

It is of note that the occupation of land by agricultural units under family administration does not exhaust the diversity of forms of territorial appropriation and collective existence of social groups living in Brazilian rural spaces. The "traditionally occupied" lands, a term used in the 1988 Brazilian Constitution, cover a wide diversity of forms of common use of natural resources, based on distinct definitions of territoriality. In the social space constituted by traditional communities and their different forms of livelihood, a vast array of common tenure systems were consolidated, as the result "*of a multiplicity of solutions historically engendered by different peasant sectors to assure access to land, notably in situations of open conflict*" (Wagner, 2010a, 2010b, p. 109). The complex cartography of territorial conflicts in contemporary Brazil includes, therefore, at the beginning of the twenty-first century, the struggle for the recognition of these social territories and the distinct identities constituted in these conflicts, in a context in which the identification of these groups as peasants, family farmers, or rural workers coexists with a series of other designations (*quilombolas*, *seringueiros* – rubber tappers, *ribeirinhos* – riverside communities, amongst others).

In Brazil, the lands currently recognized by the government as agrarian reform settlements historically emerged as the result of the conflictive dynamics of interaction between land movements and the State, reflecting a correlation of forces in Brazilian society which have decisively influenced the location of these areas, their implementation process, and the relations between settled families and public authorities. As Medeiros observed (2004), the implementation of settlement projects by the State is the result of "*a silent and continuous struggle*" in whose most recent cycle the principal protagonists have been landless farmers and their support and representative organizations, such as the Movement of Landless Workers (*Movimento dos Trabalhadores Rurais Sem Terra* – MST), rural trade unions, the Pastoral Land Commission (*Comissão Pastoral da Terra* – CPT), amongst so many others.[19]

The pressure for obtaining land and remaining on the land has allowed the placement in the Brazilian rural space of a reformed sector, whose dimensions are not negligible, although the information related to the total number of land reform settlements existing in the country is not precise. According to data published by the National Institute of Colonization and Agrarian Reform (*Instituto Nacional de Colonização e Reforma Agrária* – INCRA) on their website, in 2013 there existed in Brazil 9,114 new settlements in an area corresponding to 88,197,747 ha, with 1,288,444 settled families.[20] The data published by the Land Struggle Database (DATALUTA)[21] points, in turn, to the existence in Brazil of a total universe of 9,070 land settlement projects, created between 1979 and 2012, with 933,836 settled families on 81,781,828 ha of land (NERA/FCT-UNESP, 2013).

The controversies traditionally associated with agrarian reform figures can be attributed to various factors, including the heterogeneous conditions and trajectories that gave birth to these settlements, including: the regularization of land held by squatters; conflicts resulting from the expulsion of farmers living on land as tenant farmers; the occupation of unproductive areas by land movements; traditionally occupied lands where the so-called "alternative settlement projects"[22] were implemented, amongst others (Leite, Heredia, Medeiros, Palmeira, & Cintrão, 2004). Depending on the methodology used, lands traditionally occupied by peasants that have been regularized, without being necessarily the result of a legal process of expropriation and division of a large property (*agrarian reform*), are sometimes counted as settlements and sometimes not.

The different trajectories of creation and institutionalization of land reform settlements[23] result in the structuring of an elaborate mosaic of productive situations and social forms of organization. References to difficulties of access and transportation, lack of infrastructure, low soil fertility, and various types of insecurity are recurrent in the literature (Carter & Carvalho, 2010; Leite et al., 2004; Sparovek, 2003). People living in these settlements, in turn, possess a differentiated profile which varies significantly from region to region, and can include: squatters; sons and daughters of smallholders with scarce amounts of land; *parceiros* (sharecroppers) in search of their own land; people displaced by large infrastructure projects; rural wage workers; people living in the urban peripheral areas with varied trajectories in the labor market, often, though not always, with a rural origin; and the unemployed. Not every settlement was originally an encampment (*acampamento*) or involved in land occupations, but the large majority of settlements arose out of conflicts and pressures for the expropriation of land, sometimes involving situations of extreme violence. In a universe of 92 settlements studied by Leite et al. (2004), in areas with high concentrations of settlements in different regions of Brazil, 88 (around 96% of the universe researched) originated from land conflicts. This data is a further indicator that the creation of a reformed sector, currently consisting of almost one million settled families, emerged out of a constant process of struggle and resistance on the land, involving different social actors.

At the beginning of the 1960s, the pressure for agrarian reform gained force in the Brazilian political scene, propelled by the struggles of social movements supported by a social foundation principally consisting of squatters and sharecroppers, but with important variations from region to region. This mobilization process was interrupted with the advent of the military regime and the political repression of rural workers and peasant organizations. Following the democratization of the country, at the end of the 1970s, agrarian reform reemerged as a demand of grassroots social movements. The "agrarian question" reemerged in Brazil at this time having as protagonists a renewed set of social actors and organizations. The new identities occupying in the political scene – "*landless*," "*people displaced by dams*," "*peoples of the forest*,"[24] – were socially constructed as the result of multiple trajectories of pauperization, dispossession, and struggle for access to land. These new conflicts would involve not only resistance in traditionally occupied lands, but also the reconquest of land by a heterogeneous contingent of "*landless*" workers.

The number of rural estates expropriated through presidential decrees reached its maximum level in the 1990s, in a historical period marked by the crisis of the Brazilian agricultural sector and the intensification of the struggle for land. According to INCRA data, during Fernando Henrique Cardoso's two mandates as president (1995–1998 and 1999–2002), 4,286 settlements were created, benefitting 423,813 families (Kageyama et al., 2010).[25] During the eight years of the Lula administration (2003–2006 and 2007–2010), the total number of families settled by land reform policies, according to official sources, rose to 610,455 families (Ojeda, 2012). However, this data is strongly contested, by social movements because it includes, in the general calculation, areas traditionally occupied by family farmers whose landholdings had been legally recognized, and therefore were not settlements resulting from the expropriation of unproductive areas under the control of large landholders.[26] In the last three years, according to the Dilma Roussef presidential mandate, approximately 75,000 families have been settled (Ojeda, 2012; Reis, 2014).

There is no room here for greater details about the ongoing public debate over the "agrarian reform statistics." Nevertheless, it should be highlighted that the strengthening of the agribusiness economy has become an important obstacle for the advancement of Brazilian agrarian reform. The country registered, according to Delgado (2012), from the middle of the 1990s onward, an international boom in agricultural commodities accompanied by the implementation, with state support, of a set of public policy instruments capable of providing rural landholders with extraordinary gains (p. 100). The growing valorization of land in a market pressurized not only by the search for agricultural land, but also by the diversification of economic activities in the rural space (mining, energy production, housing projects), has become an obstacle both to the creation of new land reform settlements and the recognition and consolidation of the territorial rights of indigenous peoples and *quilombola* communities. The political and institutional strengthening of economic sectors linked to agribusiness in Brazil intensified disputes around land rights and allocation of public investments in different political arenas, including the Brazilian Congress and the judicial system. Social demands such as the allocation of unproductive land for agrarian reform, the recognition of the territorial rights of indigenous peoples and traditional communities, and the compliance of land owners with the socioenvironmental function of land have been often relegated in recent times (Intini & Fernandes, 2013; Sauer, 2013).

BETWEEN MARKETS AND PUBLIC POLICIES: THE RECONSTRUCTION OF FAMILY FARMING AND PEASANT AGRICULTURE IN LAND REFORM SETTLEMENTS

Collective dynamics aimed at gaining access to land or the recognition of rights to traditionally occupied lands are undoubtedly a key dimension in the processes of repeasantization currently underway in different regions of Brazil. Authors such as Sigaud, Rosa, and Macedo,[27] among others, have analyzed the process through which the term "movement" ("*movimento*") and the term "encampment" ("*acampamento*") have been incorporated into the repertoires of collective action of rural populations in Brazil, institutionalizing specific modalities of land conflict and the recognition of these conflicts by the State. Occupying land and setting up encampments is a practice which has its roots in the struggles of the "landless" peasants in Southern Brazil. In our time, these forms of collective action are present in the most distinct regions of the country, and have been constituted as a language, "*a way of making claims through acts*" (Sigaud et al., 2008, p. 108). In a conflictual process, the State began to accept encampments as a request for land redistribution, recognizing the social movement responsible for them as an interlocutor. Landholders also came to see the presence of encampments as a threat to their right to ownership, and began searching a number of ways, including judicial, to regain possession of occupied properties. For society in general, the encampment became a sign that the people organized in these spaces were demanding land. Undoubtedly, the Movement of Landless Workers (MST) played a fundamental role in the legitimation of this "mode of carrying out the struggle." Currently, this type of strategy has been adopted by a wide range of organizations.

Once the right of a specific group of families to the land had been officially recognized, and they are assigned to a land area that will be divided among them, a new phase begins in the life of a land reform settlement, a period which corresponds to the structuration and consolidation of the "assentamento," involving the demarcation of lots, the implementation of different types of infrastructure (houses, roads, schools, electrification, water supply, amongst others), the obtaining of essential services (health, education, leisure), access to productive support policies,[28] and the construction of relations with local authorities and the various markets. As Carter and Carvalho (2010) suggest, the "struggle for land" was transformed into the "struggle on the land."

Generally speaking, the existing literature about the economic, social, and political dynamics involved in settlement implementation processes in the different regions of the country seems to converge on some points. The first element is the centrality assumed by the relations with public authorities in the lives of settled families, in a context marked by a large range of needs and innumerable problems to be overcome. As Leite et al. (2004) observed in their comparative research on the impacts of agrarian reform settlements, which involved field research in areas of high concentration of these settlements in six different regions of the country, "settlements have become differentiated spaces of relations with the State and are subject to its administration and interference. It is this relationship which allows the settlement to exist and, as a result, settled families become a differentiated social segment from other peasants" (Leite et al., 2004, p. 111). Similarly, in comparative work involving two settlements linked to the Landless Workers Movement (MST) located in the south and northeast of the country, Wolford (2003) highlights: "once MST members receive land, the government becomes their landlord, creditor, educator and overseer."

The relationship that the settled families establish with the land is regulated either by land concession agreements or in what are called títulos de domínio (land title or deed). Through the land concession agreements the settled workers receive from the National Colonization and Agrarian Reform Institute (Instituto Nacional de Colonização e Reforma Agrária – INCRA)[29] a provisional concession to use the parcels of land, while they are not authorized to alienate, mortgage, lease, or sell the lot or the improvements existing there to third parties. INCRA is responsible in turn for ensuring access to land and to different public programs. The título de domínio transfers the rural property to the beneficiary of agrarian reform in a definitive manner, once they have fulfilled the clauses established by the concession agreement (for at least five years) and they are able to cultivate the land and pay for the deed in 20 annual installments.[30] Nevertheless, the lot of land obtained cannot be sold for 10 years.[31] The relationship which the settled families establish with the land, with the mediation of the State, has been the object of intensive debate. Some social organizations, such as MST,[32] argue that settled farmers should remain in the land reform settlements with their legal rights assured by the land concession agreements in order, on the one hand, to guarantee that the land retains its use value (and a right), not as a commodity, and, on the other hand, the maintenance of a commitment on the part of the State to the delivery of public policies in the land reform settlements.

In relation to public policies, the Second National Agrarian Reform Plan – Peace, Production and Quality of Life in the Rural Areas (II PNRA), published in 2003, and whose directives are still officially in force, allowed the implementation of a series of programs and actions which sought to assure a good quality of life in land reform settlements through a series of "productive projects suited to the regional potentials and the specificities of each biome and committed to environmental sustainability" (Brasil, 2005).

Published in the first year of the Lula Administration, the plan predicted an expansion of the demand for food and agricultural products as the result of the inclusion of a significant number of people under food insecurity in the emergency actions carried out under the Fome Zero (Zero Hunger) strategy, notably the projected inclusion of 44 million people, in four years, in cash transfer programs (Brasil, 2005, p. 7). This new demand for food was to be met by family farming and by the agrarian reform settlements. Interestingly, the noticeable reduction which has occurred in recent years in the rate of land reform settlement creation seems to reflect, however, a change in the strategy on the part of the government. Implementation of such public utilities as light, water, and housing and technical assistance to farmers has now assumed greater relevance in the governmental discourse related to the agrarian reform which is to the detriment, for example, of a more aggressive implementation of new settlements aimed at meeting the internal demand for food.[33]

Nevertheless, it is important to consider that the promotion of quality of life in land reform settlements and their productive integration into a territorial development strategy also appeared as relevant themes in the II PNRA. To achieve these objectives, the plan projected a whole set of interventions related to credit policies, technical assistance, market support, adding value to agricultural products, implementation of infrastructure (water, basic sanitation, energy, transport), and policies aimed at the universalization of fundamental rights.

Worthy of note is that the preliminary results of the research project Reforma Agrária: pesquisa SOBRE a qualidade de vida, produção e renda dos assentamentos de reforma agrária (Agrarian Reform: research on the quality of life, production, and income of agrarian reform settlements), released by MDA/INCRA in 2010,[34] indicated that a significant percentage of families still faced water access problems (a problem faced by 21% of the 16,153 families interviewed) and electricity (around 24% of the families interviewed had no access to electricity, while 33% had intermittent access). Discontent with the state of roads and access to lots, as well as poor health services, was also highlighted by the study. Approximately 52% of families in the total universe researched had access to credit through PRONAF (Programa Nacional de Fortalecimento da Agricultura) and around 63% had received financial support for the acquisition of construction materials and initial support to meet basic necessities in the first stage of their life in the new settlement (Brasil, 2010). The research thus found the existence of important deficits in relation to the implementation of public policies in land reform settlements, notwithstanding the efforts made by public authorities since 2003 to direct programs and actions toward improving the quality of life in the reformed areas.

A second point of convergence in the analyses relates to the fact that once the families had received the land, the diversity of trajectories, strategies, and life projects underlying the struggle for land as a collective enterprise become even more pronounced. Different case studies (Ferreira, 2010; Ferreira, 2013; Wolford, 2003) have called attention to the contrast existing between, on the one hand, the level of social cohesion which appears to mark, in most cases, community life in the encampments, and, on the other hand, the multiplicity of projects and strategies of social reproduction which come to influence the decisions of settled families once they have access to land. Nevertheless, it is a mistake to associate in an unequivocal manner, the recognition of the settlement by public authorities[35] with a weakening of the logics of collective action. The organizational capacity of settlements as a group is undoubtedly a fundamental ingredient of this new stage, influencing in a decisive form their possibilities of negotiation with the State, market agents, and local political groups. The format which this organization will assume involves in most cases a series of connections, impasses, and negotiations, mobilizing tensions which cut across the relationships of land reform settlers among themselves and with different social mediators.

We agree with Michelotti (2008) that the conquest of a settlement, as a fraction of a territory, should not be immediately confused with the territorialization of the peasants themselves. The author argues that obtaining land results in two important challenges. The first is related to the relative stabilization of family farmers in settlement areas, considering the economic, social, and political conditions existing there. A second element involves the construction of the relative autonomy of these peasants in relation to land, considering the dominant pattern of subordination to capital existing in the Brazilian agrarian space. The possibilities of the construction of this autonomy[36] are conditioned by constellations of factors including the relationship with different markets.

The relations which the farmers establish with agricultural markets are closely tied to a heterogeneous set of social reproduction strategies which the settler families put into practice as a way of assuring their permanence in the land reform areas. The styles of farming[37] constructed in the land reform settlements emerge in different contexts as the result of the productive profile of the settlement, its relations with its regional surroundings, the resources and strategies used individually or collectively by farmers in their relations with different actors and institutions, and the choices made over time by the settler families.

Various case studies have explored the diversity of sociocultural logics underlying productive strategies and their relationship with markets, put into practice by the settler farmers. Research carried out by Piccin (2007) revealed the diversity of productive systems of settler families in a specific project, the Ceres settlement, located in an area dominated by soybean cultivation in Southern Brazil. The analysis suggests that the different productive strategies identified in the Ceres settlement were conditioned by the social trajectories of families before going to the settlement, their collective experiences – even if differentiated – lived during the struggle for land and their positions in the field of power relations existing in the regional environment surrounding the settlement, dominated in this case by soybean cultivation and milk production. With the creation of the settlement, which occurred in a period marked by significant reduction in the price of soybeans, the researcher identified distinct productive logics and forms of relations to markets including: (i) the leasing of the productive areas to neighboring producers to grow soybeans; (ii) the structuring of productive systems aimed at the commercial cultivation of soybeans and milk; (iii) the structuring of diversified production systems and the marketing, not only of milk, but of a whole set of products previously cultivated solely for self-consumption, through short food supply chains.

Research by Ferreira (2013) in an agrarian reform settlement located in the north of the state of Rio de Janeiro shows the distinct repercussions of the involvement of land reform settlers in nonagricultural activities. Nonagricultural activities can contribute greatly to a more effective occupation of the lot, serving as an alternative source of income, reinvested in agricultural production, but can also result in limited investments in agricultural activities at farm level, as labor becomes scarce. In this case study, settled families established active relationships with different markets for food and agricultural products, developing a set of strategies which included door-to-door sales in nearby cities or in the settlement itself, the direct sale of products through small roadside shacks, access to institutional markets, the creation of a small farmers market, and the marketing of products to various types of middlemen. The formation of most of these circuits only became possible through the construction of political relations with public authorities, different local interest groups, and with the local population in a process which involved a broad set of negotiations and political exchanges developed through the settlement association, small networks of farmers, and through individual initiatives.

The study conducted by Moura (2006) in a land reform settlement located in Paraná, in the Southern Region of Brazil, where productive activities developed by a specific group of families were based in the collective organization of work, calls attention to the active role performed by these farmers in the diversification of production, the construction of small agro-industrial units, the incorporation of agro-ecological practices which seek to reduce dependence on external raw materials, and the structuring of a diversified set of commercialization strategies. The relations established by these settled families with different markets included the sale of milk, greens, bread, biscuits, and sugarcane derivatives, directly to the consumer; the organization of local farmer's markets; the distribution of products through small retailers and through institutional markets, particularly though the Food Acquisition Program (PAA). Participation in each of these circuits was constructed bit by bit in a process marked by set-backs, successes, and learning.

These case studies reinforce the active role of farmers in the construction of connections with different markets, a protagonist attitude which emerges in situations marked by high levels of uncertainty and instability in relation to access to infrastructure (water, light, roads for transport) and production support policies, in an environment also characterized, in many cases, by strong asymmetries in the relations with political and economic agents outside the land reform settlements. The commercialization strategies developed by these farmers can lead to a growing integration in agro-industrial commodity circuits, through companies, large agro-industrial cooperatives or connections to different types of middlemen. Moreover, in many situations, families were found to be part of short food supply chains: local markets, door-to-door sales in the closest town, sale of products to neighbors and relatives, etc. These tactics can be implemented individually by families or involve the participation of other settler families in associative schemes through formal or informal groups (Leite et al., 2004).

It is important to highlight that the inclusion of settler families in agro-industrial chains or in long circuits commanded by middlemen very frequently reflects a situation of fragility in relation to the agents of commercialization. Ferrante and Barone (2011) call attention to the strong asymmetries of power involved in relations established by settled farmers with the sugarcane enterprises in São Paulo. The productive integration of agrarian reform settlements into the agro-industrial system emerges in the cases analyzed by these authors, through a web of relations which come to be established among settler families, state agents, and the private sector, resulting in the loss of control of settler workers over a significant part of their land, which becomes occupied by sugarcane monoculture, based on schemes proposed by large sugar companies. In the case of the settlement studied by Ferreira (2013), based in the north of the state of Rio de Janeiro, the relationship with middlemen was presented to families as an alternative for the financing of production through the anticipated supply of inputs in a situation of extreme precariousness resulting, amongst other things, from a substantial delay in the implementation of infrastructure and productive support policies for the settlement.

Our analysis of the literature referring to agrarian reform settlements suggests that gaining a position of greater autonomy in relation to the markets, reflects in a large number of cases, not only an intrinsic sociocultural logic, informed by the prior experience of these families in the practice of peasant farming, but also their capacity to mobilize productive resources, and knowledge, and to weave social relations into different social contexts. From a symbolic point of view, the condition of *assentado* often operates as a stigma, creating a series of difficulties in the relationship of families with their social surroundings. As Leite et al. (2004) have observed, the demonstration of their productive capacity works in the case of the settlements like a positive distinction, opening paths for their entry into local society and contributing to the visibility of the positive results created by agrarian reform.

Having described some of the factors which interfere in relations between settler workers with markets and public policies in the period following the access to land, we will trace the general framework for the implementation of the PAA in agrarian reform settlements.

THE IMPLEMENTATION OF THE PAA IN LAND REFORM AREAS

The Food Acquisition Program, created in 2003, is aimed at a specific segment of farmers, identified by the Brazilian legislation as family farmers, including those settled by agrarian reform. The institutional design adopted by the program seeks to join measures supporting the sale of family farming products to a wider range of outlets aimed at the promotion of food security and nutrition in the countryside and the city. Food produced by family farmers is purchased by the Federal Government using simplified purchasing mechanisms aimed at the formation of public food stocks, the distribution of food to families experiencing food insecurity, the supply of food to popular restaurants, food banks, community kitchens, and other public facilities. The foodstuffs purchased through the PAA can be also distributed to the National School Meals Program.

The operationalization format adopted by the program allows for a diversified set of purchase mechanisms, which can be used to meet very different food demands. Resources are allocated to the Ministry of Agrarian Development and MDS in two distinct forms. In the first, money is transferred to the National Provision Company (*Companhia Nacional de Abastecimento* – CONAB)[38] and through this company, to a wide range of family farming organizations, most of whom are associations and cooperatives. The second form of implementation allows for the operationalization of the program through state and municipal governments, in partnership with the MDS.[39]

The cooperation between the federal bodies (at the federal, state, and municipal levels) is anchored on a series of administrative decentralization, participation, and social control mechanisms, stipulated in the 1988 Constitution, and is also marked by a high level of competition between local political groups for access to resources controlled by the Federal Government. The implementation formats adopted by the public authorities in the execution of governmental actions undoubtedly influence the dynamics of access of family farmers to different public programs. The social and political mediations involved in the relations which family farmers in general, and settler families, in particular, establish with public authorities, also affect the execution of policies and the construction of rural development possibilities.

In its first two years of existence (2003 and 2004), a significant part of PAA actions were aimed at agrarian reform settlements. These operations, carried out at a national level, were concentrated on a specific modality of the program, Anticipated Family Farming Purchase (*Compra Antecipada da Agricultura Familiar*), which was aimed at providing financial resources to farmers at planting time, through advanced payments to be repaid at the following harvest, with priority for food and agricultural products which could be incorporated into government stocks (e.g., beans, manioc flour, and corn). Settler workers and land struggle organizations participated actively in this initial effort to implement the program in a period marked by strong expectations in relation to possible advances in agrarian reform policies.

It is estimated that in 2003, Anticipated Family Farming Purchase operations aimed at settlements amounted to 72.8% of the total family farm units assisted by the program, allowing in 2003 and 2004 the participation of 48,000 settler families in the PAA (Schmitt et al., 2013). Anticipated Purchase operations were, however, interrupted in 2004 by a process which culminated with the suspension of this modality, which was marked by a series of tensions related, on the one hand, to the high level of default for these operations (resulting, at least in part, from the climatic adversities which affected different regions of the country that year) and, on the other, by numerous problems faced by the Federal Government in the operationalization of this public policy instrument, including delays in the release of funding, deficiencies in the technical services provided in relation to crops, flaws in the provision of agricultural insurance, etc. With the suspension of the Anticipated Purchase, those farmers settled under the agrarian reform programs continued to have access to other modalities of the program. In the following years there was a reduction in the share of the total number of agrarian reform settlers assisted by the PAA.

The study held by Schmitt et al. (2013) sought to estimate, on a national level, the presence of settler families in the total set of PAA beneficiaries. Based on PAA-related data available in the CONAB databases[40] and using the information referring to 2008–2011,[41] it was possible to observe increasing participation both in absolute numbers and in percentage terms of the settler families in the different modalities of the PAA made available by CONAB. The classification of these farmers as agrarian reform settlers, or as any other category of supplier, is done by PAA proponent organizations (associations and cooperatives), which are responsible for completing the electronic forms required to participate in the program. For example, in 2008 11.3% of the 92,307 families who sold their products in PAA through the operations implemented by CONAB were identified by the proponent organizations as agrarian reform settlers (*assentados*). In 2011 this percentage increased to 16.3% (a total number of 17,351). In 2011, this information, based on the declarations of the organizations themselves was checked through cross-tabulation of different information systems made available both by INCRA and CONAB. The results achieved in this exercise suggest that the number of agrarian reform settlers who participated in the PAA as suppliers is significantly larger than the number of family farmers identified as settlers by the organizations. Based on the cross-tabulation of the different databases it can be estimated that in 2011, 28,395 settled families participated in the PAA – 26.6% of the total number of family farm holdings assisted by the program. It appears that many families of land reform settlers were generically classified as family farmers by the organizations which participated in PAA, at the time of completing the forms (Schmitt et al., 2013).

Family Farming Purchase with Simultaneous Donation, which allows the formation at the local and territorial levels of distribution networks of family farming products for social programs, was the most accessed PAA modality, in absolute terms, by settled workers, being responsible for 80.7% of the total number of settled families who benefited from PAA in 2011. The modalities of Formation of Stocks for Family Farming and Direct Purchase from Family Farming benefitted 14.3% and 5.0%, respectively, of the total settler families who participated in the program that year.

Another important element is the spatial distribution of program operations in agrarian reform settlements across the various regions of the country. In 2011, out of a total of 9,794 settlements registered in the INCRA List of Agrarian Reform Beneficiaries, 1,744 (18% of the total) had a family farm unit benefited by the PAA, while settlements located in the Northeast and South of the country participated more strongly in the program. Nevertheless, 1,164 settlements, or 66.7% of the total settlements that benefitted from the program, had less than 10 families accessing PAA in 2011. On a national scale what predominates is a spatially dispersed pattern of access to the program, with few families accessing the program in each settlement.[42] Purchase with Simultaneous Donation operations in settlements – which corresponds in absolute terms to more than 80% of the families benefitted by the program – were distributed in 2011 among 891 municipalities in the different regions of the country, with an approximate incidence of 37 settled families accessing the PAA per municipality (Schmitt et al., 2013). Access to institutional markets via the PAA seems to occur through networks composed of a limited number of farmers, which to a certain extent restricts the territorial impact of this public policy.

It is also interesting to note that approximately 42% of settled families, who accessed the program in 2011, did this through mixed organizations in which both land reform settlers and other categories of family farmers took part. By way of example, of 1,917 family farming organizations that accessed the modality Family Farming Purchase with Simultaneous Donation in 2011, only 16% of them were solely composed of land reform settlers. These results suggest that in order to access the PAA, land reform settlers established connections with other organizations (not exclusively composed by settled families) and categories of family farmers, living in the same municipality or in municipalities adjacent to the reform areas.

Analyzed as a whole, the national data referring to the program operations carried out by CONAB, in connection with different associations and cooperatives, points to a growing and numerically significant participation of land reform settlers in the institutional supply of food distributed to social programs. Various studies (Grisa, Schmitt, Mattei, Maluf, & Leite, 2011; Le Moal, 2013; Schmitt et al., 2013) call attention to the difficulties faced by these settler workers and by family farmers in general in accessing the program, including: lack of information regarding the functioning of this public policy; numerous barriers faced in obtaining the documentation required to participate in the PAA – a problem not restricted to family farmers, but also very common at the level of the associations and cooperatives which, in order to join the program, need to comply with a series of legal requirements; the challenges related to transport and product distribution logistics; lack of technical assistance; various fragilities in accessing basic infrastructure for production (water for irrigation, all-weather roads, vehicles which allow the delivery of food, etc.); the time between the delivery of the product and payment, considered long compared to the sale of products to middlemen. These problems, which assume different shapes in the implementation of the PAA, affect the program dissemination process, which, as noted above, still involve a relatively small number of families in each settlement. The challenges faced by farmers in accessing this public policy make even more relevant the role of associations, cooperatives, and informal agricultural networks in the social construction of this market.

WEAVING THE INSTITUTIONAL MARKET: ACCESS TO MARKETS AND REPEASANTIZATION STRATEGIES IN THE BAIXO SUL OF BAHIA

This final section has the aim of analyzing the implementation of the Food Acquisition Program in the Baixo Sul territory in Bahia. It features the dynamics of the reconstruction of family farming in agrarian reform settlements. The case study shows the distinct ways that new opportunities of market access associated with institutional purchases are appropriated by farmers and their organizations in a context marked by different types of limitations and risks. What attracts attention in this case is the important role played by this public policy in the diversification of the range of products sold by settler farmers and family farmers and in the strengthening of associative organizations as social and political actors in this region.

The Struggle for Land and Peasant Reproduction Strategies in Baixo Sul Settlements

The emergence in the Baixo Sul of agrarian reform settlements is associated with the national dynamics of the struggle for agrarian reform, but also has an important connection with the transformations which occurred in the insertion of the Southern region of Bahia into global commodity markets. At the end of the 1980s, Bahian cocoa growing entered yet another of its cyclical crises, resulting from a combination of factors including competition from other producer countries in a scenario marked by an increase in global production; variations in the price of cocoa at an international level; the low qualification and demotivation of direct labor, at times working in slave like conditions (Estival, 2013); the absence of concern about product quality; and the predatory use of natural resources, particularly after the incorporation of the Green Revolution technologies (nonshaded cocoa varieties, pesticide, and chemical fertilizers). The most visible face of this crisis was the widespread dispersion of a fungicide plague known as *Witches' Broom (Crinipellis perniciosa)*, which destroyed entire crops in the region. As a result the production of cocoa in the South of Bahia, 380,000 tons in 1990, fell to 130,000 tons in 2000, though there was some level of recovery during the 2000s (Rocha, 2008). During the 1990s Brazil became an importer of cocoa beans. Due to the crisis, the principal Brazilian export companies altered their commercial strategies, coming to export products of greater added value such as cocoa butter, cocoa cake, and cocoa powder, demanding from the producers a better quality of raw material.

The crisis of the 1990s was reflected in the Baixo Sul, with the abandonment of cocoa plantations belonging to large landholders or private companies, the concentration of poor workers and the unemployed in urban centers, and the migration of workers to other regions of the country. The removal of the forests which had previously served as shade for cocoa and their replacement by pasture became a common practice in the region and cattle raising gained space as a new activity.

One of the impacts of this crisis that developed in both the central core of cocoa production as well as in its more peripheral areas was the intensification of the struggle for land in the region, though it should be noted that conflicts involving groups of squatters and the occasional establishment of settlements had been occurring in Southern Bahia since the 1980s (Meliani, 2014). The launching at the national level of the 1st National Plan of Agrarian Reform (*Plano Nacional de Reforma Agrária* – I PNRA), in 1985, marked a recognition on the part of the state of a social demand for the implementation of an agrarian reform policy. This undoubtedly contributed to the intensification of agrarian conflicts in the region and made them more visible. In the 1990s, the deepening of the cocoa growing crisis, with the abandonment of various plantations by their owners in the middle of an accumulation of labor related debts,[43] helped to propel the occupation of unproductive lands with the aim of their eventual expropriation.

In the Baixo Sul, the land conflicts of the 1980s, 1990s, and 2000s resulted in the creation, according to INCRA data, of 35 settlements, with a total land area of approximately 29,000 ha and with an installation capacity of 1,874 families. The large majority of these settlement projects were created in the 1990s, based on expropriation decrees. Nevertheless, it is important to note that the struggle for land and for the recognition of land rights of the Baixo Sul communities would historically take place on multiple fronts: in the settlement creation process, the struggle of smallholders to obtain the legal recognition of individual land deeds, and in the 2000s, the organization of *quilombola* communities in order to obtain the collective entitlement of their lands (Dutra, 2011).

The trajectory of the Dandara dos Palmares Settlement Project, located in Camamu Municipality, illustrates the many ways that families have found to remain on the land.

The 1,452 ha area, where this settlement is now located, belonged to a company called CEPEL Agropecuária Ltd. In 1997, it was occupied by a group of landless families coming from different rural communities across the municipality,[44] drawing support from the Rural Workers Union of Camamu and sectors of the Catholic Church linked to Liberation Theology. The expropriation decree which created the settlement was published in 1998, and around 65 families were settled in the region. Some abandoned cocoa growing areas were inherited from the company. Parts of these areas, where cocoa had already been grown, came to be used, at least at the beginning of the settlement, in a collective strategy, with the organization *mutirões* (collective work groups), involving family groups. The remainder was incorporated into the individual lots of settled families. In 2012, the settlement was approximately 14 years old and had accumulated a large amount of experience in its relations with public authorities, markets, and external networks. The connections with rural worker's trade unions, rural development nongovernmental organizations (NGOs) such as the Advisory Service for Popular Rural Organizations (*Serviço de Assessoria às Organizações Populares Rurais* – SASOP),[45] were fundamental for the construction of a shared collection of experiences, capacities, and strategies. These bonds and ties were a fundamental ingredient for families to be able to remain in the settlement.

When families established themselves in parts of old plantations, a significant part of the land was covered with native vegetation. The preservation of this existing forest had been a concern of settlement leadership since the establishment of the *assentamento*. The diversification of agricultural production and the implementation of agro-forestry systems was a strategy adopted by many farmers, stimulated by technical advisory organizations, particularly by SASOP,[46] with the planting of other crops in areas previously occupied by cocoa becoming a common practice (Rezende & Olalde, 2005).

At the time of the research, various families farmed on agro-ecological principles, but practices such as slash and burn and the use of pesticides still occurred. An area of approximately 4 ha, ceded by the community association, was worked by a collective group of women, and was used for the agro-ecological production of food. This space, where there is now a highly diversified agro-forestry system, had functioned since the creation of the settlement project as an important core of the social and political organization of women. Another collective group, also with the strong participation of women, was concerned with craftwork. Also of interest, as it was an important innovation, was the existence under the auspices of the settlement's community association of an environmental commission. The same association, in partnership with other organizations, sold a much diversified range of products through the Food Acquisition Program (PAA). This initiative resulted from a partnership between the settlement's community association[47] and a family farming organization which worked at the territorial level, AACAF.[48]

Working in partnership with an international NGO, the settled workers were concerned with the building of a communitarian kitchen for the production of fruit sweets and other processed foods to be sold through the institutional markets (or other commercial markets). The facilities of this collective enterprise had, however, not yet been authorized by public health inspection bodies due to the quality of the available water, considered unsuitable for human consumption. The problems associated with the water quality for the processing of food for sale undoubtedly reflect the serious challenges faced by settlers. When we carried out our research, the settled families still collected water manually in buckets from streams and springs and did not have an adequate waste treatment system in their residences. The condition of roads, especially in the rainy season, hindered the transport of students and the sale of products.

Settler family incomes were the result of a combination of differentiated sources, both agricultural and nonagricultural, including the sale of seasonal products such as cocoa and cloves, sold to middlemen; paid labor in coffee harvesting in Espírito Santo, which implied long distance seasonal migration to another state; the sale of different products in small-scale circuits, including the Camamu's market and various neighboring networks; revenues obtained through participation in governmental cash transfer programs; the sale of craftwork; sporadic work carried outside the settlement; and the sale of food through the Food Acquisition Program (PAA).

Access to institutional markets, particularly through the Food Acquisition Program (PAA) was, therefore, one of the alternatives existing in a wide-ranging set of family reproduction strategies carried out by the agrarian reform settlers at Dandara dos Palmares. Cocoa maintained its position as an important source of income, allowing farmers to receive "money on the spot" by selling to middlemen, but supplying products to the PAA allowed these families to gain monetary income, producing at the same time a diversified set of foodstuffs for self-consumption. In the beginning of the 2000s, the range of products sold by the Dandara dos Palmares settlers was quite restricted, notably to cocoa, cloves, and manioc flour (Carmo, 2003). In contrast, in the PAA sales project, presented by the association to CONAB and approved in 2010, 35 different products for sale were listed, thereby indicating an expansion of the room for maneuver for the settler families in their relations with agricultural markets, a fundamental requirement for remaining on their land.

The participation of settler workers in institutional markets, however, was only possible due to the strong involvement of those farmers in wider social and political networks, located outside the settlement.

Associative Networks and Access to Public Policies: The Implementation of the PAA in the Baixo Sul of Bahia

In the Baixo Sul, the participation of settler families in institutional markets, through the Food Acquisition Program (PAA) was found to be closely linked to the creation in the 1990s of a heterogeneous set of organizations involving rural trade unions, social movements, associations of agrarian reform settlers and family farmers, cooperatives, and advisory NGOs, all of whom came to play an important role in the struggle for land, the defense of the rights of rural populations, and the mobilization of farmers for access to public policies.

In addition to this, several organizational forms involving different segments of family farming, including fishing colonies, various associations stimulated by the actions of local politicians, and different initiatives were aimed at the production and sale of family farm products (partly organic). Furthermore, we note the emergence in the 2000s of different farmer cooperatives and associations linked to the Program for the Integrated Growth and Development with Sustainability of the Mosaic of Environmental Protection Areas of the Baixo Sul of Bahia (*Programa de Desenvolvimento e Crescimento Integrado com Sustentabilidade do Mosaico de Áreas de Proteção Ambiental do Baixo Sul da Bahia* – PDCIS), developed with the support of a private foundation, Fundação Odebrecht,[49] in partnership with the Association of Municipalities of Baixo Sul, the Sustainable Development Institute of the Baixo Sul (IDES), the State Government of Bahia,[50] amongst others. When the research was being carried out, the structuring of specific product chains (palm, manioc, aquaculture, *piaçava*) was one of the objectives pursued by the organizations linked to this network.

Research conducted in the territory strongly suggests that the commertialization experiences implemented by family farming associative organizations in the Baixo Sul of Bahia could be interpreted as a repertoire consisting of four strategies. The first had the central objective of improving the position of family farmers in existing productive chains, seeking, above all, to connect in an associative manner the commercialization of certain products, controlling whenever possible the processing stage through small agro-industries, also managed in an associative form.

Essentially, these type of iniciatives sought to reposition farmers' relations within the conventional commercialization circuits dominated by middlemen, through different forms of collective action. By way of example, in 2007 various organizations linked to the trade union movement decided to construct a new form of insertion in the guarana product chain, using funding from the territorial development policies implemented by the Ministry of Agrarian Development. This guarana processing unit was designed to process the production of 5,000 family farm units located in 14 Baixo Sul municipalities (Inhetvin, 2010). At the time of the fieldwork, this guarana processing unit had still not started operating due to a series of difficulties related to the technical specifications prepared by the public agents responsible that did not meet the technical requirements required by the legislation. This episode helps to illustrate some of the obstacles faced by farmers in their efforts to strengthen their position in conventional circuits of trade.

Another example that can be included in this strategy is the Agricultural Development Cooperative of Valença's (COOFAVA) effort to sell products such as guarana, cloves, and dendê oil through different commercialization circuits, including sales to large transnational companies such as AmBev. In 2011, this cooperative carried out, under the PAA, a project under the modality Formation of Family Farming Stocks which resulted in the purchase of 25 tons of guarana from its members, afterward to be sold on the market at a more favorable price. According to the organization this operation helped to sustain the price of this product at a regional level. Access to the PAA, thus, allowed the cooperative to pay farmers at the time of delivery, thereby expanding its space for maneuver in selling at a better price.

The network of organizations (associations, cooperatives, and teaching units) linked to the corporate responsibility actions of Fundação Odebrecht were engaged, in turn, in the construction of a somewhat more complex strategy, aimed at the verticalization of production, the stimulation of entrepreneurialism among farmers, and the integration of smallholders to large industrial chains. Some of these associations, such as the Baixo Sul Heart of Palm Producers Cooperative, were certified by various environmental quality and social responsibility certification bodies, participating in markets and exhibitions, and selling their products through long commercialization circuits, including large supermarkets.

The operationalization of these projects required very significant amounts of resources and constant advisory and market coordination work carried out by specialists linked to the partner network mobilized by Fundação Odebrecht. The sustainability of these arrangements was based, therefore in the specialized work supplied by the technical staff. In relation to this, authors such as Lima et al. (2013), analyzing the functioning of product arrangements aimed at the processing and sale of manioc starch, stimulated by the same partner network in an adjacent territory, questioned the role of family farmers (small landholders and sharecroppers) in the shaping of this product chain. In view of these authors, the smallholders linked to these supply chains still remain in a subordinated position in their relation to these markets, depending, at least at that point in time, on experts and external resources in the processing and marketing of their products.

The organizations which were part of the partner networks activated by Fundação Odebrecht in the Baixo Sul also became food suppliers to the institutional market through PAA. In 2009 *Instituto Direito e Cidadania* (IDC – Law and Citizenship Institute), a partner of the Foundation, started to link the production of family farmers in the different municipalities of the territory to institutional food demand, aimed at supplying crèches, hostels, and public hospitals, amongst other social assistance organizations. Between 2009 and 2013, with the support of CONAB, 775 family units were involved in the PAA operations promoted through the IDC, according to data published in a 2013 report (Fundação Odebrecht, 2013).

A third type of strategy in relation to the markets is the insertion of family farming organizations into a high quality market, in this specific case, the organic products market. This strategy was notably developed by farmers linked to *Projeto Onça*, whose organizational trajectory goes back to the 1980s. In 1994 the *Projeto Onça* Mixed Agricultural Cooperative was created in the municipality of Itaperoá.

Twenty-one farmers were involved in the dissemination of agro-ecological practices – including agro-forestry management systems – and the commercialization of the production of *Projeto Onça* members (Silva, da Silva, & Xavier, 2009). At the time of research, the cooperative already had more than 80 members and had experience in the exporting of organic products (especially cloves and guarana powder) to Germany. It also had some contacts with customers in large metropolitan centers, such as São Paulo.

In the 2000s, it began to sell products through the PAA. Initially its participation in the program had a total annual value equivalent to R$ 52,000 (US$23,636). At the time of the interview, the organization was implementing its fourth PAA sales project, with a value of R$ 400,000 (US $181,818), involving a significantly wider set of farmers. Cooperative members, since they were certified as organic producers, gained an additional 30% on sales for the institutional market.

A fourth set of sales strategies developed by family farmers involved the participation of farming organizations in short market circuits, including the sale of a diversified set of products in local markets and the direct sale of products through proximity networks including relatives, neighbors, and acquaintances.

Family producer associations, with the participation of agrarian reform settlers and family farmers, began to dispute space from 2009 onward in

Camamu Market, selling their production at stalls specialized in agro-ecological products. These stalls provided the families involved with a small weekly income, though many of them also sold their products to the PAA. In the specific case of Camamu, the involvement of these farmers in the so-called short commercialization circuits lacked support from municipal public authorities, notwithstanding the efforts of some administrations that were more sensitive to the needs of these farmers.

It is interesting to note that access to the institutional market through the Food Acquisition Program appears in all these cases as a complementary alternative to the different market strategies developed by organizations in the Baixo Sul. Between 2005 and 2010, food acquisitions operations through the PAA conducted in the territory (considering all municipalities), involved approximately 1,952 farming families (with repetition)[51] and around 1,200 different farming families (without repetition), while 14 different organizations acted as mediators. At least two of these organizations were able to engage operating PAA projects in the territory were able to engage agrarian reform settlers as project members. In 2011, around 38 settled families from five agrarian reform settlements sold products under the PAA through partnerships established between CONAB and different associations and cooperatives.[52]

Figs. 1 and 2 illustrate: (i) the distribution per municipality of family farmers who sold agricultural products through the PAA between 2005 and 2010 in Baixo Sul and (ii) the associations and cooperatives which acted as proponent organizations for product supply projects for the institutional market through the PAA in Baixo Sul in this period.

The operations carried out as part of this program contributed significantly, according to the statements collected from the leaders of these associations, to the strengthening of these organizations, expanding the number of farmers linked to their sales networks, reinforcing their public recognition, and strengthening their administrative capacity. Our attention here is drawn to the extensive range of products sold between 2005 and 2010, consisting of 68 different items, notably fruits and greens. Insertion into the institutional market, especially in the modality of Purchase with Simultaneous Donation, provided the farmers involved with an opportunity to expand the range of products aimed at the market, diversifying their sources of income, and allowing the sale of food which was previously wasted.

Participation in the institutional market generated at the same time a series of demands, both for the organizations as well as the public authorities, highlighting the lack of existing linkages between the different rural

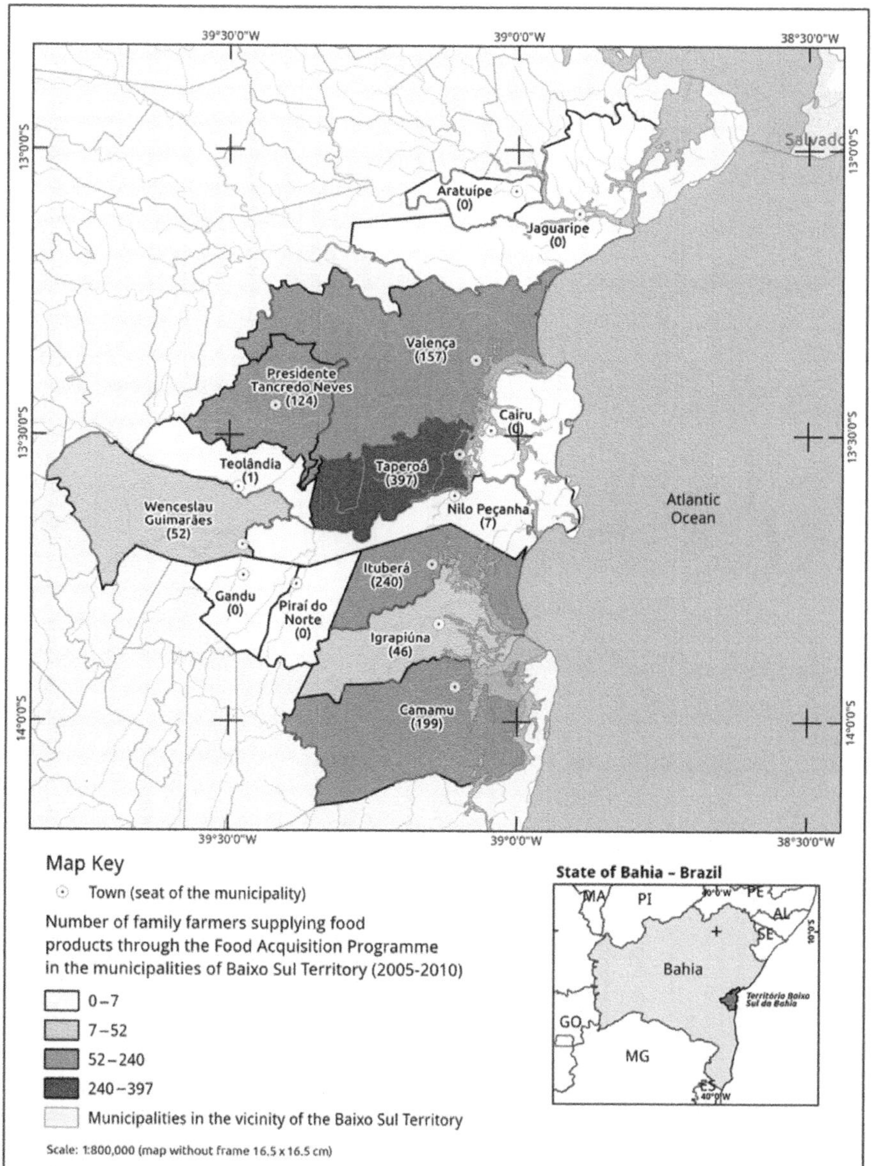

Fig. 1. Family Farmers Supplying Food Products through the Food Acquisition Program in the Baixo Sul Municipalities (2005–2010) – CONAB Operations. *Source*: IBGE/DGS. Base Cartográfica Contínua, ao milionésimo – BCIM: versão 3.0. Rio de Janeiro, 2010.

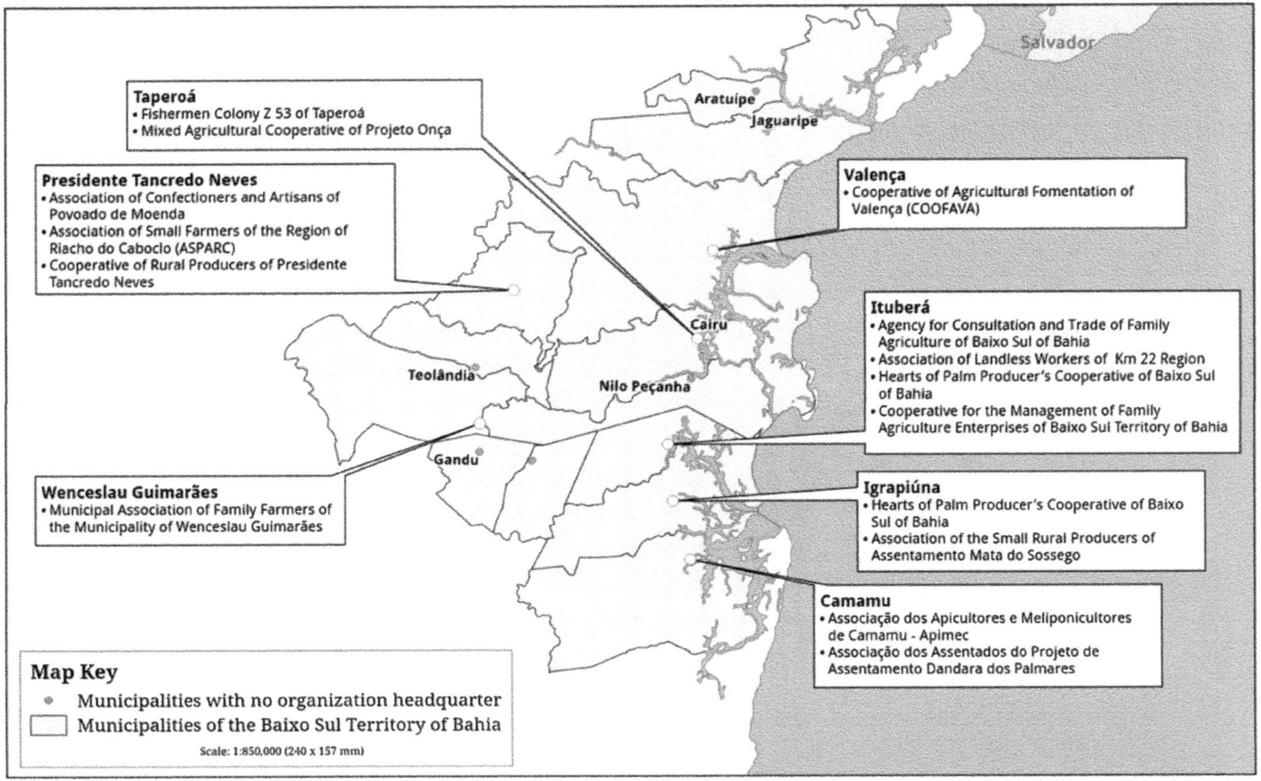

Fig. 2. Family Farming Organizations Operating Projects through the Food Acquisition Program from 2005 to 2010 in the Baixo Sul Municipalities (CONAB Operations). *Source*: IBGE/DGS. Base Cartográfica Contínua, ao milionésimo – BCIM: versão 3.0. Rio de Janeiro, 2010.

development policies, a problem which became even more dramatic in the case of the settlements. By way of example, we note the numerous problems faced by settler families in terms of infrastructure and a considerable number of families in debt with the National Program for the Strengthening of Family Farming (*Programa Nacional de Fortalecimento da Agricultura Familiar* – PRONAF), and were thus unable to get new funding. Finally, the contracting and operationalization of a sales project for the institutional market requires the use of material and human resources, including people with time and expertise available to take part in the different activities linked to commercialization, which are not included in the total project value or which can only be repaid to farmers once the products have been delivered and paid for. This hinders, or even prevents, access to the program by small associations with local bases in the settlements, which generally speaking do not have either a technical team or the resources available to cover the transaction costs associated with the contracting and administration of sales operations in the institutional market. In the Baixo Sul, the three settled worker associations which accessed PAA between 2005 and 2010 counted on the support of partner entities working at the regional level. In the settlements, the program advances through the formation of small networks and the linking of settler families with other categories of family farmers. The existence of an associative fabric capable of supporting the implementation of the program appears as a central element in the advance of this public policy in agrarian reform areas.

CONCLUSION

This chapter reflects on the limits and potentials of the Food Acquisition Program as an instrument capable of reinforcing the dynamics of the reconstruction of family farming and peasant agriculture in agrarian reform settlements in Brazil. The existence in the Brazilian rural space of almost one million productive family units created in recent decades as a response of the state to a wide set of social struggles for access to land and the recognition of territorial rights points to a slow and contradictory process of the reconstitution of family based agriculture, placing at the center of the discussion a series of questions related to the quality of life on the settlements, the styles of agriculture developed there, and their sustainability over time. The relations established by settled families with markets and with public policies are, undoubtedly, sensitive points in a delicate equation, on which the contextual definition of the conditions and possibilities of remaining on the land will be based. Rather than capturing the overall effects of the PAA as a program, or discussing its effectiveness as a support instrument for commercialization in settlements, it was sought in this text to understand the connections established by the PAA in distinct implementation contexts, considering the diversity of social reproduction strategies constructed by settler families and the different ways in which the program is accessed by family farming and agrarian reform settler organizations. The case analyzed allows us to trace a series of social dynamics which influence the implementation of the program in the context of the Baixo Sul in general, and in a more specific form within the agrarian reform settlements.

A first element to be highlighted is related to the fact that the sale of products to the institutional market through the PAA is part of a wider set of market access and income generation strategies which are used by families in order to guarantee their social reproduction and their permanence on the land they have won, in an environment strongly marked by deprivation and precariousness. In the agrarian reform settlements in the Baixo Sul, access to the institutional market did not signify the end of the asymmetrical relationship with the middlemen who controlled the commercialization of agricultural and extractive products, such as cocoa, cloves, and guarana, through long commercial circuits, but represented in the large majority of cases a step forward in the construction of a more autonomous relationship of these farmers with agricultural markets. It strengthened their intervention and negotiation capacity through collective organizational mechanisms, diversifying the range of products sold by families and increasing the potential use of resources already existing on the lots. Meeting a diversified demand for food from social programs, made feasible under PAA through the Purchase with Simultaneous Donation mechanism, also helped to reinforce the availability of foodstuffs in the settlements.

A second point is related to the role of associations and cooperatives in the implementation of the program. The existence of an associative fabric capable of making the demands of farmers visible and helping them to follow paths which allow access to different public programs, including the PAA, was found during the research to be a fundamental component in the functioning of the program. It should be highlighted here that the role of these organizations is not restricted to a single public policy, since the large majority of organizations researched have acted throughout their history as mediators of relations established between the state and rural populations.

Finally, there are the distinct forms of appropriation of purchase instruments created for the PAA by social organizations, an appropriation which allows the construction of much differentiated arrangements in relation to markets and the organization of production. Some of these arrangements sought to reinforce alternative rural development trajectories to the hegemonic model imposed by the modernization of agriculture, stimulating the diversification of productive systems, the practice of agriculture with an ecological base, the reinforcement of a community-based solidarity, and the leading role of settler families in the construction of new relations with markets. At another extreme, it is possible to identify social, organizational, and productive strategies which sought to reinforce large-scale production and its vertical integration, based on the idea of entrepreneurialism and therefore distant from a repeasantization strategy. The multiple roles assumed by the PAA in the Baixo Sul of Bahia, as well as in other parts of the country, are part of a process of social construction of this specific market, whose objectives and operational rules emerge as a result of a permanent process of negotiation and dispute between different social actors, mobilizing relations which are not restricted to the context of the settlements, involving a wider space of political articulation and decision making.

NOTES

1. In this chapter the definition of *family farming*, whenever related to public policies in Brazil, reflects the criteria defined by Law 11.326/2006. This law identifies family farmers based on the following attributes: (i) limit of land area of up to four fiscal modules (an area which varies between 5 and 110 ha, depending on the municipality); (ii) predominance of family labor in activities carried out on the farm unit or farm enterprise; (iii) a significant part of the family income is derived from economic activities carried out in the farm unit or farm enterprise; (iv) the farm unit has to be managed by the family. Retrieved from https://www.planalto.gov.br/ccivil_03/_Ato2004-2006/2006/Lei/L11326.htm (05 March 2014).

2. The concept of repeasantization, used by van der Ploeg in various works (van der Ploeg, 2007, 2008), involves the recreation in different times and places of peasant forms of agriculture and its resource base.

3. Critiques of these models can be found by authors such as Martins (1981), Garcia Jr. (1990), Shanin (1982), Long (2007), van der Ploeg (2008), Wanderley (2009), amongst others.

4. The institutional markets analyzed here cover purchase and sale operations of foodstuffs and agricultural products made by public authorities. These transactions aim to fulfill public functions such as price support, the formation of strategic grain reserves, and the supply of foodstuffs to people with food insecurity through

different social programs. In Brazil this purchasing power of the state has been also recently used as an instrument to strengthen family farming, through a set of public policies, including the *Programa de Aquisição de Alimentos* (PAA – Food Acquisition Program), which privileges the acquisition in differentiated conditions of foodstuffs produced by this specific category of farmers.

5. It is important to consider here the existence in the areas where agrarian reform policies were implemented of collective forms of organization including agricultural production and territorial administration, such as the Agricultural Production Cooperatives, stimulated by the *Movimento dos Trabalhadores Rurais Sem Terra* (MST – Movement of Landless Workers). The MST, which emerged as a political organization in the 1980s, stands as the most significant social movement fighting for land rights, social justice, and the fulfillment of the social function of land in Brazil (Brandford & Rocha, 2004; Fernandes, 1996).

6. In Brazil, the concept of family farming encompasses both peasant forms of agriculture – based in diversified and multifunctional farming systems – and a "modernized" family farm sector, marked by the intensive use of the Green Revolution technologies and highly dependent on agro-industrial capital. This "modernized" family agriculture, albeit with fluctuations over time, maintains several features of peasant agriculture (van der Ploeg, 2008; Wanderley, 2009). When we refer in this text to peasant and family farming, we seek to take into account this wide range of situations and various forms of relations with markets.

7. It is worth highlighting that the recognition of family farming as a specific category for public policy was the result of an intensive process of political mobilization led by different social organizations, particularly the different political groups representing rural labor unions, see, Picolotto (2011) and Favareto and Bittencourt (1999).

8. Included in this total are family units located in agrarian reform settlements.

9. The 2006 Agricultural Census was the first Brazilian census to incorporate the category of *family farming* in Census procedures for data collection and analysis (IBGE, 2009).

10. Taking into account various parameters such as level of commodification, access to credit, relations between agricultural and nonagricultural income, amongst others.

11. Delgado (2012) identifies the end of the 1990s and the beginning of the twenty-first century as a revitalization period of the agribusiness economy in Brazil, a movement which has resulted in (i) increasing investment in territorial infrastructure aiming to incorporate land and commercial corridors into the agribusiness economy; (ii) a strong linking of the public agricultural research system to the interests of the large multinational agro-industrial companies; (iii) weak regulation of the land market and loose compliance to land rights and the social function of land established in the Brazilian Constitution; (iv) changes in foreign exchange policies; and (v) renewed public investment in business agriculture.

12. Retrieved from http://www.agricultura.gov.br/ministerio/missao (20 February 2014). However, it is also worth noting that this Ministry also has a series of responsibilities related to family farming, including, for example, food safety, inspections of raw materials and products, agricultural research, price support policies, the development of organic agriculture, amongst others.

13. Retrieved from http://www.mda.gov.br/portalmda/institucional (20 February 2014).

14. In Brazil the remnants of *quilombo* communities are legally considered to be "the ethnic-racial groups, according to self-attributed criteria, with their own historic trajectory, and with specific territorial relations. They also carry the presumption of a black ancestry related to resistance to the historic oppression suffered." Self-definition is a central element in the recognition of these communities by the public authorities. Decree no. 4887/2003. Retrieved from http://www.planalto.gov.br/ccivil_03/decreto/2003/d4887.htm (22 February 2014).

15. The *Fome Zero* strategy was launched in 2003, the first year of the PT-led government, with the objective of expanding the access of Brazilians living under food insecurity to food, strengthening family farming, and propelling a process of mobilization and the social control of policies aiming to achieve food and nutritional security.

16. The PAA Management Group currently involves the participation of the following ministries: Ministry of Social Development and the Fight Against Hunger; Ministry of Agrarian Development; Ministry of Agriculture, Livestock and Supply represented by the *Companhia Nacional de Abastecimento* (CONAB – the National Provisioning Company); Ministry of Planning, Budget, and Management; Ministry of Finance; Ministry of Education.

17. The fieldwork which gave rise to this chapter, and which was focused on the implementation of the Food Acquisition Program (PAA) in the *Baixo Sul* of Bahia, was carried out in 2011 and 2012. The research involved the consultation of different databases, the holding of semistructured interviews and participant observation. We would like to thank here all the farmers, technical staff, and representatives of social movements and the organizations that collaborated with these research efforts, sharing information, experiences, and reflections, and most especially the team of the Advisory Service for Popular Rural Organizations (*Serviço de Assessoria às Organizações Populares Rurais* – SASOP), whose support was decisive throughout the process.

18. The fiscal module, a measurement unit, expressed in hectares, established in Brazil by the National Institute of Colonization and Agrarian Reform (*Instituto Nacional de Colonização e Reforma Agrária* – INCRA), is based on different factors, including the type of agriculture predominant in the municipality. It can vary from 5 to 110 ha. This measurement unit is used as a classification parameter and applied in different public policies.

19. Fernandes, in an article published in 2010, identified a universe of 86 movements involved in the land struggle between 2000 and 2006 (Fernandes, 2010). The 2010 report of the Land Struggle Database (DATALUTA) recorded the involvement of 116 socio-territorial movements in land conflicts between 2000 and 2012 (NERA/FCT-UNESP, 2013).

20. Retrieved from www.incra.gov.br (05 March 2014).

21. DATALUTA, the Land Struggle database, was set up in 1998–1999 by the Agrarian Reform Research and Project Group (*Núcleo de Pesquisas e Projetos de Reforma Agrária* – NERA, 2009; Law, 1994) linked to the Department of Geography of the Faculty of Science and Technology, Universidade Estadual Paulista Júlio de Mesquita Filho (Presidente Prudente Campus). Since then it has

collected data referring to the land struggle in Brazil. Data related to land reform settlements come from the National Colonization and Agrarian Reform Institute (*Instituto Nacional de Colonização e Reforma Agrária* – INCRA) and the National Association of State Governments Land Authorities (*Associação Nacional dos Órgãos Estaduais de Terra* – ANOTER). Retrieved from https://sites.google.com/site/neagagraria/dataluta (10 March 2014). See also NERA/FCT-UNESP (2013).

22. Including here the Extractivist Reserves (*Reservas Extrativistas* – RESEX), Sustainable Development Reserves, Agro-Extractive Settlement Projects, amongst others. Remnants of *quilombos* areas regularized by INCRA are not included in the statistics as land reform settlements ("assentamentos") since they follow a different process of territorial recognition.

23. Federal settlements, state settlements, and settlements created through land funding programs, amongst others.

24. The designation "peoples of the forest" emerged, especially during the 1980s, as a political identity constructed in the struggle of rubber tapers, indigenous peoples, and peasants, among other social actors, in the Brazilian Amazon.

25. For a critical reflection on processes of land redistribution carried out in the 1995–2002 period, see Pereira (2003).

26. See DATALUTA (2013).

27. See, for example, Sigaud (2005); Sigaud, Rosa, and Macedo (2008), and Schmitt (1992).

28. Particularly the National Program for the Strengthening of Family Agriculture (PRONAF), which has some specific lines of credit, both investment and funding, intended to cover the needs of settled families in the initial stages of the settlement process.

29. INCRA was created under a military regime at the beginning of the 1970s, and was originally connected to the Ministry of Agriculture. During its history, it went through different processes of restructuration, and is currently under the auspices of the Ministry of Agrarian Development. It has various responsibilities, including carrying out agrarian reform, managing the national register of rural properties, administering public land, identifying, registering, demarcating, and giving entitlements to land for land reform settlers, traditional *quilombola* communities.

30. Retrieved from http://www.incra.gov.br/index.php/reforma-agraria-2/projetos-e-programas-do-incra/titu lacao-de-assentamentos (05 March 2014).

31. Counting from the issuing of the land concession agreement, or if this is nonexistent, from the date the title was granted or its registration (Cordeiro, 2011).

32. See MST. Por que defender a concessão de uso. Retrieved from http://www.mst.org.br/jornal/302/reali dadebrasileira (05 March 2014).

33. See, for example, BRASIL, Secretaria Geral da Presidência da República. Queremos combinar a quantidade na reforma agrária com a qualidade do assentamento, afirma ministro. Retrieved from http://www.secretariageral.gov.br/noticias/ultimas_noticias/2014/02/13-02-2014-queremos-combinar-a-quantidade-na-reforma-agraria-com-a-qualidade-do-assentamento-afirma-ministro (10 April 2014).

34. This nationwide research was based on a statistically representative sample of a universe composed of 804,867 families, settled between 1985 and 2008 in the different regions of the country. Retrieved from http://www.incra.gov.br/sites/default/

files/uploads/reforma-agraria/questao-agraria/reforma-agraria/pqra_-_apresentao.pdf. (10 April 2014).

35. It is worth noting that this process of settlement recognition and the demarcation of lots, which precedes the implementation of productive support policies targeting land reform settlements, can take a number of years.

36. The idea of autonomy referred to here is associated with the construction and maintenance of a foundation of self-controlled resources, the structuring of styles of farming and patterns of market relations capable of avoiding "aggressive relations of exploitation and submission," as well as with "the practice of an agriculture which corresponds to the interests and aspirations of the producers involved in it" (van der Ploeg, 2008, pp. 48–49).

37. The definition of styles of farming is related here to the distinct ways through which farmers try to link, in a specific economic, social, and ecological context, the various social and material elements (land, labor, machines, animals, norms, knowledge, experiences, amongst others) involved in agricultural practice (van der Ploeg, 2010).

38. *Companhia Nacional de Abastecimento* (CONAB), created in 1990 based on the fusion of several governmental agencies, is a public company connected to the Ministry of Agriculture, Livestock and Supply, whose mission is to manage agricultural and supply policies, acting in areas such as stocks and warehousing, the planning and implementation of commercialization and price support policies, the supply and regulation of agricultural products in the internal market, amongst others. After 2003, CONAB also became responsible for the implementation of PAA. Retrieved from www.conab.gov.br (05 March 2014).

39. The implementation of the PAA currently involves the following modalities: (i) Family Farming Purchase with Simultaneous Donation, which allows the acquisition of products at a local and regional level for donation, which is operationalized both by CONAB and state and municipal governments; (ii) Direct Purchase from Family Farming, which focuses on the purchase of family farming products for the formation of public stocks by CONAB; (iii) Formation of Family Farming Stocks, involving the build-up of stocks by the family farming organizations, a modality operationalized via CONAB; (iv) Milk Production Incentives, an instrument centered on the acquisition of milk and fundamentally implemented in the states in the Northeast of Brazil and the north of Minas Gerais, with the strong participation of state governments; (v) Institutional purchases, which allow states, municipalities, and direct administration agencies to acquire with their own resources and without a bidding processes, food from family farming for prisons, barracks, and universities, amongst other public institutions.

40. This information only includes the operations carried out by CONAB, through the transfer of funds to family farming organizations, especially to associations and cooperatives. At a national level the available data, referring to partnerships established by the Federal government with state and municipal governments, do not allow, at least until 2010, the identification of the different beneficiary categories of program suppliers (family farmers, settled worker, agro-extractivist, small fisherman, *quilombola*, etc.) (Schmitt et al., 2013).

41. From 2008 onward, the information system used by CONAB began to register in a more systematic manner the different categories of family farmers who participated in PAA as suppliers.

42. According to INCRA data, there is an average of 104 families per settlement in Brazil. However, there is significant variation in this number across the country. Retrieved from http://painel.incra.gov.br/sistemas/index.php (20 August 2014).

43. According to the Ministry of Agriculture, Livestock and Supply, the crisis of cocoa farming in the 1990s led to the unemployment of around 250,000 rural workers (Brasil, 2009).

44. During the fieldwork we discovered that many rural communities from the region were historically constituted by squatters, who occupied vacant land or lands belonging to absentee landholders.

45. The Advisory Service for Popular Rural Organizations (SASOP) is a nongovernmental organization, created in 1989, whose actions since its foundation have been aimed at strengthening family farming and promoting agro-ecology as a technical and social alternative.

46. SASOP, in a partnership with the Federal Government, monitored the preparation of a Settlement Sustainable Development Plan (*Plano de Desenvolvimento Sustentável do Assentamento* – PDSA), a participatory planning process that resulted in the recommendation of a set of actions aimed at the sustainable management of the settlement.

47. Association of Agrarian Reform Settlers of the Dandara dos Palmares Settlement.

48. In English the acronym means Agency for Consultation and Trade for Family Agriculture of Baixo Sul of Bahia. It is a secondary organization which brings together different associations involving family farmers, agrarian reform settlers, descendants of *quilombos*, artisanal fishermen, and shellfish collectors (*marisqueiros*), represented by different associations.

49. Fundação Odebrecht is a private, nonprofit institution of public utility, created in 1965 and supported by Organização Odebrecht, a Brazilian entrepreneurial conglomerate which operates transnationally, investing in sectors such as engineering and construction, petrochemicals, oil and gas, biomass energy production, and environmental services.

50. Retrieved from http://www.fundacaoodebrecht.org.br/Imprensa/Noticias/Noticia/211/Governo-do-Estado-Amubs-e-Ides-assinam-protocolo-de-compromisso#.U52wQ_ldV1Y (15 March 2014).

51. Some of the families participated over time in more than one project.

52. This figure was obtained by cross-tabulating the CONAB database, referring to PAA operations, and the INCRA database related to settlements.

REFERENCES

Arce, A., & Long, N. (2000). *Anthropology, development and modernities: Exploring discourse, counter-tendencies and violence*. Abington: Routledge.

Brandford, S., & Rocha, J. (2004). *Rompendo a cerca: A história do MST*. São Paulo: Casa Amarela.

Brasil. (2005). Ministério do Desenvolvimento Agrário, Instituto Nacional de Colonização e Reforma Agrária. II Plano Nacional de Reforma Agrária: Paz, produção e qualidade de vida no meio rural. Brasília: MDA/INCRA. Retrieved from http://sistemas.mda.gov.br/arquivos/PNRA_2004.pdf. Accessed on March 2, 2014.

Brasil. (2009). Ministério da Agricultura, Pecuária e Abastecimento, Comissão Executiva do Plano da Lavoura Cacaueira. Nota Técnica – Programa de Recuperação da Lavoura Cacaueira – 3ª e 4ª Etapas. A crise da lavoura cacaueira, condicionantes, ação governamental, análise e recomendações. Retrieved from http://www.senado.leg.br/comissoes/CRA/AP/AP20100622_Nota%20Tecnica-2009.pdf

Brasil. (2010). *Pesquisa sobre a qualidade de vida, produção e renda dos assentamentos de reforma agrária*. Brasília: MDA/INCRA. Retrieved from http://www.incra.gov.br/index.php/reforma-agraria-2/questao-agraria/numeros-da-reforma-agraria/file/1152-pesquisa-qualidade-de-vida-nos-assentamentos-2010. Accessed on March 2, 2014.

Brasil. (2013). *Plano Agrícola e Pecuário 2013/2014*. Brasília-DF: MAPA, Secretaria de Política Agrícola.

Carmo, E. R. (2003). *Análise-diagnóstico de uma micro-região do município de Camamu: Um estudo de caso de duas comunidades*. M.Sc. thesis, Universidade Estadual de Santa Cruz, Programa de Pós-Graduação em Desenvolvimento Regional e Meio Ambiente, Brasil.

Carter, M., & Carvalho, H. M. (2010). A luta pela terra: Fonte de crescimento, inovação e desafio constante ao MST. In M. Carter (Ed.), *Combatendo a desigualdade social: O MST e a reforma agrária no Brasil* (pp. 287–330). São Paulo: Editora UNESP.

Cordeiro, M. S. S. (2011). O recebimento do título definitivo em assentamentos: Discursos acerca da propriedade da terra. Paper presented at XV Congresso Brasileiro de Sociologia, Curitiba-PR, Brasil, July, 2011.

Delgado, G. (2012). *Do capital financeiro na agricultura à economia do agronegócio: Mudanças cíclicas em meio século (1965–2012)*. Porto Alegre: Editora UFRGS.

Departamento Intersindical de Estatística e Estudos Socioeconômicos-DIEESE; Ministério do Desenvolvimento Agrário-MDA. (2011). *Estatísticas do meio rural*. São Paulo: DIEESE/NEAD/MDA.

Dutra, M. V. F. (2011). *Direitos quilombolas: Um estudo do impacto da cooperação ecumênica*. Rio de Janeiro: Koinonia – Presença Ecumênica e Serviços.

Escobar, A. (1995). *Encountering development: The making and unmaking of the third world*. Princeton, NJ: Princeton University Press.

Escobar, A. (2005). Imagining a post-development era. In M. Edelman & A. Haugerud (Eds.), *The anthropology of development and globalization: From classical political economy to contemporary neoliberalism* (pp. 341–351). Malden, MA: Blackwell Publishing Ltd.

Estival, K. G. S. (2013). *Construção social do mercado de qualidade do cacau no Brasil*. Doctoral thesis, Universidade Federal Rural do Rio de Janeiro, Brasil. Retrieved from https://www.academia.edu/4714686/Versaoposdefesa12SETEMBROfinal. Accessed on April 8, 2014.

Favareto, A., & Bittencourt, G. (1999). Agricultura e sindicalismo nos anos 90: Notas para um balanço. In J. C. Tedesco (Ed.), *Agricultura familiar: Realidades e perspectivas* (pp. 367–394). Passo Fundo: EDIUPF.

Fernandes, B. M. (1996). *MST: Formação e territorialização*. São Paulo: Hucitec.

Fernandes, B. M. (2010). Formação e territorialização do MST no Brasil. In M. Carter (Ed.), *Combatendo a desigualdade social: O MST e a reforma agrária no Brasil* (pp. 161–197). São Paulo: Editora UNESP.

Ferrante, V. L. S. B., & Barone, L. A. (2011). Parcerias com a cana-de-açúcar: tensões e contradições no desenvolvimento das experiências de assentamentos rurais em São Paulo. *Sociologias*, *13*(26), 262–305.

Ferreira, L. F. (2010). *O tempo e o voto: Uma etnografia da política no cotidiano de famílias assentadas*. Doctoral dissertation, Universidade Federal Rural do Rio de Janeiro, Programa de Pós-Graduação de Ciências Sociais em Desenvolvimento, Agricultura e Sociedade, Brasil. Retrieved from http://r1.ufrrj.br/cpda/wp-content/uploads/2011/08/tese_leticia_2010.pdf. Accessed on March 6, 2014.

Ferreira, P. C. (2013). *Entre a estrutura e a ação: As interações entre produtores e circuitos mercantis no assentamento Francisco Julião*. M.Sc. thesis, Universidade Federal Rural do Rio de Janeiro, Programa de Pós-Graduação de Ciências Sociais em Desenvolvimento, Agricultura e Sociedade, Brasil.

França, C. G., Del Grossi, M. E., & de Marques, V. P. M. A. (2009). *O Censo Agropecuário 2006 e a agricultura familiar no Brasil*. Brasília: MDA.

Fundação Odebrecht. (2013). A caminho da sustentabilidade. Relatório de desempenho do PDCIS. Edição 15. Retrieved from http://www.fundacaoodebrecht.org.br/Midias/Publicacoes/A-Caminho-da-Sustentabilidade/Edicao/15

Garcia, A. R., Jr. (1990). *Sul: O caminho do roçado. Estratégias de reprodução camponesa e transformação social*. São Paulo: Marco Zero/Brasília-DF, Editora da Universidade de Brasília/MCT-CNPq.

Grisa, C., Schmitt, C., Mattei, L., Maluf, R., & Leite, S. P. (2011). O Programa de Aquisição de Alimentos (PAA) em perspectiva: Apontamentos e questões para o debate. In J. Romano & R. Heringer (Eds.), *A política vivida: Olhar crítico sobre monitoramento de políticas públicas*. Rio de Janeiro: ActionAid-Brasil/Ford Foundation.

Hobart, M. (Ed.). (1993). *An anthropological critique of development: The growth of ignorance*. London: Routledge.

Hoffman, R., & Ney, M. G. (2010). *Estrutura fundiária e propriedade agrícola no Brasil. Grandes regiões e unidades da federação (de 1970 a 2008)*. Brasília: Ministério do Desenvolvimento Agrário.

IBGE. (2009). *Censo Agropecuário 2006. Agricultura familiar: Primeiros resultados. Brasil, Grandes Regiões e Unidades da Federação*. Rio de Janeiro: IBGE.

Inhetvin, T. (2010). *Cadeias de valor da sociobiodiversidade no Corredor Central da Mata Atlântica (Bahia e Espírito Santo) – Relatório de Estudo*. Projeto Corredores Ecológicos, GFA Consulting Group. Retrieved from http://www.corredoresecologicos.es.gov.br/publicacoes/estudo_produtos.pdf. Accessed on April 10, 2013.

Intini, J. M., & Fernandes, U. F. (2013). Bancada ruralista: A face política do agronegócio. *Revista da Associação Brasileira de Reforma Agrária – ABRA*, Special Edition July 2013, 87–96.

Kageyama, A., Bergamasco, S. P. P., & Oliveira, J. A. (2010). Caracterização dos estabelecimentos de assentados no Censo Agropecuário de 2006. *Retratos de Assentamentos*, *13*, 31–74.

Law, J. (1994). *Organizing modernity*. Oxford: Blackwell.

Le Moal, M. F. (2013). *Programa de Aquisição de Alimentos nos assentamentos rurais da reforma agrária, análise sob as lentes da multifuncionalidade da agricultura*. M.Sc. thesis, Universidade de São Paulo, Escola Superior de Agricultura Luiz de Queiroz, Brasil. Retrieved from http://www.reformaagrariaemdados.org.br/biblioteca/disserta%C3%

A7%C3%A3o-e-tese/mestrado-programa-de-aquisi%C3%A7%C3%A3o-de-alimentos-nos-assentamentos-rurais-d. Accessed on April 10, 2014.

Leite, S. P., Heredia, B., Medeiros, L., Palmeira, M., & Cintrão, R. (2004). *Impactos dos assentamentos: Um estudo sobre o meio rural brasileiro*. São Paulo: Editora UNESP.

Leonard, E., Bonnal, P., Foyer, J., & Leite, S. P. (2009). La construction normative du développement durable dans les contextes de sa "miseen politiques." Une analyse par les dépendances de sentier au Brésil et au Mexique. *Mondes en Développement*, *37*(148), 67–84.

Lima, A. dos S., Germani, G. I., & Mitidiero, M. A., Jr. (2013). Permanência camponesa e agronegócio: conflitualidade territorial na produção do espaço agrário no Vale do Jiquiriçá-BA. Paper presented at VI Simpósio Internacional de Geografia Agrária e VII Simpósio Nacional de Geografia Agrária – 1a Jornada de Geografia das Águas. João Pessoa, PB. Retrieved from http://www.geografar.ufba.br/. Acessed on March 20, 2014.

Long, N. (2007). *Sociología del desarollo: Uma perspectiva centrada em el actor*. México: Centro de Investigaciones y Estudios Superiores em Antropologia Social; El Colegio de San Luís.

Martins, J. S. (1981). *Os camponeses e a política no Brasil*. Petrópolis: Vozes.

Martins, J. S. (1996). O tempo da fronteira: Retorno à controvérsia sobre o tempo histórico da frente de expansão e da frente pioneira. Tempo Social – Revista de Sociologia da USP, *8*(1), 25–70.

Medeiros, L. S. (2004). As novas fasces do rural e a luta por terra no Brasil contemporâneo. *Nómadas*, *20*, 208–210.

Meliani, P. F. (2014). Políticas públicas e produção do espaço no Sul da Bahia: Análise da situação por município dos projetos de reforma agrária na microrregião Ilhéus-Itabuna. *Revista Movimentos Sociais e Dinâmicas Espaciais*, *3*(1), 231–255. Retrieved from http://www.revista.ufpe.br/revistamseu/index.php/revista/article/view/74/121. Accessed on March 20, 2014.

Michelotti, F. (2008). Luta pela terra e assentamentos no Sudeste do Pará. Paper presented at III Encontro da Rede de Estudos Rurais, UFCG, Campina Grande, Brasil, September, 2008.

Moura, I. F. (2006). *Assentamentos rurais: Agregação de valor e comercialização – o caso do assentamento Santa Maria (Paranacity-PR)*. M.Sc. dissertation, Universidade Estadual de Campinas, Instituto de Economia, Brasil.

Núcleo de Estudos, Pesquisas e Projetos de Reforma Agrária – NERA – FCT/UNESP. (2009). *DATALUTA – Banco de Dados da Luta pela Terra. Relatório 2008*. Presidente Prudente-SP: UNESP.

NERA/FCT-UNESP. (2013). *DATALUTA, Banco de Dados da Luta pela Terra – Relatório 2012*. Presidente Prudente-SP: FCT/UNESP. Retrieved from http://www.ippri.unesp.br/Home/pos-graduacao/desenvolvimentoterritorialnaamericalatinaecaribe/relatorio_dataluta_brasil_2012_2013.pdf.

Ojeda, I. (2012). Reforma agrária perde fôlego na agenda nacional. *Desafios do Desenvolvimento – IPEA*, *9*, 75. Retrieved from http://www.ipea.gov.br/desafios/index.php?option=com_content&view=article&id=2866:catid=28&Itemid=23. Accessed on Mach 3, 2014.

Pereira, A. (2003). Brazil's agrarian reform: Democratic innovation or oligarchic exclusion redux? *Latin American Politics and Society*, *45*(2), 41–65.

Piccin, M. B. (2007). *Lógicas socioculturais e estratégias produtivas no assentamento Menina dos Olhos dos Sem Terra*. M.Sc. dissertation, Universidade Federal Rural do Rio de Janeiro, Programa de Pós-Graduação de Ciências Sociais em Desenvolvimento, Agricultura e Sociedade, Brasil. Retrieved from http://www.dominiopublico.gov.br/pesquisa/DetalheObraForm.do?select_action=&co_obra=102073. Accessed on March 6, 2014.

Picolotto, E. L. (2011). *As mãos que alimentam a nação: Agricultura familiar, sindicalismo e política*. Ph.D. thesis, Universidade Federal Rural do Rio de Janeiro, Programa de Pós-Graduação de Ciências Sociais em Desenvolvimento, Agricultura e Sociedade, Brasil. Retrieved from http://r1.ufrrj.br/cpda/wp-content/uploads/2012/07/tese_everton_picolotto_2011.pdf. Accessed on March 6, 2014.

Reis, T. (2014). Número de famílias assentadas sobe mas é menor do que de anos FHC e Lula. Retrieved from http://m.g1.globo.com/brasil/noticia/2014/01/numero-de-familias-assentadas-sobe-mas-e-menor-que-de-anos-fhc-e-lula.html. Accessed on March 2, 2014.

Rezende, S. R., & Olalde, A. R. (2005). O Plano de Desenvolvimento como ferramenta de planejamento em áreas de reforma agrária. O caso do Projeto de Assentamento Dandara dos Palmares, Camamu-BA. Paper presented at XLIII Congresso da Sociedade Brasileira de Economia e Sociologia Rural, 2005, Riberão Preto, Brasil. Retrieved from http://www.sober.org.br/palestra/2/353.pdf. Accessed on March 17, 2014.

Rocha, L. B. (2008). *A região cacaueira da Bahia – dos coronéis à vassoura-de-bruxa. Saga, percepção, representação*. Ilhéus: Editora da UESC.

Sabourin, E. (2007). Que política pública para a agricultura familiar no segundo Governo Lula? *Sociedade e Estado*, *22*(3), 715–751.

Sauer, S. (2013). Lutas pela terra, movimentos sociais e rearticulações dos povos da terra, das águas e das florestas. *Revista da Associação Brasileira de Reforma Agrária – ABRA*, Special Edition July 2013, 69–85.

Schmitt, C. J. (1992). *O tempo do acampamento: A construção da identidade social e política do "colono sem terra."* M.Sc. thesis, Universidade Federal do Rio Grande do Sul, Programa de Pós-Graduação em Sociologia, Brasil.

Schmitt, C. J., Sérvolo de Medeiros, L., Pereira, S., Grisa, C., Cintrão, R., & Zimmermann, S. A. (2013). O Programa de Aquisição de Alimentos em assentamentos de reforma agrária: implantação, impactos e perspectivas. In Ministério do desenvolvimento social e combate à fome (Ed.), *PAA 10 Anos de Aquisição de Alimentos* (pp. 153–183). Brasilia: Grafica Brasil. Retrieved from http://www.mda.gov.br/sitemda/sites/sitemda/files/ceazinepdf/livroPAA10Anos%5Bsmallpdf.com%5D.pdf

Shanin, T. (1982). Defining peasants: Conceptualizations and de-conceptualizations: Old and new in a Marxist debate. *Sociological Review*, *30*(3), 407–432.

Sigaud, L. (2005). As condições de possibilidade das ocupações de terra. *Tempo Social – Revista de Sociologia da USP*, *17*(1), 255–280.

Sigaud, L., Rosa, M., & Macedo, M. E. (2008). Ocupações de terra, acampamentos de demandas ao Estado: Uma análise em perspectiva comparada. *Dados – Revista de Ciências Sociais*, *51*(1), 107–142.

Silva, A. M. S., da Silva, F. A., & Xavier, C. (2009). A agricultura familiar no Baixo Sul Baiano. Paper presented at 3^0 Encontro Interdisciplinar de Tecnologias, Cultura e Educação, Salvador-BA, Brasil. Retrieved from https://www.google.com.br/#q=3+interculte,+centro+universit%C3%A1rio+jorge+amado,+2008&start=20. Accessed on April 8 2014.

Soares, F. V., Nehring, R., Battaglin-Schwengber, R., Guimarães Rodrigues, C., Lambais, G., Silva Balaban, D., ... Galante, A. (2013). *Structured demand and small holder farmers in Brazil: The case of PAA and PNAE.* Brasilia: WFP Centre of Excellence against Hunger and International Policy Centre for Inclusive Growth, United Nations Development Programme. Retrieved from http://www.ipc-undp.org/pub/IPCTechnicalPaper7.pdf

Sparovek, G. (2003). *A qualidade dos assentamentos da reforma agrária brasileira.* São Paulo: Página & Letras Editora e Gráfica.

van der Ploeg, J. D. (1990). *Labor, markets and agricultural production.* San Francisco, CA: Westview Press.

van der Ploeg, J. D. (2007). The third agrarian crisis and the re-emergence of processes of repeasantization. *Rivista di Economia Agraria, 62*(3), 325–332.

van der Ploeg, J. D. (2008). *Camponeses e impérios alimentares: Lutas por autonomia e sustentabilidade na era da globalização.* Porto Alegre: Editora da UFRGS.

van der Ploeg, J. D. (2010). Farming styles research: The state of the art. Key note lecture presented at the International Workshop Historicizing Farming Styles, Melk, Austria. Retrieved from http://www.univie.ac.at/ruralhistory/Melk_Ploeg.pdf. Accessed on October 2010.

Velho, O. G. (1979). *Capitalismo autoritário e campesinato: Um estudo comparativo a partir da fronteira em movimento.* São Paulo/Rio de Janeiro: DIFEL.

Wagner, A. (2010a). Terras de preto, terras de santo, terras de índio: Uso comum e conflito. In N. G. Delgado (Ed.), *Brasil Rural em Debate: Coletânea de artigos* (pp. 104–136). Brasília: CONDRAF/MDA.

Wagner, A. (2010b). Terras tradicionalmente ocupadas: Processos de territorialização, movimentos sociais e uso comum. In N. G. Delgado (Ed.), *Brasil Rural em Debate: Coletânea de artigos* (pp. 137–213). Brasília: CONDRAF/MDA.

Wanderley, M. N. B. (2009). Raízes históricas do campesinato brasileiro. In M. de N. B. Wanderley (Ed.), *O Mundo Rural como um Espaço de Vida: Reflexões sobre a propriedade da terra, agricultura familiar e ruralidade* (pp. 155–183). Porto Alegre: Editora da UFRGS.

Wolford, W. (2003). Producing community: The MST and land reform settlements in Brazil. *Journal of Agrarian Change, 3*(4), 500–520.

CHAPTER 12

REVISITING EVOLVING WEBS OF AGRI-FOOD AND RURAL DEVELOPMENT IN THE UK: THE CASE OF DEVON AND SHETLAND

Jessica Paddock and Terry Marsden

ABSTRACT

Critically reflecting upon the role of and integrative function that relocalisation of agri-food plays in the development of what we call rural and regional 'webs' of interconnection, this chapter revisits two regional case studies in Devon and Shetland, UK. Exploring the challenges and continuities in the unfolding of the rural web, we pay particular attention to the role that agri-food initiatives play in mobilising distinctive rural and regional development processes. Although we point in both cases to the marginalisation of agri-food and its potential centrality in rural development, it is clear that this fails to disappear completely. The trends in these two rural regions, at either ends of the UK archipelago, suggest that the combinational effects of declines in multi-functional agri-food support, on the one hand, and a neo-liberalised retraction of non-agricultural rural development support on the other, are providing a potential and chaotic new governance squeeze *which is likely to severely*

Constructing a New Framework for Rural Development
Research in Rural Sociology and Development, Volume 22, 301–324

ISSN: 1057-1922/doi:10.1108/S1057-192220150000022011

reduce the massive but latent adaptive capacity embedded in the rural eco-economy. Indeed, a more multi-functional governance and policy-based approach, based upon creating conditions for the eco-economic rural web to flourish needs to find ways of harmonising different aspects of the post-carbon landscape such that its various segments (energy, tourism, agriculture, creative industries, etc.), can work in synergy with one another. To conclude, we argue that such fragmented and competing conditions as those revealed in both case study areas are unlikely to be sufficiently capable of meeting the new national and global demands for food security which have risen up the political agenda since our earlier phases of field work.

Keywords: Rural web; rural development; environment; family farm; Devon; Shetland

INTRODUCTION: CHANGING PLACES

While noting the emergence of alternative and re-embedded sets of production chains and networks, Marsden (2010) records that these are interlinked in providing stimulus for rural development. In this way, it is suggested that the re-localisation of agri-food plays an important integrative function in the development of what we call rural and regional 'webs' of interconnection (van der ploeg & Marsden, 2008), through an examination of two regional case studies – Devon and Shetland, UK. In this chapter, we revisit these case studies in a third phase of longitudinal study, exploring the challenges and continuities in the unfolding of the rural web, paying particular attention to the role that agri-food initiatives play in mobilising distinctive rural and regional development processes. Crucially, the intervening period since the first phase reported by Marsden (*ibid.*), based on data collected in 2007/2008, has witnessed wide-scale political, social and economic change under the 2010 administration of the Conservative/Liberal Democrat Coalition Government. Drawing on interviews with the same respondents interviewed in 2008 and 2010 (reported in Marsden, 2010) we find that agri-food plays an increasingly peripheral role in rural and regional development across these regions. That is, with state retreat from strategic engagement with rural development, and a concomitant squeeze on rural ways of life and livelihood making, diversifications that were previously considered new novelties move to the fore. Indeed, we might imagine that these novel diversifications were welcomed by the European Commission in its 6th Framework Programme, given their reformed focus away from a living countryside underpinned by agricultural activity, towards a more integrated rural development strategy focused on 'increased diversification, innovation and value added of products and services, both within and beyond the agricultural sector' (European Commission, 2005, p. 32). However, we argue that trends in this direction raise serious questions for governing transitions towards a more sustainable and food secure future for the UK, particularly in the context of global environmental challenges associated with climate change and biodiversity loss.

The chapter begins by outlining the concept of the 'rural web' (van der ploeg & Marsden, 2008) pointing to its continuing utility as a heuristic tool for the longitudinal study of continuity and change in rural and regional development processes. We then introduce each case study, beginning with an overview of advances and challenges across the Devon Farms Co-operative as an example of an initiative pursuing an eco-economic development pathway, before exploring the unfolding rural web in Shetland. Here, the advances of the oil industry and the burgeoning development of wind energy suggest a more bio-economic trajectory. In each case, we note the peripherality of agri-food as a novel and creative industry aligned to the support of tourism. The living countryside is, in both cases, certainly no longer based on agriculture alone nor indeed is it bestowed policy priority despite the recent alarms made about food security (see Poppy, Jepson, Pickett, and Birkett, 2014 and House of Commons Environment, 2014).

Methods

Semi-structured interviews were conducted with a total of eight members of Devon farms as well as two key development actors working for the Devon Local Authority. In Shetland, a further seven interviews were conducted with farmers, food processors, development actors to include the Local Authority as well as both protagonists and opposition to the proposed Viking Energy (VE) Wind Farm. Guiding this process are key research questions; how is the rural web configured? Have there been any changes since 2010? How is the rural development agenda framed at an institutional level and how is it understood by actors 'on the ground'?

In this way, our methodological approach is both qualitative and longitudinal, pursuing an in-depth understanding of development processes rather than statistical inferences and measurements. Our goal is not to achieve a statistically accurate description or explanation of development processes in each case, but to arrive at a greater understanding of their complexities. An important part of this pursuit is an ongoing refinement of theoretical devices such as that of the rural web. Quantitative methods such as a questionnaire survey were thus deemed unsuitable for these purposes, while not precluding the potential benefit of more statistically oriented approaches in future research. Indeed, through 're-interview' (Thomson & Holland, 2003) we are able to consider the development of narratives around rural development, food and farming over time as related to their particular locality. During interviews, an aide memoir guided discussion, leaving considerable freedom for the interviewees/interviewers to digress and to capture new insights, issues and themes. All of the interviews were tape-recorded with the interviewees' permission and later transcribed. Questions typically put to interviewees pertained to discussion of changes since 2010, any opportunities, new novelties or challenges that have arisen. All interviewees were invited to speak of their future development vision for their business as well as their county and region, as a means of garnering their insights, hopes and fears for their future.

The Rural Web

The rural web concept acts as a heuristic tool to highlight the differing responses to the squeeze on rural economies in order to maintain quality of life in rural areas at different times and places. This tool suggests that at the heart of each region's response are the intertwined institutions of society and economy of public and private life that draw differently on local resources in interaction with the wider economy, novelty modes and means of production, markets and market governance, the creation of new institutional frameworks, the co-production of sustainable ways of life and finally, the benefits of social capital. Rural development is thus grounded in and driven by a varied 'set of internally and externally generated interrelationships that shape the relative attractiveness of rural spaces economically, socially, culturally, and environmentally' (van der Ploeg & Marsden, 2008, p. vii). These sets of relationships and transactions create synergies as they come to mutually reinforce one other. That is, rural development processes are not considered the result of direct policy interventions, but are informed and shaped by the unfolding of these creative patterns that we call the rural web, as illustrated in Fig. 1.

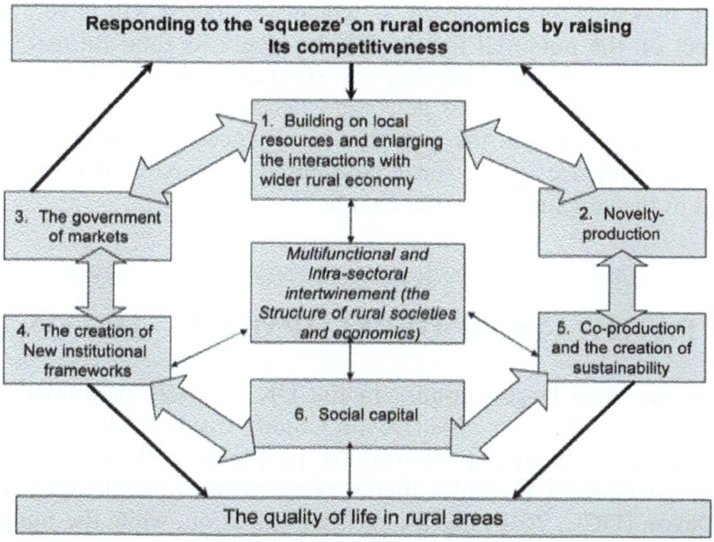

Fig. 1. A Conceptual Model of the Rural Web (Marsden, 2010).

To explore these very rural development processes, we revisit participants, actors and their networks of the 2007–2008 and 2010 study, eliciting accounts of continuity and change, of the private troubles of their 'contested countryside' (Cloke & Little, 1997) as they connect with their milieu and come to form larger structure of social, political and economic life that forms their development pathway. Indeed, reversing Mills' (1959) consideration of the city as an example of a private trouble and public issue requiring unpicking by the sociological imagination, we consider the structural fact of the rural by examining the political and economic issues that affect innumerable personal and individual milieu – what Mills (*ibid.*) calls the social setting that is directly open to her or his personal experience. In Devon, we find the rural web unfolding in ways that are more aptly characterised by eco-economy, which we define as an alternative and diverse spatial arena for the development of new endogenous production and consumption chains and networks. On the other hand, in Shetland there are clear tensions arising over the development future, with a current trajectory set to a pathway characterised by the bio-economy mode, characterised by exogenous development through corporate controlled production of biological products (fuels, mass, technology, enzymes, genomics) for global markets. In both cases, agri-food initiatives play an increasingly peripheral role, – a new agri-food 'squeeze' – which we suggest will have a calamitous effect on the potential for the UK to secure its food futures, and for the broader co-evolution of rurality and rural development. The conceptual and policy implications of this new agnosticism to the agricultural and the rural are occurring just at the time that society needs to consider the future sustainable resilience of its rural land-based resources. This paradox is explored in the conclusions to the chapter.

PATHWAYS OF DEVELOPMENT – DEVON

Devon is the third largest county in the UK, sparsely populated by just under 754,000 residents in 2008 (Devon County Council, DCC, 2010, p. 9). Moreover, there is a lower proportion of people of working age compared with the rest of the UK, and a higher proportion of people aged over 50. Thus, Devon (DCC, 2010) has an ageing population, while the numbers of young people are in decline. The population is concentrated in the South of the county, with urban areas such as Exeter providing home to over 33% of Devon's population, while urban areas in the North of the county account for 11% of the county's population. However, more than half of the population live in rural areas, villages and small towns. Administratively, the landscape of the county is complex, being split into eight districts, 357 parish and town councils with nine parliamentary constituencies. Two national park authorities – Exmoor and Dartmoor – act as planning authorities for protected landscapes. Noting the uniqueness of their economy, DCC report that the most significant contribution to the increase in Devon's output between 1998 and 2008 were in industrial sectors – construction (7.8%), distribution (13.7%), and business services (30.4%). These three dominant sectors together contributed some 52% of the increase in total output for the county. The agricultural sector, including crop and animal production, hunting, forestry, fishing and aquaculture, has the lowest labour productivity in Devon. It is also less productive when compared to the country, with output at 83% of the national average. This may be partly accounted for by the topography that lends itself best to livestock, dairying and lowland cattle and sheep and upland hill farming, which tend to be more labour intensive. While the outbreak of Foot and Mouth Disease in 2001 marked a low-point, the share of output contributed by the agriculture and forestry sector grew in this period up to 2008, which DCC note as the result of diversification.

> Not only has the growth of the agricultural sector outstripped the overall growth for the Devon economy – increasing its relative share – it has also outstripped the national growth rates. The national economy grew by just 5.4%, the Devon economy grew by 6.2% but the agricultural sector in Devon expanded by 12.5%. In Devon the agricultural sector expanded almost six times faster than the sector nationally (growing by just 2.4%). In the ten years to 2008 agriculture was the fastest growing sector in the Devon economy. As a result the relative contribution made by the agricultural sector almost doubled – from 2% to 3.6%. Whilst agriculture makes an important contribution to the Devon economy in terms of critical natural capital, the sector is the least productive in terms of output per worker. (DCC, 2010, p. 58)

Moreover, food and drink contributes just 10% of the total manufacturing output (around 1% of total output), a share that DCC report as falling over the 10 years to 2008, while DCC report that agriculture in Devon 'contributes *four times more* to output than it does in the national economy' (*ibid.*, p. 56). With such a decline in agricultural output, alongside an increasing focus on diversifying agricultural output towards value-added products and services, what is the development destiny for rural ways of life? To explore this question, in February/March 2014 we revisited the same members of the Devon Farms Co-operative interviewed across the intervening periods of 2008 and 2010, asking them to discuss the changes and continuities in the challenges they face operating a farm business, as well as the diversified aspect of their business; farm tourism. This retreat from mainstream agricultural productivism, characterised by the shift towards intensification, extensification and diversification, marks an outlook on farming that is less well understood as what Drummond, Campbell, Lawrence, and Symes (2000) term a 'crisis' but as a longer process wherein the extent to which farm households are able to depend upon their farm for their livelihood is increasingly challenged.

Devon Farms

In March 2014, the Devon Farms Co-operative of 110 farms providing bed and breakfast as well as self-catering accommodation to visitors celebrated their 25 year anniversary. Over this period they have supported each other to develop the diversified aspect of the farm business, not least, advertising and promoting themselves as one co-operative. While they comprise separate businesses, the farm and the accommodation components complement each other in providing a unique landscape and experience for visitors, while the generated income relieves pressure on farm productivity and the widely noted 'cost-price squeeze' explored by Horlings and Marsden

(2011), Darnhofer (2005) and van der Ploeg (2000). Indeed, the story of Devon Farms speaks to the persistence of a business form that has largely disappeared elsewhere (Whatmore, Munton, Little, & Marsden, 1987), that is, the combining of family ownership of assets with managerial control as an institutional unit. Indeed, while Lobley and Potter (2004) find in their survey of agricultural households in England, that the economic centrality of agriculture for the family farm business had declined, we also suggest that Devon Farms offers an example of the collective reconfiguration of the farm business towards an eco-economical form of endogenous adjustment and development to the cost squeeze in agriculture, echoing what has been termed the new rural development paradigm in Europe (Horlings & Marsden, 2014).

Indeed, Evans and Ilbery (1989) devise a conceptual framework for the investigation of farm-based accommodation and tourism in Britain, using a political economy perspective as advocated by Marsden (1984) that interrogates the interactions between market and family relations that coalesce around the family farm. Here, external institutions shape farm investment through the supply of capital for the development of farm tourism accommodation; from high street banks and heritage organisations to direct government influence in the form of grant aid for the establishment of alternative enterprise. Furthermore, the internal farm environment demands diversified activity to boost family income and farm profitability. As the external capitalist environments pressures the internal farm environment to restructure, Evans and Ilbery (*ibid.*) argue that a diversification to farm accommodation may not necessarily reduce reliance upon external capitals, but in some ways deepens this relation of dependence through loss of control over business assets and management rights. Here, they also note the emergence of farm-based accommodation and tourism as an important phenomenon for agricultural restructuring, one that received little serious attention, scholarly or otherwise. While this has somewhat been redressed by further studies in advertising (Evans & Ilbery, 1992a), marketing (Clarke, 1999) and in communication (Clarke, 1996), further work by Evans and Ilbery (1992b) has returned to the conceptual framework outlined above, arguing that outside organisations are increasingly involved with farm-based accommodation, thus facilitating the penetration of agriculture by private and public capitals.

These trends mark commentary on the resilience of the family run farm business, one that we seek to develop by means of revisiting the conceptual framework of the 'rural web'. This section now draws upon the experience of *X* number of respondents as related to the thematic categories derived from the analysis of each interview. We focus here on a common thread that permeates each narrative: (i) the growing economic centrality of the tourism aspect of the farm business, (ii) the travails of meeting the demands of a shift towards the novelty driven customer-facing service sector and (iii) the perceived and real retreat of the state from the support of family farming agriculture as a mode of commodity production. These shifts, when taken together, we argue, represent a devalorisation of food and food production as a centrifugal force in rural economies that will serve to undermine the balance of a sustainable rural web of interconnections now and in the future.

Novelty as Economic Centrality in Diversified Family Farming

Speaking of the bookings that returning customers make annually, Respondent 1 (pseudonym) reflects upon the intertwining and co-production of the farm and service aspects of the farm business. Crucial to note here is that the agricultural aspect is not only called into question in the first instance in terms of its profit-making potential, but is considered only in terms of its capacity to generate income and profit for the tourism aspect. Agriculture is *itself* the value added.

> For instance, Easter is fully booked and has been, well, apart from the fact that the schools have messed up and they're going back Easter week this year, but the two weeks before Easter, the school holidays if you like, have been booked for a year, because people book before they leave, because they want their children to experience lambing. So therefore from a research point of view, or a cost analysis thing, how do you work out how important the sheep are? Is that profitability for the sheep, or is that profitability for the cottages? And inevitably, it's very interlinked.
>
> (Respondent 1: Livestock)

Indeed, Respondent 1 and her husband began as dairy farmers, working with 100 acres of land. Recognising the somewhat limited capacity for productivity with this size of farm – 'It's going to make you money but you're not going to live on it' – He developed the cottages for farm-stays. The cottage business then became 'absolutely key in providing our family with an income', which was not necessarily noted at the time as being quite so central to the business. Rather, farming 'was the most important thing', and the cottages were considered a bonus, as a little 'pin-money for the wife'. Noting a considerable shift in emphasis since what she describes as the 'most amazing agricultural downturn', he explains that:

> Those bits of cottages on the side were probably the only things making any money on a lot of farms, and certainly hugely important in the farm income, and that has changed the way that women have run them, because I think women if you like, I think I'm being very rude and very categorising, but I think women went from something they did and, you know, the husbands were pleased that they did it and it was quite nice and everything – to actually realising how important it was, and also when really it didn't particularly matter if they sold 20 weeks or 22 or 18 or 30, then suddenly it really did matter, so those women became much more professional in what they wanted to achieve, because they needed this business to make money, because it was a key part of the farm, and as such was being respected as such by the farmers.
>
> (Respondent 1: Livestock)

The professionalisation of service provision on Devon farms thus also points towards an often underappreciated and less well understood aspect of the farm business as ecological entrepreneurship – the contributions made by women (Gasson, 1992). While many women are not perceived to consider themselves entrepreneurs, and, as noted by Little (2002), are therefore less likely to apply for Local Authority grants to support the development of their business endeavours. Indeed, with the shift from government to governance, the sorts of project funded at local partnership levels tend to focus on masculine interpretations of development centred upon the 'bricks and mortar' projects with literal concrete outputs, rather than those focused around community development. This is not to even mention the competitive and corporate style application, a process found to be unfamiliar and typically uncomfortable for women. It seems worthy to point towards the benefits of the eco-economical trajectory of endogenous development that has brought recognition, professionalisation empowerment for women who begin to see centrality of their contribution to the business as more than a fringe activity. For another participant;

> I mean, there's a long way to go for all of us [women], in various – you know, we all have our different strengths, but I would say over the fourteen years, I've seen a lot of people realise that they are actually running a successful business, and that it is a business, it's not pin money, it's not something you do on the side, it's integral to the business of the farm.
>
> (Respondent 1: Livestock)

Moreover, interviewing husband and wife farmers, Respondents 2 and 3, they go further in emphasising the economic centrality of the tourism aspect of the farm business. Crucially, it is the farm that provides the building block for the success of the tourism business;

> R2: And I think lots of the men farmers have realised that their wife's got a lot of input into their farm industry combining them both. The farm might have been struggling

and then suddenly they've got these barns that they've converted and two things; the value of the farm's gone up because they've got not just a shitty old barn, they've got another house sort of thing and it's supplemented the income without using up any land in a way. So we've never really relied on the land as income. It's been more what I call an attraction, that's why we've got the sheep and so the guests can see it. We did have outdoor pigs and that's why we put in the woodland, 40 acres of woodland, and that was all to –

R3: Make it more attractive for our visitors.

(Respondents 2 and 3)

Developing further this narrative of economic centrality of the diversified aspects of the farm business is the growing sense that the family business and its resilience as a whole suffers, still, from the widely recognised problem of succession (Gasson & Errington, 1993).

How are you going to get the next generation in? Which you know, if you're doing agricultural things, you'll know. The trouble with these businesses, they're so capital-intense. My husband and I are both in our middle fifties. This business is very profitable, it's a nice business, it's a lovely place to live and all the rest of it. There's not room for one of our children here. We have three children. We employ, effectively, we did a study the other day on it, we worked it all out – we effectively employ one full-time person, by the time we've contracted out the cleaning and painting, you know, you have a contractor to come and bale the hay or a contractor to cut the hedges or whatever it might be. If you add up all the hours of people that help us run the business, it's almost one full-time person. Well, it probably is one full-time person. Probably 50, 60% of that on minimum wage. Well, our children don't want to work for minimum wage! (Laughter). Well, you know, they don't. I mean, they're all university-educated. Ruby, get down! It's a shame, isn't it? So, I mean, although this business has made us a good living and has brought up three children and helped them through uni and all the rest of it and we're making a nice living, it requires us both to work full-time and there's no way that any of our children could carry it on, which is a challenge, isn't it, if you like, in the rural community?

(Respondent 4: Livestock)

Indeed, these challenges are exacerbated by those of meeting the demands now of a service industry defined and led by consumer demands for services to be delivered at digital pace. Speaking not only of the shift to online booking, the use of card payment terminals and the provision of wireless internet, there is the growing sense of demand for high-spec fittings, furnishings and decoration;

From our business perspective it's how I keep abreast of everything, and how you have the energy to keep abreast as well, because I think that not only have you got the changing electronic market, I think people's expectations have massively changed over the last fourteen years. When I was a child, we used to go on holiday to a holiday cottage, and you were delighted that you were away, and whoever owned the cottage, it was all

> great-granny's old furniture and it was all mix and match and it was just chaos, but that was fine. And then it became that that was completely unacceptable, and now it's really ... better than home, almost. It's meeting that balance of not going down the iPad route, but providing them with access ... Because if you just say, 'Well, this has been good enough for all our guests up until now,' you'll drift backwards, and I don't want to drift backwards, but sometimes I don't like to be dragged forward! (Laughter).
>
> (Respondent 1: Livestock)

Meeting more specific and novel customer demand is similarly a struggle for Respondents 5 and 6, whose farm cottages undergo continuous refurbishment and investment. Painting, updating bathroom suites and increasing access to digital services through the provision of wireless internet and flat-screen televisions are but only the beginning in the potential for the growth of the farm tourism business. Indeed, they find a market for the provision of childcare on the farm, corporate retreats and team-building trips as well as cooking holidays for groups of friends and families celebrating holidays and special events such as birthdays and anniversaries. Indeed, catering to these events requires further investment in specialist cooking equipment requested from customers, time to be spent in party planning and decorating, all of which they provide without increasing prices, in fear of the loss of custom. This, we argue, represents a second squeeze, that is, upon the diversified resource of the family farm;

> R5: We're finding that people are asking more and more and more and we don't quite know how we need to package it or ... Because, you know, it's spending more time doing it but 'Oh yeah, course we'll dress it,' but then that's taking you ...
>
> R6: Well that's right, we had find somebody who makes gluten free cakes, that was the last one, birthday cake, we had to find those sorts of things.
>
> R5: We were thinking about what to do because this is ridiculous that we spend all these hours ...
>
> R6: But it's hard because somebody just asks you, 'Could you hang up some balloons?' Well, yeah, I could really. But course then it's, 'Can you do the balloons and can you find me someone who (inaudible 00:39:20) and can you ...?' and then it adds up. But is that the best way, though, because of the experience, is that the best way to optimise a second booking? You know. The experience will far exceed by me hanging up some balloons than it would to be petty and charging £5 for hanging up some balloons.
>
> (Respondents 5 and 6: Livestock)

Trepidation over raising prices to cover the cost of inputs to the farm tourism business is not unique to Respondents 5 and 6. Indeed, this sentiment resounds across interviews with each of the participants revisited in this round of study, with concern expressed over the potential loss of custom if one was to charge for an evening meal, charging a premium for local and farm produce sold directly to farm stayers, to reflect the costs of refurbishing converted farm buildings to such high specifications, or simply raising prices to cover the costs of services now charged to individual businesses such as recycling and rubbish collection.

> I think more people are more aware of being customer driven, rather than, 'I've got a nice house and if you don't like it, well that's up to you.' Now it's actually, more people are saying, 'Okay, if you don't like my house like this or you want me to put in whatever, or you want me to provide meals or get the shopping in for you, of course we will,' sort of attitude, I think.
>
> (Respondent 1: Livestock)

This customer-driven focus, we argue, represents an added form of self-exploitation that has been widely noted as unique to the family farm business. Here, individuals may be more exposed to exploitation within the privacy of their own family business than anywhere else in the economy (Errington & Gasson, 1994). Indeed, while the flexibility of primarily family owned and operated farm businesses afford the weathering of hard times better than other business models typical of the wider economy, farm tourism adds a further string to this bow of resilience. However, the further restructuring of the agricultural business towards the provision of not only accommodations, but also the tourism services associated with entertaining, add a further labour burden, without immediate remuneration, thus complicating the strong vision of leadership presented by Horlings and PADT (2013) in their comparative analysis of farm diversification initiatives across Europe. That is, while the additional labour associated with entertaining is treated as a trade-off for the long-term profitability of the business, or a benefit to be repaid through inheritance of the farm business in the longer-term future, without the concomitant rise on prices charged to the customer, this restructured farm business is figured, we argue, in a further exploitative relation that adds to the devalorisation of agriculture, rural ways of life and the services and benefits that can be derived from it.

Crucially, this cost-price squeeze on the service aspect of the farm business, as has been the case with the agricultural dimension, is coupled by a decisive retreat of state investment and support for development. While the Local Enterprise Partnership (LEP) is presented by DCC as a means for such rural business development, it is widely perceived by farmers and more specifically the Devon Farms network, as biased in favour of capital intense businesses with direct employment returns, amounting to an urban bias. From an interview with DCC, it is clear that future pathways for development for the county as a whole are focused upon attracting new businesses in the 'knowledge economy and digital services sector' as outlined by the Heart of the South West Local Enterprise Partnership's Strategic Economic Plan 2014–2030 (DCC, 2014). Better transportation links are considered key to bringing employment to rural areas, as rural dwellers may commute more easily to take up employment in the towns and cities across Devon. This a far removed from an endogenous rural development policy or strategy; and it is left to farm families and other rural entrepreneurs to create endogenous developments. Moreover, speaking of his experience of the dwindling institutional support for family and more diversified farming, Respondent 7 explains that:

> Because you certainly don't get any sort of help from institutions in terms of Devon County Council now. That's all gone. I've had a go with the LEP as well and they're not particularly ... I mean they're interested and they pretend to be terribly ... oh yes, but you don't get anywhere. Because we're not a high sort of capital type job which could create employment.
>
> (Respondent 7: Livestock)

Furthermore, speaking of the deterioration of the local village amenities, Respondent 5 speaks also to the feeling of isolation as a rural business;

> Yes, I mean, there is so much really deprivation in the rural areas in our villages reflected in that. Like we only have now, you know, one bus a week, we don't have a shop anymore, you know, it is becoming ... and the roads – It's only going to get worse. It's all getting worse because the investment is not happening in the rural areas at all. So you're becoming even more isolated within rural economies actually.
>
> (Respondent 5: Livestock)

Given the sense of abandonment felt here, what are we to make of the unfolding of the rural web in the case of Devon Farms? While as a co-operative, Devon Farms demonstrate use of their collective social capital, capacity for diversification through introduction of new novelties while drawing upon endogenous resources afforded by the Devon landscape to boost their resilience in the aftermath of agricultural downturn. However, the wider financial crisis, shifts from government to governance (Rhodes, 1997), and the provision of knowledge services as key strategic development focus, alongside growing disaffection with food and agriculture in the context of apparent plentiful global supply, what role for food in rural development in the UK? While Marsden (2010) has suggested that the re-localisation of agri-food plays an important integrative function in the development of what we call rural and regional 'webs' of interconnection (van der ploeg & Marsden, 2008), there is little confidence among Devon Farm members that food represents more than a side-line role in supporting a business focused on the provision of tourism related services.

> There are lots of issues within the agriculture industry, like food security I think is something that the Government never addresses, never thinks it should invest in sort of a structured agriculture sort of kind of policy at all really; it's just from hand to mouth.
>
> (Respondent 5: Livestock)

Should this particular configuration of the rural web of interconnections continue to unfold in such a way as to cement the 'hand-to-mouth' approach to rural development, we suggest there is further cause for concern for the family farm business as food is increasingly fragmented into obliteration. While Gasson and Errington (1993) argue that the family farm business will indeed survive, they note that it will not necessarily do so 'in the form that we know today' (*ibid.*, p. 305). Twenty years on, with increased diversification, innovation and value added of products and services within the agricultural sector, we are led to critically explore the implications for UK food security, as food production is increasingly relegated as a marginal and non-productive sector. To do so, we first consider the accounts of participants who represent and account for experience of the divergent development trajectory of Shetland.

PATHWAYS OF DEVELOPMENT – SHETLAND

The Shetland Islands are the most northerly Local Authority area of the UK, with a development history characterised by the rapid expansion of the petroleum industry since the 1970s. Given the unprecedented level of economic prosperity brought by the oil industry, Shetland remains relatively wealthy today, owing also to the continued success of a long-standing fisheries sector and a well-resourced system of public administration, which remains the largest employer on the islands (Shetland Islands Council, SIC, 2012). Indeed, according to data compiled by the Office for National Statistics (2014), Shetland has considerably lower unemployment rates (1.3%) compared with the rest of Scotland (4.3%) and the rest of Great Britain (3.8%). Individuals who are economically active in Shetland also surpass the average figures for the rest of Scotland and the UK, with 81.3% economically active compared to 70.7% in Scotland and 70.1% in Great Britain. These figures are also higher than other island communities.

Orkney, for example, has 79.3% economically active, and an unemployment figure of 1.5%. The number employed full-time in shellfish aquaculture across Shetland is growing each year, while there has been a steady increase in the number of fish processing firms and factories from 11 and 15 in 1977 to 18 and 19 in 2011, respectively.

Speaking of the development and investment plans for Shetland, a representative of the SIC economic development branch states that support is now geared towards the development of business projects that 'bring value to the economy' (Interview, SIC, 2014) rather than circulating 'what is already there' (*ibid.*). This support for exogenous development is further demonstrated by its support for a wind farm proposed by a partnership between VE Shetland LLP and Scottish and Southern Energy (SSE) Viking Ltd, which is a subsidiary of SSE plc. The proposed wind farm consists of 103 turbines, to be located on the central mainland, which would be the third largest wind farm in Scotland and the most productive onshore wind farm in the world. Running alongside this proposed development are tensions between other development trajectories that have traditionally represented the mainstay of the Shetland economy; fisheries and agriculture. While the wind farm poses little known or direct threat to the fisheries sector, it tears a fault line through the heart of the agricultural community, and for many Shetlanders alike. A voluntary organisation – 'Sustainable Shetland' – was set up to directly oppose the development of the wind farm. With a membership of approximately 870–900, they hold more support than the number of votes that Labour, the SNP and the Tories combined in Shetland.

Indeed, while Kanemasu, Sonnino, Marsden, and Schneider (2008) suggested that it was unclear in 2008 what role the VE wind farm project would play in the unfolding of the rural web – would the farm represent a bio-economical replacement of oil, or a mode of endogenous development on the basis of multi-functional use of land and resources? Indeed the 50:50 partnership structures between VE Ltd and SSE Viking Ltd implicates considerable community ownership, for VE Ltd is 90% owned by the Shetland Charitable Trust. However, differing interpretations over the use of these Charitable Trust funds lie at the heart of the controversy, and, we suggest are representative of competing ideas as to the pursuit *bio*-economy or *eco*-economy development trajectory for a sustainable Shetland. That is, the future is undecided, with clear support from the SIC to continue on the bio-economy mode; but with considerable trepidation on behalf of communities, particularly those represented by 'Sustainable Shetland', over the use of the reserve community funds for investment in what they consider a risky project, that may not deliver the returns for further community investment. In other words, there is fear that the wind farm will lock Shetland into one bio-economical pathway of development that will disable potential for a multi-functional eco-economy. Several interviewed to different stakeholders were carried on of which we give some items. Seeing the wind farm as a potential to replace oil as its primary industry, stakeholder 1 speaks to the view that the wind farm will bring long-term community benefits.

> Looking ahead we have got renewable energy, a wind farm looking to be built towards the end of this decade which will be quite a lot of investment and work as well, and big income. Because the wind farm is going to be 45% owned by the Shetland community itself it is going to be a huge amount of money coming in to help the community build its future. A lot of that money will be able to use for our economic development potentially. Nobody has decided what the money will be used for yet, they won't discuss it because it is not in the bag yet. And humans have got this aversion to count their chickens before they are hatched I suppose. But I see that money which could be £20/£30 million pounds a year coming into the public ... into this trust charity that is owned by the community [...] so we can use it for developing industry. And no other community in Britain will have that sort of vast amount of money for such a small number of people to use to build a stronger future.
>
> (Interview: Stakeholder 1)

Opposition, however, arises from severe scepticism over the financial statements made by Stakeholder 1. Indeed, while they suggest there are long-term community benefits to be derived from profits, due to the unique ownership structure of this wind farm – they anticipate only a successful outcome for the project. Furthermore, there is perceived to be little discussion of the high risk and other community-based opportunity costs involved in investing £180m of Shetland Charitable Trust resources in the project. Sustainable Shetland emphasise that the best-case-scenario publicised by VE is based on financial conjecture, as the final build costs, cost of energy transmission to the mainland and the final price of electricity to be sold are all unknown. In this case, conflict over two differing potential outcomes are sorely debated, and divide communities and families across Shetland. This painstaking process has been met with sustained opposition, starting with a petition to the Court of Session in Edinburgh to review consent granted by Scottish Ministers under section 36 of the Electricity Act 1989. This process culminated in judicial review in September 2013, wherein the application made by the VE partnership was found to be 'incompetent', for they did not hold a licence to generate electricity. Furthermore, Ministers were found to have failed to address issues under the Wild Birds Directive as concerning the whimbrel. During this phase of fieldwork, the project strives to meet concerns and awaits approval, while the opposition suggest the VE wind farm project is 'dying a slow death' (Interview: Stakeholder 2). The explicit undercurrent of this conflict is debated over competing sustainable and post-carbon visions and pathways for Shetland's development. Will the rural web unfold in ways that support a bio-economical trajectory through the export of energy, as wind power gradually comes to replace oil as the mainstay of Shetland industry? Or, will the VE wind farm project create new sets of relationships and transactions that create synergies as they come to mutually reinforce one other? Indeed, while revisiting interviewees from the previous round of study, it is clear there is thirst for the latter mode, which, if the wind farm were to go ahead, would be seen to stifle any such opportunity for the creative unfolding of these patterns and interactions.

> But I'm thinking smaller. If something big comes along fine, but not to the exclusion of all else. I think we're not big enough to sustain failure on a big scale but we can manage lots of small ones, lots of small failures and lots of small successes. It's not going to be headline news but it creates a really healthy diverse economy. [The wind farm project has] also stopped sensible renewable things going ahead because we can't think about a smaller scheme because we've got this one big one. So it stopped a new power station being built, because it could have been built five years ago and so our emissions could have been far lower five years ago but they didn't do it because they were waiting on this wind farm and waiting on this cable. So it's an opportunity lost. I think that's the biggest thing is the opportunity cost because it's difficult to measure. What we else have we really done with the time?
>
> (Interview: Stakeholder 2)

Speaking of future challenges and opportunities, there is clear verve for Shetland's development strategy to be hinged upon endogeneity and multifunctionality;

> I think the kind of reality check in that we're a lump of rock in the middle of the ocean. We can't change geography no matter how much we pretend we want to. So I think recognition of transport links and where we're physically sitting and making use of the assets that we've got. We've still, despite the cuts and closures, we've still got a relative egalitarian society compared to a lot of places so that regardless of someone's background there's a good chance they'll get reasonable care and attention through the education system.
>
> (Interview: Stakeholder 2)

This is similarly echoed as we revisit a local business and branding consultant, who has been active in building Shetland's brand 'Pride of Place' in order to advance the reputation of Shetland across the rest of the UK and worldwide, boosting the attractiveness of Shetland as a place to live as well as for tourism. While reflecting upon changes and challenges arising, the bio-economical pathway of development in Shetland is subject to further trepidation.

> I think I would want to try and realise ... I'm quite wary of lots of eggs in one basket. And I think we've suffered to some extent to that in some ways, in relation particularly to oil. But I think it would be good to ... and I know everybody says this, we need to diversify. But I really think we need to make more of some of the things we do at the moment which we're not doing enough of. And I'm thinking particularly about the food sector away from fishing. I think there are things we need to do in terms of fishing as well. Mainly to do with value adding, provenance, there is more to be done there ... But we need to do more in terms of other kinds of food production. Certainly the agricultural sector, the sheep, cattle.
>
> (Interview: Stakeholder 3)

Large-scale oil and indeed energy and biological products are thus considered to be detracting potential to realise a more multi-functional eco-economy characterised by the social management of the reproduction of ecological resources in ways designed to 'mesh with and enhance regional and local regional ecosystems' (Kitchen & Marsden, 2009). This not only presents a picture of a contradictory and contested development landscape, but is also the site of struggle and tension over the potential to become *locked into* the bio-economy to the exclusion of all else. Again as with Devon, the Shetland case is most acute in the apparently growing peripherality of agri-food initiatives, which, for van der Ploeg and Marsden (2008), play a crucial role in mobilising distinctive rural and regional development processes in the unfolding of the rural web. Indeed, efforts to develop agri-food initiatives by the Shetland Livestock Marketing Group (SLMG, 2014) are now found to have been met with some disinterest from the SIC, who instead focus on what they call 'big projects' synonymous with the bio-economy. Indeed, while the wind farm project presents in such potential development, the singular focus upon fish and fisheries is frustrating to those with a more holistic view of a rural development landscape that embraces also an agri-food dimension;

> Well, the food and farming is ... unless you're into fish you don't matter anymore. The SIC don't do agriculture anymore, they've removed all the support payments that they had for various grant schemes and they have no development officer dedicated to it, so as far as agriculture's concerned that's a dead stop and ... so any development that goes on now we'd basically have to try to do it ourselves and so as chair of the cooperative then I try to if possible foster schemes that I think may have potential that we might be in a position to persuade people to help fund. I mean we're involved in a

> couple of projects at the moment which Development weren't interested in at all. One project on climate mitigation and carbon sequestration in sheep production on the peat moorland and we've been involved with the University of Aberdeen in a knowledge transfer partnership and the figures suggest that if livestock management is maintained at a certain level the whole system can be viewed as being carbon benign, can actually sequester carbon as well as producing lambs and wool, which is probably a first anywhere in Europe for an agricultural system to be showing a positive balance in climate change mitigation, so we've tried to do things like that, things that no other agency is willing to take on, but obviously we have no resources at all, so whatever we do we basically have to cheat and swindle our way. We have to be very quick and very shrewd in going about any kind of development, it's just simply not something that's encouraged.
>
> (Interview: Stakeholder 4)

Development concentration focused around oil and fish resulted in a fragmented experience of Shetland's economic 'boom'. Indeed, the volatility of Shetland's oil industry since the 1970s is thought to be forgotten with the boost to the construction, service and transport sectors since decisions were made to build a new and refurbish the existing gas terminal. The benefits of which are therefore enjoyed by only particular sectors of the Shetland community.

> That bit is booming, but you go out to the village here and you look through the streets and you try and find where it's booming down there. It's not booming with your average person. There's huge disparity there, so if you are told that Shetland's economy is booming – only for some.
>
> (Interview: Stakeholder 4)

This exogenous focus is, moreover, considered by a representative of the Stakeholder 4 as damaging to the potential to develop initiatives that have impact within the wider community, for a pound spent locally through traditional industry circulates within the local economy for a longer period of time.

> I mean that's the frustrating thing about the Shetland example at the moment is ... some years ago I learnt the use of the word synergy, there's no synergy here. It's all pigeonholed. The same as if you ever get into battles with the Civil Service you'll find that Civil Servants all sit in their own little pigeonholes and they're basically not interested in anything else outside their realm and the consequences of that are ridiculous legislation, ridiculous regulation and that's what's happening here. You have people who, 'Oh fishing, fishing, fishing, fishing,' and ignore everything else. The multiplier effect was on spending a pound within a local economy on a local product because it went around and it stayed within that local economy for a long period of time before it disappeared out, whereas the pound spent on imports was like giving it to Tesco, it was bye bye. You'd think a Development Agency, be it either the Development Department

> of the SIC or the HIE would grasp that and be actually saying, 'Hold on, why not do this? Why do you persist in doing something that's obviously costing the local economy lots of money?' Nobody does it. Nobody does it.
>
> (Interview: Stakeholder 4)

The profits gained by the oil industry are understood to be leaving Shetland. This focus upon one development pathway is met with further exasperation, compounded by what is perceived as an obstructive attitude on behalf of the SIC towards the continued development of traditional industries on Shetland, including agriculture in particular. This is exacerbated by not only the expense of imported food, but also the profits that do not circulate in ways that boost the local economy.

A LANDSCAPE OF FOOD INSECURITY: FRAGMENTING THE RURAL WEB IN THE POST-CARBON ECONOMY

Following the trajectories of the rural webs in Devon and Shetland have unearthed some significant generic as well as local results. The longitudinal (2007–2014) research has allowed us to begin to assess how the 'pathways towards rural sustainability' are being shaped and articulated. A major finding in both regions is the realisation that moves towards a sustainable rural development trajectory under more post-carbon conditions are not likely or necessarily likely to lead to more cohesive rural web developments. Agri-food in particular can play a potentially leading and synergising role. Yet left to their own state-led and governance devices, since 2010, both regions show that attempts at sustainable place making is showing more signs of fragmentation, contestation and a diminution of cohesive rural webs built upon synergy, facilitative institutional arrangements and endogeneity. In both regions there has been a diminution of state support for agri-food developments, especially when it involves struggling multi-functional family and micro businesses (as in Devon), and the arrival of bio-economical mega projects in Shetland.

In this context, and to be critical of our earlier conceptual formulations, we have underestimated the growing and powerful exogenous forces linked to both the bio-economy (the attractiveness of wind power developments in Shetland), and shifts towards neo-liberalised and urban biased, spatial governance (in Devon); both of which prioritise (and by implication devalorise) small and middle-sized endogenous rural business development, especially in the multi-functional agri-food sector. These new exogenous factors, combined with those that we did incorporate in our earlier models of the rural web (such as the severe cost-price squeeze on agriculture) also now combine to marginalise and peripheralise small land-based businesses and the networks (social capital, etc.) upon which they are based.

This does not necessarily devalue the conceptual power of our rural web. Rather it shows that its very dynamic and contingent mobilisation is indeed a site and a place of dynamic and valuable struggle. A struggle we see clearly in our Devon Farms Network; a network which has been developing over 25 years, but having to adapt and self-exploit itself and its members in ways which allow it to continue to innovate in ways of providing an increasing array of novelties to their growing and more demanding tourist consumers. These practices and network building activities increasingly operate *outside of the state* and its institutional and regulatory frameworks. The latter are now less interested in encouraging endogenous rural and sustainable development – at least for the time being.

Also, although we point in both cases to the marginalisation of agri-food and its potential centrality in rural development, it is clear that this fails to disappear completely. It is a central part of the construction of landscape value ('eco-system services') in both regions, and central for the maintenance of ecological biodiversity. *But it is not, at the moment, or indeed in the foreseeable future being valorised as such.* However, there are real generational and reproductive vulnerabilities on the social and economic fabric of multi-functional family farming in both regions, as family occupancy ages and actual farm-derived income continues to fall.

If we are in Europe to manage the post-carbon transition we will have to devise ways of re-valorising the socio-ecological infrastructures upon which it depends. The trends in these two rural regions, at either ends of the UK archipelago, suggest that the combinational effects of declines in multi-functional agri-food support, on the one hand, and a neo-liberalised retraction of non-agricultural rural development support on the other, are providing a potential and chaotic *new governance squeeze* which is likely to severely reduce the massive, but latent adaptive capacity embedded in the rural eco-economy. One implication is therefore that we need to create new and more reflexive pathways for good governance so as to harness this potential if we are to protect and build resilient rural communities.

Indeed, a more multi-functional governance and policy-based approach, based upon creating conditions for the eco-economic rural web to flourish needs to find ways of harmonising different aspects of the post-carbon landscape such that its various segments (energy, tourism, agriculture, creative industries, etc.) can work in synergy with one another. This is very much what the Devon Farms Network is trying to do, but largely outside governance frameworks, and at considerable (potentially unsustainable) self-exploitative cost to themselves. Such fragmented and competing conditions as those revealed in both case study areas are unlikely to be sufficiently capable of meeting the new national and global demands for food security which have gained prominence on the political agenda since our earlier phases of fieldwork.

REFERENCES

Clarke, J. (1996). Farm accommodation and the communication mix. *Tourism management*, *17*, 611–616.

Clarke, J. (1999). Marketing structures for farm tourism: Beyond the individual provider of rural tourism. *Journal of Sustainable Tourism*, *7*, 26–47.

Cloke, P. J., & Little, J. (1997). *Contested countryside cultures: Otherness, marginalisation, and rurality*. Routledge, London: Psychology Press.

Darnhofer, I. (2005). Organic farming and rural development: Some evidence from Austria. *Sociologia Ruralis*, *45*, 308–323.

Devon County Council (DCC). (2010). Devonomics: The Devon economy at your fingertips.

Devon County Council (DCC). (2014). Strategic economic plan.

Drummond, I., Campbell, H., Lawrence, G., & Symes, D. (2000). Contingent or structural crisis in British agriculture? *Sociologia Ruralis*, *40*, 111–127.

Errington, A., & Gasson, R. (1994). Labour use in the farm family business. *Sociologia Ruralis*, 34(4), 293–307.

European Commission. (2005). Territorial state and perspectives of the European Union, towards stronger territorial cohesion in the light of Lisbon and Gothennburg ambitions Scoping document endorsed by Ministers of Spatial Development and the European Commission. Ministerial Meeting on Regional Policy and Territorial Cohesion.

Evans, N. J., & Ilbery, B. W. (1989). A conceptual framework for investigating farm-based accommodation and tourism in Britain. *Journal of Rural Studies*, *5*, 257–266.

Evans, N. J., & Ilbery, B. W. (1992a). Advertising and farm-based accommodation: A British case study. *Tourism Management*, *13*, 415–422.

Evans, N. J., & Ilbery, B. W. (1992b). Farm-based accommodation and the restructuring of agriculture: Evidence from three English counties. *Journal of Rural Studies*, *8*, 85–96.

Gasson, R. (1992). Farmers' wives – Their contribution to the farm business. *Journal of Agricultural Economics*, *43*, 74–87.

Gasson, R., & Errington, A. J. (1993). *The farm family business*. London: CAB International.

Horlings, I., & PADT, F. (2013). Leadership for sustainable regional development in rural areas: Bridging personal and institutional aspects. *Sustainable Development*, *21*, 413–424.

Horlings, L., & Marsden, T. (2011). Towards the real green revolution? Exploring the conceptual dimensions of a new ecological modernisation of agriculture that could 'feed the world'. *Global Environmental Change*, *21*, 441–452.

Horlings, L., & Marsden, T. (2014). Exploring the 'new rural paradigm' in Europe: Eco-economic strategies as a counterforce to the global competitiveness agenda. *European Urban and Regional Studies*, *21*, 4–20.

House of Commons Environment, F. A. R. A. C. (2014). Food security: Second Report of Session 2014–15 House of Commons.

Kanemasu, K., Sonnino, R., Marsden, T., & Schneider, S. (2008). Testing the web: A comparative analysis. In J. D. van der Ploeg & T. Marsden (Eds.), *Unfolding webs: The dynamics of regional rural development*. Assen, The Netherlands: Van Gorcum.

Kitchen, L., & Marsden, T. (2009). Creating sustainable rural development through stimulating the eco-economy: Beyond the eco-economic paradox? *Sociologia Ruralis*, *49*(3), 273–294.

Little, J. (2002). *Gender and rural geography: Identity, sexuality and power in the countryside*. New York, NY: Prentice Hall.

Lobley, M., & Potter, C. (2004). Agricultural change and restructuring: Recent evidence from a survey of agricultural households in England. *Journal of Rural Studies*, *20*, 499–510.

Marsden, T. (1984). Capitalist farming and the farm family: A case study. *Sociology*, *18*, 205–224.

Marsden, T. (2010). Mobilizing the regional eco-economy: Evolving webs of agri-food and rural development in the UK. *Cambridge Journal of Regions, Economy and Society*, *3*, 225–244.

Mills, C. W. (1959). *The sociological imagination*. New York, NY: Oxford University Press.

Poppy, G. M., Jepson, P. C., Pickett, J. A., & Birkett, M. A. (2014). Achieving food and environmental security: New approaches to close the gap. *Philosophical Transactions of the Royal Society B*, *369*, 1–7. doi:10.1098/rstb.2012.0272

Rhodes, R. A. (1997). *Understanding governance: Policy networks, governance, reflexivity and accountability*. Buckingham: Open University Press.

Shetland Island Council (SIC). (2012). Shetland partnership: Our community plan.

SLMG. (2014). *Initiatives*. Retrieved from http://www.slmg.co.uk/

Office for National Statistics. (2014). Regional Labour Market Statistics October 2012.

Thomson, R., & Holland, J. (2003). Hindsight, foresight and insight: The challenges of longitudinal qualitative research. *International Journal of Social Research Methodology*, *6*, 233–244.

van der Ploeg, J. D. (2000). Revitalizing agriculture: Farming economically as starting ground for rural development. *Sociologia Ruralis*, *40*, 497–511.

van der Ploeg, J. D., & Marsden, T. (2008). *Unfolding webs, the dynamics of regional rural development*. Assen, The Netherlands: Van Gorcum.

Whatmore, S., Munton, R., Little, J. O., & Marsden, T. (1987). Towards a typology of farm businesses in contemporary British agriculture. *Sociologia Ruralis*, *27*, 21–37.

CHAPTER 13

CONCLUSION: REPRODUCING FUTURE IN RURAL AREA

Pierluigi Milone, Flaminia Ventura and Jingzhong Ye

ABSTRACT

Peasants play a key role in the processes of growth and development of rural areas. But the practices and the organizational forms or arrangements can be very different in relation to the context or territory of origin. This has resulted in a multiplicity of solutions unlikely to be repeated in other sectorial or scientific context. This heterogeneity of responses allows the peasants model to strengthen the resilience of rural areas and offer itself as an alternative model of agricultural modernization paths increasingly ineffective in managing the modern complexity. This is a common element that emerges in all experiences of rural development in Brazil, China, and Europe, which are compared in this book. In addition to this, this chapter highlights some commonalities that can be used to delineate the attributes of the new peasantry and its consolidation and dissemination in space and time.

Keywords: Rural development; peasants; autonomy; market; path-dependency; multifunctionality

Constructing a New Framework for Rural Development
Research in Rural Sociology and Development, Volume 22, 325–333

ISSN: 1057-1922/doi:10.1108/S1057-192220150000022022

In recent years, there have been overwhelming changes in spatial, cultural, and political boundaries that have had a profound effect on farmers and citizens alike. In the agrarian domain, these changes have been characterized by three main driving forces all of which have emerged as the result of new scarcities:

1. climate change and the need to maintain the resilience of natural systems;
2. food security becoming increasingly defined in terms of food safety and access to food;
3. commodities, markets, globalization, and price volatility.

The pressing nature of these concerns has led to an enlargement of the domains of agricultural and rural development which now include new and different actors: "*rural development is actively shaped by the many actors, social movements and/or state apparatuses that are involved in it*" (van der Ploeg, Ye, & Schneider, 2015). As a consequence, rural development is increasingly being constructed through the many and multi-faceted encounters between these actors who engage in complex and, often, contradictory practices (see Long, 2015).

In this ongoing process of socially and culturally constructing rural development, political negotiations between the different participating actors have acquired an increased importance. These negotiations can be rife with conflict, not necessarily over the main goals of development, but more over the practical choices that need to be made. A multitude of different solutions are emerging. Some of these solutions increase the pressure on natural resources, already vulnerable and scarce and often the main limiting factors in rural development. In this chaotic and dynamic arena, new and heterogeneous peasant practices, activities, and solutions are emerging in different parts of the world. These practices emerge from the peasantry's recognition of the central value of reproducing their resource base in a way that increases their autonomy from the market and loosens ecological constraints.

This path is paved by the innovations that have emerged from the creativity of the peasantry. This behavior stems from "*the rational choices of peasants' social instincts and external changes*" (Ye & Fu, 2015). In this volume of work, we represent this "social instinct" as stemming from "*the notions, capabilities and eagerness of peasants to go forward under the influences of the social environment* (*ibid.*)." The "external changes" that Ye and Fu refer to include the new institutions, policies, or forms of control that influence and change the traditional environment that the peasantry lives in. Peasant innovations and grassroots activities are reactions to these external changes that are based on their social instinct (*ibid.*).

These innovations are practical responses to the emerging scarcities that threaten the survival of farmers as a social group. These responses "... *require[s] doggedness, passion, resistance and the like. Thus, it can be argued that rural development practices very much (co-)shape the actors involved into the people they are*" (van der Ploeg et al., 2015). Over time, these practices increase farmers' agency and *"more importantly they are tools/strategies for regaining and/or enlarging autonomy. Even when there is considerable state support, the unfolding of these practices represents a search for enlarging autonomy. This search for autonomy subsequently translates into a search for endogeneity, building as much as possible (but not exclusively) on locally available resources in order to avoid getting entrapped in new dependency relations. It also translates into novelty production, the search for local and original solutions which helps to avoid dependency on externally developed innovations* (*ibid.*)*."*

The innovative practices documented in this volume can be found across the globe: in Europe, Brazil, and China. One feature they share in common is that they are not embedded in hierarchical logics or models, but instead originate from new "horizontal" networks where reciprocity plays a key role. Within these new networks, new forms of cooperation are developed, which allow farmers to regain market and political power. In the first case, farmers are seeking to increase the influence that they have over market variables and achieve a better remuneration for their assets (mainly labor, knowledge, and land). In the second, power allows farmers more opportunities to influence the constricting process of new institutional frameworks (the external changes discussed above).

An unusual aspect of this redistribution of power is that it is hardly generating any conflict. "*This is due to the recognition by all actors, first and foremost consumers, of the importance of the role of the peasantry in creating responses to various contingencies, mostly unexpected, which not only impact on farming, but on the quality of life of citizens and consumers*" (Milone & Ventura, 2015). This new empowerment of the peasantry is part of a growing societal recognition of the need for agriculture and thriving rural regions. Within farming this process is characterized by *"the shifts from agriculture back to farming" [...] Farming is what farmers do and have done through millennia: [...] manage the natural conditions of their activity, with all their uncertainties and risks, including the vagaries of climate and the biochemical tendency to soil degradation unless measures are taken to maintain and restore the fertility of land. Successful farming, then, requires high levels of knowledge of ecological conditions and a willingness to devise and adopt better methods of cultivation within acceptable boundaries of uncertainty and risk* (Bernestein, 2010, p. 62).

The present differs from the past in that there has recently been an uncontrollable increase in risk (climate change, animal and plant diseases, etc.) and in uncertainty (price volatility, market segmentation, economic and financial crises, etc.). The logic of modernization, based solely on scientific and technological knowledge of production methods, is found to be lacking in responding to these changes. By contrast, the numerous responses of the peasantry (documented in this volume) demonstrate the existence of a deep pool of knowledge, skills, and attitudes in rural areas that can be harnessed to manage risk and uncertainty. These practices are unfolding in different ways in different parts of the world and within different Technological Administrative Task Environments, yet they share some commonalities that go some way to explaining their success in meeting the multi-dimensional challenges of sustainability. These commonalities can be used to delineate the attributes that characterize the new peasantry:

1. a tendency toward autonomy;
2. an ability to instinctively manage the unknown; and
3. a sense of responsibility toward their own social group and community.

We examine each of these three aspects in turn in the rest of this chapter.

THE TENDENCY TOWARD AUTONOMY

The closed-loop nature of the peasant model, which is based on the continuous reproduction and valorization of the peasant's resource base (including family labor), increases farmers' control over these resources. It is an approach that substantially reduces dependency on external inputs and pressures. The circularity that farmers seek is based on their knowledge and ability to decide what, when, and how to produce and reproduce. This freedom to decide provides the space needed to effectively respond to, and maneuver within, a rapidly and dynamic changing external environment. This is the main incentive for the peasantry's creativity. The boundaries of creativity are set by the peasants' attitudes toward risk and their ability to read and interpret the external contexts and redefine the ways they interact with these. This creativity is a key aspect of the identity of the peasantry and helps define their different farming styles.[1]

The drive for autonomy is one of the common factors in the different case studies in this volume. But the different ways in which this autonomy is achieved and strengthened depend on cultural, historical, and institutional contexts. The capacity to acquire autonomy in such different contexts emphasizes the value of the peasant approach and its centrality in the new, more sustainable, paradigm of rural development.

On-farm food processing and direct sales are but two examples of practices that farmers have introduced in order to increase their autonomy and respond to market instabilities. These practices also contribute to the ongoing transition of the socio-technical food regime. Schneider and Gazolla (2015) argue that this is fostering the development of new markets and changes in the institutional environment in which farms operate. This is due to the development of new interfaces between farm families and other social actors, institutions, and organizations, especially in co-constructing the knowledge required to generate novelties and create nested markets.

Autonomy can be understood as a way for the peasantry to manage its interfaces with other actors and to revalorize proximity which leads to the emergence of the following behaviors (Bernstein, 2010, p. 64):

1. *maintaining soil fertility through the use of green and animal manures sourced on or near the farm, as well as through systems of fallowing and crop rotation – termed "closed-loop agro-ecological systems";*
2. *the pooling of labor between neighboring households at critical moments of the farming calendar, for example, to ensure timely planting and harvesting, especially when weather conditions are uncertain; and*
3. *the provision by local artisans of goods and services farmers might not produce themselves, including some of the tools they used.*

These behaviors are seen repeatedly in the case studies within this volume and show the importance of farmers not only creating autonomy for themselves and their families, but also in the wider rural economy. Such behaviors were observed in the development of micro-technologies for on-farm food processing and sales in Italy, in the distributive cooperatives in Brazil, the Dutch environmental cooperatives and in the autonomous innovations of peasants in Zhejiang Province which have created opportunities for them to break through institutional barriers and overcome economic and social exclusion.

THE ABILITY TO INSTINCTIVELY MANAGE THE UNKNOWN

The motivations and roots of peasant innovativeness are another common element in the case studies. All the researchers in the different countries involved in this volume specifically investigated this element. They were guided by two predefined research questions. Where does the innovative spirit of peasants come from? And, how can institutions foster this spirit?

A first answer came from Brazil. Schneider and Gazzolla (2015) identified *farmers' ingenuity* as a central source for the development of differentiated products. Their use of the term ingenuity comes from the work of Gaglio (2011) that describe ingenuity as a combination of creativity talent and capacity and as a driving force for novelty production.

The peasantry's ingenuity stems from what conventional economists would define as their "limited rationality": the direct consequence of the co-production process with nature that is characterized by unpredictable events. Nature is the peasants' first source of creativity. The ability to manage co-production with nature requires specific knowledge and enables peasants to acquire creative skills that are enhanced and strengthened over time by their own, and their colleagues', experiences.

A second answer comes from the Chinese case studies. Here innovation lies in the autonomous strategies adopted to overcome the vulnerabilities of rural life. "*The innovations devised by peasants result from their rational choices. [...] When an ideal life was not forthcoming or foreseeable, but a problem of subsistence was on the rise in the collective work and management of the commune system, peasants did not sit back and do nothing, but started to innovate and reform the production and management system without changing the collective ownership structure*" (Ye and Fu, 2015). This autonomous strategy of innovation is linked to the desire to maintain the social structure: we call this the "social instinct" of peasants, which is the well-spring of peasants seeking to introduce processes of innovation.

A third answer comes from the analysis of step by step processes of innovation by the peasantry (Milone, 2009). The peasantry's innovation capabilities are linked to its innate propensity for "methodological pragmatism." This attitude encourages the peasant to enter onto a largely unknown pathway. As long as visible progress is being made the peasant is confident of finding a solution to the problems facing him or her. This behavior has sustained the survival of peasant farms throughout history as it provides the flexibility required to make new transformations and innovations. This behavior is rooted in increasing autonomy through developing the multifunctionality of key resources (knowledge, labor, land, animal and plant biodiversity) and avoiding the extreme specialization promoted and required by the modernization model, which forces farmers into making excessive investments and becoming locked into "path-dependency" (Saccomandi, 1994).

In a situation where the survival of farm families and communities depends on farmers' choices and their creativity in responding to external changes, peasants have developed a social instinct of resistance and conservationism. Farmers' instincts translate into the ability to look at the future and to construct solutions that reduce the consequences of scarcities. This attitude is linked with an awareness that "*the broader the space of the known, the wider the boundaries of the unknown*" (Milone, Ventura, & Ye, 2015).

This way of thinking allows farmers to make changes without calculating all the possible alternatives in front of them. It gives them confidence in their own abilities, and those of other actors, to find solutions or practices that will improve their wellbeing and that of their family and their community. Peasants are so aware of the enormity of the everyday risks of their activities that they are not afraid to take additional risks.

SOCIAL AND COMMUNAL RESPONSIBILITY

Innovation in farming can have profound ecological and social consequences as farming continuously mobilizes a common pool of (social and natural) resources. The availability and the quality of the resources available for mobilization are directly dependent on the way that individuals use them. The peasantry is innately aware of this dependency: this awareness is one of the key features that distinguishes peasant farming from the "modern" agriculture model.

One of the main consequences of this awareness is the peasantry's attitude toward social responsibility and the sense of belonging. Both elements are now emerging as key criteria for market competitiveness in the era of globalization. Social responsibility leads to people adopting strategies that are based on reputation and reciprocities. In turn these reduce transaction costs and enhance consumer loyalty. The sense of belonging that they engender reduces local conflicts over the use of resources and encourages the development of new institutional arrangements, new forms of market governance, and the creation of nested markets (Milone & Ventura, 2014). Social responsibility and a sense of belonging can both be communicated to consumers through ICTs, thereby overcoming geographical barriers and boundaries and creating a new proximity based on shared cultural and social values.

These factors and attitudes appear to be the main driving forces behind the innovative practices of the peasantry. These innovative practices appear to offer a more sustainable future than the ones they are displacing. Van der Ploeg et al. (2015) note that actors are shaped by the practices they construct and that the policies that sustain certain practices have a direct impact on the reproduction or disappearance of different types of actors. The development and the strengthening of the seeds and sprouts of new peasant practices can foster the reproduction of future farmers who follow the historic peasants' approach. This is a basic pre-condition for maintaining and developing the capacity to create social and sustainable innovations which serve as a motor for rural development. However, as shown in this book, these practices emerge through very varied development process and our understanding of the sociological and economic forces at play needs to be further refined if we wish to develop a more robust analysis of the theoretical and methodological frameworks within which sustainable rural development occurs and can be fostered.

NOTE

1. For a discussion and definition of farming styles see van der Ploeg (1990).

REFERENCES

Bernstein, H. (2010). *Class dynamics of agrarian change*. Canada: Fernwood Publishing.

Gaglio, G. (2011). *Sociologie de l'innovation, PUF, collection « Que sais-je? PUF editor*. Paris: Presses Universitaires de France.

Long, N. (2015). Activities, actants and actors: Theoretical perspectives on development practice and practitioners. In P. Milone, F. Ventura, & J. Ye (Eds.), *Constructing a new framework for rural development* (Vol. 22). Research in Rural Sociology and Development. Bingley, UK: Emerald Group Publishing Limited.

Milone, P. (2009). *Agriculture in transition: A neo-institutional analysis* (p. 256). The Netherlands: Van Gorgum.

Milone, P., & Ventura, F. (2014). The visible hand in building new markets for rural economies. In P. Hebinck, S. Schneider, & J. D. van der Ploeg (Eds.), *Rural development and the construction of new markets*. London: Routledge.

Milone, P., & Ventura, F. (2015). Is multifunctionality the road to empowering farmers? In P. Milone, F. Ventura, & J. Ye (Eds.), *Constructing a new framework for rural development* (Vol. 22). Research in Rural Sociology and Development. Bingley, UK: Emerald Group Publishing Limited.

Milone, P., Ventura, F., & Ye, J. (2015). Introduction. In P. Milone, F. Ventura, & J. Ye (Eds.), *Constructing a new framework for rural development* (Vol. 22). Research in Rural Sociology and Development. Bingley, UK: Emerald Group Publishing Limited.

Saccomandi, V. (1994). La concentrazione produttiva dell'agricoltura italiana: Alcune considerazioni, in atti del convegno "Giornate Tassinari sull'Economia e la Politica agraria: Il sistema di agrimarketing e le reti di impresa", Assisi 14–15 luglio, CESAR.

Schneider, S., & Gazzolla, M. (2015). Seeds and sprouts of rural development: Innovations and nested markets in small scale on-farm processing by family farmers in South Brazil. In P. Milone, F. Ventura, & J. Ye (Eds.), *Constructing a new framework for rural development* (Vol. 22). Research in Rural Sociology and Development. Bingley, UK: Emerald Group Publishing Limited.

van der Ploeg, J. D. (1990). Labor, markets, and agricultural production. *Westview Special Studies in Agriculture Science and Policy*. Boulder: Westview Press.

van der Ploeg, J. D., Ye, J., & Schneider, S. (2015). Rural development: Actors and practices. In P. Milone, F. Ventura, & J. Ye (Eds.), *Constructing a new framework for rural development* (Vol. 22). Research in Rural Sociology and Development. Bingley, UK: Emerald Group Publishing Limited.

Ye, J., & Fu, H. (2015). Peasant innovation and grassroots action in China. In P. Milone, F. Ventura, & J. Ye (Eds.), *Constructing a new framework for rural development* (Vol. 22). Research in Rural Sociology and Development. Bingley, UK: Emerald Group Publishing Limited.

ABOUT THE AUTHORS

Huiyang Fu is PhD candidate, major in development studies in the College of Humanities and Development Studies (COHD), China Agricultural University. Her doctoral dissertation converges on the political ecology of agricultural development, and researches she engaged in include food security, rural transformations, peasant innovation and grassroots action.

Marcio Gazolla is Professor at the Federal University of Santa Maria (UFSM-CAFW) – Campus Frederick – RS. He got the PhD in Rural Development at the Federal University of Rio Grande do Sul. His main research interests include Rural Development, Rural Economy, Rural Sociology, Food Security, Family Agriculture, Public Policy for Rural Development, Family Agribusiness, Agricultural and Rural Markets and Food Innovations.

Norman Long is Professor Emeritus at Wageningen University. His main research interests include different theoretical perspectives, such as discourse analysis, knowledge/power frameworks, post-modernism, actor-network theory and new modes of 'materialism'. His early career was at universities in the United Kingdom, notably at University of Manchester (Lecturer), then the University of Durham (Reader and Professor). In 1981 he became Professor of Rural Development Sociology at Wageningen University in the Netherlands until 2001 when he retired.

Terry Marsden is Director of the Research Institute and Professor of Environmental Policy and Planning in the School of Planning and Geography. He is also Dean of the University Graduate College. He has a broad range of research and policy experience based around the themes of international rural development, sustainability and the rural environment. He is currently a member of the Strategic Advisory Committee of the ESRC's Rural Economy and Land Use Research Programme in the United Kingdom.

Pierluigi Milone is Researcher in rural and agricultural economics and sociology at the University of Perugia. He got the PhD in rural sociology at Wageningen University. His research interests include agricultural and rural sociology and economics, development intervention and rural transformation, contemporary rural politics and governance. He was a member of the technical cabinet of the former Italian agricultural Minister in the period 2002–2006 and from 2009 he is the coordinator of technical advisor group in the Molise Rural Development Program. He obtained in 2013 a national qualification for Associate Professor in Sociology.

Henk Oostindie is Assistant Professor at the Rural Sociology Chair of Wageningen University and Research Centre. He is a PhD candidate at Wageningen University. His main research interests include: heterogeneity of farming styles and farming strategies, rural policy and food chain dynamics, new rural development activities and multifunctional farming.

Jessica Paddock is Research Associate at the Sustainable Places Research Institute (PLACE), Cardiff University, and Guest lecture at School of Social Science, Cardiff University. Her research interests include the links between natural resource use, inequalities, cultural differentiation and food security, with the aim of informing policy development in the governance of coupled social-ecological systems.

Paulo F. Petersen is Executive Coordinator of the Brazilian NGO AS-PTA – Family Farming and Agroecology and board member of the Brazilian Association of Agroecology. He is a PhD student at Universidad Pablo de Olavide, España. He is Chief-Editor of Revista Agriculturas experiências em Agroecologia and Member of the Editorial Council of Agroecology and Sustainable Food Systems and Revista Brasileira de Agroecologia. Currently, he is member of National Council on Agroecology and Organic Production, body linked to the General Secretariat of the Presidency of the Brazilian Republic, and member of the Permanent Forum on Agroecology of the Brazilian Agricultural Research Enterprise (Embrapa).

Claudia Job Schmitt is Adjunct Professor at the Social Sciences Graduate Studies Program on Development, Agriculture and Society at the Federal Rural University of Rio de Janeiro, Brazil. Her research interest includes family farming, agroecology, rural development and public policies. She got the PhD in Sociology at the Federal University of Rio Grande do Sul and worked with NGOs, social movements and public institutions as advisor and consultant.

Sergio Schneider is Professor of Rural Sociology and Development Studies at the Federal University of Rio Grande do Sul (UFRGS), Porto Alegre, Brazil. He has a degree in Social Sciences, Master and PhD in Sociology.

His main interest is related to sociology of food, agrarian and rural development, family farming and rural policies. He is editor of the Rural Studies Series.

Bart Soldaat is Researcher, private consultant and Secretary of the Groupe de Bruges, an independent think tank on European Agricultural and Rural Development Policy. He graduated at the University of Wageningen in rural sociology and have been involved in many research in Italy and in Netherlands. He was a co-ordinator of different Dutch-Local Action Groups (LAG) in the Initiative Leader + and in the Leader framework of the Rural Development Programme 2007–2013.

Rudolf van Broekhuizen is Researcher and project manager, Rural Sociology Group, Wageningen University, The Netherlands. He has thirty years of experience in international research on farming styles, physical and spatial planning, rural development, multifunctional agriculture, food supply chains, dairy breeding and rural estates. He also worked as rural planner and programme manager of the Government Service for Land and Water Management of the (former) Ministry of Agriculture.

Laurent Van de Poele is Professor Emeritus at the Catholic University of Leuven and former Director for Rural Development at the European Commission. His research interest includes history of European integration, European politics and policy, rural development and bottom up approach. He was nominated by the Dutch Minister for Agriculture for the period 2008–2012 as member of the supervisory board of the Wageningen University.

Jan Douwe van der Ploeg is Professor of Rural Sociology at Wageningen University and adjunct Professor of Rural Sociology at Chiana Agricultural University in Beijing. His main research interests include peasants agriculture, rural development, differential degrees of commoditization, differential responses to technology development, cultural repertoire and farmers' strategies and rural politics and social problems. He was advisor of Italian minister of agriculture and chairman of Mansholt Institute, a research School for the social sciences at Wageningen University.

Flaminia Ventura is Researcher in rural and agricultural politics and sociology at the University of Perugia. She got the PhD in rural sociology at Wageningen University. Her research interests include agricultural and rural sociology, development intervention and rural transformation, contemporary rural politics and governance. She was the head of the technical cabinet of the former Italian agricultural Minister in the period 2002–2006 and from 2008 she is one of the coordinator of National Rural Network. She obtained in 2013 a national qualification for Associate Professor in Sociology.

Jingzhong Ye is Professor of development studies and deputy dean at the College of Humanities and Development Studies (COHD), China Agricultural University. His research interests include development intervention and rural transformations, rural social problems, rural left-behind population, rural education, agrarian sociology and land politics.

Printed and bound by CPI Group (UK) Ltd, Croydon, CR0 4YY

15/09/2026

14962364-0003